Feb 1993

Kenya

a travel survival kit

Geoff Crowther
Hugh Finlay

Kenya - a travel survival kit
1st edition

Published by
Lonely Planet Publications
Head Office: PO Box 617, Hawthorn, Vic 3122, Australia
US Office: PO Box 2001A, Berkeley, CA 94702, USA

Printed by
Singapore National Printers Ltd, Singapore

Photographs by
Geoff Crowther (GC)
Hugh Finlay (HF)
Tony Wheeler (TW)
Greg Herriman (GH)
Rona Abbott (RA)
Mark Savage (MS)
George Pavlu (GP)

Front Cover: Hippo (Guido Alberto Rossi), The Image Bank
Back Cover: Kenyan sunrise (HF)

Safari Guide illustrations by
Matt King

First Published
February 1991

Although the author and publisher have tried to make the information as accurate as possible, they accept no responsibility for any loss, injury or inconvenience sustained by any person using this book.

National Library of Australia Cataloguing in Publication Data

Crowther, Geoff
    Kenya, a travel survival kit.

    Includes index.
    ISBN 0 86442 103 6.

1. Kenya - Description and travel - 1981 -   - Guide-books.
I. Finlay, Hugh. II. Title.

916.762044

text © Geoff Crowther & Hugh Finlay 1991
maps © Lonely Planet 1991
photos © photographers as indicated 1991
illustrations © Lonely Planet 1991

Geoff Crowther

Hugh Finlay

Born in Yorkshire, England, Geoff took to his heels early on in the search for the miraculous. The lure of the unknown took him to Kabul, Kathmandu and Lamu in the days before the overland bus companies began digging up the dirt along the tracks of Africa. His experiences led him to join the now legendary but sadly defunct alternative information centre BIT in the late '60s.

In 1977, he wrote his first guide for Lonely Planet – *Africa on the cheap*. He has also written *South America on a shoestring*, travel survival kits to *Korea* and *East Africa* and has co-authored LP's guides to *India*, *Malaysia, Singapore & Brunei*, and *Morocco, Algeria & Tunisia*.

Though they still travel extensively, Geoff and Hyung Pun have discovered the joys of working on over-drive with their two-year-old son, Ashley Choson. They recently moved out of a banana shed which had been home for 10 years into a new house that Geoff (et al) built in Korean/mediaeval English style in the Northern Rivers area of New South Wales. When not travelling or writing, Geoff devotes his time to landscaping, dreaming up impossible schemes, arguing with everyone in sight, pursuing noxious weeds and brewing Davidson's plum wine.

After deciding there must be more to life than a career in civil engineering, Hugh first took off around Australia in the mid '70s, working at everything from parking cars to prospecting for diamonds in the back blocks of South Australia, before heading further afield. He spent three years travelling and working in three continents, including a stint on an irrigation project in Saudi Arabia, before joining Lonely Planet in 1985.

Hugh has also written the Lonely Planet guide *Jordan & Syria – a travel survival kit*, co-authored *Morocco, Algeria & Tunisia – a travel survival kit*, and has contributed to others including *Africa on a shoestring* and *India – a travel survival kit*.

Hugh and Linda are now finding life considerably enlivened by their daughter, Ella. When not travelling and writing, Hugh spends a good deal of time striving for the perfect home-brew beer.

From the Authors
As with all LP guides, this book is partially the result of research undertaken by the authors and feedback from travellers carrying copies of *Africa on a shoestring* and/or *East Africa – a travel survival kit*. There's also been a significant amount of input from Kenyans in various parts of the country and expatriates who live and work there.

Without listing them in any order of preference, Geoff would like to sincerely thank the following people for their help, encouragement, friendship, hospitality and constructive criticism:

George Pavlu of Brisbane, Australia, who accompanied me on the trip to Kenya, contributed to the research, maintained his usual highly explosive degree of humour, and amazed all and sundry by his prodigious consumption of Tusker lager. A professional photographer and film scriptwriter, George was particularly instrumental in introducing me to many facets of Kenya which I might otherwise have remained ignorant of.

Malcolm Gascoigne of Yare Safaris, Nairobi, Kenya, who enthusiastically allowed me to clutter up his office, rummage through his files, introduced me to a host of people in the safari business and never missed a recreational session at Buffalo Bill's or the Florida 2000. A good head and shoulders above anyone else I met in Kenya and twice the size of his girlfriend, Susan. Malcolm's humour was contagious, his consumption of Tusker lager at least the equal of George's, and his knowledge of East Africa extremely valuable. May your Maralal hostel, camel and gorilla safaris prosper!

Jeannette Wittermans, a computer graphics artist and painter of Den Haag, Holland, for her smile, her quiet good humour and resourcefulness on a somewhat disastrous safari to Lake Turkana and a much less problematical one to the Aberdares, Mt Kenya and Samburu.

Willem and Yoke Wittermans of Nairobi, Kenya, for their matchless hospitality on two separate occasions and for the loan of their camping equipment.

Rachel Newphry of Yelverton, UK, for putting us up on two seperate occasions and maintaining such a mellow atmosphere at her rented villa in Kilifi.

Lillian Nabude of Nairobi, Kenya, who rescued me from the intricacies of the Kenyan telephone system, introduced me to Buffalo Bill's, put me onto works of African literature I would never otherwise have encountered, saved me a small fortune through her command of several African languages, and expanded my consciousness with stories of growing up in Africa, being a refugee and an unmarried mother there, and for her laughter and determination in the face of adversity. I hope your son didn't wreck the bicycle too soon!

Mark Savage of Nairobi, Kenya, for the loan of his Land Rover, camping equipment, tools, and his irreplaceable large-scale maps of northern Kenya for a safari to Lake Turkana. Mark has been an enthusiastic member of the Mountain Club of Kenya for many years and is the co-author of the excellent, *Mt Kenya Map & Guide* – the best available.

Sarah Zaituni Nakubulwa of Nairobi, Kenya, for her captivating smile and mellow friendship which made me think seriously about leaving.

Suh Ja-Lee (known to everyone as 'Sue'), the resolute and dedicated proprietress of Buffalo Bill's, Nairobi, for maintaining the best watering hole in Kenya. Hang in there, Sue!

Hugh would like to thank Peter Pickernell for his outstanding hospitality and an interesting insight into the *wazungu* in Kenya.

Thanks also to Tony Wheeler for additional information on Hyrax Hill, Rhino Rescue, Gedi and Lamu.

From the Publisher

Back at Lonely Planet, Melbourne, Diana Saad was the editor for this edition. Proofreading was done by Sharan Kaur. The maps, illustrations, layout and cover were done by Valerie Tellini, with additional help from Chris Lee Ack and Margaret Jung. Special thanks to Matt King for the Safari Guide illustrations.

Warning & Request

Things change, prices go up, schedules change, good places go bad and bad ones go bankrupt – nothing stays the same. So, if you find things better or worse, recently opened or long since closed, please write and tell us about it.

Between editions, when it is possible, we'll publish the most interesting letters and important information in a Stop Press section at the back of the book.

All information is greatly appreciated, and the best letters will receive a free copy of the next edition or any Lonely Planet book of your choice.

Contents

MAP LEGEND

BOUNDARIES

▬ ▬ ▬ ▬	International Boundaries
▬ ▪ ▬ ▬ ▪ ▪	Internal Boundaries
▪ ▬ ▪ ▪ ▪ ▪ ▬	National Parks, Reserves
▬ ▬ ▬ ▬	The Equator
⋯⋯⋯⋯⋯	The Tropics

SYMBOLS

◉ NEW DELHI	National Capital
● BOMBAY	Provincial or State Capital
● Pune	Major Town
● Barsi	Minor Town
▲	Post Office
✈	Airport
i	Tourist Information
◓	Bus Station, Terminal
66	Highway Route Number
☪ ✝ ✝	Mosque, Church, Cathedral
∴	Temple, Ruin or Archaeological Site
▲	Hostel
✚	Hospital
✳	Lookout
⚐	Camping Areas
⌐⌐	Picnic Areas
⌂	Hut or Chalet
▲	Mountain
⊹⊹	Railway Station
⫽	Road Bridge
⊬⊬⊬	Road Rail Bridge
⫽	Road Tunnel
⊬⊬	Railway Tunnel
⌒⌒	Escarpment or Cliff
⫽	Pass
∿∿	Ancient or Historic Wall

ROUTES

————	Major Roads and Highways
- - - - - - - -	Unsealed Major Roads
————	Sealed Roads
- - - - - - - -	Unsealed Roads, Tracks
————	City Streets
+++++++++++++	Railways
▬▬◉▬▬	Subways
⋯⋯⋯⋯⋯	Walking Tracks
- - - - - - - -	Ferry Routes
++ ++ ++ ++	Cable Car or Chair Lift

HYDROGRAPHIC FEATURES

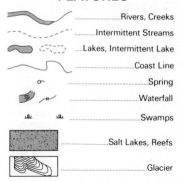

	Rivers, Creeks
	Intermittent Streams
	Lakes, Intermittent Lake
	Coast Line
	Spring
	Waterfall
	Swamps
	Salt Lakes, Reefs
	Glacier

OTHER FEATURES

	Parks, Gardens and National Parks
	Built Up Area
	Market Place and Pedestrian Mall
	Plaza and Town Square
	Cemetery

Note: Not all the symbols displayed above will necessarily appear in this book

Introduction

In past centuries the main visitors to Kenya were the Arab traders who plied their dhows along the eastern coast of Africa. These days it's tourists and adventurers who come to Kenya in large numbers – currently around one million annually – and little wonder as it has an amazing variety of attractions.

For many people Kenya means wildlife and in this field alone it is one of the best places in Africa. Millions of wildebeest on their annual migration, and equally large numbers of pink flamingos massing on the shores of the Rift Valley soda lakes are breathtaking sights. For sheer majesty it's hard to beat the sight of a herd of elephants crossing the flat plains with Africa's most famous mountain, the evocative snow-capped Kilimanjaro, rising in the background. Kenya is also the heart of safari country and a trip through a few of Kenya's spectacular reserves is a memorable experience.

If relaxation is on your mind then head for the coast. Mombasa is a town with a history and from here any of the superb picture-postcard beaches are easily accessible. But without doubt the highlight of the coast is the island of Lamu, where the Arab influence is evident and the pace of life definitely a few steps behind the rest of the country – the perfect place to unwind for a week, or two...

Those people seeking more energetic pursuits will find no shortage of challenges – Kenya has some excellent mountains to climb, especially the very popular Mt Kenya with its unusual alpine flora, and the much less visited Mt Elgon in the west on the Ugandan border. Organised camel treks through the semidesert north of the country also attract a steady stream of hardy souls.

The heart of this relatively prosperous country is the bustling capital, Nairobi, a friendly, modern and efficient city where things work and business can be taken care of in a snap – a far cry from so many other African countries where even simple things like a telephone call can be a major exercise. Added to this is the fact that Kenya has excellent air connections with Europe, Asia and elsewhere in Africa, making it the ideal place for a short visit, or the starting or finishing point for a longer sojourn in Africa. Either way it's a great place – don't miss it.

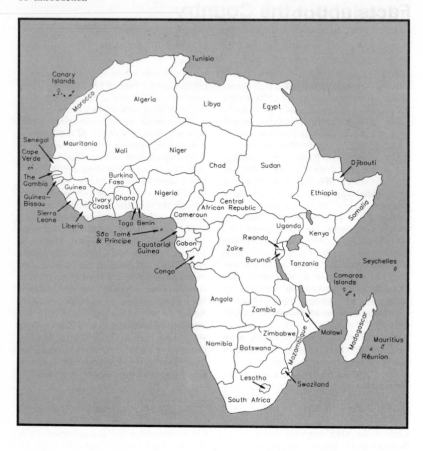

Facts about the Country

HISTORY

The Birthplace of Humanity

The Rift Valley, which runs through the centre of Kenya, has been established as the 'cradle of mankind' as a result of the now famous digs of the Leakey family in Olduvai Gorge (Tanzania) and around Lake Turkana (Kenya). Their discoveries of several hominoid skulls, one of which is estimated to be 2½ million years old, have radically altered the accepted theories on the origin of humans.

Before the East African digs, the generally accepted theory was that there were two different species of the ancestors of modern humans: the apelike *Australopithecus africanus* and the *Australopithecus robustus*. It was believed one of these died out while the other gave rise to *Homo sapiens*. The Leakey discoveries suggested that there was a third contemporary species, *Homo habilis*, and that it was this one which gave rise to modern humans while both the Australopithecus species died out, leaving no descendants.

The Tribes

This area of Africa has a large diversity of peoples – Kenya is home to almost every major language stock in Africa. Even Khoisan, the 'click' language spoken by the Bushmen and Hottentots in southern Africa, has its representatives, although these days they are only a tiny community close to the Tana River near the coast. This diversity is clear evidence that Kenya has been a major migratory pathway over the centuries.

The first wave of immigrants were the tall, nomadic, Cushitic speaking people from Ethiopia who began to move south around 2000 BC. They were pastoralists and depended on good grazing land for their cattle and goats, so when the climate began to change and the area around Lake Turkana became more arid, they were forced to resume their migration south. They were to reach as far as central Tanzania. A second group of pastoralists, the Eastern Cushitics, followed them around 1000 BC and occupied much of central Kenya. The rest of the ancestors of the country's medley of tribes arrived from all over Africa between 500 BC and 500 AD though there was still much movement and rivalry for land right up to the beginning of the 20th century. Even today it hasn't ended completely. The Bantu speaking people (such as the Gusii, Kikuyu, Akamba and Meru) arrived from West Africa while the Nilotic speakers (such as the Maasai, Luo, Samburu and Turkana) came from the Nile Valley in southern Sudan.

The Arabs

While migrations were going on in the interior, Muslims from the Arabian Peninsula and Shirazis from Persia (now Iran) began to visit the East African coast from the 8th century AD onwards. They came to trade, convert and settle, rather than conquer as they had done in North Africa and Spain. Their dhows would head down on the northeast monsoon bringing glassware, ironware, textiles, wheat and wine and return with ivory, slaves, tortoiseshell and rhino horn.

This trade soon extended right across the Indian Ocean to India and beyond. Even China entered the fray at one point early in the 15th century, with a fleet of 62 ships and an escort of some 37,000 men, after the king of Malindi had sent the Chinese emperor a gift of a giraffe! Many of the traders stayed to settle and intermarry with the Africans. As a result, a string of relatively affluent and Islamic-influenced coastal towns sprang up along the East African coast from Somalia to Mozambique, acting as entrepôts for the cross-Indian Ocean trade. Though there was naturally rivalry between these towns from time to time, up until the 16th century life was relatively peaceful. All this was to be rudely shattered with the arrival of the Portuguese.

Kenya

0   100   200 km

The Portuguese

While the Spanish Crown was busy backing expeditions to the Americas, the Portuguese were determined to circumvent the Ottoman Turks' grip on trade with the Far East, particularly the trade in spices which were worth more than their weight in gold in Europe. Throughout the 15th century, the Portuguese had been exploring further and further down the western coast of Africa until, in 1498, they finally rounded the Cape of Good Hope and headed up the eastern coast under the command of Vasco da Gama.

They were given a hostile reception both at Sofala on the Mozambique coast and at Mombasa but were lucky to find a friendly sultan at Malindi who provided them with a pilot who knew the route to India. Da Gama was back again with another expedition in 1502, after selling the first expedition's cargo of spices in Portugal and earning a small fortune.

The main Portuguese onslaught began with Dom Francisco de Almeida's armada of 23 ships and some 1500 men in 1505. Sofala was burned to the ground and looted, Kilwa was occupied and garrisoned, and Mombasa was taken after a naval bombardment and fierce street fighting. Mombasa was sacked again by Nuña da Cunha in 1528. The Arab monopoly of Indian Ocean trade had been broken. Though the Ottoman Turks attempted to wrest it back from the Portuguese in 1585 and again in 1589, they were unsuccessful.

After the original onslaught, there followed two centuries of harsh colonial rule. Tribute was demanded and levies were imposed on all non-Portuguese ships visiting the coastal towns. Severe retribution was the reward for the slightest offence. Economic exploitation came hand in hand with a drive to convert the local population to Catholicism but they never had much success at this and, whenever they abandoned an outpost, those who had been 'converted' reverted back to Islam. Mombasa came to be their principle outpost following the construction of Fort Jesus there in 1593.

The Portuguese task was made easier since they were able to play one sultan off against another, but their grip over the East African coast was always tenuous since their outposts had to be supplied from Goa in India, where the Viceroy had his headquarters. Delays were inevitable. The colonial bureaucracy also became moribund because of the sale of offices to the highest bidder. And, in the final analysis, Portugal was too small a country with insufficient resources to effectively hold onto a worldwide empire.

The beginning of the end came in 1698 when Fort Jesus fell to the Arabs after a siege lasting 33 months and, by 1720, the Portuguese had packed up and left the Kenyan coast for good.

The Omani Dynasties

The Arabs were to remain in control of the East African coast until the coming of the British and Germans in the late 19th century. The depredations of the Portuguese period, however, had exacted a heavy price and the constant quarrelling among the Arab governors who succeeded them led to a decline in the trade and prosperity which the East African coast had once enjoyed. Political and economic recovery had to wait until the beginning of the 19th century.

Throughout the 18th century, Omani dynasties from the Persian Gulf entrenched themselves along the East African coast. They were nominally under the control of the Sultan of Oman but this control was largely ineffective until Seyyid Said came to the Omani throne in 1805. The Omanis had gradually built up a relatively powerful navy during the latter part of the 18th century and Seyyid Said decided to use this to bring the East African dynasties into line. In 1822 he sent an army to subdue Mombasa, Paté and Pemba, which were then ruled by the Mazrui clan.

The Mazruis appealed to Britain for help, which it provided the following year in the form of two warships on a survey mission. The commander of one of these ships, Captain Owen, decided to act first and ask questions later, so the British flag was raised over Fort Jesus and a protectorate was declared. A small garrison was left in charge, but three years later the British government repudiated the protectorate and the flag was hauled down. Seyyid Said reasserted his control the following year, garrisoned Fort Jesus and began to lay out clove plantations on Zanzibar. In 1832, he moved his court to Zanzibar.

19th Century Colonialism

By the mid-19th century, several European nations were showing an interest in the East African coast, including the British and the Germans. The British were interested in the suppression of the slave trade and when Seyyid Said moved to Zanzibar they set up a consulate at his court. Later an agreement was reached between the British and the Germans as to their spheres of interest in East Africa. Part of the deal was that the Sultan of Zanzibar would be allowed to retain a 16 km-wide strip of the Kenyan coastline under a British Protectorate. It remained as such right up until independence when the last Sultan of Zanzibar, Seyyid Khalifa, ceded the territory to the new government.

Since it was occupied by the Maasai pastoralists, the Kenyan interior, particularly the Rift Valley and the Aberdare highlands, remained impregnable to outsiders until the 1880s. Their reputation as a proud warrior tribe had been sufficient to deter Arab slavers and traders and European missionaries and explorers up to that date. But with the rest of Africa being combed by European explorers, Kenya's turn was soon to follow.

Notable early explorers who lived to tell the tale were Gustav Fischer (a German whose party was virtually annihilated by Maasai at Hell's Gate on Lake Naivasha in 1882), Joseph Thomson (a Scot who reached Lake Victoria via the Rift Valley lakes and the Aberdares in 1883), and Count Teleki von Szek (an Austrian who explored the Lake Turkana region and Mt Kenya in 1887). James Hannington, an Anglican bishop who set out in 1885 to set up a diocese in Uganda, wasn't quite so fortunate. Though he discovered Lake Bogoria (known as Lake Hannington during colonial days) he was killed when he reached the Nile.

By the late 19th century, the Maasai were considerably weakened and their numbers reduced by years of civil war between two opposing factions, the Ilmaasai and the Iloikop. The dispute was about which of the two were the true descendants of Olmasinta, the legendary founder of the tribe. Rinderpest (a cattle disease), cholera, smallpox and famine had also taken their toll between 1880 and 1892. Because of this, the British were able to negotiate a treaty with Olonana (these days known as Lenana), the *laibon* (chief, or spiritual leader of the Maasai). Armed with this treaty, the British were able to construct the Mombasa-Uganda railway through the heart of the Maasai grazing lands. The approximate halfway point of this railway is where Nairobi stands today.

White Settlement

With the railway completed and the headquarters of the colonial administration moved from Mombasa to Nairobi, White settlers began to move into the fertile highlands north of Nairobi in search of farming lands. Their interests naturally clashed with those of the Maasai, prompting the colonial authorities to pressure Olonana into restricting the Maasai to two reserves, one on either side of the new railway. Though this was a blow to Maasai independence, worse was to follow since the White settlers soon wanted the northern reserve as well. In 1910-11 those Maasai who lived there were forced to trek south, despite Olonana's objections.

Though it's probably true that it was the Maasai who had the greatest amount of land taken from them by the White settlers, the Kikuyu, a Bantu agricultural tribe which occupied the highlands around the western side of Mt Kenya, also suffered. The Kikuyu came to nurse a particular grievance about the alienation of land by White settlers later on in the 20th century. Many of the numerically larger tribes such as the Luo and Luyha and the tribes of the north-east were hardly affected, if at all.

White settlement in the early years of the 20th century was led by Lord Delamere, a pugnacious gentleman farmer from Cheshire, England. Since he was not familiar with the land, its pests and its wildlife, his first ventures – into sheep farming and, later, wheat growing – were disastrous failures. By 1912, however, following the move to the highlands, Delamere and his followers had put the colony onto a more realistic economic footing by establishing mixed agricultural farms. Other European settlers established coffee plantations about the same time, including Karen von Blixen and her hunter husband, Bror. Her memoirs are to be found in the book *Out of Africa*, which has also been made into a very successful film.

WW I interrupted settlement of Kenya for four years during which time some two-thirds of the 3000 White settlers formed impromptu cavalry units and went off in search of Germans in neighbouring Tanganyika, leaving their wives behind to manage the farms. They were not entirely successful but they did eventually manage to drive the German forces into Central Africa with assistance from Jan Smut's South African units. However, Vorbeck's intrepid unit of 155 Germans and 3000 Africans remained undefeated when the armistice was signed in November 1918. Under the Treaty of Versailles, Germany lost Tanganyika and the British were given a mandate by the League of Nations to control the territory.

Settlement of Kenya resumed after the war under a scheme where veterans of the European campaign were offered land in the highlands, either at rock-bottom prices or on long-term loans. The effect of this was to raise the White settler population to around 9000 by 1920. By the 1950s it had reached 80,000.

African Nationalism

While all this was going on, more and more Kikuyu were migrating to Nairobi or being drawn into the colonial economy in one way or another. They weren't at all happy about the alienation of their land and this led to the formation of a number of associations whose principle concern was the return of land to the Kikuyu.

One of the early leaders of the Kikuyu political associations was Harry Thuku. Shortly after he was arrested for his activities by the colonial authorities in March 1922, a crowd of Africans gathered outside the Nairobi Central Police Station where he was being held. Reports differ as to what happened next but by the time the police had stopped shooting, between 21 and 100 people had been killed. Thuku was eventually exiled to Kisimayo and was only finally released from jail in 1930 after he had agreed to cooperate with the colonial authorities. His cooperation cost him his leadership of the Kikuyu movement since he was thenceforth regarded as something of a collaborator. This early Sharpeville led to the politicisation of the Kikuyu and was the start of a sustained campaign for political, social and economic rights.

While Harry Thuku's star was on the wane, that of another member of the tribe was on the rise. His name was Johnstone Kamau, later changed to Jomo Kenyatta, who was to become independent Kenya's first president. Kenyatta was born in 1892 in the highlands north of Nairobi, the son of a peasant farmer. He spent the early years of his life as a shepherd tending his father's flocks. When he was in his teens he ran away to a nearby Church of Scotland mission school where he picked up an education.

At the age of 29 he moved to Nairobi. He worked there as a court interpreter and water meter reader but his real skills lay elsewhere – as an orator. He soon became the propaganda secretary of the East Africa Association which had been set up to campaign for land reform, better wages, education and medical facilities for Africans. At this time, Africans were barred from hotels and restaurants and were only considered for the most menial jobs within the colonial administration. Although it was official British government policy to favour African interests over those of the settlers in the event of conflicts, this was often ignored in practice because of the dominance of Lord Delamere's lobby in the Whites-only Legislative Council which had been formed after the protectorate became a colony. Recognising this, Kenyatta soon moved to the more outspoken Kikuyu Central Association as its secretary-general.

Shortly afterwards, in 1929, with money supplied by Indians with communist connections, he sailed for London to plead the Kikuyu case with the British colonial secretary. Though the colonial secretary declined to meet him, Kenyatta teamed up with a group called the League Against Imperialism which took him to Moscow and Berlin and then back again to Nairobi. He returned to London the following year and remained there for the next 15 years. He spent his time perfecting his oratory with Trafalgar Square crowds, studying revolutionary tactics in Moscow, visiting cooperative farms in Scandinavia and building up the Pan-African Federation with Hastings Banda (who later became the president of Malawi) and Kwame Nkrumah (who later became the president of Ghana). By the time he returned to Kenya in 1946, he was the recognised leader of the Kenyan liberation movement.

During WW II, the Belgian, British, French and Italian governments all recruited African troops to fight. The overall effect on Africans (as well as soldiers from other colonised peoples) was a realisation that the Europeans were not omnipotent. They could be defeated or, at the least, forced to come to terms with African aspirations for the same benefits and opportunities as their European overlords. Africans had also been trained in the use of arms. When the war ended, therefore, the returning soldiers were in no mood to accept the status quo and began to actively campaign for changes.

The main African political organisation involved in the confrontation with the colonial authorities was the Kenya African Union (KAU), first headed by Harry Thuku and then by James Gichuru who himself stood down in favour of Kenyatta on the latter's return from Britain. The Kikuyu Central Association had been banned in 1940 along with many other similar organisations.

The Mau Mau Rebellion

As the demands of the KAU became more and more strident and the colonial authorities less and less willing to make concessions, oath-taking ceremonies began to spread among various tribes like the Kikuyu, Maasai and Luo. Some of these secret oaths bound the participants to kill Europeans and their African collaborators.

The first blow was struck early in 1953 with the killing of a White farmer's entire herd of cattle. This was followed, a few weeks later, by the massacre of 21 Kikuyu loyal to the colonial government. The Mau Mau rebellion had started. The government declared an emergency and began to herd the tribespeople into 'protected villages' surrounded by barbed wire and booby-trapped trenches which they were forbidden to leave during the hours of darkness. Some 20,000 Kikuyu 'Home Guards' were recruited to assist British army units brought in to put down the rebellion and to help police the 'protected villages'. By the time it came to an end in 1956 with the defeat of the Mau Mau, the death toll stood at over 13,500 Africans – Mau Mau guerrillas, civilians and troops – and just over 100 Europeans, only 37 of which were settlers. In the process an additional 20,000 Kikuyus had been thrown into detention camps.

Only a month after the rebellion started, Kenyatta and several other KAU leaders were arrested and put on trial for allegedly being the leaders of the Mau Mau. It's very doubtful that Kenyatta had any influence over the Mau Mau commanders, let alone that he was one of their leaders, but he was, nevertheless, sentenced to seven years jail in the remote Turkana region after a trial lasting five months. He was released in 1959 but was immediately sent to Lodwar under house arrest.

The rebellion shook the settlers to the roots and gave rise to a number of White political parties with opposing demands, ranging from partition of the country

Mt Kenya's Unusual Alpine Flora

As in other alpine areas of the tropics such as the Andes, the Himalayas, Borneo and on neighbouring Mt Kilimanjaro, there are a number of unusual plant species to be found on the upper slopes of Mt Kenya. Some of these are so characteristic as to be one of the major features of the area. The most prominent are the giant lobelia and the giant groundsel.

The giant lobelia are unmistakable with their unbranched treelike stems topped by a wild looking mop of thick, hairy leaves which, depending on the species, grow to a height of between two and nine metres. The hairs are an adaptation to the severe climate which the plants experience at these altitudes. The stems, nevertheless, remain largely non-woody. Like other lobelia species, the giants have blue to purple flowers borne in clusters on long, terminal spikes which project above the foliage. However, unlike the smaller annual species, giant lobelias flower only once in their lifetime.

There are three giant species found in Kenya. In the wetter forests between 1200 and 2700 metres high, the most usual is *Lobelia gibberoa* which grows up to a height of nine metres. The other two, *Lobelia aberdarica* and *Lobelia telekii*, which grow to a height of two metres, are found between 2100 and 3400 metres, though some hardy individuals grow even as high up as 4600 metres. ■

Giant lobelia & giant groundsel (MS)

The Maasai

It is the Maasai more than anyone who have become the symbol of 'tribal' Kenya. With an (often exaggerated) reputation as fierce warriors and a supercilious demeanour, the Maasai have largely managed to stay outside the mainstream of development in Kenya and still maintain their cattle herds in the area south of Nairobi straddling the Tanzanian border.

They first came to the region from the Sudan and eventually came to dominate a large area of central Kenya until, in the late 19th century, they were decimated by famine and disease, and their cattle herds routed by rindepest. Up until the Masai Mara Game Reserve was created in the early 1960s, the Maasai had plenty of space for cattle grazing, but at a stroke much of this land was put off limits. As their population increased (both the cattle and the Maasai) pressure for land became intense and conflict with the authorities constant. Settlement programmes have only been reluctantly accepted as Maasai traditions scorn agriculture and land ownership is a foreign concept to them.

Another consequence of the competition for land is that many of the ceremonial traditions can no longer be fulfilled. Part of the ceremony where a man becomes a warrior *(moran)* involves a group of young men around the age of 14 going out and building a village *(manyatta)* after their circumcision ceremony. Here they spend as long as eight years alone, and while the tradition and will survives, the land is just not available.

Tourism provides an income to some, either through selling everyday items (gourds, necklaces, clubs and spears), dancing or simply posing for photographs. However, while a few can make a lot of money from tourism the benefits are not widespread. ■

Maasai men - Tsavo West National Park (TW)

between Blacks and Whites to the transfer of power to a democratically elected African government. It should have been obvious to anyone with eyes to see that the latter view would have to prevail in the end, but it wasn't adopted as official policy until the Lancaster House Conference in London in 1960. The rebellion did lead, however, to an exodus of White settlers who packed their bags and headed off to Rhodesia, South Africa and Australia. At the conference, independence was scheduled for December 1963 and the British government agreed to provide the new Kenyan government with US$100 million in grants and loans so that it would be able to buy out European farmers in the highlands and restore the land to the tribes from whom it had been taken.

In the meantime a division occurred in the ranks of KAU between those who wanted a unitary form of government with firm centralised control in Nairobi and the others who favoured a federal setup in order to avoid Kikuyu domination. The former renamed their party the Kenya African National Union (KANU) and the latter split off under the leadership of Ronald Ngala to become the Kenya African Democratic Union (KADU). Many of the White settlers, who had come to accept the inevitable, supported KADU.

Kenyatta was released from house arrest in mid-1961 and assumed the presidency of KANU. Despite his long period of incarceration by the colonial authorities, he appeared to harbour no resentment against the Whites and indeed set out to reassure the settlers that they would have a future in the country when independence came. At a packed meeting of settlers in Nakuru Town Hall in August 1963, he asked them to stay, saying that the country needed experience and that he didn't care where it came from. He assured them of the encouragement and protection of the new government and appealed for harmony, saying that he wanted to show the rest of the world that different racial groups were capable of living and working together. It did the trick. Kenyatta's speech transformed him, in the eyes of the settlers, from the feared and reviled spiritual leader of the Mau Mau into the venerable *mzee* (respected elder) of the post-independence years.

Most of the White settler farms have been bought out by the government over the years and the land divided up into small subsistence plots which support 15 to 20 people. This may well have appeased the pressure for land redistribution in a country with the world's highest birth rate but it has led to a serious decline in agricultural production (and therefore a diminishing tax base for the government) and has threatened to damage the region's delicate ecology. By 1980, Kenya was forced to import half its grain needs whereas in 1975 it was self-sufficient in these. The government is keen to halt the break-up of the 100-odd settler farms which remain but the prospects of being able to do this in a land-hungry nation are not good.

Independent Kenya

The two parties, KANU and KADU, formed a coalition government in 1962, but KANU and Kenyatta came to power in May 1963 following elections. Independence came on 12 December 1963 with Kenyatta as the first president. He was to rule Kenya until his death in 1978. Under Kenyatta's presidency, Kenya developed into one of Africa's most stable and prosperous nations. Unlike many other newly independent countries, there was no long string of coups and counter-coups, military holocausts, power-crazy dictators and secessionist movements. It wasn't all plain sailing but he left the country in a much better state than he found it and, although there were excesses, they were minor by African standards. By the time he died, there were enough Kenyans with a stake in their country's continued progress to ensure a relatively smooth succession to the presidency. Violence and instability would have benefited few people. Kenyatta's main failings were that he was excessively biased in favour of his own tribe and that he often regarded honest criticism as tantamount to treason.

Control of the government and large sectors of the economy still remain in the hands of the Kikuyu, to the social and financial detriment of other ethnic groups. Corruption in high places remains a problem and once prompted J M Kariuki, a former Mau Mau fighter and later an assistant minister in the government, to remark that Kenya had become a nation of '10 millionaires and 10 million beggars'. There are indeed great disparities in wealth. Many destitute squatters and unemployed people, especially in Nairobi, have little hope of ever finding employment – but this is hardly a problem peculiar to Kenya.

Jomo Kenyatta

In 1964, Kenya effectively became a one-party state following the voluntary dissolution of the opposition KADU party. With it died the party's policy of regionalism and the two-chamber Legislature became a single chamber, the National Assembly. However, when Oginga Odinga, a Luo, was purged from the KANU hierarchy in 1966 over allegations that he was plotting against the government, he resigned from the vice-presidency and formed his own opposition party, the Kenya People's Union. The party was later banned and Odinga was jailed. He was released when he agreed to rejoin KANU, but was imprisoned again in 1969 on spurious charges. After his release in 1971 he was banned from running for public office until 1977.

Similarly, Tom Mboya, an intelligent young Luo who was widely regarded as future presidential material, was murdered by a Kikuyu gunman in 1969. The ambitious Mboya was feared by influential Kikuyu who felt that he might have designs on succeeding Kenyatta as president. J M Kariuki, a very popular Kikuyu who spoke out stridently and often about the new Black elite and their corrupt practices, met a similar fate. He was assassinated in 1975. Other politicians who opposed Kenyatta – however mildly – found themselves arrested and held for long periods, often without trial.

Kenyatta was succeeded by Daniel arap Moi, a member of the Tugen tribe and regarded by Kikuyu power brokers as a suitable front man for their interests. Lacking the charisma of Kenyatta and the cult following which he enjoyed, Moi was even less willing to brook criticism of his regime and his early years were marked by the arrest of dissidents, the disbanding of tribal societies and the frequent closure of the universities. There were allegations of conspiracies to overthrow the government whose details were often so labyrinthine they could have come straight out of a modern spy novel. Whether these conspiracies were real or just a convenient facade to justify Moi's consolidation of power is hard to tell since rarely were any names or details released.

What certainly was real was the attempted coup by the Kenyan Air Force in August 1982. It was put down by forces loyal to the government but, by the time it was over, about 120 people had been killed and there was widespread looting of the major shopping areas. Twelve ringleaders were subsequently sentenced to death and 900 others received jail sentences. The entire Kenyan Air Force was disbanded and replaced by a new unit. Since then, other alleged conspiracies have come to light but, again, rarely are the details made known. The most publicised of these clandestine opposition groups was Mwakenya which supposedly centred around a number of lecturers at Nairobi University along with the exiled novelist and playwright, Ngugi wa Thiong'o. Certainly Ngugi has made his opposition to the Kenyan government quite plain but there's little evidence to support the claim that he was a leading light behind the movement.

President Moi was re-elected in March 1987 in an election which was most notable for the controversial voting system used. Candidates could only run in the secret ballot election after gaining a set percentage of the vote in a preliminary election whereby voters queued behind the candidate of their choice. If the candidate gained more than 70% of the queue vote, they were automatically elected and did not have to take part in the secret ballot election. The outcome was that at least 45 constituencies had no secret ballot as the candidate who had received over 70% of the turnout in the queue vote was automatically elected (it didn't matter that in one case the turnout was less than 9% of registered voters). In other constituencies, the number of candidates was significantly reduced because the nominees failed to win sufficient support at the preliminary election.

After the election Moi considerably expanded his cabinet to 33 ministers – many on the basis of political patronage – and, as a result, the government's (and therefore Moi's) position seems totally secure. With the fall of a couple of outspoken politicians in the 1987 elections (amid allegations of vote rigging) it is unlikely that parliamentary opposition to Moi on major issues in the immediate future will be anything more than a whisper. Perhaps more significantly, changes to the constitution were rushed through parliament unopposed in late 1987 which gave Moi increased powers as President, including the right to dismiss senior

judges and public servants without redress. The independence of the judiciary had been a much admired cornerstone of the Kenyan political system ever since independence and the changes were viewed with alarm by many sections of society.

In view of the above changes, there is now no effective political opposition within the parliamentary system and the party has further strengthened its hold by augmenting the ranks of the KANU Youth Brigade who essentially serve as pro-government vigilantes. They are frequently unleashed to disrupt demonstrations, harass opposition figures and maintain a climate of intimidation amongst those who might have similar thoughts.

These days, opposition comes only from groups in the civil field, notably the leaders of various Christian sects and especially the bishops of the Anglican Church. Many have come in for virulent public condemnation for their attacks on the government by various ministers and Moi himself, and there have been demands for their removal and even arrest on charges of sedition. So far, this hasn't happened but it may only be a question of time.

That the government feels under threat from these various civil opposition groups and Western opinion is all too obvious. In late 1989, a programme of screening all residents of Somali origin was announced. The intention behind it was to 'flush out' those who were in Kenya illegally – and there were certainly quite a lot including many who, though they'd never admit it, were involved in the slaughter of rhino and elephant. It's possible that the screening was insensitively handled and it certainly led to the flight of many to neighbouring Uganda and Tanzania, but what enraged the Kenyan government most was a press report in a Canadian newspaper which was highly critical of the exercise. The issue blew up into a full-scale diplomatic row which came close to the recall of ambassadors by both countries. Kenya regarded it as interference in its internal affairs while Canada upheld the freedom of the press. Tempers have since cooled but

Western journalists are now viewed with suspicion by immigration officials on arrival.

Apart from political opposition, the government's main worry is the economy. The budget deficit stands at over US$600 million and is unlikely to improve in the foreseeable future. The main reason for this is the continuing population expansion of around 4% per annum (one of the highest in the world) which is going to see Kenya's population grow from 22-23 million at present to 37-38 million by the end of the century. This is already putting considerable strain on health and educational facilities and is likely to result in increasing social, economic and political turmoil. Of the estimated 400,000 school leavers who come onto the job market each year, only around 30,000 manage to find formal jobs. Or, put another way, of the labour pool of some seven million, there are only about one million formal wage-paying jobs. By the end of the century, it's estimated that the labour pool will double.

Other causes for the budget deficit include heavy maize purchases during 1986-87, increased university intake, the hosting of the All Africa Games in 1987, the 1988 elections, and the Nyayo and Silver Jubilee celebrations of 1988. If it goes ahead – as seems likely – the huge Times Media Complex in Uhuru Park, Nairobi, will further add to national indebtedness. The cost of this project has been set at over US$200 million, most of it coming from overseas banks in the form of a 10 year loan.

It's fair to say beyond the doom and gloom, on the other hand, that Kenya enjoys a healthier economic outlook than any of its neighbours. Tourism is booming, the tea and coffee sectors are relatively efficiently handled (though sales are restricted by international quotas) and the country is now self-sufficient in maize (the national staple food). The country has never had to experience lunatic dictators like Idi Amin followed by multiple civil wars (as in Uganda) or rigid 'socialist' dogmatism coupled with eco-

nomic mismanagement (as in Tanzania). And it's still relatively stable despite political repression.

GEOGRAPHY
Kenya straddles the equator and covers an area of some 583,000 square km which includes around 13,600 square km of inland water in the form of part of Lake Victoria. It's bounded in the north by the arid bushlands and deserts of Ethiopia and Sudan, to the east by Somalia and the Indian Ocean, to the west by Uganda and Lake Victoria, and to the south by Tanzania.

The country can be roughly divided into four main zones: the Coastal Belt, the Rift Valley & Central Highlands, Western Kenya and the North & East of Kenya.

The Coastal Belt
This area covers some 480 km of Indian Ocean littoral including coral reefs and beaches, the Lamu archipelago, the Tana River estuary (Kenya's principal river) and a narrow, low lying and relatively fertile strip suitable for agriculture. Beyond this, the land rises fairly steeply towards the central plateau and gives way to bushland and scrub desert.

The Rift Valley & Central Highlands
These regions form the backbone of the country and it's here that Kenya is at its most spectacular scenically. The lake studded Rift Valley runs the whole length of the country from Lake Turkana to Lake Magadi and is peppered with the cones of extinct volcanos. It's bounded on the eastern side by the thickly forested slopes of the Aberdare mountains and, further to the east, by the massif of Mt Kenya – Africa's second highest mountain at 5199 metres. This is the most fertile area of the country and the lower slopes of the mountains are intensively cultivated. Nairobi, the capital, sits at the southern end of the central highlands.

Western Kenya
The west of the country consists of an undulating plateau stretching from the Sudanese

border to Tanzania in the south. The northern part, particularly around the shores of Lake Victoria, is fertile, well watered and intensively cultivated and it's here that Mt Elgon is situated – Kenya's second highest mountain at 4321 metres. Further south the land gradually merges into scrub and savannah and is suitable only for cattle grazing but it's here that Kenya's largest and most popular wildlife sanctuaries are situated – Masai Mara, Amboseli and Tsavo. To the south of Amboseli rises the spectacular massif of Mt Kilimanjaro – Africa's highest mountain.

The North & East of Kenya
These two regions cover a vast mountainous area of bushland, scrub and desert where rainfall is sparse and where the land is suitable only for cattle grazing. It's this area, however, where Kenya is at its wildest and most untouched by the modern world.

CLIMATE
Because of Kenya's diverse geography, temperature, rainfall and humidity vary widely but there are effectively four zones about which generalisations can be made.

The undulating plateau of western Kenya is generally hot and fairly humid with rainfall spread throughout the year though most of it falls in the evenings. The highest falls are usually during April when a maximum of 200 mm may be recorded whilst the lowest falls are during June with an average of 60 mm. Temperatures range from a maximum of 30-34°C to a minimum of 14-18°C.

The central highlands and Rift Valley enjoy perhaps the most agreeable climate in the country though there's quite a variation between the hot and relatively dry floor of the central Rift Valley and the snow-covered peaks of Mt Kenya. Rainfall varies from a minimum of 20 mm in July to 200 mm in April and falls essentially in two seasons – March to May (the 'long rains') and October to December (the 'short rains'). The Aberdares and Mt Kenya are the country's main water catchment areas and falls of up to 3000 mm per year are often recorded.

Average temperatures vary from a maximum of 22-26°C to a minimum of 10-14°C.

The vast semiarid bushlands, deserts and lava flows of northern and eastern Kenya are where the most extreme variations of temperature are to be found, ranging from up to 40°C during the day in the deserts down to 20°C or less at night. Rainfall in this area is sparse and when it does fall it often comes in the form of violent storms. July is generally the driest month and November the wettest. The average annual fall varies between 250 mm and 500 mm.

The fourth climatic zone is the coastal belt which is hot and humid all year round though tempered by sea breezes on the coast itself. Rainfall varies between a maximum of 240 mm in May to a minimum of 20 mm in February. The average annual fall is between 1000 mm and 1250 mm. Average temperatures vary little throughout the year ranging from a maximum of 30°C to a minimum of 22°C.

FLORA & FAUNA
Flora
With its range of geographical types, Kenya has a corresponding diversity in its flora. The vast plains of the south are characterised by the distinctive flat-topped acacia trees, and interspersed with these are the equally distinctive bottle-shaped baobab trees and thornbushes.

On the slopes of Mt Elgon and Mt Kenya the flora changes with altitude. Above about 1000 metres it is thick evergreen temperate forest which continues to around 2000 metres and then gives way to a belt of bamboo forest to about 3000 metres. Above this height is mountain moorland which is characterised by the amazing groundsel tree (*dendrosencio*) with its huge cabbagelike flowers, and giant lobelias with long spikes.

In the semidesert plains of the north and north-east the vegetation cover is unremarkable – scruffy thornbushes seem to go on forever. In the northern coastal areas mangroves are prolific and the trees are cut for export, mainly to the Middle East for use as scaffolding; mangrove wood is termite resistant and is in high demand.

Fauna

Kenya has such a dazzling array of wildlife that game viewing in the national parks is one of the main attractions of a visit to this country. All of the 'Big Five' (lion, buffalo, elephant, leopard and rhino) can be seen in at least two of the major parks, and there's a huge variety of other less famous but no less impressive animals.

To aid identification of animals while you're game spotting on safari, refer to the Safari Guide at the back of the book. For a full treatment of Kenya's animals, *A Field Guide to the Mammals of Africa* (Collins, 1988) has excellent colour plates to aid identification as does the smaller *A Field Guide to the Larger Mammals of Africa* (Collins, 1986). The main trouble with both these books is the relatively poor index (which lists many animals only by their Latin names) and the dispersion of the colour

plates which are often far from the actual description of the animals in question. *Animals of East Africa* (Hodder & Stoughton, 1960) has good descriptive notes of the animals' habits and appearance, but the

sketches are not the greatest and the notes on distribution are out of date.

The birdlife is equally varied and includes ostriches, vultures and a variety of eagles, waterbirds such as flamingos, storks, pelicans, herons, ibis and cormorants, and others such as the yellow weaver birds which you'll see everywhere. The best reference source for twitchers is *A Field Guide to the Birds of East Africa* by John G Williams. It is widely available in Kenya.

National Parks & Game Reserves

Kenya's national parks and game reserves rate among the best in Africa. Obviously the tremendous variety of birds and animals are the main attractions, and the more popular parks such as Masai Mara Game Reserve and Amboseli National Park see huge numbers of visitors – from the budget campers to the hundreds of dollars a day Hilton hoppers. In the peak season (January-February) on a game drive, you can observe at close quarters the daily habits of the prolific Nissan Urvan. Other smaller parks, such as Saiwa Swamp National Park, near Kitale in the country's western highlands, would be lucky to see a handful of visitors a day at any time of year.

As well as the wildlife to be seen, some parks have been gazetted to preserve the landscape itself, and these too can be exciting and rewarding places to visit – places such as Mt Kenya, Mt Elgon, Hell's Gate, Mt Longonot and the Kakamega Forest are all worth investigating. Marine life is also in abundance and the marine national parks of Malindi and Watamu off the central coast both offer excellent diving prospects.

What probably helps to make Kenyan parks such a draw card for the budget traveller is that the competition among safari companies for the traveller's dollar is so fierce that a safari of at least a few days is within the reach of the vast majority of travellers. For those at the other end of the scale the competition is equally brisk and there are lodges and tented camps within the major parks which have superb facilities and are a real experience – if you can afford them.

As Kenya relies so heavily on tourism for

income, and because it's the animals which people have chiefly come to see, the government has placed a high priority on the conservation of the wildlife and the eradication of poaching. To this end it has appointed Richard Leakey, grandson of Louis Leakey, head of the Ministry of Wildlife, and he has not been afraid to stick his neck out and get things done. Poaching patrols are now much more efficient, extremely stiff penalties for poaching are now in effect, and the estimated 500 of the ministry's Land Rovers which had been left to rot due to lack of maintenance are gradually being refurbished and pressed into service. It was Leakey who recommended that President Moi should take a high profile stance on Kenya's anti-ivory policy and burn the stockpile of confiscated ivory in 1989. This action got good press coverage abroad but was widely criticised at home by people who thought that the ivory should have been sold and the money (estimated at around three million dollars) put to good use.

It's a moot point since although the tourist industry brings in some US$400 million a year, the budget for the national parks was, until very recently, only a tiny fraction of this amount and depended heavily for its anti-poaching measures on gifts from Western governments and environmental groups.

Yet, despite the risks, poaching still goes on and the war (for that is virtually what it is) between the Kenyan government and the poachers has escalated with the poachers turning to robbing tourists when denied elephants and rhino. It's easy to see why. There is big money in ivory and rhino horn and as long as the Taiwanese government and various Arab governments – notably the two Yemens, Oman and Kuwait – refuse to ban their importation, the slaughter of Kenya's wildlife is likely to continue. A kg of ivory is worth about US$300 wholesale and rhino horn is US$2000 a kg (or up to US$30,000 for a single horn). In the Middle East, rhino horn is prized for dagger handles whilst in China and Korea, in powdered form, it's a supposed aphrodisiac.

Although poaching has been going on for many years, it took on a new dimension in 1972 as a result of the drought in North-East Africa which rendered some 250,000 Somali pastoralists destitute as their sheep, goats and camels died by the million. Many drifted south armed with weapons ranging from bows and arrows to WW II guns and found poaching to be a suitable antidote to poverty. Meanwhile, corruption in the Kenyan wildlife department deepened with officials taking cutbacks in return for turning a blind eye to the poachers' activities. By 1976, it was plain that the number of elephants being slaughtered by poachers far exceeded those dying as a result of the drought and the deforestation and it was estimated that there were over 1300 poachers operating within Tsavo National Park alone.

Worst was yet to come. In 1978, waves of Somalis hungry for ivory and rhino horn and encouraged by official corruption swept across the border and into the national parks, only this time they came with modern automatic weapons issued to them by the Somali government during the 1977 war with Ethiopia. They killed everything in their path including any Kenyan tribal poachers who they came across. By the end of the decade, some 104,000 elephants (about 62% of the total) and virtually the entire rhino population had been slaughtered.

There was little improvement during the early '80s despite the setting up of anti-poaching patrols armed with modern weapons, high speed vehicles and orders to shoot on sight. Part of the reason was the patrols' reluctance to engage the Somalis who have a reputation for toughness and uncompromising violence. By 1989, however, following George Adamson's murder by poachers in the Kora National Reserve and attacks on tourists in other national parks, the Kenyan government signalled its determination to seriously address the problem. Following Leakey's appointment, corrupt wildlife officials were sacked and the antipoaching units beefed up, even to the extent that 200 US-trained paramilitary personnel were deployed in 1990 on shoot-to-kill patrols.

The measures have had a large degree of success though it appears that some poachers, denied ivory, are turning to robbing tourists. A few tourists have actually been shot dead and others seriously injured but the numbers are very small – less than 10 so far. Put in the context of around 800,000 to one million tourists who visit Kenya each year, that's still a pretty good safety record and it's only fair to add that some areas are worse than others. Masai Mara, Amboseli and Samburu are considered safe, for example, whereas parts of Tsavo East and Meru are more dubious.

Entry Fees The entry fees to all national parks and to Masai Mara Game Reserve is KSh 220 per person per day plus KSh 50 for a car or KSh 60 for a truck. Camping costs KSh 50 per person per night. Entry fees to game reserves other than Masai Mara vary because they are administered by local county councils but to be on the safe side it's best to assume they are the same as for national parks. If you find them less, consider it a bonus.

Maps If you are driving your own vehicle it's a good idea to equip yourself with maps of the parks before you set out. The best are all published by the Survey of Kenya and obtainable either from the Public Map Office or bookshops in Nairobi. The ones you will need are SK 87 *Amboseli National Park*, SK 86 *Masai Mara Game Reserve*, SK 82 *Tsavo East National Park* and SK 78 *Tsavo West National Park*.

Getting to the National Parks Since you are not allowed to walk in the national parks (with the exception of Hell's Gate, Saiwa Swamp and certain designated areas within Nakuru) you will have to hitch a ride with other tourists, hire a vehicle or join an organised tour.

Hitching is really only feasible if the people you get a ride with are going to be camping. Since this requires some considerable preparation in terms of food, drink and equipment, people with their own cars are naturally reluctant to pick up hitchhikers. If they are going to be staying at the lodges then you have the problem of how to get from the lodge to the camp site at the end of the day. Lodges and camp sites are often a long way apart and driving in the parks is not allowed between 7 pm and dawn. You'll then have to face the problem of transport the following day for game drives and again when you want to leave. All in all, it can be very problematical and it's probably not worth the effort.

Most travellers opt to go on organised safaris. There are scores of different companies offering safaris and they cater for all pockets and tastes. The cheaper ones involve camping and a degree of self-help (erect your own tent, help with the catering, etc) and are for people who don't expect much in the way of comfort but do want an authentic experience in the African bush.

For a full description of safari possibilities, costs and company addresses, etc see the section on organised safaris in the Getting Around chapter.

The alternative to an organised safari is to get a group together and rent a vehicle. If you're looking for other people to join you on a safari using a rented vehicle then check out the notice boards at the Youth Hostel, Mrs Roche's or the Hotel Pigale in Nairobi. As with safaris, a full description of costs and conditions for vehicle hire can be found in the Getting Around chapter.

Accommodation Camping out in the bush is, of course, the authentic way of going about a safari. There's nothing quite like having just a sheet of canvas between you and what you would normally see only on the residents' side of a zoo. Full-on contact with the bush, its potential dangers and rewards is surely what you are looking for. Anything more luxurious than this is going to dilute the experience and remove the immediacy of it all.

It's true there are some beautifully conceived and constructed game lodges and, if you have the money, it's probably worth spending a night or two at one or another of them though it's probably true to say they are mainly for those who prefer to keep the bush at arm's length and a glass of ice-cold beer within arm's reach. Or for those who are simply on a package tour or short holiday and prefer creature comforts and predictability to the rigours of camping. Certainly the way in which some game lodges attract wildlife to their door is somewhat contrived. Hanging up shanks of meat in a tree which a 'resident' leopard comes to feed off 10 minutes later – despite the spotlights – is hardly the essence of Africa. You might as well feed your domestic cat at home and smoke a joint. It's only fair to add, on the other hand, that not all game lodges go in for this sort of circus.

Animal Spotting In the parks and reserves you'll be spending a lot of time craning necks and keeping watchful eyes out for the animals and birds you've come so far to see. There are few telltale signs, as well as a few things you can do to maximise your chances. Most of them are just common sense but it's amazing the number of people who go belting around noisily expecting everything to come to them:

Drive slowly and, where possible, quietly, keeping eyes trained not only on the ground ahead but also to the side and in the branches above.

Go in search in the early morning or the late afternoon, although in the more popular parks such as Amboseli and Masai Mara the animals are actually changing their normal hunting habits to fit in with the tourists, so at midday, when most people are safely back in their lodges stuffing their faces, the carnivores are out hunting in the hope that they may be able to do the same thing – in peace.

Vultures circling are not necessarily an indication of a kill below, but if they are gathering in trees and seem to be waiting you can reasonably assume they are waiting their turn on the carcass.

In wooded country, agitated and noisy monkeys or baboons are often a sign that there's a big cat (probably a leopard) around.

Do's & Don'ts In their quest for the perfect photo opportunity some drivers do some crazy things to that end. Again, a healthy dose of common sense goes a long way, but too many drivers seem to lack one.

Never get too close to the animals and back off if they are getting edgy or nervous. On the safari I was on a female cheetah (with cub) became extremely agitated when she was totally surrounded and hemmed in by a dozen minibuses, all full of excited visitors trying to get their 'shot'. She reacted by dropping the cub and bolting.

Never get out of your vehicle, except at designated points where this is permitted. The animals may look tame and harmless enough but this is not a zoo – the animals are wild and you should treat them as such.

Animals always have the right of way. Don't follow predators as they move off – you try stalking something when you've got half a dozen minibuses in tow.

Keep to the tracks. One of the biggest dangers in the parks today is land degradation from too many vehicles crisscrossing the countryside. Amboseli's choking dust is largely a result of this, and although Masai Mara is less fragile, it too needs to be treated with care.

Don't light fires, and dispose of cigarettes thoughtfully.

Don't litter the parks and camp sites. Unfortunately the worst offenders are often the safari drivers and cooks who toss everything and anything out the window with gay abandon, and leave camp sites littered with all manner of crap. It won't do any harm to point out to them the consequences of what they're doing, or clean it up yourself.

GOVERNMENT
Kenya is a one-party state with the Kenya African National Union (KANO) being the only legal political party. The government consists of the president, who holds executive power, and a legislative assembly of 188 members, 176 of whom are elected. There's a high degree of political patronage (Kikuyu being the major beneficiaries) and, following the 1988 elections, it's probably true to say that the executive's hold on power is unassailable. Opposition within the party and government does exist but there are definite limits to which it is tolerated and accusations of treason against those who oppose executive policy are not uncommon.

The judiciary were, until 1987, independent of government pressure and free to interpret both the constitution and the laws passed by the legislative assembly. In that year, however, parliament rushed through a bill giving the president the right to dismiss judges without recourse to a tribunal, thus effectively silencing them as a source of opposition. The measure was viewed with dismay by many sectors of Kenyan society, but it's now generally accepted that if you have anything negative to say about the government and its policies then you'd better not do it in public. Detention without trial is a common result of indiscretion. Indeed, it would not be inappropriate to slightly misquote Louis XIV's classic statement:

L'état?

C'est Moi!

ECONOMY

The cornerstone of Kenya's capitalist economy is agriculture which employs around 80% of the population, contributes some 31% to the GDP, and accounts for over 50% of the country's export earnings. The principal food crops are maize, sorghum, cassava, beans and fruit while the main cash crops are coffee, tea, cotton, sisal, pyrethrum and tobacco. The bulk of the food crops are grown by subsistence farmers on small plots of land whereas most of the cash crops originate from large, privately owned plantations employing contract labour though there's a significant input from smaller growers. Coffee and tea are the largest of the agricultural export earners with annual production being around 120,000 tonnes and 160,000 tonnes respectively.

While such figures might be a healthy sign for the country's balance of payments (tea fetches between US$2.70 and US$4 per kg on the world market), there's a great deal of discontent among the small farmers and labourers who are paid just US$0.10 per kg (for tea). In 1989-90, the country witnessed riots over this paltry sum. The dispute was handled badly by the Kenya Tea Development Authority (KTDA) and, although several heads have rolled and price increases were promised, there's still a long way to go before a settlement is reached. The situation

is similar in the coffee sector and exacerbated by quotas imposed by the international cartel controlling this product which limits Kenya's ability to dispose of its stockpile. Coffee exports amounted to about 40% of export earnings in 1987.

On the other hand, tourism has replaced coffee as the country's largest export earner with arrivals up from 665,000 in 1987 to around one million in 1990. It seems likely that this growth will continue although there are concerns that the continued depletion of the wildlife in Kenya's game parks through poaching may lead to a fall-off, with Tanzania becoming the preferred destination. This issue is now being addressed and strict conservation measures are being implemented.

In addition to agriculture and tourism, Kenya has a relatively well developed industrial base which accounts for some 15% of GDP though the bulk of this is concentrated around Nairobi and Mombasa. The principal manufactures include processed food, vehicles and accessories, construction materials, engineering, textiles, glass and chemicals. Initially, this sector of the economy was developed with import substitution in mind but the bias has now changed in favour of joint-venture, export-oriented industries as a result of increasing deficit in the balance of payments and IMF loan conditions. Kenya's external debt of around US$4 billion is still considered to be low but the most worrying thing is the proportion of the country's foreign exchange earnings which goes into servicing foreign debt – currently around 35%.

Mining is a relatively small contributor to GNP and centred around the extraction of soda and fluorspar for export. There are other minerals, which include silver, gold, lead and limestone, but these have yet to be developed commercially.

Kenya's major export trading partners are the UK (17%), Germany (11.5%), Uganda (about 9%), the USA (about 7%) and the Netherlands (6.5%).

Some 75% of domestic energy requirements are imported, mainly in the form of oil from Saudi Arabia, but geothermal projects are being developed and there are four hydroelectric plants in operation along the Tana River. These will soon be joined by a huge new hydroelectric plant built in the Turkwel Gorge which is due to come on line in 1990.

Kenya's major sources of imports are Saudi Arabia (18.5%), the UK (about 14%), Japan (10%), Germany (8%) and the USA (5.5%).

POPULATION & PEOPLE

Kenya's population stands at around 23 million and is made up almost entirely of Africans with small (although influential) minorities of Asians (about 80,000), Arabs (about 40,000) and Europeans (about 40,000). The population growth rate of 3.8% is one of the highest in the world and is putting great strain on the country's ability to expand economically, provide reasonable educational facilities and other urban services. It has also resulted in tremendous pressure to increase the area of land under cultivation or for grazing with its associated environmental problems.

The Africans

There are more than 70 tribal groups among the Africans, although the distinctions between many of them are already blurred and are becoming more so as Western cultural values become more ingrained. Traditional values are disintegrating as more and more people move to the larger towns, family and tribal groups become scattered and the tribal elders gradually die off.

Yet even though the average African may have outwardly drifted away from tribal traditions, tribe is still the single most important part of a person's identity. When two Africans meet and introduce themselves they will almost always say right at the outset what tribe they are each from. Although nominally Christian for the most part, a surprising number of people still practice traditional customs. Some of the more inhumane customs, such as cliterodectomy (female circumcision), were outlawed by the British, usually with the aid of the local

missionaries, but circumcision still remains the principal rite of passage from childhood to adulthood for boys.

The most important distinguishing feature between the tribes is language. The majority of Kenya's Africans fall into one of two major groups: the Bantu speakers and the Nilotic speakers. The Bantu people arrived in East Africa in waves from West Africa over a period of time from around 500 BC. Among the Bantu the largest tribal groups

Maasai warrior

are the Kikuyu, Meru, Gusii, Embu, Akamba, Luyha and Mijikenda. The Nilotic speakers migrated to the area from the Nile Valley some time earlier but then had to make room for the migrations of Bantu speaking people. Nilotic speaking groups include the Maasai, Turkana, Samburu, Pokot and Kalenjin. All these tribal groups account for something over 90% of the total African population in Kenya. The Kikuyu and the Luo are by far the most numerous groups, and between them hold practically all the positions of power and influence in the country.

A third language grouping, and in fact the

first migrants into the country, are the Cushitic speakers who occupy the north-east of the country and include such tribes as the El-Molo, Somali, Rendille and the Galla.

On the coast the Swahili is the name given to the local people who, while having various tribal ancestries, have in common the fact that they have been mixing, trading and intermarrying both among themselves and with overseas immigrants for hundreds of years.

The Asians

The economically important Asian minority is made up largely of people of Indian descent whose ancestors originated from the western state of Gujarat and from the Punjab. Unlike the situation in Uganda, sensibility prevailed and the Asians here were not thrown into exile, largely because their influence was too great. Uganda is still trying to get its economy back on track.

India's connections with East Africa go back centuries to the days when hundreds of dhows used to make the trip between the west coast of India or the Persian Gulf and the coastal towns of East Africa every year. In those days, however, the Indians came as traders and only a very few stayed to settle. This all changed with the building of the Mombasa-Uganda railway at the turn of the century. In order to construct it, the British colonial authorities brought in some 32,000 indentured labourers from Gujarat and Punjab. When their contracts expired many of them decided to stay and set up businesses. Their numbers were augmented after WW II with the encouragement of the British.

Since they were an industrious and economically aggressive community they quickly ended up controlling large parts of the economies of Kenya, Tanzania and Uganda as merchants, artisans and financiers. Not only that, but they kept very much to themselves, regarding the Africans as culturally inferior and lazy. Few gave their active support to the Black nationalist movements in the run-up to independence despite being urged to do so by Nehru, the Prime Minister of India. And when independence came, like many of the White settlers, they were very hesitant to accept local citizenship, preferring to wait and see what would happen. To the Africans, therefore, it seemed they were not willing to throw their lot in with the newly independent nations and were there simply as exploiters.

As is well known, Idi Amin used this suspicion and resentment as a convenient ruse to enrich himself and his cronies. Uganda's economy collapsed shortly afterwards since Amin's henchmen were incapable of running the industries and businesses which the Asians had been forced to leave. Asians have fared somewhat better in Tanzania though nationalisation of many of their concerns has considerably reduced their control over the economy. It is in Kenya that they have fared best of all. Here they have a virtual stranglehold over the service sector (the smaller hotels, restaurants and bars, road transport and the tourist trade), the textile trade, book publishing and bookshops, and they are very important in the construction business.

For a time in the 1970s it seemed that there was little future for them in Africa. Governments were under heavy pressure to 'Africanise' their economies and job markets. Even in Kenya thousands of shops owned by Asians who had not taken out Kenyan nationality were confiscated in the early 1970s and they were forbidden to trade in the rural areas. Those days appear to have passed and African attitudes towards them have mellowed. What seemed like a widespread demand that they should go 'home' has been quietly dropped and the Asians are there to stay. The lesson of what happened to the economy of Uganda when the Asians were thrown out is one reason for this.

The Dispossessed

Kenya, being a relatively stable country with opportunities to make a living or at least working the tourists for hand-outs, is a natural magnet for refugees from strife-torn neighbouring countries. Nairobi and

Mombasa and, to a lesser degree, the coastal resort towns, are the favoured destinations. You'll come across plenty of these people on your travels and it's relatively easy to remain anonymous if you can make enough money to stay off the streets.

There's nothing remarkable about this as such – it happens all over the world. What is remarkable in Kenya are the number of unattached teenage mothers – many of them Kenyan but also quite a lot from Uganda, Sudan, Ethiopia and even Rwanda. With the break-up of many traditional communities as a result of colonial policies that were designed to bring people into the money economy, and the continuation of this system under post-colonial regimes, there has been large-scale movement of people to urban areas. Most arrive with nothing and are forced to live in overcrowded shantytowns (some 60% of Nairobi's population live in these places) with little hope of anything resembling a steady job with reasonable pay. As a result, all the facets of urban alienation can be found in these places with drunkenness, theft and rape (particularly of schoolgirls) being fairly commonplace. But this isn't confined to the major urban areas. It appears to be fairly widespread everywhere outside of tribal areas that are still traditional.

As far as the girls are concerned, once they become pregnant they're expelled from school (in other words, it's the end of their educational prospects) and, as likely as not, rejected by their families, too. In 1986, the number of young girls who found themselves in this position (according to official figures) was 11,000 and it's been rising steadily ever since. The options for those to whom this happens are extremely limited. A few shelters do exist (usually run by Christian organisations) but it's only the lucky few who get in. For the rest, it's very poorly paid domestic work or the flesh market.

Laws regarding the responsibilities of paternity in Kenya either don't exist or are hardly ever enforced – it's definitely a man's world – and establishment Kenyan society remains tight-lipped about the problem.

What it remains even more tight-lipped about is the practice of well-to-do Kenyan families recruiting little girls from the bush as domestic servants. Those recruited are even more circumspect.

Though clothed and fed and, if lucky, paid a pittance which varies between US$1 and US$16 a month, these children work on average 15 to 17 hours a day with no days off. Some get no pay at all with just food and clothing provided in lieu of salary. The reason their parents push them into this, apart from the wages which they expect to recoup, is the hope that their children will acquire a training and education of sorts. The reality is often quite different. These girls are often raped by either the man of the house or his sons and thrown out when they become pregnant. Like their more fortunate counterparts who did actually go to school before being expelled, these girls, as likely as not, join the flesh market.

Whatever you may think of prostitution, it's a hard life in Kenya. Minimal rentals, even in rough areas of Nairobi, are around KSh 2000 (about US$95) a month. In better areas it's frequently KSh 4000 to KSh 5000 (US$190 to US$240) a month. Add on decent clothes and footwear and medical attention when necessary, that's a lot of money to be made even to make ends meet – let alone save anything. It's not surprising, therefore, that those who do manage to get their heads above water head for the bars and discos frequented by expatriate workers and tourists since it's more lucrative and there is the vague possibility of marriage or, at least, a long-term friendship. Even so, it's not that easy. Ever since the advent of AIDS, there's been a profound reluctance to tempt fate and prostitutes now carry condoms out of economic necessity as well as to protect themselves from infection.

It isn't just pregnant young girls who find themselves dispossessed of course. The conditions under which young boys have to work in the coffee, sisal and rice plantations are equally onerous and many find their way onto the streets of Nairobi and Mombasa along with other jobless adult males.

Blaming the government for this state of affairs is all too easy for those from rich Western countries but is, to a large degree, unfair. Because of Kenya's high birth rate and the limited amount of funds available, the government is already flat out keeping pace with the demand for schools, hospitals and other social services, the transport infrastructure, and paying interest on its foreign loans. Given this, it's unlikely that much can be done in the foreseeable future for those who fall under the category of the dispossessed.

RELIGION

It's probably true to say that most Kenyans outside of the coastal and eastern provinces are Christians of one sort or another whilst most of those on the coast and in the eastern part of the country are Muslim. Muslims make up some 30% of the population. In the more remote tribal areas you'll find a mixture of Muslims, Christians and those who follow their ancestral tribal beliefs.

As a result of intense missionary activity from colonial times to the present, just about every Christian sect is represented in Kenya, from Lutherans to Catholics to Seventh Day Adventists and Weslyans. The success which all these weird and wonderful sects have enjoyed would be quite mind boggling if it were not for the fact that they have always judiciously combined Jesus with education and medicine – two commodities in short supply until recently in Kenya. Indeed, there are still many remote areas of Kenya where the only place you can get an education or medical help is at a mission station and there's no doubt that those who volunteer to staff them are dedicated people.

On the other hand, the situation is often not as simple as it might at first appear. As with Catholicism in Central and South America which found it necessary to incorporate native deities and saints into the Roman Catholic pantheon in order to placate local sensibilities, African Christianity is frequently syncretic. This is especially so where a tribe has strong ancestral beliefs. There are also many pure home-grown African Chris-

tian sects which owe no allegiance to any of the major Western cults. The only thing they have in common is the Bible though their interpretation of it is often radically different. It's worth checking out a few churches whilst you're in Kenya if only to get an understanding of where the religion is headed and even if you can't understand the language which is being used, you'll certainly be captivated by what only Africans can do with such beauty and precision – unaccompanied choral singing.

The upsurge of home-grown Christian sects has much to do with cultural resurgence, the continuing struggle against neocolonialism, and the alienation brought about by migration to urban centres far from tribal homelands in search of work. Some of these sects are distinctly radical and viewed with alarm by the government. The Tent of the Living God, for instance, was denounced by the President as being anti-Christ and three of its leaders were arrested at a gathering in Eastleigh, Nairobi, in late January 1990. The charges against them were thrown out of court the following week and the men released but the government's action was perhaps an indicator of how it intends to deal with such perceived threats to the status quo in the future.

It isn't just the radical sects which worry the government, however. In the absence of any effective political opposition within the party, even mainstream church leaders have taken to criticising the government from the relative safety of their pulpits. They have likewise been denounced and accused of treason though none have yet been arrested.

As far as Islam is concerned, most Muslims belong to the Sunni branch of the faith and, as a result, the Sunni communities have been able to attract substantial Saudi Arabian funding for schools and hospitals along the coast and elsewhere.

Only a small minority belong to the Shia branch of Islam and most are to be found among the Asian community. On the other hand, Shiites have been coming to East Africa from all over the Eastern Islamic world for centuries, partially to escape persecution but mainly for trading purposes. They didn't come here to convert souls and there was a high degree of cooperation between the schismatic sects and the Sunnis which is why there's a total absence of Shiite customs in Swahili culture today.

Among the Asian community, there are representatives of virtually all Shiite sects but the most influential are the Ismailis – followers of the Aga Khan. As with all Ismailis, they represent a very liberal version of Islam and are perhaps the only branch of the faith which is strongly committed to the education of women at all levels and their participation in commerce and business. It's obvious that the sect has prospered well in Kenya, going by all the schools and hospitals dedicated to the Aga Khan which you will come across in most urban centres.

Hinduism, as is the case in India, remains a self-contained religion which concerns only those born into it. You'll come across a considerable number of temples in the larger urban areas where most of those of Indian origin live. There are literally scores of different sects of Hinduism to be found in Kenya which are too numerous to mention here but many are economically quite influential.

For a superb and very detailed account of each and every Asian-derived sect of both Islam and Hinduism see *Through Open Doors – A View of Asian Cultures in Kenya*, by Cynthia Salvadori (Kenway Publications, Nairobi, 1989). This is a large-format, hardback book with many illustrations on sale in most of Nairobi's bookshops. It's one of the best researched and readable books I've ever come across.

HOLIDAYS & FESTIVALS

January
  New Year's Day
March-April
  Good Friday
  Easter Monday
  Id-ul-Fitr (end of Ramadan, 1991-93)
May
  Labour Day (1st)

June
  Madaraka Day (1st)
October
  Kenyatta Day (20th)
December
  Independence Day (12th)
  Christmas Day (25th)
  Boxing Day (26th)

LANGUAGE

English and KiSwahili are the official languages and are taught in schools throughout Kenya, but there are many other major tribal languages which include Kikuyu, Luo and Kikamba as well as a plethora of minor tribal languages. Most urban Kenyans and even tribal people involved in the tourist industry speak English so you shouldn't experience too many problems making yourself understood. Italian and German are also spoken by many Kenyans but usually only among those associated with the tourist trade on the coast.

It's extremely useful, however, to have a working knowledge of KiSwahili, especially outside of urban areas and in remote parts of the country since this will open doors and enable you to communicate with people who don't speak English. It's also the most common language which speakers of different tribal languages use to communicate with each other. Even tribespeople who haven't been to school will be able to speak *some* KiSwahili as a rule. Not only that, but if you're planning on visiting Tanzania then you'll find it extremely useful as it's essentially become the official language there (though English is still used extensively).

A *Swahili Phrasebook* by Robert Leonard is available in the Lonely Planet language survival kit series.

Pronunciation

KiSwahili vowels are pronounced as follows:

a	as the 'a' in 'father'
e	as the 'e' in 'better'
i	as the 'ee' sound in 'bee'
o	as the 'a' in 'law'
u	as the 'oo' in 'too'

Double vowels, or any two vowels together, are pronounced as two separate syllables. Thus *saa* (time/hour) is pronounced 'sa-a', and *yai* (egg) is pronounced 'ya-i'. There are no diphthongs as in English.

General Rules

KiSwahili relies heavily on prefixes; adjectives change prefix according to the number and class of the noun. Thus *mzuri, wazuri, vizuri* and *kizuri* are different forms of the word 'good'.

Verbs use a pronoun prefix:

I	*ni*
you	*u*
he/she	*a*
we	*tu*
you	*m*
they	*wa*

and a tense prefix:

present	*na*
past	*li*
future	*ta*
infinitive	*ku*

giving you:

We are going to Moshi.
Tunakwenda Moshi.
Shall I take a picture?
Nitapiga picha?
Juma spoke much.
Juma alisema sana.

Some Useful Words & Phrases

hello*
jambo or *salama*
welcome
karibu
How are you?
habari?
I'm fine, thanks
mzuri
goodbye
kwaheri

yes
ndiyo
no
hapana
thank you
asante
thanks very much
asante sana
What's your name?
unaitwa nani?
It is...
ninaitwa...

How was the journey?
habari ya safari?
How much/how many?
ngapi?
where?
wapi?

money
pesa
today
leo
tomorrow
kesho
guest house
nyumba ya wageni
toilet
choo
eat
kula
sleep
lala
want
taka
come from
toka
there is
kuna
there isn't
hakuna
White people
wazungu

* There is also a respectful greeting used for elders: *shikamoo*. The reply is *marahaba*.

Food

food
  chakula
rice
  mchele or *wali*
bananas
  ndizi
bread
  mkate
vegetables
  mboga
salt
  chumvi

meat
  nyama
beef
  ng'ombe
goat
  mbuzi
chicken
  kuku
fish
  samaki
egg(s)
  (ma)yai

milk
  maziwa

water
  maji or *mai*

Numbers

½	*nusu*
1	*moja*
2	*mbili*
3	*tatu*
4	*nne*
5	*tano*
6	*sita*
7	*saba*
8	*nane*
9	*tisa*
10	*kumi*
11	*kumi na moja*
20	*ishirini*
30	*thelathini*
40	*arobaini*
50	*hamsini*
60	*sitini*
70	*sabini*
80	*themanini*
90	*tisini*
100	*mia*

Facts for the Visitor

VISAS

Visas are required by all except nationals of Commonwealth countries (excluding nationals of Australia and Sri Lanka and British passport holders of Indian, Pakistani and Bangladeshi origin), Denmark, Ethiopia, Germany, the Irish Republic, Italy, Norway, Spain, Sweden, Turkey and Uruguay. Those who don't need visas are issued on entry with a Visitor's Pass valid for a stay of up to six months. Three months is the average but it depends what you ask for.

If you enter Kenya through a land border no-one will ever ask you for an onward ticket or 'sufficient funds'. This isn't always the case if you enter by air. A lot depends on what you look like, whether you're male or female, what you write on your immigration card and which immigration officer you deal with. If it's fairly obvious that you aren't intending to stay and work then you'll generally be given the benefit of the doubt. Put yourself in a strong position before you arrive: look smart and write the name of an expensive hotel on your immigration card in the appropriate section.

Single women have been told at times that 'sufficient funds' in the absence of an onward ticket were suspect 'because women lose money easily'! Perhaps the appropriate rejoinder should be that 'men spend money faster'. To balance these experiences, it should be said that we've never heard of anyone being refused entry to Kenya even if, as a last resort, they've had to buy a refundable onward ticket.

So long as your visa remains valid you can visit either Tanzania or Uganda and return without having to apply for another visa. This does not apply to visiting any other countries. There is, however, a charge at the border for doing this – usually about US$4.

Embassies

Visas can be obtained from the following Kenyan diplomatic representatives in:

Australia
  33 Ainslie Ave, Canberra (tel 474788)
Belgium
  1-5 Avenue de la Joyeuse, 1040 Brussels (tel 2303065)
Canada
  Ottawa, Ontario (tel 5631773)
Egypt
  20 Boulos Hanna St, PO Box 362, Dokki, Cairo (tel 704455)
Ethiopia
  Fikre Miriam Rd, Hiher Kebelle 01, PO Box 3301, Addis Ababa (tel 610033)
France
  3 Rue Cimaros, 75116 Paris (tel 4553 3500)
Germany
  5300 Bonn-Bad Godesburg 2, Micael Plaza, Villichgasse 17, Bonn (tel 356042)
India
  E-66 Vasant Marg, 110057 New Delhi (tel 672280)
Italy
  Icilio No 14, 00153 Rome (tel 5781192)
Japan
  24-20 Nishi-Azobu 3-Chome, Minato-Ku, Tokyo (tel 7234006)
Nigeria
  52 Queens Drive, Ikoyi, PO Box 6464, Lagos (tel 682768)
Pakistan
  Sector G-6/3, House 8, St 88, PO Box 2097, Islamabad (tel 811243)
Rwanda
  Boulevard de Nyabugogo just off the Place de l'Unité Nationale, PO Box 1215, Kigali (tel 72774)
Somalia
  Km 4 Via Mecca, PO Box 618, Mogadishu (tel 80857)
Sudan
  Street 3 Amarat, PO Box 8242, Khartoum (tel 40386)
Sweden
  Birger Jarlsgatan 37, 2tr, 10395 Stockholm (tel 218300)
Tanzania
  NIC Investment House, Samora Ave, PO Box 5231, Dar es Salaam (tel 31526)
Uganda
  Plot No 60, Kira Rd, PO Box 5220, Kampala (tel 231861)
UK
  45 Portland Place, London W1N 4AS (tel 6377861)

USA
  2249 R St NW, Washington DC 20008 (tel 3876101)
Zaïre
  5002 Ave de l'Onganda, BP 9667, Gombe, Kinshasa (tel 30117)
Zambia
  Harambee House, 5207 United Nations Ave, Lusaka (tel 227938)
Zimbabwe
  95 Park Lane, PO Box 4069, Harare (tel 790847)

Where there is no Kenyan embassy or high commission, visas can be obtained from the British embassy or high commission.

The cost of visas generally increases with the distance from Kenya and so do the hassles of getting them. We've had cliff-hanger stories from Australia where the high commission took 1½ months to issue a visa. All this time they hung on to the person's passport who only got it back (with a visa) *one* day before the departure date. This is not at all typical but it does indicate that you should apply well in advance if you're flying direct.

In New York visas cost US$10, and you must have two photographs and an onward ticket or a letter from your bank saying you have at least US$2000 in your account. They're issued in 24 hours and are valid for a stay of six months. In London they cost £5, you do not need photographs or onward tickets, and they are issued in 15 minutes. In Australia they cost A$17, require three photos and are *usually* issued within 10 days if you send your passport from another city. Visas are also available on arrival at Jomo Kenyatta International Airport in Nairobi for US$10.

Closer to Kenya things are generally simpler and less time consuming:

Rwanda The embassy is on the Boulevard de Nyabugogo just off the Place de l'Unité Nationale next to the Panafrique Hotel and is open Monday to Friday from 8.30 am to noon and 2 to 4.30 pm. Visas cost RFr 700, require two photographs and are issued the same day if you apply before 11.30 am. No

onward tickets or minimum funds are asked for.

Tanzania The embassy is on the 14th floor, NIC Investment House, Samora Ave at the junction with Mirambo St, Dar es Salaam. Visas cost TSh 700, require two photographs and take 24 hours to issue. The embassy is open Monday to Friday from 9 am to noon.

Uganda The high commission (tel 31861) is at Plot No 60, Kira Rd near the Uganda Museum. It's open Monday to Friday from 8.30 am to 12.30 pm and 2 to 4.30 pm. Visas cost US$3, are issued in 24 hours and two photos are required. If you make your application before noon the visa can usually be issued the same day.

Zambia In Lusaka they cost Kw 15, require two photographs and are issued in 24 hours. No onward ticket is required.

Visa Extensions
Visas can be renewed in Nairobi at Immigration (tel 332110), Nyayo House (ground floor), on the corner of Kenyatta Ave and Uhuru Highway or at the office in Mombasa (tel 311745) during normal office hours. A single re-entry permit costs US$8 and a multiple-entry permit US$40. You must pay in foreign currency. No onward tickets or 'sufficient funds' are demanded. Remember that you don't need a re-entry permit if you're only going to visit Tanzania or Uganda *so long as your visa remains valid*. The staff here are friendly and helpful.

Other Visas
Since Nairobi is a common gateway city to East Africa and the city centre is easy to get around, many travellers spend some time here picking up visas for other countries which they intend to visit. If you are going to do this you need to plan ahead because some embassies only accept visa applications in the mornings, others only on certain days of the week. Some take 24 hours to issue, others 48 hours. Some visas (Sudan,

for instance) may have to be referred to the country's capital city but this is rare.

If you're heading for Zaire get the visa here, where it costs around US$8, rather than in Uganda, Rwanda or Tanzania where you'll pay at least US$70!

Burundi The embassy is on the 14th floor, Development House, Moi Ave (tel 728340). Visas cost KSh 200, require two photographs and take 24 hours. The visa is good for a visit from one to 60 days, depending what you put on the form, and is valid for three months from the date of issue. You can only apply on Mondays and Wednesdays, and collect on Tuesday and Thursday at 4 pm. The embassy is open Monday to Thursday from 8.30 am to 12.30 pm and 2 to 5 pm.

Egypt The embassy is at Chai House, Koinange St (tel 25991). It's open Monday to Friday from 9 am to noon. One month, single-entry visas cost KSh 380, require two photos, an onward ticket and vaccination certificate for yellow fever and cholera. They take 48 hours to issue and you can collect them in the afternoons only from 2 to 3.30 pm.

Ethiopia The embassy is on State House Ave (tel 723035). It's open Monday to Friday from 8.30 am to 12.30 pm and 2.30 to 5 pm. Tourist and transit visas all cost KSh 90, require one photo and take between 24 and 48 hours to issue. Entry and exit is by air only and you must have an onward ticket.

Madagascar There is no Malagasy embassy/consulate as such in Nairobi but visa applications are processed at the Air Madagascar office in the Hilton Hotel block (City Hall Way). Visas cost KSh 170, require four photographs and an onward ticket and are issued in 24 hours.

Rwanda The embassy (tel 334341) is on the 12th floor, International House, Mama Ngina St, Nairobi. It's open Monday to Friday from 8.30 am to 12.30 pm and 2 to 5 pm. One month visas cost KSh 200, require

two photos and take 24 hours to issue. On the application form it will ask you the date when you want to enter Rwanda. Think carefully about this as the visa will run from then.

Somalia The embassy is at International House, Mama Ngina St (tel 24301). Visa applications are only accepted on Monday and Tuesday mornings. One month visas cost KSh 300, require two photographs and are issued in 24 hours. You must have a letter from your embassy stating your profession and a valid reason for visiting Somalia. It's then up to the embassy staff to decide if you qualify for an entry visa – it's by no means assured.

Sudan The embassy is on the 7th floor, Minet ICDC House, Mamlaka Rd (tel 720853). A one month visa costs KSh 200, requires two photographs and takes around one month to issue as all applications have to be forwarded to Khartoum. An onward ticket is necessary.

Tanzania The high commission is on the 4th floor, Continental House, on the corner of Harambee Ave and Uhuru Highway (tel 331056/7). It's open Monday to Friday from 9 am to 5 pm. Visas cost from KSh 100 to KSh 600 (depending on your nationality), require two photographs and take 48 hours to issue.

Uganda The visa section of the high commission is on the 4th floor, Baring Arcade, Phoenix House, Kenyatta Ave. It's not a good place to get a visa as they cost US$20 which must be paid in cash dollars or by travellers' cheque! The office is open from 9.30 am to 12.30 pm and 2.30 to 4 pm. The two week visas take 24 hours to issue and require one photo.

Zaïre The embassy is in Electricity House, Harambee Ave (tel 29771). A one month visa costs KSh 160, a two month visa costs KSh 280 and a three month visa is KSh 350. There is no extra charge for multiple entry; just request it on your visa application form. Four photographs and a letter of introduction from your own embassy are required, and the visas take 24 hours to issue. The staff are pleasant and the embassy is open Monday to Friday from 9 am to noon.

Zambia The high commission is on Nyerere Rd next door to the YWCA (tel 724796). It's open only on Mondays and Fridays from 8.30 am to 12.30 pm and 2 to 4.30 pm, and on Wednesdays from 8.30 am to 12.30 pm. One month, single-entry visas cost KSh 200, require three photographs and take 48 hours to issue. Double entry visas cost KSh 400, multiple entry KSh 600.

Francophone Countries The French Embassy (Embassy House, Harambee Ave; tel 339783) issues visas for French speaking countries which don't have embassies in Nairobi, such as Chad and Central African Republic, for instance. See the Tourist Information section later in this chapter for a full list of foreign diplomatic missions in Kenya.

Working in Kenya

Foreigners will find that jobs are hard to find and working permits are even harder to obtain. Basically the rule of thumb is that if an African can do the job there's no need to hire a *mzungu* (White person). The only real possibilities are teaching jobs and working for one of the international aid agencies. All this sort of work has to be arranged, and permits obtained, before you arrive in Kenya.

MONEY

The unit of currency is the Kenyan shilling (KSh), which is made up of 100 cents. Notes in circulation are KSh 500, 200, 100, 50, 20 and 10; coins are KSh 5 (seven-sided) and KSh 1, and 50, 10 and 5 cents.

The official bank rates fluctuate according to the international currency markets but not by a great deal. The Kenyan shilling is virtually a hard currency, especially in surrounding countries.

US$1	=	KSh 22.00
UK£1	=	KSh 35.30
A$1	=	KSh 17.00
Y100	=	KSh 15.66
C$1	=	KSh 18.60

Import and export of local currency is allowed up to KSh 100 and, when you leave the country, customs officials will ask you if you are carrying any. If you say you are not that's generally the end of the matter. If you're only leaving the country for a short while and intend to return via the same border and don't want to convert all your Kenyan shillings into another currency, you can leave any excess at a border post against a receipt and pick it up again when you get back.

When leaving via Nairobi airport it's possible to reconvert any amount of Kenya shillings to hard currency as long as you have the bank receipts to cover the amount. This is only possible at the airport, and not only is the exchange rate a little low but they charge KSh 100 commission! This facility is obviously meant for those who are leaving the country and have excess shillings (which you can't legally export) but they don't ask to see your air ticket at the time so presumably anyone could do this.

It used to be possible, and still may be, to cash US dollar travellers' cheques at banks in Kenya and get US dollars cash for them, but it's becoming harder. At most banks you'll be met with a flat 'No' but some people are successful. Certainly you have to prove that you are leaving the country within 48 hours (air ticket, dated visa) and you generally need a convincing story about why you need cash dollars.

You can get cash dollars with no problems if you make a withdrawal against your home account using a Visa card at Barclays Bank. So long as you don't want more than US$150 to US$200 per day it takes about 20 minutes. One traveller reported that she was able to get US$1000 in cash though that required a telex to the bank in her home country. Asked why she wanted that amount, she told them she was going to Tanzania where hotel bills and national park entry fees had to be paid in hard currency. Several other travellers have used the same explanation with success. Another traveller reported that it's possible to change your travellers' cheques to gambling chips at the casino in Nairobi, then after a while go back to the cashier and change the chips back to cash dollars.

Bank Charges

Travellers' cheques attract a 1% commission at some banks but none at all at others (at Barclays there's generally no commission). Barclays is probably the best bank to change cheques at since there's hardly any red tape and the transaction takes just a few minutes. Banking hours are Monday to Friday from 8 or 9 am to 2 pm and on the first and last Saturdays of the month from 9 to 11 am.

The Black Market

There is a black market for hard currency in Nairobi but as you only get a few shillings over the bank rate, it's only worth it if you are on a real shoestring budget. You will no doubt be approached by people (mainly in Nairobi) who offer to buy US$ and UK£ from you at a rate which you almost can't refuse (KSh 30 for the US dollar). It's more than likely you are being set up for a rip-off. There is no way *anyone* is going to give you KSh 30 to the US dollar.

If you do want to change money on the black market then it obviously has to be with money which is not declared on your currency form (see below). Keep away from the street hustlers and deal direct with shopkeepers. The travellers' grapevine is the best source of info as to who is currently offering the best rates.

Currency Declaration Forms

Currency declaration forms are usually issued on arrival although you may have to ask for one at the Namanga border between Kenya and Tanzania. These are collected when you leave, but not scrutinised. You cannot change travellers' cheques without a currency form so it's to your advantage to make sure you obtain one.

If for any reason you don't get one, or lose yours, they can be obtained from the Central Bank of Kenya, 9th floor, Ukulima House, Haile Selassie Ave, Nairobi, without any fuss (it takes about 10 minutes). Before you report to the bank you must first get a declaration from the police station on the corner of Harry Thuku Rd and University Way near the university stating that you have lost your original form. There is no fuss about this, just tell them your story.

Currency declaration forms can also be obtained from the Customs desk in the main post office in the larger towns (such as Kisumu, Eldoret and Mombasa).

Currency forms and bank receipts have to be produced when buying international flight tickets in Kenya. If you are intending to do this plan ahead because if you leave the country and then return you will no longer have your original currency form and you will have lost credit for the money which you changed on your first visit. See the Getting There chapter for further details on how this affects you.

Transferring Money

Kenya is a good place to have funds transferred to. It generally takes only a few days. You can collect your money entirely in US dollars travellers' cheques but the money is transferred first into Kenyan shillings then back into dollars. If you are going to spend all the money in Kenya it's worth getting Kenya shillings travellers' cheques and saving yourself a few percentage points commission.

Travellers' cheques issued in Kenya are sometimes stamped 'Non-negotiable in the Republic of South Africa'. If you intend to go there, this is going to cause problems. It is, after all, your money and not the bank's. Some travellers regard this sort of interference as totally unacceptable and have spent the best part of a day arguing with bank officials. Some have been successful. Barclays Bank does this, which is nonsense since they have scores of branches in South Africa.

It's also possible to get cash (dollars or shillings) with a Visa card at Barclays Bank.

At the Bank of Kenya's Bureau de Change at Jomo Kenyatta International Airport, Nairobi, you can exchange shillings for cash dollars up to any amount so long as you have bank receipts to cover the transaction.

COSTS

The cost of budget accommodation in Kenya is very reasonable so long as you're happy with communal showers and toilets. Clean sheets are invariably provided and sometimes you'll also get soap and a towel. For this you're looking at US$3 a single and US$5 a double and up. It can be slightly cheaper on the coast, especially at Lamu. If you want your own bathroom costs rise to around US$5 a single and US$7 a double and up. Again, it can be slightly cheaper on the coast but more expensive in Nairobi.

There are plenty of small cafés in every town, usually in a certain area. They cater to local people and you can get a traditional meal for about US$1. Often the food isn't up to much but sometimes it can be excellent. For a little more the Indian restaurants are great value. Some offer all-you-can-eat lunches for around US$2. They're not only tasty but you won't need to eat for the rest of the day either. A splurge at a better class restaurant is going to set you back between US$5 and US$10.

The price of beer and soft drinks is regulated by the government. At any place other than a tourist hotel (officially known as a Class D establishment), soft drinks are up to KSh 3, and the excellent local beer (Tusker, White Cap and Pilsner) is around KSh 15. At a Class D place you'll pay up to KSh 8 and KSh 30 respectively.

Public transport is very reasonable and the trains are excellent value. To travel from one end of Kenya to the other (Mombasa to Malaba) on the train in 2nd class is going to cost you about US$18. In 3rd class it's less than half of that. Buses are priced about halfway between the 3rd and 2nd class train fares.

The thing that is going to cost you most in Kenya is safaris. A safari for three nights and four days, for instance, by companies which cater for budget travellers is priced around US$130; seven days costs around US$200. This includes transport, food, hire of tents, national park entry fees, camping fees and the wages of the guides and cooks. In other words, more or less everything except a few drinks and tips.

Car hire is even more expensive and is probably out of reach of most budget travellers. A 4WD Suzuki costs around US$500 per week with unlimited mileage; petrol is extra. If you don't want 4WD then a small car, such as a Nissan Sunny, costs around US$400 per week.

TIPPING

With such an active tourist industry, Kenya is a country where tipping is expected. Obviously there's no need to tip in the very basic African eateries or hotels, in *matatus* (local minibuses) or when using other public transport. In better restaurants 5% to 10% of the bill is the usual amount. Porters at hotels and railway stations get around KSh 5 per bag.

If you take a safari then it's also expected that you tip your driver, guide and cook, or at least give them a useful gift of some description. In money terms, KSh 30 per day for the driver, less for cooks and assistants, is about the right amount. This is the cost per person and how much you give obviously depends on whether they have worked well to make your safari enjoyable.

TOURIST INFORMATION

Considering the extent to which the country relies on tourism, there is very little in the way of printed information available, and it's incredible to think that there's not even a tourist office in Nairobi! There are a couple of free weekly pamphlets which go some way towards filling the gap, but they are by no means comprehensive. The best of them is the *Tourist's Kenya*, and it is available at the larger hotels and travel agents in Nairobi. It lists major hotels and airlines and gives schedules for trains, Kenya Airways and the Lake Victoria ferries. It also has a non-exhaustive list of car hire and safari operators. Another one is the monthly *Tourist Index.*

Local Tourist Offices

The only tourist offices in the country are the ones in Mombasa on Moi Ave (tel 311231) and in Malindi on Lamu Rd.

Overseas Reps

The Ministry of Tourism maintains several overseas offices:

France
    Kenya Tourist Office, 5 Rue Volney, Paris 75002
Germany
    Kenya Tourist Office, Hochstrasse 53, 7 Frankfurt
Sweden
    Kenya Tourist Office, Birger Jarlsgatan, S 102 95 Stockholm
Switzerland
    Kenya Tourist Office, Bleicherweg 30, CH-8039 Zurich
UK
    Kenya Tourist Office, 13 New Burlington St, London WIX IFF
USA
    Kenya Tourist Office, 9100 Wilshire Blvd, Doheney Plaza Suite 111, Beverly Hills CA 90121
    Kenya Tourist Office, 60 East 56th St, New York NY 10022

Foreign Embassies

Countries which have diplomatic representation in Kenya (all in Nairobi) include:

Algeria
    Matungulu House, Mamlaka Rd, PO Box 53902 (tel 724634)
Australia
    New Chancery, Riverside Drive, PO Box 30360 (tel 749955)
Belgium
    Silopark House, Mama Ngina St, PO Box 30461 (tel 20501)
Burundi
    Development House, Moi Ave, PO Box 44439 (tel 728430)

Canada
    Comcraft House, Haile Selassie Ave, PO Box 30481 (tel 334033)
Denmark
    HFCK Building, Koinange St, PO Box 40412 (tel 331088)
Egypt
    Chai House, Koinange St, PO Box 30285 (tel 25991)
Ethiopia
    State House Ave, PO Box 45198 (tel 723035)
France
    Embassy House, Harambee Ave, PO Box 41784 (tel 339783)
Germany
    Embassy House, Harambee Ave, PO Box 30180 (tel 26661)
Ghana
    Muthaiga Rd, PO Box 48534 (tel 65417)
India
    Jeevan Bharati Building, Harambee Ave, PO Box 30074 (tel 22566)
Japan
    ICEA Building, Kenyatta Ave, PO Box 60202 (tel 332955)
Libya
    Jamahiriya House, Loita St, PO Box 60149 (tel 337493)
Malawi
    Bruce House, Standard St, PO Box 30453 (tel 21174)
Nigeria
    Lenana Rd, Hurlingham, PO Box 30516 (tel 564116)
Pakistan
    St Michael's Rd, Westlands, PO Box 30045 (tel 61666)
Rwanda
    International House, Mama Ngina St, PO Box 48579 (tel 334341)
Somalia
    International House, Mama Ngina St, PO Box 30769 (tel 24301)
Sudan
    Minet ICDC House, Mamlaka Rd, PO Box 48784 (tel 720853)
Tanzania
    Continental House, Harambee Ave, PO Box 47790 (tel 331056)
Uganda
    Phoenix House, Baring Arcade, Kenyatta Ave
UK
    Bruce House, Standard St, PO Box 30465 (tel 335944)
USA
    Embassy Building, corner Haile Selassie Ave & Moi Ave, PO Box 30137 (tel 334141)
USSR
    Lenana Rd, PO Box 30049 (tel 722462)

Zaïre
> Electricity House, Harambee Ave, PO Box 48106 (tel 29771)

Zambia
> Nyerere Rd, off Central Park, PO Box 48741 (tel 724796)

Zimbabwe
> Minet ICDC Building, Mamlaka Rd, PO Box 30806 (tel 721071)

GENERAL INFORMATION
Post

The Kenyan postal system is very reliable. Letters sent from Kenya rarely go astray but do take up to two weeks to reach Australia or the USA. Incoming letters to Kenya take around a week to reach Nairobi.

Parcels or books sent by surface mail take up to 4½ months to arrive – but they do get there. I can vouch for this – I've sent plenty of stuff this way!

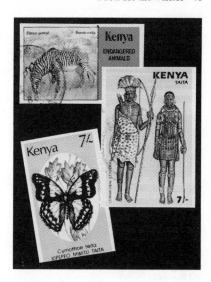

Postal Rates The airmail rates in KSh for items posted from Kenya are:

Item	Africa	Europe	USA & Australia
letter	4.40	5.50	7.70
postcard	2.80	3.90	5.50
aerogramme	3.40	3.40	3.40

The surface mail rates in KSh for parcels posted in Kenya are:

Weight	Europe	USA	Australia
5 kg	160	183	135
10 kg	211	326	168
15 kg	274	469	207
20 kg	328	608	246

Parcel Post Kenya is a good place to send home parcels of goodies, or excess gear. In the main post office in Nairobi you'll always see at least a couple of people busily taping and wrapping boxes to send home. You have to take the parcel *unwrapped* to be inspected by customs at the post office not later than 3.30 pm. You then wrap and send it. The whole process is very simple and, apart from wrapping the parcel, takes only a few minutes.

Right outside the post office in Nairobi there's usually a guy selling all the things you'll need to safely wrap a parcel. When he's there, he hangs out right at the foot of the steps to the bridge across Haile Selassie Ave. Trouble is, he's not always there so it's best to bring along your own cardboard, paper, tape and string. The cheapest place to get this stuff is the supermarket on Koinange St between Kenyatta Ave and Standard St in Nairobi. Otherwise go to Biba on Kenyatta Ave at the junction with Muindi Mbingu St.

Receiving Mail Letters can be sent care of poste restante in any town. Virtually every traveller uses Nairobi as a mail drop and so the amount of mail in poste restante here is amazing. The vast majority of it finds its way into the correct pigeon holes though there's naturally the occasional mistake. Most of the mistakes are entirely the fault of the letter writer. Make sure you write the addressee's name in block capitals and underline it! I can only admire the ingenuity of the postal staff in sorting out poste restante letters into the correct pile after seeing the way that some people address letters. You'd think some people had never been to school! Don't blame the Nairobi postal staff – blame your friends. Nevertheless, if you're not getting expected letters, try looking under all possible initials including 'M' (for M, Mr, Mrs, Ms, if you're an English or French speaker), 'S' (for Señor, Señora, etc, if you're a Spanish or Portuguese speaker), etc.

Some travellers use the American Express Clients Mail Service and this can be a useful alternative to poste restante. Officially you are supposed to have an Amex card or be using their travellers' cheques to avail yourself of this service but no check of this is made at the office in Nairobi. The postal addresses in Nairobi and Mombasa are:

American Express Clients Mail Service
Express Kenya Ltd
PO Box 40433
Nairobi

Express Mombasa
PO Box 90631
Mombasa

The Nairobi office is in Bruce House on Standard St (tel 334722), while the Mombasa office is on Nkrumah Rd (tel 312461).

Telephones

As you might expect, the phone system also works well.

International Calls International calls are easy to make from Nairobi, Mombasa and Kisumu where you can either go through the operator or dial it yourself using a phonecard. These are available from the post office counter in denominations of KSh 200, 400 and 1000. A KSh 200 card gives you around three minutes to Australia or the USA, slightly more to Europe and the UK.

In Nairobi there is one card phone at the main post office and another in the Extelcoms office in Haile Selassie Ave. There are also two in the lobby of the Kenyatta Conference Centre and these are by far the best to use as there's little background noise here. In Mombasa and Kisumu there's one phone at the main post office.

Operator connected calls are also easy to make. The Extelcoms office in Nairobi is open from 8 am to midnight. Again, the Kenyatta Conference Centre is the best place to ring from as there's an international call office in the lobby and this is much quieter and less frantic than the Extelcoms office. It is only open until 6 pm, however.

In other towns calls can be made from the post office, although there may be some delay in getting through to the international operator in Nairobi.

Internal Calls Local and trunk calls are also quite straightforward. There are public phone boxes in every town and these all seem to work. The only problem is that there aren't enough of them, especially in Nairobi where you'll find a queue of four or five people at each box. Local calls cost KSh 1, while STD (long-distance) rates vary depending on the distance. Call boxes accept only KSh 1 and KSh 5 coins. When making an internal call, make sure you put a KSh 1 coin into the machine first (regardless of what you insert after that). If you don't, you may have problems.

Calls to Tanzania are only STD calls, not international.

Electricity

Kenya uses the 240 volt system. The power supply is reliable and uninterrupted in most places.

Time

Time in Kenya is GMT plus three hours all year round.

One thing that must be borne in mind is that Swahili time is six hours out of whack with the way we tell the time, so that midday and midnight are 6 o'clock (*saa sitta*) Swahili time, and 7 am and 7 pm are 1 o'clock (*saa moja*). Just add or subtract six hours from the time you are told and hopefully from the context you'll be able to work out whether it's am or pm the person is talking about! You don't come across this all that often unless you speak Swahili but you still need to be prepared for it – I met one person who missed the one daily bus from a particular town on two consecutive days because he was at the station six hours late.

Business Hours

Government Offices & Businesses These offices are open Monday to Friday from 8 or 8.30 am to 1 pm, and 2 to 5pm. Some private businesses are also open on Saturday mornings from around 8.30 am to 12.30 pm.

Banks Banking hours are Monday to Friday from 9 am to 2 pm. Banks are also open on the first and last Saturday of the month from 9 to 11 am.

In Nairobi and Mombasa there are branches of Barclays Bank which stay open until 4.30 or 5 pm Monday to Saturday. The branch of Barclays Bank at Nairobi airport is open 24 hours.

Outside normal banking hours you may be able to change at one of the five-star tourist hotels, although many are reluctant to help unless you're a guest.

MEDIA
Newspapers & Magazines

Tabloid newspapers are printed in both English and Swahili. Of the three English language papers, the best is probably the *Daily Nation*, which has a surprising amount of both local and overseas coverage. The others are the *Kenya Times* (the KANU party rag) and the *Standard*.

If your Swahili is up to it there's the *Kenya Leo)* (the Swahili version of the *Kenya Times*) and the *Taifa Leo* (the Swahili version of the *Daily Nation*).

There is also a surprising range of locally produced magazines in both English and Swahili. Principal among them is the *Weekly Review* (KSh 20) which is the Kenyan equivalent of Time/Newsweek. Radicals berate this magazine as being a tool of government propaganda but it does, nevertheless, discuss issues in much greater detail than any of the daily newspapers and it's well worth a read. There are plenty of other weekly magazines but they're largely titillative and cater to the lowest common denominator (much like the

News of the World in the UK or *The Sun* in Australia).

Foreign newspapers (up to a week old) in English, French and German are readily available in Nairobi and Mombasa (but expensive!), as are current affairs magazines such as *Time, Newsweek* and the like (at the usual price you'd pay at home).

Radio & TV

The Voice of Kenya radio has transmissions in English, Swahili and more specialised languages such as Hindi and African languages.

The BBC World Service transmits to East Africa on short wave around 12 hours a day and has programmes in English and Swahili.

TV is widespread and most programmes are imported from Europe and the USA.

HEALTH

Kenya is a fairly healthy country to visit. Malaria is endemic and you need to take precautions against chloroquine-resistant strains. Chloroquine-based malaria tablets are available over the counter even in tiny stores out in the country.

Tap water throughout the country is safe to drink but treat with suspicion water obtained from other sources, especially wells and bores.

Travel health depends on your pre-departure preparations, your day-to-day health care while travelling and how you handle any medical problem or emergency that does develop. While the list of potential dangers can seem quite frightening, with a little luck, some basic precautions and adequate information few travellers experience more than upset stomachs.

Travel Health Guides

Two useful books are *The Traveller's Health Guide* by Dr A C Turner (Lascelles, London) and *Preservation of Personal Health in Warm Climates* published by the Ross Institute of Tropical Hygiene, Keppel St, London WC1. Another helpful book on health is David Werner's *Where There is No Doctor: a village health care handbook* (Macmillan

Press, London). *Travel with Children* by Maureen Wheeler (Lonely Planet Publications, Hawthorn) includes basic advice on travel health for younger children.

Pre-Departure Preparations

Medical Insurance Get some! You may never need it, but if you do you'll be very glad to have it. Medical treatment in East Africa is not free and public hospitals are often very crowded. Don't expect the same quality of medical treatment in an East African public hospital as you get back home either. There are many different travel insurance policies available and any travel agent will be able to recommend one.

Before you choose one collect several different policies and read through them for an hour or two, as the cost of a policy and the sort of cover offer can vary considerably. Many pitch themselves at the family package tour market and are not really appropriate for a long spell in Africa under your own steam. Usually medical insurance comes in a package which includes baggage insurance and life insurance, etc. You need to read through the baggage section carefully as many policies put a ceiling on how much they are prepared to pay for individual items which are lost or stolen. Check the small print:

1. Some policies specifically exclude 'dangerous activities' which can include scuba diving, motorcycling, even trekking. If such activities are on your agenda you don't want that sort of policy.
2. You may prefer a policy which pays doctors or hospitals direct rather than you having to pay on the spot and claim later. If you have to claim later make sure you keep all documentation. Some policies ask you to call back (reverse charges) to a centre in your home country where an immediate assessment of your problem is made.
3. Check if the policy covers ambulances or an emergency flight home. If you have to stretch out you will need two seats and somebody has to pay for them!

Medical Kit A small, straightforward medical kit is a wise thing to carry. A possible kit list includes:

1. Aspirin or Panadol – for pain or fever.
2. Antihistamine (such as Benadryl) – useful as a decongestant for colds, allergies, to ease the itch from insect bites or stings or to help prevent motion sickness.
3. Antibiotics – useful if you're travelling well off the beaten track, but they must be prescribed and you should carry the prescription with you.
4. Kaolin preparation (Pepto-Bismol), Imodium or Lomotil – for stomach upsets.
5. Rehydration mixture – for treatment of severe diarrhoea, this is particularly important if travelling with children.
6. Antiseptic, mercurochrome and antibiotic powder or similar 'dry' spray – for cuts and grazes.
7. Calamine lotion – to ease irritation from bites or stings.
8. Bandages and Band-aids – for minor injuries.
9. Scissors, tweezers and a thermometer (note that mercury thermometers are prohibited by airlines).
10. Insect repellent, sunscreen, suntan lotion, chap stick and water purification tablets.

Ideally antibiotics should be administered only under medical supervision and should never be taken indiscriminately. Overuse of antibiotics can weaken your body's ability to deal with infections naturally and can reduce the drug's efficacy on a future occasion. Take only the recommended dose at the prescribed intervals and continue using the antibiotic for the prescribed period, even if the illness seems to be cured earlier. Antibiotics are quite specific to the infections they can treat; stop immediately if there are any serious reactions and don't use it at all if you are unsure if you have the correct one.

In many countries if a medicine is available at all it will generally be available over the counter and the price will be much cheaper than in the West. However, be careful of buying drugs in developing countries, particularly where the expiry date may have passed or correct storage conditions may not have been followed. It's possible that drugs which are no longer recommended, or have even been banned, in the West are still being dispensed in many Third World countries.

Health Preparations Make sure you're healthy before you start travelling. If you are embarking on a long trip make sure your teeth are OK; dentists are few and far between in Africa and treatment is expensive.

If you wear glasses take a spare pair and your prescription. Losing your glasses can be a real problem, although in many places you can get new spectacles made up quickly, cheaply and competently.

If you require a particular medication take an adequate supply, as it may not be available locally. Take the prescription, with the generic rather than the brand name (which may not be locally available), as it will make getting replacements easier. It's a wise idea to have the prescription with you to show you legally use the medication – it's surprising how often over-the-counter drugs from one place are illegal without a prescription or even banned in another.

Immunisations Before you're allowed to enter most African countries you must have a valid International Vaccination Card as proof that you're not the carrier of some new and exotic plague. The essential vaccinations are cholera (valid for six months) and yellow fever (valid for 10 years). In addition, you're strongly advised to be vaccinated against typhoid (valid for one year), tetanus (valid for five to 10 years), tuberculosis (valid for life) and polio (valid for life). Gamma globulin shots are also available for protection against infectious hepatitis (Type A) but they are ineffective against serum hepatitis (Type B). Protection lasts three to six months. There is a vaccine available for Type B but it's only recommended for individuals at high risk. It's expensive, and the series of

three injections takes six months to complete.

You need to plan ahead for these vaccinations, as they cannot all be given at once and typhoid requires a second injection about two or three weeks after the first. Cholera and typhoid jabs usually leave you with a stiff and sore arm for two days afterwards if you've never had them before. The others generally don't have any effect. Tetanus requires a course of three injections.

If your vaccination card expires whilst you're away, there are a number of medical centres in African cities where you can be revaccinated. There's usually a small fee for these but sometimes they are free.

Avoid turning up at borders with expired vaccination cards, as officials may insist on you having the relevant injection before they will let you in and the same needle may be used on a whole host of people.

Your local physician will arrange a course of injections for you or in most large cities there are vaccination centres which you can find in the telephone book:

Belgium
>Ministère de la Santé Publique et de la Famille, Cité Administrative de l'État, Quartier de l'Esplanade, 1000 Brussels
>Centre Médical du Ministère des Affaires Etrangères, 9 Rue Brederode, 1000 Brussels

France
>Direction Départementale d'Action Sanitaire et Sociale, 57 Boulevard de Sevastopol, 75001 Paris (tel 4508 9690)
>Institut Pasteur, 25 Rue du Docteur Roux, 75015 Paris (tel 4566 5800)

Holland
>Any GGD office or the Academical Medical Centre, Amsterdam

Switzerland
>L'Institut d'Hygiène, 2 Quai du Cheval Blanc, 1200 Geneva (tel (022) 438075)

UK
>Hospital for Tropical Diseases, 4 St Pancras Way, London, NW1 (tel (071) 387 4411). Injections here are free but they're often booked up about a month ahead.
>West London Designated Vaccination Centre, 53 Great Cumberland Place, London W1 (tel (071) 262 6456). No appointment is necessary; the fees vary depending on the vaccine.
>British Airways Immunisation Centre, Victoria

Terminal, Buckingham Palace Rd, London, SW1 (tel (071) 834 2323). Try to book a few days in advance, or you might have to wait around for a few hours before they can fit you in.
British Airways Medical Centre, Speedbird House, Heathrow Airport, Hounslow, Middlesex (tel (081) 759 5511).

General Health

The main things which are likely to affect your general health while you're abroad are diet and climate. Stomach upsets are the most likely travel health problem but the majority of these upsets will be relatively minor. Don't become paranoid, trying the local food is part of the experience of travel after all.

Water Avoid drinking unboiled water anywhere it's not chlorinated, unless you're taking it from a mountain spring. Unboiled water is a major source of diarrhoea and hepatitis, as are salads that have been washed in contaminated water and unpeeled fruit that has been handled by someone with one of these infections.

Avoiding contaminated water is easier said than done, especially in the desert, and it may be that you'll have to drink water regardless of where it came from. This is part of travelling and there is no way you can eliminate all risks. Carrying a water bottle and a supply of water-purifying tablets is one way around this. Halazone, Potable Aqua and Sterotabs are all good for purifying water but they have little or no effect against amoebas or hepatitis virus. For this you need a 2% tincture of iodine – five drops per litre in clear water and 10 drops per litre in cloudy water. Wait 30 minutes and it's safe to drink.

Food & Nutrition Cheap food from cafés and street stands tends to be overcooked, very starchy (mainly maize and millet) and lacking in protein, vitamins and calcium. Supplement your diet with milk or yoghurt (where it's available and pasteurised) and fresh fruit or vitamin/mineral tablets. Avoid untreated milk and milk products – in many countries herds are not screened for brucellosis or tuberculosis. Peel all fruit. Read up

on dietary requirements before you set off. And watch out for grit in rice and bread – a hard bite on the wrong thing can lead to a cracked tooth.

Climate In hot climates you sweat a great deal and lose a lot of water and salt. Make sure you drink sufficient liquid and have enough salt in your food to make good the losses (a teaspoon of salt per day is generally sufficient). If you don't make good the losses, you run the risk of suffering from heat exhaustion and cramps. Heat can also make you impatient and irritable. Try to take things at a slower pace. Hot, dry air will make your hair brittle, so oil it often with, say, refined coconut oil. Take great care of cuts, grazes and skin infections otherwise they tend to persist and get worse. Clean them well with antiseptic or mercurochrome. If they're weeping, bandage them up since open sores attract flies. Change bandages daily and use an antibiotic powder if necessary.

A temporary but troublesome skin condition from which many people from temperate climates suffer initially is prickly heat. Many tiny blisters form on one or more parts of your body – usually where the skin is thickest, such as your hands. They are sweat droplets which are trapped under your skin because your pores aren't large enough or haven't opened up sufficiently to cope with the greater volume of sweat. Anything which promotes sweating – exercise, tea, coffee, alcohol – makes it worse. Keep your skin aired and dry, reduce clothing to a loose-fitting minimum and keep out of direct sunlight. Calamine lotion or zinc oxide-based talcum powder helps to soothe the skin. Apart from that, there isn't much else you can do. The problem is one of acclimatisation and shouldn't persist more than a few days.

Adjustment to the outlook, habits and social customs of different people can take a lot out of you too. Many travellers suffer from some degree of culture shock. This is particularly true if you fly direct from your own country to an African city. Under these conditions, heat can aggravate petty irritations which would pass unnoticed in a more temperate climate. Exhausting all-night, all-day bus journeys over bad roads don't help if you're feeling this way. Make sure you get enough sleep.

Everyday Health A normal body temperature is 98.6°F or 37°C; more than 2°C higher is a 'high' fever. A normal adult pulse rate is 60 to 80 per minute (children 80 to 100, babies 100 to 140). You should know how to take a temperature and a pulse rate. As a general rule the pulse increases about 20 beats per minute for each °C rise in fever.

Respiration (breathing) rate is also an indicator of illness. Count the number of breaths per minute: between 12 and 20 is normal for adults and older children (up to 30 for younger children, 40 for babies). People with a high fever or serious respiratory illness (like pneumonia) breathe more quickly than normal. More than 40 shallow breaths a minute usually means pneumonia.

Many health problems can be avoided by taking care of yourself. Wash your hands frequently – it's quite easy to contaminate your own food. Clean your teeth with purified water rather than straight from the tap. Avoid climatic extremes: keep out of the sun when it's hot, dress warmly when it's cold. Avoid potential diseases by dressing sensibly. You can get worm infections through walking barefoot or dangerous coral cuts by walking over coral without shoes. You can avoid insect bites by covering bare skin when insects are around, by screening windows or beds or by using insect repellents. Seek local advice: if you're told the water is unsafe due to jellyfish, crocodiles or bilharzia, don't go in. In situations where there is no information, discretion is the better part of valour.

Medical Problems & Treatment
Potential medical problems can be broken down into several areas. First there are the climatic and geographical considerations – problems caused by extremes of temperature, altitude or motion. Then there are diseases and illnesses caused by insanitation,

insect bites or stings, and animal or human contact. Simple cuts, bites or scratches can also cause problems.

Self-diagnosis and treatment can be risky, so wherever possible seek qualified help. Although we do give treatment dosages in this section, they are for emergency use only. Medical advice should be sought before administering any drugs.

An embassy or consulate can usually recommend a good place to go for such advice. So can five-star hotels, although they often recommend doctors with five-star prices. (This is when that medical insurance really comes in useful!) In some places standards of medical attention are so low that for some ailments the best advice is to get on a plane and go somewhere else.

Climatic & Geographical Considerations
Heat Stroke This serious, sometimes fatal, condition can occur if the body's heat-regulating mechanism breaks down and the body temperature rises to dangerous levels. Long, continuous periods of exposure to high temperature can leave you vulnerable to heat stroke. You should avoid excessive alcohol or strenuous activity when you first arrive in a hot climate.

The symptoms are feeling unwell, not sweating very much or at all and a high body temperature (39°C to 41°C). Where sweating has ceased the skin becomes flushed and red. Severe, throbbing headaches and lack of coordination will also occur, and the sufferer may be confused or aggressive. Eventually the victim will become delirious or convulse. Hospitalisation is essential, but meanwhile get patients out of the sun, remove their clothing, cover them with a wet sheet or towel and then fan continually.

Fungal Infections Hot weather fungal infections are most likely to occur on the scalp, between the toes or fingers (athlete's foot), in the groin (jock itch or crotch rot) and on the body (ringworm). You get ringworm (which is a fungal infection, not a worm) from infected animals or by walking on damp areas, like shower floors.

Sisal Baskets

Sisal baskets, or *kiondos*, are probably the most distinctive Kenyan souvenir and are now popular and widely available in the West. They are still an excellent buy here and the range is staggering – take a look in the market in Nairobi (although buying here is expensive). They come in a variety of sizes, colours and configurations with many different straps and closures. Expect to pay around KSh 60 for a basic one up to around KSh 250 for a large one with a leather 'neck'. Some of the finer ones have the bark of the baobab tree woven into them and this bumps up the price considerably. ■

Soapstone

Soapstone carvings come from Kisii in the west of Kenya. The soft, lightly coloured soapstone is carved into dozens of different shapes – from ashtrays to elephants. The best place for buying Kisii soapstone carvings is not in Kisii, as you might expect, but in Kisumu on Lake Victoria. The only problem is that it's extremely heavy and a kg or two of dead weight in your rucksack is not something to be taken lightly. ■

Makonde

Makonde carvings, which are made from ebony, a very black and very heavy wood, are the best pieces of woodcarving and also the most expensive. This genre of carving had its origins in the highlands on both sides of the Ruvuma River in southern Tanzania but, because of its popularity, has been copied by other carvers all over East Africa. Done with inspiration, attention to detail, and an appreciation of the life force which motivates its imagery, it's a unique art form. Unfortunately, too many imitators create inferior products. Much of what is passed off as ebony is lighter (and cheaper) wood blackened with Kiwi boot polish and the quality of the carving is often slap-dash. A quality piece of makonde carving is always superbly finished.

Maybe you don't care too much about this. Perhaps you like what you imagine to be the slightly rough quality of 'ethnic art'. But, if you do, you're not buying makonde, you're buying repro rubbish.

Before you buy any of this type of carving, do the rounds of the expensive craft shops in Nairobi and see what it ought to look like. Better still, buy it in Tanzania where it's much cheaper anyway. And, when you've seen the real thing, don't get too fetishistic about ebony. There are some excellent Kenyan carvers even if they do it on local hardwoods and employ Kiwi boot polish as the finish.

Basically, there are two forms of this art – the traditional and the modern – and they're instantly distinguishable. The modern stuff is pure Modigliani, though the carvers have doubtless never heard of the man or seen any of his works.

The best pieces, available from the expensive craft shops, are probably made in Tanzania, but you shouldn't pass up the opportunity of having a good look at what is hawked around the bars of Nairobi. Some of it is good; most of it is rubbish. If you're interested, heavy bargaining is the name of the game. ∎

Makonde carvings (HF)

Fabrics & Batik

Kangas and *kikois* are the local sarongs and they serve many useful purposes.

Kangas are colourful prints on thin cotton. Each bears a Swahili proverb and they are always sold in pairs – one to wrap around your waist and one to carry your baby with on your back – though you can buy just one if you prefer. Biashara St in Mombasa is the kanga centre in Kenya, and here you'll pay upwards of KSh 150 for a pair, depending on the quality.

Kikois are made of a thicker cotton and just have stripes. They are originally from Lamu and this is still the best place to buy them, although the kanga shops in Mombasa also stock them. These days they are also made into travellers' clothes in Lamu.

Batiks are another good buy and there's a tremendous range, although the good ones are not cheap. The cheapest ones are printed on cotton and you can expect to pay around KSh 300 for one measuring about one metre by one metre, although the price also varies depending on the artist.

Batiks printed on silk are of superior quality and the prices are generally in the thousands rather than the hundreds of shillings. ∎

Batik cloth (HF)

Jewellery & Tribal Souvenirs

Most of the jewellery on sale is of tribal origin, although very little of it is the genuine article. The colourful Maasai beaded jewellery is the most striking and the most popular, and items include long earrings and the sets of three 'collars', all made with brightly coloured beads.

Other Maasai items include the decorated *calabash* – dried gourds used to store a mixture of blood and milk which is then left to ferment for a few days before it is drunk. Before the mixture is placed in the gourd, specific grasses are burnt inside it, and the soot deposit imparts a certain flavour and aids in fermentation. As you might imagine, these gourds often smell a bit, but are quite strikingly decorated with Maasai beads. Spears and shields are also popular although these are all made specifically for the tourist trade these days.

One of the best places to pick up Maasai souvenirs is at Namanga on the Tanzanian border. This is where all the minibuses headed for Amboseli pass through and stop for a few minutes, so prices are outrageous. However, with some persistent bargaining you can reduce the prices to realistic levels. They know as well as you that the prices they ask are ridiculous, but there are plenty of well heeled tourists passing through here who have more money than sense. For instance, the starting price for earrings is KSh 100 per pair, but they are quite happy to sell them for KSh 10; similarly I expressed an interest in a calabash and was quoted KSh 500 – and eventually paid KSh 35!

All this stuff is bought cheaper out in the bush away from the tourist circuits but buying still demands judicious haggling. ■

Maasai jewellery (HF)

Maasai calabash (HF)

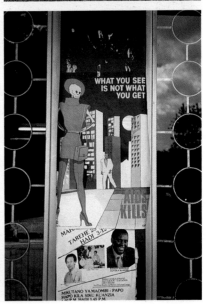

Top Left: Market stall, Naivasha (RA)
Top Right: Wildebeest, Amboseli National Park (GC)
Bottom Left: Kikuyu woman married into Maasai tribe (GH)
Bottom Right: AIDS poster, Nairobi (GP)

Top: Masai giraffes (HF)
Bottom: Kenyan flora (GC)

To prevent fungal infections wear loose, comfortable clothes, avoid artificial fibres, wash frequently and dry carefully. If you do get an infection, wash the infected area daily with a disinfectant or medicated soap and water, and rinse and dry well. Apply an antifungal powder like the widely available Tinaderm. Try to expose the infected area to air or sunlight as much as possible and wash all towels and underwear in hot water as well as changing them often.

Tropical Ulcers These are sores which often start from some insignificant scratch or blister which doesn't seem to heal up. They often get worse and spread to other areas of the body and they can be quite painful. If you keep clean and look after any sores which you get on your arms and legs (from ill-fitting shoes, accidents to your feet, or from excessive scratching of insect bites) then it's unlikely you will be troubled by them. If you do develop sores which won't clear up then you need to hit the antibiotics quickly. Don't let them spread.

Altitude Sickness Acute Mountain Sickness or AMS occurs at high altitude and can be fatal. The lack of oxygen at high altitudes affects most people to some extent. Take it easy at first, increase your liquid intake and eat well. Even with acclimatisation you may still have trouble adjusting – headaches, nausea, dizziness, a dry cough, insomnia, breathlessness and loss of appetite are all signs to heed. If you reach a high altitude by trekking, acclimatisation takes place gradually and you are less likely to be affected than if you fly straight there.

Mild altitude problems will generally abate after a day or so but if the symptoms persist or become worse the only treatment is to descend – even 500 metres can help. Breathlessness, a dry, irritative cough (which may progress to the production of pink, frothy sputum), severe headache, loss of appetite, nausea, and sometimes vomiting are all danger signs. Increasing tiredness, confusion, and lack of coordination and balance are real danger signs. Any of these symptoms individually, even just a persistent headache, can be a warning.

There is no hard and fast rule as to how high is too high: AMS has been fatal at altitudes of 3000 metres, although 3500 to 4500 metres is the usual range. It is always wise to sleep at a lower altitude than the greatest height reached during the day.

Motion Sickness Eating lightly before and during a trip will reduce the chances of motion sickness. If you are prone to motion sickness try to find a place that minimises disturbance – near the wing on aircraft, close to midships on boats, near the centre on buses. Fresh air usually helps, reading or cigarette smoke doesn't. Commercial anti-motion-sickness preparations, which can cause drowsiness, have to be taken before the trip commences; when you're feeling sick it's too late. Ginger is a natural preventative and is available in capsule form.

Diseases of Insanitation
Diarrhoea Sooner or later most travellers get diarrhoea, so you may as well accept the inevitable. You can't really expect to travel halfway around the world without succumbing to diarrhoea at least once or twice, but it doesn't always mean that you've caught a bug. Depending on how much travelling you've done and what your guts are used to, it can be merely the result of a change of food. If you've spent all your life living out of sterilised, cellophane-wrapped packets and tins from the local supermarket, you're going to have a hard time until you adjust.

If and when you get a gut infection, avoid rushing off to the chemist and filling yourself with antibiotics. It's a harsh way to treat your system and you can build up a tolerance to them with overuse. Try to starve the bugs out first. Eat nothing and rest. Avoid travelling. Drink plenty of fluids. Have your tea with a little sugar and no milk. Diarrhoea will dehydrate you and may result in painful muscular cramps in your guts. The cramps are due to a bad salt balance in your blood, so take a small amount of salt with your tea. If you can find it, tincture of opium (known as 'paregoric' and often mixed with kaolin – a stronger version of Milk of Magnesia) will relieve the pain of cramps. Something else you may come across, called RD Sol, also helps to maintain a correct salt balance and so prevent cramps. It's a mixture of common salt, sodium bicarbonate, potassium chloride and dextrose. Two days of this regime should clear you out.

If you simply can't hack starving, keep to a *light* diet of curd, yoghurt, toast, dry biscuits, rice and tea. Stay away from butter, milk, sugar, cakes and fruit.

If starving doesn't work or you really have to move on and can't rest for a couple of days, try Pesulin (or Pesulin-O which is the same but with the addition of a tincture of opium). The dosage is two teaspoons four times daily for five days. Or try Lomotil – the dosage is two tablets three times daily for two days. Avoid overuse of Lomotil.

If you have no luck with either of these, change to antibiotics or see a doctor. There are many different varieties of antibiotics and you almost need to be a biochemist to know what the differences between them are. They include tetracycline, chlorostep, typhstrep, sulphatriad, streptomagma and thiazole. If possible, have a word with the chemist about their differences. Overuse will do you more harm than good but you must complete the course otherwise the infection may return and then you'll have even more difficulty getting rid of it.

Giardia Giardia is prevalent in tropical climates and is characterised by swelling of the stomach, pale-coloured faeces, diarrhoea and, after a while, depression and sometimes nausea. Many doctors recommend Flagyl – seven 250 mg doses over a three day period should clear up the symptoms, repeated a week later if not. Flagyl, however, has many side effects and some doctors prefer to treat giardia with Tinaba (tinadozole). Two grams taken all at once normally knocks it right out but if not you can repeat the dosage for up to three days.

Dysentery Dysentery is, unfortunately,

quite prevalent in some places. It's characterised by diarrhoea containing blood and lots of mucus, and painful gut cramps. There are two types. Bacillary dysentery is short, sharp and nasty but rarely persistent – it's the most common variety. Amoebic dysentery is, as its name suggests, caused by amoebic parasites. This variety is much more difficult to treat and often persistent.

Bacillic dysentery comes on suddenly and lays you out with fever, nausea, painful cramps and diarrhoea but, because it's caused by bacteria, responds well to antibiotics. Amoebic dysentery builds up more slowly and is more dangerous. You cannot starve it out and if it's untreated it will get worse and permanently damage your intestines. If you see blood in your faeces persistently over two or three days, seek medical attention as soon as possible.

Flagyl (metronidazole) is the most commonly prescribed drug for amoebic dysentery. The dosage is six tablets per day for five to seven days. Flagyl is both an antibiotic and an antiparasitic as well. It is also used for the treatment of giardia and trichomoniasis. Flagyl should not be taken by pregnant women. If you get bacillic dysentery, the best thing for slowing down intestinal movements is codeine phosphate (30mg tablets – take two once every four hours). It's much more effective than Lomotil or Imodium and cheaper. Treatment for bacillic dysentery consists of a course of tetracycline or bactrim (antibiotics).

Hepatitis Hepatitis is a liver disease caused by a virus. There are basically two types – infectious hepatitis (known as Type A) and serum hepatitis (known as Type B). The one you're most likely to contract is Type A. It's very contagious and you pick it up by drinking water, eating food or using cutlery or crockery that's been contaminated by an infected person. Foods to avoid are salads (unless you know they have been washed thoroughly in purified water) and unpeeled fruit that may have been handled by someone with dirty hands. It's also possible to pick it up by sharing a towel or toothbrush with an infected person.

An estimated 10% of the population of the Third World are healthy carriers of Type B but the only ways you can contract this form are by having sex with an infected person or by being injected with a needle which has previously been used on an infected person.

Symptoms appear 15 to 50 days after infection (generally around 25 days) and consist of fever, loss of appetite, nausea, depression, complete lack of energy and pains around the base of your rib cage. Your skin will turn progressively yellow and the whites of your eyes yellow to orange. The easiest way to keep an eye on the situation is to watch the colour of your eyes and urine. If you have hepatitis, the colour of your urine will be deep orange no matter how much liquid you've drunk. If you haven't drunk much liquid and/or you're sweating a lot, don't jump to conclusions. Check it out by drinking a lot of liquid all at once. If the urine is still orange then you'd better start making plans to go somewhere you won't mind convalescing for a few weeks. Sometimes the disease lasts only a few weeks and you only get a few really bad days, but it can last for months. If it does get really bad, cash in that medical insurance you took out and fly back home.

There is no cure as such for hepatitis except rest and good food. Diets high in B vitamins are said to help. Fat-free diets have gone out of medical fashion, but you may find that grease and oil make you feel nauseous. Seeking medical attention is probably a waste of time and money although you are going to need a medical certificate for your insurance company if you decide to fly home. There's nothing doctors can do for you that you can't do for yourself other than run tests that will tell you how bad it is. Most people don't need telling; they can feel it! Wipe alcohol and cigarettes right off the slate. They'll not only make you feel much worse, but alcohol and nicotine can do permanent damage to a sick liver.

Think seriously about getting that gamma globulin vaccination.

Typhoid Typhoid fever is another gut infection that travels the faecal-oral route – ie, contaminated water and food are responsible. Typhoid is very infectious and vaccination against it is not totally effective. It is one of the most dangerous infections so medical help must be sought.

In its early stages typhoid resembles many other illnesses: sufferers may feel like they have a bad cold or flu on the way, as early symptoms are a headache, a sore throat, and a fever which rises a little each day until it is around 40°C or more. The victim's pulse is often slow relative to the degree of fever present and gets slower as the fever rises – unlike a normal fever where the pulse increases. There may also be vomiting, diarrhoea or constipation.

In the second week the high fever and slow pulse continue and a few pink spots may appear on the body; trembling, delirium, weakness, weight loss and dehydration are other symptoms. If there are no further complications, the fever and other symptoms will slowly go during the third week. However you must get medical help before this because pneumonia (acute infection of the lungs) or peritonitis (burst appendix) are common complications.

The fever should be treated by keeping the victim cool and dehydration should also be watched for. Chloramphenicol is the recommended antibiotic but there are fewer side affects with ampicillin. The adult dosage is two 250 mg capsules, four times a day. Children aged between eight and 12 years should have half the adult dose; younger children should have one-third the adult dose.

Patients who are allergic to penicillin should not be given ampicillin.

Worms These parasites are most common in rural, tropical areas and a stool test when you return home is not a bad idea. They can be present on unwashed vegetables or in undercooked meat and you can pick them up through your skin by walking in bare feet. Infestations may not show up for some time, and although they are generally not serious, if left untreated they can cause severe health problems. A stool test is necessary to pin-point the problem and medication is often available over the counter.

Diseases Spread by People & Animals

Tetanus This potentially fatal disease is found in undeveloped tropical areas. It is difficult to treat but is preventable with immunisation. Tetanus occurs when a wound becomes infected by a germ which lives in the faeces of animals or people, so clean all cuts, punctures or animal bites. Tetanus is known as lockjaw, and the first symptom may be discomfort in swallowing, or stiffening of the jaw and neck; this is followed by painful convulsions of the jaw and body.

Rabies Rabies is found in many countries and is caused by a bite or scratch by an infected animal. Dogs are a noted carrier. Any bite, scratch or even lick from a mammal should be cleaned immediately and thoroughly. Scrub with soap and running water, and then clean with an alcohol solution. If there is any possibility that the animal is infected medical help should be sought immediately. Even if the animal is not rabid, all bites should be treated seriously as they can become infected or can result in tetanus. A rabies vaccination is now available and should be considered if you are in a high-risk category – eg, if you intend to explore caves (bat bites could be dangerous) or work with animals.

Meningococcal Meningitis Sub-Saharan Africa is considered the 'meningitis belt' and the meningitis season falls at the time most people would be attempting the overland trip across the Sahara – the northern winter before the rains come. Other areas which have recurring epidemics are Mongolia, Vietnam, Brazil, the Nile Valley and Nepal.

This very serious disease attacks the brain and can be fatal. A scattered, blotchy rash, fever, severe headache, sensitivity to light and neck stiffness which prevents forward bending of the head are the first symptoms. Death can occur within a few hours, so immediate treatment is important.

Treatment is large doses of penicillin given intravenously, or, if that is not possible, intramuscularly (ie, in the buttocks). Vaccination offers good protection for over a year, but you should also check for reports of current epidemics.

Tuberculosis Although this disease is widespread in many developing countries, it is not a serious risk to travellers. Young children are more susceptible than adults and vaccination is a sensible precaution for children under 12 travelling in endemic areas. TB is commonly spread by coughing or by unpasteurised dairy products from infected cows. Milk that has been boiled is safe to drink; the souring of milk to make yoghurt or cheese also kills the bacilli.

Bilharzia This is caused by blood flukes (minute worms) which live in the veins of the bladder or the large intestine. The eggs which the adult worms produce are discharged in urine or faeces. If they reach water, they hatch out and enter the bodies of a certain species of freshwater snails where they multiply for four or more weeks and are then discharged into the surrounding water. If they are to live, they must find and invade the body of a human being where they develop, mate and then make their way to the veins of their choice. Here they start to lay eggs and the cycle repeats itself. The snail favours shallow water near the shores of lakes and streams and they are more abundant in water which is polluted by human excrement. They particularly like reedy areas. Generally speaking, moving water contains less risk than stagnant water but you can never tell.

Bilharzia is quite a common disease in Africa so stay out of rivers and lakes. If you drink water from any of these places, boil it or sterilise it with chlorine tablets. The disease is painful and causes persistent and cumulative damage by repeated deposits of eggs. If you suspect you have it, seek medical advice as soon as possible – look for blood in your urine or faeces that isn't associated with diarrhoea. The only body of water in

Africa which is largely free of bilharzia is Lake Malawi. Keep out of lakes Victoria, Tanganyika, Mobutu Sese Seko, Edward (Idi Amin) and Kivu and the River Nile. As the intermediate hosts (snails) live only in fresh water, there's no risk of catching bilharzia in the sea.

Sexually Transmitted Diseases Sexual contact with an infected sexual partner spreads these diseases. While abstinence is the only 100% preventative, using condoms is also effective. Gonorrhoea and syphilis are the most common of these diseases; sores, blisters or rashes around the genitals, discharges or pain when urinating are common symptoms. Symptoms may be less marked or not observed at all in women. Syphilis symptoms eventually disappear completely but the disease continues and can cause severe problems in later years. The treatment of gonorrhoea and syphilis is by antibiotics.

There are numerous other sexually transmitted diseases, for most of which effective treatment is available. However, there is no cure for herpes and there is also currently no cure for AIDS. AIDS, also known as 'Slim' in East Africa, is prevalent in Uganda, Rwanda, Burundi and Eastern Zaïre, although less so in Kenya and Tanzania. Most of those who have it are not aware of the fact, and hospitals (if they ever get to them) are likely to diagnose their symptoms as something more mundane. The obvious way to pick it up is to have sex with someone who has the disease. The obvious way to avoid it is to be celibate. Not everyone can do this so if you do have sex make sure you cut the risk as far as you can by using condoms. You are still a long way from 100% safe if you do this but the message has definitely got through and most sexually active Africans living in urban areas carry them.

There are two other ways you can pick it up. The first is if you need a blood transfusion. Blood donors in East Africa are rarely screened for AIDS and if you receive blood from an infected donor you will be exposed to the virus. Your options are probably limited if you get into the sort of strife which requires a transfusion. It is also possible to pick up the virus if you are injected with an unsterilised needle. If you do have an injection in Africa try to ensure the needle is either new or properly sterilised.

Insect-Borne Diseases
Malaria Malaria is caused by a blood parasite which is spread by certain species of night-flying mosquito (anopheles). Only the female insects spread the disease but you can contract it through a single bite from an insect carrying the parasite. Start on a course of antimalarial drugs before you set off and keep it up as you travel.

The drugs are fairly cheap in some places but horrendously expensive in others – the USA and Scandinavia in particular. There are basically two types: Proguanil (or Paludrine) which you take daily and Chloroquine which you take once or twice per week (depending on its strength). Both are marketed under various trade names. In some areas of Africa the parasite is beginning to acquire immunity to some of the drugs. This is particularly true in East and Central Africa. Here you will need to take Maloprim in addition to Chloroquine. You would be very unlucky to contract malaria if you are taking one or more of these drugs but they are not a 100% guarantee.

If you do develop malarial symptoms – high fever, severe headaches, shivering – and are not within reach of medical advice, the treatment is one single dose of four tablets (600 mg) of Chloroquine followed by two tablets (300 mg) six hours later and two tablets on each following day. As an alternative (or in Chloroquine-resistant areas) take a single dose of three tablets of Fansidar.

Other than the malaria hazard, mosquito bites can be troublesome and although it's probably useless to say this, *don't scratch the bites*. If you do, and they don't heal quickly, there's a chance of them becoming infected with something else. You'll come across people in Africa pockmarked with angry sores which started out as insignificant mosquito bites – the owners couldn't resist the urge to scratch them. Don't join them. Will-power works wonders, as does antihistamine cream. To keep the mosquitoes off at night, use an insect repellent or sleep under a fan. Mosquitoes don't like swift-moving currents of air and will stay on the walls of the room in these circumstances.

There is not yet a vaccination against malaria. Take those pills.

Trypanosomiasis (Sleeping Sickness)
This is another disease transmitted by biting insects, in this case by the tsetse fly. Like malaria, it's caused by minute parasites which live in the blood. The risk of infection is very small and confined to areas which are only a fraction of the total area inhabited by the tsetse fly. The flies are only found south of the Sahara but the disease is responsible for the absence of horses and cattle from large tracts of central Africa particularly central and eastern Tanzania.

The fly is about twice the size of a common housefly and recognisable from the scissorlike way it folds its wings while at rest. The disease is characterised by irregular fevers, abscesses, local oedema (puffy swellings caused by excess water retained in body tissues), inflammation of the glands and physical and mental lethargy. It responds well to treatment.

Yellow Fever Yellow fever is endemic in much of Africa. Get that vaccination before you set off and you won't have to worry about it.

Cuts, Bites & Stings
Cuts & Scratches Skin punctures can easily become infected in hot climates and may be difficult to heal. Treat any cut with an anti-septic solution and mercurochrome. Where possible avoid bandages and Band-aids, which can keep wounds wet. Coral cuts are notoriously slow to heal, as the coral injects a weak venom into the wound. Avoid coral cuts by wearing shoes when walking on reefs, and clean any cut thoroughly.

Bites & Stings Bee and wasp stings are usually painful rather than dangerous. Cala-mine lotion will give relief or ice packs will reduce the pain and swelling. There are some spiders with dangerous bites but antivenenes are usually available. Scorpion stings are notoriously painful and in Mexico can actu-ally be fatal. Scorpions often shelter in shoes or clothing.

There are various fish and other sea crea-tures which can sting or bite dangerously or which are dangerous to eat. Again, local advice is the best suggestion.

Snakes To minimise your chances of being bitten always wear boots, socks and long trousers when walking through undergrowth where snakes may be present. Don't put your hands into holes and crevices, and be careful when collecting firewood.

Snake bites do not cause instantaneous death and antivenenes are usually available. Keep the victim calm and still, wrap the bitten limb tightly, as you would for a sprained ankle, and then attach a splint to immobilise it. Then seek medical help, if possible with the dead snake for identifica-tion. Don't attempt to catch the snake if there is even a remote possibility of being bitten again. Tourniquets and sucking out the poison are now comprehensively discred-ited.

Jellyfish Local advice is the best way of avoiding contact with these sea creatures with their stinging tentacles.

Fleas, Lice & Bedbugs Unwanted passen-gers you're likely to come across are fleas, lice and bedbugs. There isn't a lot you can do about fleas. They vary considerably in numbers from one season to another; some places have a lot, others none at all. The less money you pay for a bed or a meal, the more likely you are to encounter them.

You can generally avoid lice by washing yourself and your clothes frequently. You're most likely to pick them up in crowded places like buses and trains, but you might also get them by staying in very cheap hotels. You'll occasionally meet tribespeople whose hair is so matted and so unwashed that it's literally crawling with lice. However, it takes a while for lice to get stuck into you so you should get a companion to have a look through your hair about once a week to see if you've acquired any eggs. They are always laid near the base of the hairs. If you find any, you can either pick them out one by one (very laborious) or blitz them with insecticide shampoo like Lorexane or Sulco. We've had letters from people who have doused their hair in petrol or DDT. You're certainly guaranteed total wipeout this way but it does seem mildly hysterical!

With luck you won't come across bedbugs too often. These evil little bastards live in the crevices of walls and the framework of beds where they hide during the day. They look like lice but they move like greased lightning once you become aware of their presence and switch on the light to see what's happening. Look for telltale bloodstains on the walls near beds in budget hotels. If you see them, find another hotel.

Women's Health

Gynaecological Problems Poor diet, lowered resistance due to the use of antibiotics for stomach upsets and even contraceptive pills can lead to vaginal infections when travelling in hot climates. Keeping the genital area clean, and wearing skirts or loose-fitting trousers and cotton underwear will help to prevent infections.

Yeast infections, characterised by a rash, itch and discharge, can be treated with a vinegar or even lemon-juice douche or with yoghurt. Nystatin suppositories are the usual medical prescription. Trichomonas is a more serious infection; symptoms are a discharge and a burning sensation when urinating. Male sexual partners must also be treated, and if a vinegar-water douche is not effective medical attention should be sought. Flagyl is the prescribed drug.

Pregnancy Most miscarriages occur during the first three months of pregnancy, so this is the most risky time to travel. The last three months should also be spent within reasonable distance of good medical care, as quite serious problems can develop at this time. Pregnant women should avoid all unnecessary medication, but vaccinations and malarial prophylactics should still be taken where possible. Additional care should be taken to prevent illness and particular attention should be paid to diet and nutrition.

Don't Panic

The health section might seem long and off-putting. It isn't meant to be. Most travellers arrive healthy and leave even healthier. If you do pick up something, however, it's useful to know what to do about it.

DANGERS & ANNOYANCES
Theft

Travelling in Kenya is basically trouble free but you definitely do need to keep your wits about you. The time when you face the biggest risk is within the first couple of days of arriving in the country. The people who make a living by relieving people of their possessions can often spot new arrivals by their uncertain movements and general unfamiliarity with the place. This is particularly true in Nairobi, and in fact the number of people who get their passports and money knocked off on the No 34 public bus in from the airport is amazing. The thieves use the 'instant crowd' technique, you'll find yourself jostled and before you know it your bag or money-belt strap has been slashed. Personally, I wouldn't use this bus for quids but, instead, take the Kenya Airways minibus, or even a taxi and get into Nairobi with your valuables intact.

Never leave your gear unattended anywhere as chances are it won't be there when you get back, no matter how short a time you are away. In hotel rooms your gear is generally safe but use your common sense and never leave valuables such as passport, other documents, money and preferably camera equipment in any hotel room. In some places (particularly the real cheapies/brothels) the door locks are purely cosmetic.

The place to carry your passport, money and other precious documents is in a pouch

The Kima Killer

Early this century when the railway line was being pushed through from Mombasa to Kampala and beyond, a remarkable incident occurred at Kima, a small siding on the line, about 110 km along the track south-west of Nairobi.

A rogue lion had been terrorising the track gangs and had in fact claimed a few victims. In an attempt to eradicate this menace, a superintendent of the Uganda Railways stationed in Mombasa, Charles Ryall, decided to mount a night vigil in a railway carriage specially positioned at the Kima siding. The station staff wanted nothing to do with the escapade and had locked themselves firmly in the station buildings.

Ryall left the carriage door open, in the hope that the lion would be lured in, and sat back with rifle at the ready and waited. Inevitably he fell asleep and just as inevitably the lion showed up. The struggle that ensued caused the sliding door on the compartment to shut and the lion was trapped inside with a firm grip on Ryall's neck. Accompanying Ryall in the carriage were two European merchants who were travelling to Nairobi and had hitched a ride with Ryall, agreeing to the overnight stop in Kima. So petrified were they that one of them ducked into the toilet and bolted the door, while the other watched transfixed as the lion wrested the body out the train window!

A reward was offered by Ryall's mother for the capture of the offending lion but it was only after a trap, baited with a live calf, was devised that the human-eater was snared. It seems there was no reason for the lion to have turned human-eater as it was a healthy beast and there was abundant herds of game animals in the vicinity – it just seems to have developed a liking for human flesh.

The railway carriage involved in this incident is preserved today in the Nairobi Railway Museum, while the tombstone of Ryall, which bears the inscription 'He was attacked whilst sleeping and killed by a man-eating lion at Kima', is in the Hill Cemetery, also in Nairobi. ■

against your skin, either around your waist or your neck. Neither method is foolproof but both give a good measure of security and make it much harder to lose things. Leather pouches are far more comfortable to have against your skin than synthetic ones, and the moisture from perspiration is far less likely to turn your precious documents into a soggy pulp.

If you are the victim of a snatch theft, think twice before yelling 'thief' and trying to catch the guy. Once caught, brutal and often lethal punishment is often meted out on the spot by angry crowds, so either be prepared to defend your assailant or give up your possessions as lost.

Confidence Tricks

In Nairobi the chances are you'll come across people who play on the emotions and gullibility of foreigners. People with tales about being 'refugees', usually from Uganda or South Africa, can sound very convincing as they draw you into their net but they all end up asking for money. If you do give any, expect to be 'arrested' by plainclothes 'police', complete with fake ID cards, who then extract a 'fine' from you on the basis that 'it's illegal to give money to foreigners'. It's actually only illegal to give them foreign currency. Stories such as this abound and the number of travellers who get taken in is legend. The best policy is to ignore all such requests for money even though by doing this you'll occasionally be turning down what is a genuine request for help.

Another trick in Nairobi is the envelope full of money which gets dropped on the footpath in front of you. The idea is that, as you are reaching to pick it up, someone else (the accomplice of the person who dropped it) grabs it and then suggests to you that as you both found it you should go somewhere and share your 'good luck'. If you go along the only thing that will be shared is your money in a side alley somewhere.

Another tried and tested con trick is what appears to be a school student who approaches you with a photostated sponsorship form headed by the name of a school.

He tells you his school needs funds to buy equipment and can you give a donation? Look at the form and you'll find the names of two or three wonderfully philanthropic people (usually from the USA, Germany or the UK) who have apparently donated KSh 700 or even KSh 900 to this worthy cause. If you fall for this then you need your head examined. If the person proves persistent, just ask him to go along with you to a telephone so you can confirm that the request is genuine and that the person is a registered student at the school in question.

In Nakuru they don't lack ingenuity either. A trick that has been popular for years involves tourists with cars. Locals splash oil on your wheels, then tell you that your wheel bearings, differential or something else had failed, and then direct you to a nearby garage where their friends would 'fix' the problem – for a substantial fee. We've even had reports of oil being splashed on the back wheels and then the driver being told that the rear differential had failed even though the car was front wheel drive!

Mugging

Foreigners do occasionally get mugged but if you're sensible the chances of it happening to you are extremely small. There are certain places in Nairobi and on the coast where it's not recommended to walk at night, but other than that it's just a matter of common sense: don't go out boozing in the nightclubs carrying your valuables and then go rolling home down the street; don't wear your wealth, or you become a very tempting target. Leave valuable jewellery at home, keep cameras out of sight and don't pull out wads of money to pay for something. Always have enough small change for everyday transactions handy and keep the rest concealed. Take a cue from the taxi drivers of Nairobi who stash their money in at least half a dozen places on their body and in various articles of clothing.

Lastly, be wary on crowded matatus. It's not the ragamuffins you should watch but those who appear to be well dressed and on their way home from work. Plenty of these people work the matatus and you, as a tourist, are just one of their targets. Kenyans get hit, too.

WOMEN TRAVELLERS

Sexual harassment of women is far less prevalent in Kenya than in many countries though essentially this relates only to White women. If you're Black and walking the streets alone after 7 pm, there's a very good chance you'll be arrested, accused of being a whore and pressured into bribing your way out. KSh 200 is the usual amount. Refuse to pay and you could well spend the night in a cell at the central police station, taken to court the following morning and fined KSh 1000. From the people I've met whom this has happened to, you break no ice protesting your innocence even if you're married and your husband happens to be back at a hotel room or elsewhere. It can even happen if you're a Black woman in the company of a White man. The obvious way around this is to take taxis at night if you're going anywhere.

White women come under the category of 'tourists' and enjoy a somewhat dubious though privileged status. If you're one of these, you may get the occasional hassle but it's rarely persistent if treated with the cold shoulder. There are certain areas in Nairobi where you wouldn't want to walk alone at night, but that applies equally to men, though usually for different reasons.

FILM & PHOTOGRAPHY
Film

Film is widely available in Nairobi and the price is fairly competitive with what you'd pay at home. You'll need plenty of it – Kenya has heaps to photograph, and anyone with a camera inevitably gets very shutter-happy in the game parks looking for that 'perfect' shot.

It's wise to take with you films of varying ASAs. If you're using a zoom or long focal length camera (recommended) you're going to need film of at least 200 ASA to give you enough light, especially as the best photo opportunities are early and late in the day

when the light is not as bright as the middle daylight hours. Higher speed film also makes it possible to take photos with a higher shutter speed, which is important when you're trying to photograph moving animals while at the same time you're being bumped around inside a minibus.

Some of the lodges have salt licks which the animals are attracted to at night, so with 800 or 1600 ASA or higher film non-flash photos are a possibility.

You'll find 64, 100, 200 and 400 ASA slide film readily available in Nairobi and Mombasa but 800 ASA hard to find and 1600 ASA almost impossible to find. The same is true for colour negative film. As an indication of price, slide film in Nairobi costs KSh 322 for Kodachrome 64 (36 exposures, processing included). Colour negative film costs KSh 177 for Ektachrome 200 (36) and KSh 140 for Fujichrome 100 (36).

Cameras & Lenses

Wildlife Photography For serious wildlife photography a SLR (single lens reflex) camera which can take long focal length lenses is necessary. If all you have is a little generic 'snapomatic' you may as well leave it behind. Although they are becoming more sophisticated these days, the maximum focal length is around 70 mm – still too small for getting decent shots.

Zoom lenses are probably the best for wildlife photography as you can frame your shot easily to get the best composition. This is important as the animals are constantly and often quickly on the move. The 70 mm to 210 mm zoom lenses are popular and the 200 mm is really the minimum you need to get good close-up shots. The only problem with zoom lenses is that with all the glass (lenses) inside them they absorb about 1½ 'f' stops of light, which is where the 200 and 400 ASA film starts to become useful.

Telephoto (fixed focal length) lenses give better results than zoom lenses but you're limited by having to carry a separate lens for every focal length. A 400 mm or 500 mm lens brings the action right up close, but again you need the 200 or 400 ASA film to make the most of them. You certainly need a 400 mm or 500 mm lens if you're keen on photographing birdlife.

Another option is to carry a 2x teleconverter, which is a small adaptor which fits between the lens and the camera body, and doubles the focal length of your lens, so a 200 mm lens becomes 400 mm. These are a good cheap way of getting the long focal length without having to buy expensive lenses. They do, however, have a couple of disadvantages. The first is that, like the larger lenses themselves, a teleconverter uses about 1½ 'f' stops of light. Another disadvantage is that, depending on the camera and lens, teleconverters can make it extremely difficult to focus quickly and precisely, which is an important consideration when both you and the animals are on the move.

When using long lenses a tripod can be extremely useful, and with anything greater than about 300 mm it's a necessity. The problem here is that in the confined space of the hatch of a minibus (assuming you'll be taking an organised safari) it is impossible to set up the tripod, especially when you are sharing the confined space with at least three or four other people. Miniature tripods are available and these are useful for setting up on the roof of the van, although you can also rest the lens itself on the roof, provided that the van engine is switched off to kill any vibration.

Whatever combination of camera, lenses and accessories you decide to carry, make sure they are kept in a decent bag which will protect them from the elements, the dust, and the knocks they are bound to receive. It's also vital to make sure that your travel insurance policy includes your camera gear if it gets stolen.

Camera Hire

If you don't have the inclination or the resources to buy expensive equipment but still want some decent pictures of your safari, it is possible to hire SLR cameras and lenses in Nairobi. You're looking at around KSh 100 per day for the camera, and as much again for a 70 mm to 210 mm zoom lens.

Places to try include Elite Camera House on Kimathi St, or Expo Cameras and Camera Experts on Mama Ngina St.

Selling Cameras

With the high duty placed on imported goods, you may be surprised to find that your old used camera is worth quite a bit in Kenya. Obviously the better the condition of the camera, the more it will be worth. There are a few camera shops in Nairobi which deal in second-hand equipment, so check them out. One place to try is Expo Cameras on Mama Ngina St. If you do sell your camera chances are they'll pay you in Kenyan shillings, so if it's at the end of your stay you'll need to have enough bank exchange certificates to reconvert the shillings to hard currency at the airport.

Film Processing

There are plenty of one hour film processing labs in Nairobi, and at least one in all other major towns. They handle colour print film only and can process any film speeds. The cost is reasonable and the results just as good as what you'd get back home. One good place is the lab next to the Coffee House on Mama Ngina St. This place also has a wide variety of film for sale. Developing and mounting of slides costs around KSh 95 for 36 exposures.

Photographing People

As is the case in any country where you are a tourist, this is a subject which has to be approached with some sensitivity. The colourful people in Kenya, such as the Maasai and the Samburu, have had so many rubbernecks pointing cameras at them for so many years that they are utterly sick to death of it – with good reason. There are even signs up in Namanga and Amboseli that it is prohibited to take photos of the Maasai. This doesn't mean that you can't, but just that you'll have to pay for it. Much as you may find this abhorrent, it is nevertheless an aspect of the tourism industry you'll just have to accept – put yourself in their position and try to think what you'd do.

It is of course possible to take pictures of people with zoom lenses but, most of the time, what's the point? By paying or giving some sort of gift, you can not only get a better picture by using a smaller lenses but you have some interaction with your subject. You might even get an invitation to see the family (and possibly photograph them).

ACCOMMODATION

Kenya has a good range of accommodation from the very basic US$3 a night budget hotels up to luxury tented camps in the national parks for up to $500 a night!

Hotels

Real bottom of the range hotels (known everywhere as Boardings & Lodgings; 'hotels' are often only restaurants) are generally brothels first and hotels second. This in itself is not a problem as long as you don't mind the noise, disruption and general atmosphere. Most places don't mind renting out rooms all night, although in some you get distinctly strange looks when they discover that not only do you want the room for the whole night, but that you want to spend it alone! These places are also not all that clean – you'll have to ask for clean sheets, the rooms are often claustrophobic cells, the common facilities smell and the whole place exudes a seedy air. On the other hand, you do occasionally come across cheap places which are clean and pleasant places to stay, so don't dismiss them totally; there's usually at least one cheap Boarding & Lodging in each town. On the plus side, they are cheap. Expect to pay around KSh 50/85 for a single/double room.

Things improve dramatically if you have a few shillings more to spend, although there are always exceptions. For around KSh 95/145 a single/double, you will get a clean room with private bath and soap and towel supplied. These places often have a restaurant and bar (usually noisy). They really have no advantage over the really cheap places except perhaps that you get your own bathroom.

Those who prefer a mid-range hotel are well catered for. If you're willing to spend US$10 to US$25 a night then you can expect all the basic comforts and sometimes even a touch of luxury including clean sheets and beds, your own shower and toilet with hot water, towels, soap and toilet paper, a table and chair and often a telephone and room service.

At the top end of the market you have all the usual international chain hotels with prices to match. These start at around KSh 600/800 for a single/double and head up from there. Some of these places are old colonial buildings with bags of atmosphere, but most are modern and somewhat characterless. The resort hotels on the coast and the lodges in the game parks also fall into this category, although some of the latter are superb places to stay if you can afford it – having animals come to drink at the salt lick in front of your lodge as you sit on the verandah sipping a cool drink is just great, but pleasures such as this set you back around KSh 2000/2500 for full board.

Youth Hostels

The only youth hostels affiliated with the IYHA are in Nairobi and Malindi though the one operated by Yare Safaris in Maralal is a member of the national network. If you like youth hostels, they are fine. At KSh 60 for a dorm bed they are not that cheap but, as usual, they are good places to meet people.

Camping

There are enough opportunities for camping that it is worth considering bringing a tent. It is also possible to hire camping equipment in Nairobi and elsewhere but it's not the sort of lightweight gear you could carry without a vehicle.

There are camp sites in just about every national park and game reserve and these are usually very basic. There'll be a toilet block with a couple of long-drops, usually a water tap but very little else. Private sites are few and far between but where they do exist they offer more in the way of facilities. Often it's possible to camp in the grounds of a hotel but this is obviously not an option in the bigger towns where space is limited.

Camping out in the bush is also possible though you would be advised to ask permission first. On the coast this is not advisable and sleeping on the beaches would be just asking for trouble.

Just in case you thought that the tented camps in the game parks might be a cheap option – forget it. They are luxury camps with all the facilities laid on, and high prices. The 'tents' barely justify the name – they usually just have canvas or mosquito netting for walls, but otherwise have a roof and bathroom.

FOOD

For the main part Kenyan cuisine consists largely of stodge filler and is really just survival food for the locals – maximum filling-up potential at minimum cost. It is still possible to eat cheaply and well although the lack of variety becomes tedious after a while. People with carnivorous habits are far better served by the local tucker than vegetarians.

The most basic local eateries (often known as *hotelis*) hardly warrant being called restaurants. These places usually have a limited menu and are open only for lunch – the main meal of the day. If you're on a tight budget you'll find yourself eating in these places most of the time. However, if you have the resources, even in the smaller towns it's usually possible to find a restaurant that offers more variety and better food at a higher price. Often these places are connected with the mid-range and top-end hotels.

Putting together your own food is a viable option if you are camping and carrying cooking gear. Every town has a market and there's usually an excellent range of fresh produce available.

Fast food has taken off in a big way and virtually every town has a place that serves food that rates high in grease and low in price. Fried chips with lashings of lurid tomato sauce are a basic filler, but sausages, eggs, fish and chicken are also popular. In Nairobi there are literally dozens of these places, and they can be handy places to pick up a snack.

The only place where any sort of distinctive cuisine has developed is on the coast where the Swahili dishes reflect the history of contact with the Arabs and other Indian Ocean traders – coconut and spices are used heavily and the results are generally excellent.

As might be expected with the large number of Asians in Kenya, there are also Indian restaurants, although these are mainly confined to Nairobi and Mombasa.

Vegetarians are not well catered for. Away from the two main cities there are virtually no vegetarian dishes to accompany the starch. Beans are going to figure prominently in any vegetarian's culinary encounters in Kenya! Buying fresh vegetables in the market can help relieve the tedium – and perhaps the constipation – which no doubt results.

Snacks

Sambusas are probably the most common snack and are obvious descendants of the Indian samosa. They are deep-fried pastry triangles stuffed with spiced mince meat. Occasionally you come across sambusas with vegetarian filling, but this is usually only in the Indian restaurants. If you can find them freshly made and still warm, sambusas can be excellent. However, more often by the time you get them they are at least several hours old, are cold and have gone limp and greasy from the oil saturation...

Another item that fits into the pure starch category is that curious beast known as the *mandazi*. It's a semisweet, flat doughnut and, once again, when they're fresh they can be very good. They are usually cooked and eaten at breakfast time and as often as not are dunked in tea. Should you decide to eat one later in the day, chances are it will be stale and hard.

Something that you don't come across that often but which makes an excellent snack meal is *mkate mayai* (literally bread-eggs). This was originally an Arab dish and is now found in countries as far ranging as Kenya and Singapore. Basically it's a wheat dough which is spread into a thin pancake, is filled with minced meat and raw egg and is then folded into a neat parcel and fried on a hotplate. The Iqbal Hotel in Nairobi is a good place to try this snack.

Seemingly on every second street corner you come across someone trying to make a few bob selling corn cobs roasted on a wire grille over a bed of hot coals. You pay only a couple of shillings for these. Another street-corner snack is deep-fried yams, eaten hot with a squeeze of lemon juice and a sprinkling of chilli powder.

Main Dishes

Basically it's meat, meat and more meat, accompanied by starch of some sort. The meat is usually in a stew with perhaps some potato or other vegetables thrown in, and is often as tough as an old boot. Beef, goat and mutton are the most commonly eaten.

The starch comes in three major forms: potatoes, rice and *ugali*, the last of these is maize meal which is cooked up into a thick porridge until it sets hard. It's then served up in flat bricks. It's incredibly stodgy, almost totally devoid of any flavour and tends to sit on the stomach like a royal corgi, but most Kenyans swear it's the bees' knees. It's certainly the equivalent of mashed potato for the Pommies or sticky rice for the Chinese and Koreans but it certainly isn't a culinary orgasm. Freshly cooked it's palatable; when stale, just about inedible. Naturally, you must try it at least once and some travellers actually get to like it, but don't hold your breath! The only thing it has going for it is that it's cheap.

Cooked red kidney beans are always an alternative to meat and are widely available in local eateries.

Roast chicken and steak are popular dishes in the more upmarket restaurants of the bigger towns. Food in this sort of place differs little from what you might get at home.

Fruit

This is where Kenya really excels. Because of the ranges in climate found in the country, there's an excellent array of fruits. The tropical ones are especially good. Depending on the place and the season you can buy mangoes, papaya, pineapple, oranges, guavas, custard apples, bananas (many varieties) and coconuts. Prices are cheap and the quality very high.

Menus

Menus, where they exist in the cheaper places, are usually just a chalked list on a board on the wall. In better restaurants they are usually just in English.

The list which follows gives the main words you are likely to come across when trying to decipher Swahili menus.

food	*chakula*
raw	*mbichi*
ripe	*mbivu*
sweet	*tamu*
cup	*kikombe*
fork	*uma*
glass	*glasi*
knife	*kisu*
napkin	*kitambaa*
plate	*sahani*
table	*mesa*
teaspoon	*kijiko*
aubergine	*biringani*
cabbage	*kabichi*
capsicum	*pilipili baridi*
carrots	*karoti*
cassava	*muhogo*
garlic	*vitunguu saumu*
kidney beans	*maharagwe*
lettuce	*salad*
onions	*vitunguu*
plantains	*ndizi*
potatoes	*viazi*
spinach	*sukuma wiki*
tomatoes	*nyanya*
vegetables	*mboga*

beef	*nyama ya ngombe*
meat	*nyama*
mutton, goat	*nyama ya mbuzi*
pork	*nyama ya nguruwe*
steak	*steki*

crab	*kaa*
fish	*samaki*
lobster	*kamba*
squid	*ngisi*

bananas	*ndizi*
coconut (green)	*dafu*
coconut (ripe)	*nazi*
custard apples	*stafeli*
dates	*tende*
fruit	*matunda*
grapefruits	*madanzi*
guava	*pera*
limes	*ndimu*
mangoes	*maembe*
oranges	*machungwa*
papayas	*paipai*
passionfruit	*pasheni*
pineapples	*mananasi*
sugar cane	*miwa*
watermelon	*tikiti*

boiled spinach	*sukuma wiki*
curry	*mchuzi*
kebabs	*mushkaki*
maize meal porridge	*ugali*
mashed plantains & maize	*matoke*
meat stew	*karanga*
rice	*wali*
soup	*supu*
vegetable stew	*mboga*

boiled	*chemka*
fried	*kaanga*
roast	*choma*

hot/cold	*moto/baridi*
hot (spicy)	*hoho*

bread	*mkate*
butter	*siagi*
egg(s)	*yai(mayai)*
Indian bread	*chapati*

pepper	*pilipili*
salt	*chumvi*
sauce	*mchuzi*
sugar	*sukari*
yoghurt	*maziwalala*

DRINKS
Tea & Coffee
Despite the fact that Kenya grows some of the finest tea and coffee in the world, getting a decent cup of either can be difficult.

Tea *(chai)* is the national obsession and is drunk in large quantities. It bears little resemblance to what you might be used to but as long as you look on it as just a different hot drink and not actually tea it can be quite good. Be warned that it is generally very milky and horrendously sweet. Chai is made the same way in Kenya as it is in India: all the ingredients (tea, milk and masses of sugar) are put into cold water and the whole lot is brought to the boil and stewed. Finding a good honest cup of tea is virtually impossible outside the fancy restaurants. For tea without milk ask for *chai kavu*.

Coffee is similarly disappointing. Instant coffee is what is generally used, and in small quantities, so, once again, you're looking at a sweet milky concoction which is not quite what you might be expecting. However, as each cup is individually made it's somewhat easier to order one tailored to your own liking.

Beer
Kenya has a thriving local brewing industry and formidable quantities of beer are consumed. It's probably true to say that beer is the most widely available manufactured product in the country. Go to just a tiny group of *dukas* (local stores) by the side of the road somewhere and chances are one of them will either be a bar, or it will stock beer. Sure, it won't be cold, but then even in the most upmarket places beer is available both chilled and warm. Why warm you might ask as your face wrinkles in horror?! The answer is because most Africans appear to prefer it that way. I've certainly never seen them drink cold White Cap though you'll occa-

sionally see an African drinking cold Pilsener or Premium. My co-author, Hugh, who's a true-blue Aussie, reckons the Poms love it warm but that's a barrel of bullshit. Kenyan beer bears no resemblance to that fine brew produced in the British Isles which, to be at its best, has to be served at a specific temperature – neither too cold nor too warm and preferably pumped from the barrel. Kenyan beers are essentially lagers and they're all bottled.

Their names are White Cap, Tusker and Pilsner and they're sold in 500 ml bottles. Like Australian commercial beers they are basically the same product with different labels (though there is a discernible difference in taste) but most people end up sticking to just one brand. White Cap and Tusker also have 300 ml upmarket beers – Export and Premium respectively – and these are slightly stronger and more expensive. Guinness is also available but tastes and looks nothing like the genuine Irish article (or even the bastardised English variety outside of Kilburn High Road).

Until early November 1989, beer prices were strictly controlled by the government and there was only a very slight price difference between a beer in a spit-and-sawdust shack and a five-star hotel. That all changed with deregulation but, because of the competition for the nation's beer money, prices have once again stabilised after a short period of greed and opportunism.

They are cheapest bought from a supermarket where a 500 ml bottle will cost you around KSh 12. Bought from a normal bar, you are looking at KSh 14 to KSh 15. Even in the tourist hotels the top whack seems to be about KSh 35 on the coast, KSh 25 in Nairobi, so it's still affordable, though you will occasionally come across a place which wants KSh 40 a bottle.

Wine

Kenya also has a fledgeling wine industry and the Lake Naivasha Colombard wines are said to be quite good. This is something that cannot be said about the most commonly

encountered Kenyan wine – papaya wine. It tastes foul and even the smell is unbearable.

On the other hand, you can get cheap imported European wine by the glass for around KSh 40 in Nairobi restaurants. This is expensive when compared to the price of beer but is actually not too bad.

Local Brews

Although it is strictly illegal to brew or distil liquor this doesn't stop it going on. Pombe is the local beer and is usually a fermented brew made with bananas or millet and sugar. You may get the chance to sample it here and there and it shouldn't do you any harm. The same cannot be said for the distilled drinks, known locally as *changa*, as these are often very effective poisons – inefficient/amateur distilling techniques ensure various percentages of methyl alcohol creep into the brew. They'll blind you if you're lucky; kill you if you're not. Leave it alone!

Soft Drinks

All the old favourites are here – Coke, Pepsi, Fanta, etc – and they go under the generic term of soda. As with the beer, prices have been deregulated so they vary depending on where you buy. In most places you pay around KSh 3.50 per bottle but in the more exclusive places you can pay up to KSh 10 though a more usual price would be KSh 8. There are no such predictable prices for freshly squeezed fruit juices which range from KSh 10 to KSh 30 per glass.

BOOKS

You can walk into any decent bookshop in Europe, America or Australasia and find countless books on Western and Eastern history, culture, politics, economics, religion/philosophy, craft and anything else you care to name. Finding the same thing for Africa is somewhat more difficult except where it relates to European or American history. Things are improving, however, but so far only in the large format, hardback, photo-essay genre. What you will be hard-pressed to find is a good selection of novels, plays and biographies by contemporary

African authors, many of them published by the African branches of major Western publishing houses. Heinemann's African Writers Series offers a major collection of such works but they're generally only available in large African cities. In East Africa, the bookshops of Nairobi carry an excellent selection but the choice is considerably more limited in Dar es Salaam and Arusha. In Western countries, they're to be found only in specialist bookshops.

General Books

There are some excellent but quite expensive photo-essay hardbacks which you may prefer to look for in a library. They include *Journey though Kenya* by Mohammed Amin, Duncan Willets & Brian Tetley (Bodley Head 1982). There is a companion volume entitled *Journey through Tanzania* by the same authors and publisher.

Other colourful books on the region include *Africa Adorned* by Angela Fisher (Collins, 1984), *Ivory Crisis* by Ian Parker & Mohammed Amin (Chatto & Windus 1983), *Isak Dinesen's Africa* by various authors (Bantam Books, 1985), *Africa: A History of a Continent* by Basil Davidson (Weidenfield & Nicolson, 1966) and *Through Open Doors: A View of Asian Cultures in Kenya* by Cynthia Salvadori (Kenway Publications, Nairobi, 1983).

History, Politics & Economics

There are numerous books on the history of Africa which include *The Penguin Atlas of African History* by Colin McEvedy (Penguin, 1980), *A Short History of Africa* by Roland Oliver & J D Fage (Penguin, 1962), and *The Story of Africa* by Basil Davidson (Mitchell Beazley/Channel Four, 1984). Also excellent reading is *The Africans – A Triple Heritage* by Ali A Mazrui (Guild Publishing 1986) which was published in conjunction with a BBC TV series of the same name.

For the origins and development of the coastal Swahili culture and the effect on them of the arrival of the Portuguese in the Indian Ocean, the standard work is *The Por-tuguese Period in East Africa* by Justus Strandes (East African Literature Bureau, 1961). For a radical African viewpoint of the effects of colonialism in general, Walter Rodney's *How Europe Underdeveloped Africa* (Bogle L'Ouverture, 1976) is well worth a read.

Worthwhile contemporary accounts include the extremely readable but rather discouraging *The Africans* by David Lamb (Vintage Books/Random Books, 1984). Or there's *The Making of Contemporary Africa* by Bill Freund (Indiana, 1984) and *A Year in the Death of Africa* by Peter Gill (Paladin, 1986). On contemporary Kenyan politics, it's well worth reading Oginga Odinga's *Not Yet Uhuru* (Heinemann) and *Detained – A Prison Writer's Diary* by Ngugi wa Thiong'o (Heinemann, 1981) for a radically different view from that put out by the Kenyatta and Moi regimes.

The *Africa Review*, an annual production by World of Information (NTC Publishing Group, UK), offers an overview of the politics and economics of every African country as well as detailed facts and figures. It's well balanced and researched and makes no attempt to curry favours with any particular regime.

Travellers & Other Accounts

Dian Fossey's research with the mountain gorillas of Rwanda is recounted in her book *Gorillas in the Mist* (Penguin, 1983). *The White Nile* by Alan Moorehead (Penguin, 1973) is a superbly evocative account of the exploration of the upper Nile and the rivalry between the European powers.

Journey to the Jade Sea by John Hillaby (Paladin, 1974) recounts this prolific travel writer's epic trek to Lake Turkana in northern Kenya in the days before the safari trucks began pounding up the dirt in this part of Kenya. Other books to look for include *Initiation* by J S Fontaine (Penguin, 1985), *A Bend in the River* by V S Naipaul (Penguin, 1979) and *Travels in the Congo* by André Gide (Penguin, 1927).

Two women's accounts of life in East Africa earlier this century have been recent best sellers. *Out of Africa* by Karen Blixen (Isak Dinesen) is published by Penguin books and has also been made into a hugely popular movie. *West with the Night* by Beryl Markham (North Point Press) has also been a major best seller.

African Fiction

Heinemann's African Writers Series probably has the greatest range of contemporary African authors. There's a list of their writers on the first page of each of their books. Two of Kenya's best authors are Ngugi wa Thiong'o and Meja Mwangi whose books are a good introduction to what's happening in East African literature at present. Ngugi is uncompromisingly radical and his harrowing criticism of the neocolonialist politics of the Kenyan establishment landed him in jail for a year, lost him his job at Nairobi University and forced him into exile. His books, on the other hand, are surprisingly not banned in Kenya even though he's considered a dangerously subversive thorn in the side of the government. Meja Mwangi sticks more to social issues and urban dislocation but has a brilliant sense of humour which threads its way right through his books.

Titles worth reading by Ngugi wa Thiong'o include *Petals of Blood* (1977), *A Grain of Wheat* (1967), *Devil on the Cross* and *Weep Not Child*. Titles by Meja Mwangi include *Going Down River Road, Kill me Quick* (1974) and *Carcass for Hounds* (1974). All these titles are published by Heinemann.

For a hilarious but at times poignant account of the higher education system and its relationship with the political system you probably can't beat *The People's Bachelor* by Austin Bukenya (East Africa Publishing House, Nairobi, 1972). Though set at Makerere University in Kampala, Uganda, shortly after independence, its theme is relevant to virtually all British ex-colonies. Another author whose books are well known even outside Africa is Chinua Achebe. Although Achebe is a Nigerian and his material is drawn from his experiences in that country, many of the themes and issues are

relevant to contemporary East Africa. His most famous title is *Things Fall Apart* (Heinemann, 1958). Another well worth reading is *Ant Hills of the Savannah*, a much more recent publication. Another Nigerian author who writes about similar themes is Elechi Amadi. Try his *The Concubine* (Heinemann, 1968).

For writing by women in Africa try *Unwinding Threads* (Heinemann, 1983), a collection of short stories by many different authors from all over the continent.

Travel Guides

Africa on a shoestring by Geoff Crowther (Lonely Planet, 1989) covers more than 50 African countries, concentrating on practical information for budget travellers.

Insight Kenya, edited by Mohammed Amin & John Eames (APA Productions, 1985), is another of the popular APA guidebook series with many excellent photographs and a lively text. It concentrates more on the country's history, its peoples, cultures, sights and wildlife rather than on practical information and is a good book to read either before you go or whilst you're there.

Guide to Mt Kenya & Kilimanjaro, edited by Iain Allan (Mountain Club of Kenya, Nairobi, 1981), has been written and added to over the years by dedicated enthusiasts. It contains trail descriptions, maps, photographs, descriptions of fauna and flora, climate and geology, even mountain medicine. Unfortunately, it appears to be out of print at present but you may be able to find a copy at MCK's clubhouse at Wilson Airport in Nairobi.

More recent practical guides to East Africa which would be excellent companions for the one you are reading are those by David Else who spends a great deal of his time walking and trekking in various parts of Africa. The *Camping Guide to Kenya* (Bradt, 1990) covers every camp site in Kenya – the cities, national parks and mountain areas – and contains information and advice for campers and backpackers venturing off the main routes into the more remote areas of

Kenya. *Mountain Walking in Kenya* (Robertson-McCarta, 1990) covers a selection of walking routes through the mountain and highland regions of Kenya including everything from easy strolls around Lake Naivasha to expeditions on Mt Kenya. There's an equipment guide as well as accurate maps and colour wraps. *Mountain Walking in Tanzania, Malawi & Zimbabwe* (Robertson-McCarta, 1991) is a companion volume in the same style.

Field Guides

A Field Guide to the Larger Animals of Africa by Jean Dorst & Pierre Dandelot (Collins, 1970) together with *A Field Guide to the Birds of East Africa* by J G Williams & N Arlott (Collins, 1963) should suffice for most people's purposes in the national parks and wildlife reserves.

MAPS

Largely as a result of the prosperous tourism industry, there's a wide range of maps available, although many are just made to look pretty and have very little practical use.

One of the best maps of the region is the Hallwag map of *Kenya & Tanzania* which also covers Uganda, Rwanda, Burundi and the very eastern part of Zaïre. Covering a similar area, but not as well, is the Hildebrand's travel map of *East Africa*. The Michelin maps are usually pretty reliable but their only one which covers this area (No 155, Southern Africa) really covers too wide an area to give enough detail.

The *Tourist Map of Kenya*, printed and published in Kenya, gives good detail and there are a few similar ones.

Macmillan publish a series of maps to the game parks and these are not bad value at KSh 75.

At the Public Map Office next to the Kenyatta Conference Centre in Nairobi they have a stock of government survey maps covering the whole country. The most popular ones (Mt Kenya, Mt Elgon and those covering the game parks) are often out of stock but it's worth getting hold of these maps if possible. The only trouble with maps

published by the Survey of Kenya other than those available in the bookshops is that they're not available to the general public without official authorisation. This is hard to get and takes time so, if you're a tourist with limited time, you can forget it. Even people with credentials, such as Kenyan residents of the Mountain Club of Kenya (MCK), have great difficulty or find it simply impossible to get hold of detailed maps of the country.

ACTIVITIES
Diving & Snorkelling

Malindi and Watamu are the spots for scuba diving, the latter being the preferred of the two. At Watamu, diving is from a boat not far offshore. A typical anchor dive is made at 12 to 15 metres depth. Visibility is often only fair and in fact Kenyan diving visibility has a poor reputation due to the plankton in the water. There is, however, usually plenty of fish in the water even if the coral is not that spectacular. A typical dive costs KSh 400, plus KSh 50 extra for transport if the dive is from Watamu. For more information contact the Dive Shop, Driftwood Club, Malindi.

Windsurfing

Most of the resort hotels south and north of Mombasa have windsurfers for hire, and the conditions are ideal – the waters are protected by the offshore reefs and the winds are usually reasonably strong and constant. The going rate at most places seems to be about KSh 80 per hour, more if you need instruction.

Beaches

One of the great attractions of Kenya is the superb beaches which line the coast. Many travellers find themselves staying much longer than they anticipated. This is real picture postcard stuff – coconut palms, dazzling white sand and clear blue water. The only problem is that for the most part the resort hotels have a virtual monopoly on accommodation, although there are a couple of budget options both south and north of Mombasa.

The beach at Diani is one of the best

although it's dotted fairly solidly with resorts. Tiwi Beach, between Diani and Mombasa, is much lower key and you can camp right on the beach at the Twiga Lodge. There are similar possibilities north of Mombasa.

Caving

For information on this bizarre activity contact the Cave Exploration Group of East Africa, PO Box 47583, Nairobi.

Desert Grandeur

There's the opportunity to experience this on either side of Lake Turkana and for a considerable distance south of there on the eastern side of the lake. For most travellers, this is one of the highlights of their trip to Kenya.

On the western side access to the lake is easy with a bitumen road all the way from Kitale, and there's at least one bus and often a matatu or two every day in each direction. If you're heading up this way then don't miss the opportunity of exploring the Cherangani Hills east of the Kitale-Lodwar road using the Marich Pass Field Centre as your base.

The eastern side is perhaps more challenging since the mountains and the desert begin much further south but public transport is much more limited. The Turkana, Samburu and Rendille tribespeople are also fascinating and, like the Maasai, have hung on to their traditional ways. It's certainly an area which you shouldn't miss at any cost.

Climbing & Walking

Mt Kenya is the obvious one, but other promising and relatively unexplored territory includes Mt Elgon on the Uganda border, the Cherangani Hills north of Eldoret and even the Ngong Hills close to Nairobi. For more information refer to the relevant chapter or contact the MCK at their clubhouse at Wilson Airport (meetings every Tuesday at 8.30 pm – visitors welcome), or at their Nairobi address (tel 501747, PO Box 45741).

Gliding

The Gliding Club of Kenya has its headquar-ters in Mweiga near Nyeri in the Aberdares, and there are flights every day except during July and August. For more information contact the Gliding Club of Kenya (tel Nyeri 2969), PO Box 926, Nyeri.

Ballooning

Balloon safaris in the game parks are an absolutely superb way of seeing the savannah plains and of course the animals, but without the intrusion of vehicles and dozens of other tourists doing the same thing. The most popular of these trips is that in the Masai Mara Game Reserve. The hot-air balloons depart daily from Keekorok Lodge just after dawn and return around mid-morning. The flight includes a champagne-style breakfast on the plains. The cost is KSh 4000 (about US$190). Bookings can be made through Block Hotels (tel 335807), PO Box 47557, Nairobi, or at Keekorok Lodge.

There's another outfit which offers balloon trips in Taita Hills Game Reserve. Bookings for this can be made through the Hilton International (tel 334000), PO Box 30624, Nairobi.

Fishing

The Kenya Fisheries Department operates a number of fishing camps in various parts of the country. They are really only an option if you have your own transport as the sites are off the main roads. Before you head off you need to get a fishing licence from the Fisheries Department. Advance bookings are not taken so it's just a matter of turning up at the site. For full details of the exact locations of the camps, see the Fisheries Department in Nairobi; the office is near the National Museum.

White-Water Rafting

Rafting is still in its infancy in Kenya, perhaps because of the limited possibilities – there are only two major rivers in Kenya, the Athi/Galana and Tana. The Tana flows through relatively flat country so it's sluggish and unsuitable for rafting. The Athi/Galana, on the other hand, has substantial rapids, chutes and waterfalls. The only outfit which can fix you up with a trip down this river is operated by Mark Savage (tel 521590), PO Box 44827, Nairobi. He has two units of the Avon Ranger 3 river rafts.

A day trip from Nairobi consists of putting in just above Sagana on the Athi River and finishing about four km above the Masinga dam. The trip starts with about two km of mild rapids followed by six km of smooth water and then two km of Grade 4-plus rapids without a breather and another two km of the same grade but with a few calm stretches for bailing out. This is followed by porterage around a waterfall and a further 13 km of smooth water to the takeout point.

There's also an exciting three day trip available from Yatta Gap on the Athi down to Tsavo Safari Camp (74 km) and, if permission can be obtained from the National Parks Authority, trips all the way down to Malindi may be available in 1991.

THINGS TO BUY

Kenya is an excellent place for souvenirs, although much of the cheap stuff available is just pure junk mass produced by hand for the tourist trade. Look carefully at what's available before parting with your money.

Nairobi and Mombasa are the main centres but much of the stuff comes from the various regions, so it's often possible to pick up the same at source, although you then have the problem of transporting it.

The best buys include *makonde* carvings made from ebony, a very black and very heavy wood, sisal baskets (*kiondos*), jewellery & tribal souvenirs, including colourful Maasai beaded jewellery, the decorated *calabash* (dried gourds) and spears and shields. There are also batiks, local sarongs (*kangas* and *kikois*), and soapstone carvings from Kisii in the west of Kenya.

Elephant Hair Bracelets

On the streets of Nairobi you'll undoubtedly be approached by hawkers trying to flog you 'elephant hair' bracelets. Despite all the protestations to the contrary, these bracelets are made either from reed grass, which is then covered in boot polish, or from slivers of cow

horn. You can safely assume that none of them are the real McCoy.

WHAT TO BRING

Bring the minimum. One thing that many travellers in Kenya find once they actually get there is that they have far too much gear. This is not only an uncomfortable inconvenience, it also means that instead of taking back some special reminders of Kenya you'll be taking back the same extra pullover and jeans that you set off with. Unless it's absolutely essential, *leave it at home!*

A rucksack is far more practical than an overnight bag, and is essential if you plan to climb Mt Kenya or do any amount of walking. It is worth buying a good quality bag right at the start – African travel soon sorts out the good stuff from the junk, and if it's the latter you've opted for you'll be cursing it the whole way.

What type of pack you buy is largely a matter of personal preference. I find that the travel packs with the straps which zip into a compartment in the back are excellent. Although expensive, they are a compromise solution to a number of different problems; they are not really suited for specialised activities such as climbing or serious walking. Of the other types of packs, internal frame ones seem to be the best as they have less protuberances and straps to catch on things.

A day pack is a worthwhile item, if only for keeping your camera dry and out of the incredible dust which seems to permeate every crack and crevice when you're on safari, especially at Amboseli. For those reasons and for security, it needs to be one which zips shut. Quite a few travellers use the local kiondos which are fine if they suit your purpose.

A sleeping bag is more or less essential if you are travelling overland beyond Kenya, but in the country itself there are enough hotels for you not to need one. On the other hand, carrying a sleeping bag and closed-cell foam mat does give you a greater degree of flexibility and means that if you take a safari you know you'll have adequate gear. Sleeping bags are the one thing which all camping safari companies require you to provide.

There's always much discussion about the pros and cons of carrying a tent, and basically it boils down to what sort of travelling you want to do, and how much weight you're prepared to carry. As with a sleeping bag, a tent is far from essential if you're just travelling from town to town, but carrying your own portable shelter opens up a whole stack of exciting possibilities. The same applies to carrying a stove and cooking gear, so give some careful thought as to what you want to do, and how. On the other hand, the full range of camping equipment can be hired from various places in Nairobi (principally Atul's on Biashara St) and from certain hotels elsewhere in the country (principally the Naro Moru River Lodge on the northern side of Mt Kenya).

Quite a few travellers carry a mosquito net, and with the risk of malaria, there is no doubt that this is not a bad idea. Personally I found that with judicious use of insect repellent and mosquito coils, I was never unduly discomfited. On the topic of insect repellent, bring a good supply and make sure that whatever you bring has as the active ingredient NN-diethyl-m-toluamide, commonly known more sensibly as DEET. This has been found to be the most effective against mosquitoes. Brands which have this include Mijex and Rid. Mosquito coils are what the locals use (when they use anything at all, that is) to keep the mozzies at bay, and local brands such as Doom (!) are available in even the smallest stores.

Clothes need to be both practical and take into account local sensibilities. Although Kenya straddles the equator, the large variations in altitude lead to equally large variations in climate. The coast is hot and steamy year-round, while Nairobi and the western highlands get decidedly cool in the evenings in July and August, so you need to carry one decent warm pullover as well as warm weather gear. A windproof and waterproof jacket also comes in handy, particularly during the rainy season. Most travellers seem to get around in T-shirts and shorts which is fine in most areas, but you should be a little more circumspect on the Muslim-dominated coast, particularly in Lamu. Here women should wear tops that keep the shoulders covered and skirts or pants which reach at least to the knees. Shorts on men are likewise not particularly appreciated.

Overlooked by many people but absolutely indispensable is a good pair of sunglasses. The amount of glare you experience in the bright tropical light is not only uncomfortable but can damage your eyes. A hat which shades your face and neck is also well worth considering. A water bottle is well worth any slight inconvenience it may cause. It needs to be unbreakable, have a good seal, and hold at least one litre.

Also important are little things which can make life just that little bit more comfortable: a Swiss Army knife, a small sewing kit (including a few metres of fishing line and a large needle for emergency rucksack surgery), a 10 metre length of light nylon cord for a washing line, and a half tennis ball makes a good fits-all washbasin plug.

Most toiletries – soap, shampoo, toothpaste, toilet paper, tampons – are available throughout the country.

The one thing that you're really going to appreciate in Kenya is a pair of binoculars, whether they be pocket ones or larger field binoculars. When out in the game parks you can put them to constant use and they are essential for identifying the dozens of species and animals and birds that you'll come across. If you don't plan on going to the game parks they are less essential, but are still handy just for the scenery, or perhaps for trying to spot that potential lift coming over the horizon when you're stuck out in the north somewhere...

Getting There

Unless you are coming overland, flying is just about the only – and the most convenient – way of getting to Kenya. Nairobi is the main hub for flights and the route on which you are most likely to get a relatively cheap ticket but it's worth checking out cheap charter flights to Mombasa from Europe too.

Buying an ordinary economy class ticket is not the most economical way to go, but it does give you maximum flexibility and the ticket is valid for 12 months.

Students and those under 26 can often get discounted tickets so it's worth checking first with a student travel bureau to see if there is anything on offer. Another option is an advanced purchase ticket which is usually between 30% and 40% cheaper than the full economy fare but has restrictions. You must purchase your ticket at least 21 days in advance (sometimes more) and you must stay away for a minimum period (usually 14 days) and return within 180 days (sometimes less). The main disadvantage is that stopovers are not allowed and if you have to change your dates of travel or destination then there will be extra charges to pay. Standby fares are another possibility. Some airlines will let you travel at the last minute if there are seats available just before departure. These tickets cost less than the economy fare but are usually not as cheap as the advance purchase fares.

Of all the options, however, the cheapest way to go is via the so-called 'bucket shops'. These are travel agents who sell discounted tickets. Airlines only sell a certain percentage of their tickets through bucket shops so the availability of seats can vary widely, particularly in the high season. You have to be flexible with these tickets although if the agents are sold out for one flight they can generally offer you something similar in the near future.

Most of the bucket shops are reputable organisations but be careful as there is always the occasional fly-by-night operator who sets up shop, takes your money for a bargain-basement ticket and then either disappears or issues you with an invalid or unusable ticket. Check carefully what you are buying before you hand over money although I've used bucket shops for years and been handed the most weird and wonderful tickets. For example, tickets issued in East Berlin but bought in London for a flight from London to Malaysia with stopovers in New Delhi, Bangkok and Kuala Lumpur. They've all been sweet.

Bucket shops generally advertise in newspapers and magazines and there's a lot of competition and different routes available so it's best to telephone first and then rush round if they have what you want. In Europe, the market for these sort of tickets to American and Asian destinations has been well developed over many years, but little has been available to African destinations south of the Sahara until fairly recently. Fares are becoming more flexible but the options are still limited. Luckily, Nairobi is one of the few destinations that does have plenty of options.

FROM NORTH AMERICA
Air

In the USA, the best way to find cheap flights is by checking the Sunday travel sections in the major newspapers such as the *Los Angeles Times* or *San Francisco Examiner-Chronicle* on the west coast and the *New York Times* on the east coast. The student travel bureaus are also worth trying – STA or Council Travel.

North America is a relative newcomer to the bucket shop traditions of Europe and Asia so ticket availability and the restrictions attached to them need to be weighed against what is on offer on the more normal advance purchase or full economy price tickets.

Return tickets to Nairobi from New York on Pan Am cost US$1785 in the low season (September 15 to November 30 and February 1 to May 14), and US$2745 in the high season (May 15 to September 14 and December 1 to January 31). Pan Am also has flights from Los Angeles for US$2939 in the low season and US$3139 in the high season.

From Canada, Lufthansa offers flights from Vancouver to Nairobi for US$2635 in the low season and US$3290 in the high season. It also flies from Toronto for US$2415 in the low season and US$3070 in the high season.

It may well be cheaper in the long run to fly first to London from the east coast of the USA using Virgin Atlantic (for around US$225 one way or US$560 return), or standby on the other airlines for a little more, and then buy a bucket shop ticket from there to Kenya with or without stopovers. But you must do your homework to be sure of this. All the main magazines which specialise in bucket shop advertisements in London will mail you copies so you can study current prices before you decide on a course of action.

FROM EUROPE
Air

You can find bucket shops by the dozen in London, Paris, Amsterdam, Brussels, Frankfurt and a few other places too. In London, there are several newspapers with lots of bucket shop ads which will give you a good idea of current fares as well as specialist magazines catering entirely to the travel industry.

Trailfinder is a magazine put out three times a year by Trailfinders (tel (071) 938 3366), 42-50 Earls Court Rd, London W8 6EJ. It's free if you pick it up in London but if you want it mailed it costs £8 for three issues in the UK or Eire and £12 or the equivalent for three issues in Europe or elsewhere in the world (airmail). Trailfinders can fix you up with all your ticketing requirements for anywhere in the world as well as insurance, immunisation and books. They've been in business for years and can be highly recommended. All their staff are experienced travellers so they speak your language. Trailfinders is open Monday to

Saturday from 9 am to 6 pm (7 pm on Thursday).

Africa Travel Now is a newspaper put out quarterly by Africa Travel Centre (tel (071) 387 1211), 4 Medway Court, Leigh St, London WC1H 9QX. It's free and, as its name indicates, it specialises entirely in travel to and around Africa. It contains an excellent rundown of discounted flight prices to most major cities in Africa as well as what safaris are available once you get there along with costs. You can book all your safaris in advance at this place in addition to getting your airline ticket if you care to do that. Office hours are Monday to Friday from 9.30 am to 5.30 pm and on Saturday from 10 am to 2 pm. As with Trailfinders, they're highly recommended.

Time Out (tel (071) 836 4411), Tower House, Southampton St, London WC2E 7HD, is London's weekly entertainment guide and it's available from all bookshops and newsagents. Subscription enquiries should be addressed to Time Out Subs, Unit 8 Grove Ash, Bletchley, Milton Keynes MK1 1BZ, UK.

The price of airline tickets from London to Nairobi advertised in the above magazines varies from £210 to £263 one way and from £370 to £390 return (the full fare is around £630). The airlines used are generally Aeroflot and other Eastern European and Middle Eastern airlines but this isn't always the case. Both Trailfinders and Africa Travel Centre can also fix you up with multistopover tickets such as Kenya, Madagascar, Réunion, Mauritius, Seychelles, Kenya for around £360 (valid 21 days) or £560 (valid for a year); London, Cairo, Nairobi, London for £447; London, Nairobi, Johannesburg, London for £655. There are also 'open jaws' tickets available (fly into one city/country and out of another) such as London-Kigali (Rwanda) plus Nairobi-London or vice versa for about £400. On these sort of tickets you make your own travel arrangements between where you arrive and where you leave from.

If you plan to head further east or to Australasia after Africa they can fix you up with this too. Nairobi, Delhi, Kathmandu,

Bangkok, Singapore, Perth, for instance, costs around £620 while Nairobi-Delhi costs around £190 one way (comparable to anything you'll be offered at the bucket shops in Nairobi).

There is no advantage in buying a one-way ticket to Nairobi and then another one-way ticket back to Europe from there. You'll end up paying more than buying a return ticket in the first place. You may also run foul of immigration on arrival in Kenya without an onward ticket and be forced to buy one on the spot – an expensive exercise in lack of forethought.

A Round the World (RTW) ticket is another economic option if that's what you want to do and have the time but only very few of these include African stopovers. Starting and finishing in London with stopovers in Delhi, Singapore, Sydney, Auckland, Honolulu, Los Angeles, Rio, Johannesburg, and Nairobi, you're looking at around £2000.

Don't take advertised fares as gospel truth. To comply with truth in advertising laws, UK companies must be able to offer *some* tickets at their cheapest quoted price but they might only have one or two of them each week. If you are not one of the lucky ones, you may find yourself looking at tickets which cost up to £50 more (one way or return). The best thing to do, therefore, is to start looking into tickets well before your intended departure date so you have a very good idea what is available.

Remember that discounted tickets cannot generally be paid for with a credit card. You must pay with cash or with a bank cheque.

TO/FROM ASIA
Air

You may safely assume that flying is the only feasible way of getting between the Indian subcontinent and Kenya. There are plenty of flights between East Africa and Bombay due to the large Indian population in Kenya. There are bucket shops of a sort in New Delhi, Bombay and Calcutta and most of the discounted tickets will be with Air India. In New Delhi I'd recommend Tripsout Travel,

72/7 Tolstoy Lane behind the Government of India Tourist Office, Janpath.

Typical fares from Bombay to Nairobi are around US$440 return with either Ethiopian Airlines, Kenya Airways or PIA (via Karachi).

In Nairobi there are a lot of bucket shops offering tickets to Karachi, Islamabad, New Delhi, Bombay and Calcutta. Most of these will be with Air India or PIA.

Sea

There are no longer any passenger ships from India or Pakistan to Kenya. Don't believe any rumours that there are such ships. There are about four or five dhows which do the journey from Zanzibar and Mombasa to Karachi and Bombay each year via Somalia, South Yemen and Oman, but they are extremely difficult to locate and to get onto. The days of the dhows were numbered decades ago and those you find in Mombasa harbour will only be plying between Lamu, Mombasa, Pemba and Zanzibar.

FROM AUSTRALASIA
Air

There are no longer tight constraints on ticket discounting in Australia, but for Australians and New Zealanders there are simply very few route options to Africa. The only direct connection is the weekly Qantas flight from Perth to Harare (Zimbabwe) which costs about A$2230 (low season) and A$2560 (high season) return. Sydney-Harare costs around A$2600 (low season) and A$2990 (high season) return.

Sydney-Harare via Perth is the most expensive way to go, however. It's cheaper to go via Singapore and Bombay to Nairobi with Air India or a combination of Singapore Airlines and Air India. The published price for this is around A$2500 return but a good travel agent should be able to get it for you for around A$2300 return.

It obviously makes sense for Australasians to think in terms of a RTW ticket or an Australia/New Zealand-Europe round trip ticket with stopovers in Asia and Africa. It shouldn't be too much trouble for a travel agent to put together a ticket which includes various Asian stopovers plus a Nairobi stopover. Having Nairobi added to such a ticket bumps up the price a little and you may have to go through several travel agents before you get satisfaction as many of them know very little about deals via Africa.

It's probably best to start your search for a ticket by looking in the travel section of the Saturday issue of either the *Sydney Morning Herald* or the *Age* and by visiting a student travel bureau. It's also worth writing or telephoning for a copy of *Airfares Guide* from The Travel Specialists (tel (02) 262 3555), 62 Clarence St, Sydney, NSW 2000. They've been putting out this guide for a number of years now and it will give you a very good idea of what's available.

TO/FROM SOMALIA
Overland
With the current state of internal strife in Somalia it is not considered safe to travel overland between the two countries, although that has not stopped a few intrepid (crazy?) travellers in the past. There is also the problem of well-armed *shifta* (bandits) to contend with who are getting more desperate and mean by the week as a result of the Kenyan government's determined crackdown on Somali poachers. Buses and other vehicles along this route have become fair game and although they travel with an army escort, don't assume the soldiers are going to use the guns which they carry.

Kisimayo to Garissa There is usually one daily bus between Kisimayo and the tiny Somali border settlement of Liboi. There is a small adobe guest house here as well as a couple of basic eateries and a small market. The Kenyan bus arrives in Somali Liboi at around 9 am on Wednesday, Friday and Sunday for the seven hour journey to Garissa. Obviously you need to clear Somali customs and immigration before getting on the bus. It stops on the Kenyan side for customs formalities which take half an hour or so.

In Kenyan Liboi there is the *Cairo Hotel* which has basic rooms and meals.

TO/FROM SUDAN
Air
Kenya Airways and Sudan Airways operate direct flights between Khartoum and Nairobi.

Overland
As is the case with Somalia, the internal strife within Sudan has put the overland route through the south of that country off limits to travellers.

TO/FROM TANZANIA
Air
The cheapest options to fly between Tanzania and Kenya are the flights between Dar es Salaam and Nairobi (about US$50) and Zanzibar and Mombasa (about US$28), though you must add the US$20 departure tax to these prices. The Zanzibar-Mombasa flight by Kenya Airways is very popular so there's heavy demand for tickets. You need to book at least two weeks ahead if you want to be sure of getting a seat.

Overland
Dar es Salaam to Mombasa There are a number of bus companies (such as Coast, Cat and Tawfiq) which do the run from Dar es Salaam to Mombasa via Tanga and vice versa though usually only once per week in either direction. The trip takes anything from 16 to 24 hours or eight to 12 hours from Tanga. The border at Lunga Lunga-Horohoro is quite straightforward but it takes as much as four hours to clear all 50 or so people through both posts. The fare from Dar es Salaam to Mombasa is TSh 2500. The Cat bus office in Dar es Salaam is on Msimbazi St close to the Kariakoo Market and the Caltex station.

If you're going to take one of these buses it's worth considering doing the journey partly by train. It's much more comfortable, and costs only about TSh 300 more, to take the overnight train 1st class from Dar es Salaam to Tanga. From Tanga, pick up one of the buses running between Dar es Salaam and Mombasa at around 8 am. The trip from Tanga to Mombasa costs TSh 700.

You can also do the journey the hard way. From Tanga to the Tanzanian border post at Horohoro there are a couple of buses per day along the rough single-lane dirt road which cost TSh 300. From Horohoro it's a six km walk to the Kenyan border post at Lunga Lunga and there's very little traffic so hitching is difficult. Once through the Kenyan border post, however, there are frequent matatus for the one hour journey to Mombasa.

Arusha & Moshi to Nairobi Kilimanjaro Bus Service operate a regular luxury bus between Arusha/Moshi and Nairobi. The bus departs Arusha at 9 am on Monday, Thursday and Saturday and arrives in Nairobi at 3.30 pm. There's also another service which departs Moshi at 7 am on Monday, Thursday and Saturday, arrives in Arusha at 9 am and Nairobi at 2.30 pm. In the opposite direction the bus departs Nairobi at 9 am on Tuesday, Friday and Sunday arriving in Arusha at 3.30 pm. The fares are KSh 150/TSh 1250 (Nairobi-Moshi) and KSh 140/TSh 1150 (Nairobi-Arusha). You need to book in advance for these buses as there's heavy demand for tickets. The booking office in Nairobi is at Goldline (tel 25279), Cross Rd. In Arusha and Moshi the bus office is at the bus station.

It's just as easy to do this journey in stages and since the Kenyan and Tanzanian border posts are next to each other at Namanga, there's no long walk involved. There are frequent matatus and shared taxis from Arusha to Namanga every day which go when full and cost TSh 500/1000 to TSh 1300 (negotiable) respectively. The taxis normally take about 1½ hours though there are a number of kamikaze drivers who are totally crazy and will get you there in just one hour. From the Kenyan side of the border there are frequent matatus and shared taxis which go when full and cost KSh 80 and KSh 120 respectively. The journey by taxi takes about two hours and by matatu about three

hours. Both have their depot outside the petrol station on Ronald Ngala St close to the junction with River Rd.

Moshi to Voi & Musoma to Kisii The crossing between Moshi and Voi via Taveta is also reliable as far as transport goes (buses, matatus and shared taxis) but between Musoma and Kisii in the north there's very little traffic and you'll have to rely on hitching a ride or doing a lot of walking especially in the border area.

Boat

It used to be possible to get from Pemba, Zanzibar or Dar es Salaam to Mombasa by the *Virgin Butterfly* hydrofoil but the service has been suspended. There are now only occasional dhows between these places. In Dar es Salaam you'll have to make enquiries down at the Malindi dhow dock but it could take you several days to find one. The fare should be around TSh 3000 and the journey will take anything from 24 to 36 hours depending on the currents.

Between Zanzibar and Mombasa it's much easier. There are motorised dhows and other boats usually once or twice per week in either direction. To find out when they go and make a booking you need to go to the Institute of Marine Science workshop on Mizingani Rd – there's a small sign at the gate here (which is flanked by the Tanzanian and Zanzibari flags) which says, 'Tickets for Dar, Pemba, Mombasa'. The fare is TSh 2000 or US$11 and the journey takes about 12 hours but can take quite a bit longer depending on the currents.

Bring adequate supplies of food and drink with you if you take any of these boats.

There are no steamers on Lake Victoria which connect Kenya with Tanzania.

TO/FROM UGANDA
Overland

The two main border posts which most overland travellers use are Malaba and Busia with Malaba being by far the most commonly used.

Kampala to Nairobi via Malaba Between Jinja (USh 1500, two hours) or Kampala (USh 2200, three hours) and Malaba there are frequent matatus until the late afternoon. There are also frequent matatus in either direction between Tororo and Malaba (Uganda) which cost USh 200 and take less than one hour. The road has recently been resurfaced and is excellent, although it does mean that the drivers can get up to terrifying speeds, especially between Jinja and Kampala. There's also a train from Tororo to Kampala but it only runs three times a week and is diabolically slow.

The Ugandan and Kenyan border posts are about one km from each other at Malaba and you will have to walk. When leaving Uganda you will probably be asked for your currency declaration form, which isn't checked, and whether you have any Ugandan shillings in your possession (it's officially illegal to export them) but otherwise there's no fuss or baggage searches. Entering Kenya you have to fill in a currency form but there's no searches or other inconvenience. On the Kenyan side there are hordes of money-changers who will greet you, both while on your way through neutral territory to the Kenyan post and after you clear Kenyan immigration. The rate is not too bad.

There are trains from Malaba to Nairobi via Eldoret and Nakuru on Wednesday, Saturday and Sunday at 4 pm, arriving in Nairobi the next day at 9.30 am. The fares are KSh 440 in 1st class, KSh 207 in 2nd class and KSh 107 in 3rd class. The trains do not connect with the Ugandan system.

If you don't want to take the train, there are daily buses by different companies between Malaba and Nairobi which depart at around 7.30 pm arriving at about 5.30 am the next day. The fare is KSh 160. If you prefer to travel by day there are plenty of matatus between Bungoma and Malaba which cost KSh 20 and take about 45 minutes. If you stay in Bungoma overnight there are plenty of cheap hotels to choose from. From Bungoma there are several daily buses to Nairobi which leave at about 8 am and arrive about 5 pm the same day.

The other main entry point into Kenya from Uganda is via Busia further south. There are frequent matatus between Jinja and Busia and between Busia and Kisumu.

LEAVING KENYA

Nairobi is the best city in East Africa (and perhaps in the whole of Africa) to pick up cheap airline tickets for international flights. There is a lot of competition between travel agents so most of them lean over backwards to give you whatever discounts they can. They are the equivalent of bucket shops in Europe. Only a few of the airlines sell discounted tickets through these agents and none of them sell them directly from their own offices. The most common discounters are Aeroflot, Air India, EgyptAir, Olympic Airways, PIA and Sudan Airways and most of the cheap tickets available are for flights to Europe, although there are others to India, Pakistan and Singapore and sometimes to Madagascar, Mauritius and Réunion.

Tickets are paid for in local currency but to comply with government regulations it's usually necessary to produce your currency declaration form and bank receipts for the full amount you would pay if you bought the ticket direct from the airline concerned. It's important to bear this in mind if you are going to be leaving Kenya for a while and then returning later to buy your ticket, since your currency form will be collected at the border so you will lose the exchange credits recorded on it. The best thing to do in these circumstances is to buy your ticket just before you leave Kenya for the first time. You can also pay for your ticket in foreign currency, travellers' cheques or with a credit card in which case you don't need bank receipts.

A Nairobi-London ticket on Aeroflot or Sudan Airways currently goes for KSh 6000 to KSh 7800 (about US$286 to US$371). The cheaper tickets typically involve flights which touch down in several places before reaching their final destination and, in some cases, may involve stopovers of up to three days before there's a connecting flight. You may or may not find this an interesting prospect. The more expensive tickets are usually for nonstop flights.

There may also be deals on Air Madagascar and Air Mauritius if you're looking for a ticket to take you to the Comoros Islands, Madagascar, Mauritius or Réunion.

Departure Tax

The airport departure tax for international flights is US$20. You must pay this in foreign currency; Kenyan shillings are not accepted. It is possible to change US$ travellers' cheques to US$ cash in Nairobi but there are certain limitations which are discussed in the Money section in the Facts for the Visitor chapter.

Getting Around

AIR

Kenya Airways Kenya Airways, the national carrier, connects the main cities of Nairobi, Mombasa, Kisumu and Malindi. It's advisable to book in advance and essential to reconfirm 48 hours before departure if you're coming from either Malindi or Kisumu and have to connect with an international flight from either Nairobi or Mombasa airports. Otherwise you may well find that your seat has been reallocated. The flight schedules can be found in the respective city chapters.

Private Airlines There are also a number of private airlines which connect the main cities with smaller towns and certain national parks. From Nairobi's Wilson Airport, the main one is Kenya Aviation which connects Nairobi with Amboseli National Park, Masai Mara Game Reserve, Eldoret, Lamu, Lodwar, Loyangalani, Nanyuki and Nyeri. The flight schedule can be found in the Nairobi chapter.

Other private airlines connect Mombasa with Malindi and Lamu. They are Eagle Aviation, Prestige Air Services, Skyways Airlines and Equator Airlines. Their flight schedules can be found in the Mombasa, Malindi and Lamu chapters.

BUS

Kenya has a network of regular buses, matatus (normally minibuses), shared taxis and normal private taxis. The cheapest form of transport are buses, next matatus and lastly private taxis (expensive). There's not a lot to choose in terms of journey times between normal buses and matatus but there is a lot in terms of safety.

Regular Bus

Bus fares are generally about halfway between what you would pay on the railways in 2nd class but journey times are quicker.

Unlike the trains, which usually travel at night, many buses travel during the day so you may prefer to take a bus if you want to see the countryside. All the bus companies are privately owned but some of them run better buses than others. Coastline Safari, Goldline, Tana River Bus Company, Malindi Bus and Garissa Express are about the best of the bunch. Mawingo Bus Service and Akamba Bus Service are somewhat cheaper but their buses are older. It's worth paying that little extra for a good bus on a long journey.

Some Kenyan towns have what you might call a 'bus station', although this is often nothing more than a dirt patch. In others each bus company will have its own terminus though these are often close to each other. There are exceptions and these are indicated on the street maps. Matatu and shared taxi ranks sometimes share the same stations as buses but this isn't always the case, especially in Nairobi.

Matatu

Most matatu drivers are under a lot of pressure from their owners to maximise profits so they tend to drive recklessly and overload their vehicles. They also put in long working days. Stories about matatu smashes and overturnings in which a few people are killed and many injured can be found almost daily in the newspapers. There has been a determined police crackdown on such practices but bribery continues to undermine the success of it. Of course, many travellers use them and, in some cases, there is no alternative, but if there is (such as a bus or train) then take that in preference. The Mombasa-Nairobi road is notorious for smashes.

Overcrowding, on the other hand, isn't confined to matatus. I once counted 136 people getting off a Malindi-Mombasa bus at Kilifi excluding the driver and his mate.

As in most East African countries, you can always find a matatu which is going to the next town or further afield so long as it's not too late in the day. Simply ask around among the drivers at the park. Sometimes it's shared with the bus station. Matatus leave when full and the fares are fixed. It's unlikely you will be asked for more money than what other passengers are paying.

TRAIN

Kenyan Railways are excellent; they're a very popular way of travelling, generally run on time and they're considerably safer than travelling by bus or matatu. The main railway line runs from Mombasa to Malaba on the Kenya-Uganda border via Voi, Nairobi, Nakuru and Eldoret with branch lines from Nakuru to Kisumu, Nairobi to Nanyuki, Voi to Taveta and Eldoret to Kitale. There are no passenger services on the Nairobi-Nanyuki or Eldoret-Kitale branches. Although the Kenyan tracks are continuous with both the Tanzanian and Ugandan systems, there are no international services at present.

Classes

First class consists of two-berth compartments with a washbasin, drinking water, a wardrobe and a drinks service. There's a lockable door between one compartment and the adjacent one so, if there are four of you travelling together, you can make one compartment out of two, if you wish. They're usually very clean.

Second class consists of four-berth compartments with a washbasin and drinking water supply. Third class is seats only. All the compartments have fans. Sexes are separated in 1st and 2nd class unless you book the whole compartment. Third class can get a little wearing on the nerves on long journeys especially if they are overnight (which most are). Second class is more than adequate in this respect and 1st class is definitely a touch of luxury as far as budget travel goes.

There is a dining car on most trains offering dinner and breakfast (two sittings). Dinner on the Nairobi-Mombasa or Mombasa-Nairobi runs is an East African experience you should not miss at any price,

but try to go to the second sitting as you can hang around afterwards and continue your conversation. The food is excellent and plentiful. You are served four courses on starched white linen with silver-plated cutlery by usually immaculately dressed waiters, though some of the uniforms are getting decidedly tatty at the edges. Dinner costs KSh 120 and breakfast is KSh 80. Smaller portions are available for children at KSh 60 and KSh 40 respectively.

Reservations

You must book in advance for both 1st and 2nd class – two to three days is usually sufficient – otherwise you'll probably find that there are no berths available and will have to go 3rd class. If you're in Malindi and planning on taking the Mombasa-Nairobi train, bookings can be made with agents in Malindi. Compartment and berth numbers are posted up about 30 minutes prior to departure. Bedding (sheets, pillow and blanket) is available for KSh 25 if you don't have a sleeping bag and mattresses can be hired for KSh 15. Attendants will come round to ask you if you want bedding before the train departs.

BOAT
Lake Victoria Ferries

Ferries connect Kisumu with Kendu Bay, Kuwur, Homa Bay, Mfangano and Mbita but there are no international services connecting these Kenyan ports with those of Tanzania or Uganda.

Dhows

Sailing on a dhow along the East African coast is one of Kenya's most worthwhile and memorable experiences. There's nothing quite like drifting along the ocean in the middle of the night with the moon up high, the only sounds the lapping of the waves against the side of the boat and subdued conversation. It's enjoyable at any time of day, however, even when the breeze drops and the boat virtually comes to a standstill.

There are no creature comforts aboard these dhows so when night comes you simply bed down wherever there is space. You'll probably get off these boats smelling of fish since fish oil is used to condition the timbers of the boat – nothing that a shower won't remove! Take drinking water and food with you although fish is often caught on the way and cooked up on deck over charcoal. Dhows can be picked up in Mombasa, Malindi and Lamu.

Many of the smaller dhows these days have been fitted with outboard motors so that progress can be made when there's no wind. The larger dhows are all motorised and most of them don't even have sails.

Large, motorised dhows connect Mombasa with the Tanzanian islands of Pemba and Zanzibar and with Dar es Salaam though there's usually only one per week.

DRIVING

If you are bringing your own vehicle to Kenya you should get a free three month permit at the border on entry, so long as you have a valid carnet de passage for it. If you don't have a carnet you should be able to get a free one week permit at the border on entry after which you must get an 'Authorisation permit for a foreign private vehicle' which costs KSh 3900 (about US$244). Before you do this, however, get in touch with the Automobile Association in Nairobi.

When you are driving your own vehicle there are certain routes in north-east Kenya where you must obtain police permission before setting out. This is just a formality but there will be a roadblock to enforce this. The main stretch where this applies is between Isiolo and Marsabit where all transport must travel in convoy at a particular time of day unless you're turning off to go somewhere else.

Road Safety

Kenyan roads in the south-western part of the country – west of a line drawn through Malindi, Isiolo and Kitale – are excellent. In fact they're some of the best in Africa. North and north-east of this line and in the national

parks they are all gravel roads, usually in a reasonable state of repair though there are long sections of corrugated gravel in some parts. Driving on these, at the necessary speed to avoid wrecking a vehicle, can be agony on your kidneys after several hours, especially if you're on a bus which has had a double set of unyielding springs fitted to it. Naturally, there are washouts on some of these gravel roads during the rainy seasons and, under these circumstances, journey times can be considerably longer.

Right up in the north on the eastern side of Lake Turkana, especially in the Kaisut and Chalbi deserts, you can make good headway in the dry season and the roads (which would be better described as tracks) are often surprisingly smooth and in good condition. This is certainly true of the road from Wamba to North Horr via Parsaloi, Baragoi, South Horr and Loyangalani. After rain, however, it's another story, particularly on the flat parts of the deserts. They turn into treacherous seas of mud, often as much as a metre deep in places. Only a complete fool would attempt to drive in these circumstances without 4WD, sand ladders, adequate jacking equipment, shovels, a tow rope or wire, drinking water and spare metal jerrycans of fuel. This is particularly true of the stretches of track between North Horr and Maikona and on any of the tracks leading off the Marsabit-Isiolo road to South Horr.

To get out of the mud, if you're really stuck, you're going to be entirely dependent on the small number of vehicles which *may* pass by and *may* stop and help (they won't want to get stuck either), or on a passing herd of camels. It's going to cost you money either way. Not only that but you can sometimes drive for hours only to find that it's impossible to cross a river, which may not even exist in the dry season, and have to drive all the way back again. Fuel is very difficult to find in this region and is usually only available at mission stations at up to three times what you would pay for it in Nairobi – and they'll only sell you a limited amount. Make adequate preparations if you are driving your own vehicle.

Top: Voi bus station (TW)
Bottom Left: Nairobi-Mombasa train (GC)
Bottom Right: Masai Mara Game Reserve (HF)

Top: Turkana camp, Lake Turkana (HF)
Bottom: Lamu waterfront (GP)

Vehicle Hire

Hiring a vehicle to tour Kenya (or at least the national parks) is a relatively expensive way of seeing the country but it does give you freedom of movement and is sometimes the only way of getting to the more remote parts of the country. On the other hand, if you're sharing costs, it's quite a feasible option.

There are a number of factors to take into consideration before deciding what type of vehicle to take and which company to go through, and there's no real substitute for sitting down with pen and paper and working out as near as possible what the total cost will be. To do this you'll need as many hire charge leaflets as you can get hold of and a distances table.

The other major consideration is what type of vehicle is going to be suitable to enable you to get where you want to go. Outside of the rainy season, a 2WD vehicle may be perfectly adequate in some parts of the country including Masai Mara Game Reserve and Amboseli and Tsavo national parks, but it won't get you to Lake Turkana and would restrict your movements in the Aberdare and Meru national parks and the Buffalo Springs and Samburu game reserves. Most companies also have a policy of insisting that you take a 4WD vehicle if you're going upcountry and off the beaten track.

Hire Charges This is something of a minefield since the daily/weekly base rates vary quite a lot as do the km (mileage) charges. What initially looks cheap often works out just as expensive as anything else. No company offers unlimited free km on a daily basis; to get this you must hire on a weekly basis. Again, some of the so-called 'unlimited' km rates are not quite that. Most have a ceiling of 1200 km to 1400 km per week free after which you pay the excess at the normal km rate. Some companies also offer the option of 500 km or 1200 km to 1400 km per week free of charge with corresponding lower or higher base rates. If you're not planning on going too far then it may be more economical to opt for the lower

free km rate. Also, some companies include insurance in the weekly rates; others don't.

To give you some idea of average costs, the base rates for a 2WD saloon car are between KSh 300 and KSh 500 per day plus mileage or KSh 2750 and KSh 4000 per week plus mileage. 'Unlimited' km weekly rates for this type of car vary between KSh 6200 and KSh 6600.

In the next category, an average small 4WD vehicle such as a Suzuki Sierra costs between KSh 500 and KSh 600 per day plus mileage or KSh 3200 and KSh 7500 per week plus mileage. 'Unlimited' km rates are between KSh 8600 and KSh 15,000.

In the highest category – a 4WD Isuzu Trooper, for instance – daily rates vary between KSh 900 and KSh 1350 plus mileage or KSh 8100 and KSh 16,250 per week plus mileage. The 'unlimited' km rates are between KSh 12,000 and KSh 29,000.

If you're not hiring on the basis of 'unlimited' mileage then average rates are KSh 4 (2WD saloon cars), KSh 5.50 (4WD Suzuki Sierra) and KSh 9 (Isuzu Trooper) per km.

Minimum Mileage Conditions Where you're paying a km charge, some companies stipulate 50 km per day for saloon cars, 65 km per day for station wagons and 100 km per day for 4WD and camping vehicles. Other companies make no such conditions.

Insurance Third party insurance is compulsory but this does not cover you for damage to the vehicle or damage to anyone else's property. That being the case, you could be in big trouble financially if you have an accident and particularly if your vehicle is a write-off. The only way around this is to take out additional Collision Damage Waiver (CDW) insurance which usually absolves you of any financial responsibility except for the first KSh 1000 (or less – depends on the insurance company) in the event of an accident. Most companies strongly recommend that you cover yourself in this way. CDW usually doesn't cover tyres or tools nor does it usually cover windscreens.

Average daily rates for CDW cover are KSh 280 for saloon cars and KSh 400 for 4WD vehicles.

Deposits There's a wide variation in the deposits charged on hired vehicles. It's usually the estimated total hire charges (base rate plus km) plus KSh 4000 to KSh 5000. If you don't take out CDW cover then the KSh 4000 to KSh 5000 may be increased to the full replacement value of the vehicle. On the other hand, if you do take out CDW cover then the KSh 4000 to KSh 5000 excess is usually waived. No deposit is necessary if you are paying by credit card.

Driving Licences & Driver's Age An international driving licence or your own national driving licence is standard. Some companies stipulate a minimum age of 23 but with others it is 25. There are occasionally stipulations about endorsements on licences (clean licences preferred) and that you must have been driving for at least two years.

Quality of Maintenance Although it's not always the case, it's probably true to say that the more you pay for a vehicle, the better condition it will be in. It's worth paying attention to this especially if you're planning on going a long way. It doesn't necessarily mean that the cheaper companies neglect maintenance but, in some cases, they certainly do as our feedback mail indicates.

The other factor related to maintenance is what the company will do for you, if anything, in the event of a major breakdown. The major companies *may* deliver you a replacement vehicle and make arrangements for recovery of the other but with most you'll be entirely responsible for getting it fixed and back on the road. Only when you return the vehicle will you be refunded and you'll need receipts to prove what you spent.

Equipment Some companies provide you with adequate tools to tackle breakdowns, others with just sufficient to change a tyre. If you have mechanical skills, it's worth enquiring about what tools are provided. The only company which includes a full complement of camping equipment including tents in their hire charges on 4WD vehicles is Habib's. With other companies you'll have to hire this separately.

One-Way Rates If you want to hire a vehicle in one place and drop it in another there will be additional charges to pay. These vary depending on the vehicle and the company but range from KSh 1000 to KSh 3000.

Taking a Hired Vehicle to Tanzania Only the larger (and more expensive) companies cater for this and there are additional charges. Briefly, these are KSh 1000 for insurance and KSh 2500 for documentation (both payable to the hire company) plus US$100 for Tanzanian road tax (payable to the Tanzanian customs on entry).

Which Company? At the top end of the market are two companies:

Hertz
> PO Box 42196, Nairobi, tel (331960, 331973/4)
> PO Box 84782, Mombasa (tel 316333/4, 315079)
> PO Box 365, Malindi (tel 20069, 20040)

Avis
> Kenyatta Ave, Nairobi (tel 336703/4)
> Moi Ave, Mombasa (tel 23048)
> Sitawi House, Malindi (tel 20513)

Both these companies have branch offices at Jomo Kenyatta International Airport (Nairobi), Moi Airport (Mombasa) and at many of the beach resort hotels both north and south of Mombasa and at Malindi.

In much the same league but considerably less expensive on weekly rates is Europcar (tel 334722/3/4/5/6), PO Box 40433, Nairobi, and PO Box 90631, Mombasa (tel 312461). They also have a branch office at Jomo Kenyatta International Airport .

Similar, but for no discernible reason since their vehicles are not new and, in some cases, quite tatty, is Glory (tel 24428, 22910), PO Box 66969, Nairobi; PO Box 85527, Mombasa (tel 21159, 313561); and PO Box 994, Malindi (tel 20065).

Budget also slot into this category but, if their Australian operations are anything to go by, they may be in receivership. If not, they're at PO Box 59767, Nairobi (tel 23304, 24081), and Moi Ave, Mombasa (tel 24600, 24065).

Beneath the above there's an excellent choice of good, reliable companies with well maintained vehicles and they all have approximately the same rates. What they don't have is large fleets of vehicles so it's important to book in advance if you want to be sure of getting what you want – particularly a 4WD vehicle. Typical daily rates would be KSh 1200 (2WD saloon), KSh 1650 (4WD Suzuki Sierra) and KSh 3000 (4WD Isuzu Trooper). Corresponding weekly rates without 'unlimited' mileage would be KSh 7000, KSh 10,500 and KSh 20,500. Remember to add CDW charges to the above rates. Companies which we can recommend in this category include:

Habib's
PO Box 48095, Agip House, Haile Selassie Ave, Nairobi (tel 20463, 23816, 20985)
Central Rent-a-Car
PO Box 49439, Fedha Towers, Standard St, Nairobi (tel 22888, 332296)
PO Box 99753, Moi Ave, Mombasa (tel 20171, 312070)
Let's Go Travel
PO Box 60342, Caxton House, Standard St, Nairobi (tel 29539/40, 340331)
Market Car Hire
PO Box 49713, Market Service Station, Koinange & Banda streets, Nairobi (tel 25797, 335735)
Payless
PO Box 49713, Olympic House, Koinange St, Nairobi (tel 338400)
Nutty Car Hire, Tours & Travel
PO Box 45833, Puri Building, Muindi Mbingu St, Nairobi (tel 542605, 542696)
Galu Safaris Ltd
PO Box 56707, Standard St, Nairobi (tel 20365, 336570)
PO Box 99143, Ambalal House, Nkrumah Rd, Mombasa (tel 314174, 314226)

HITCHING

Hitching is usually good on the main roads and may well be preferable to travelling by matatu, but if you are picked up by an African driver and are expecting a free lift then make this clear from the outset. Most will expect a contribution at least. Hitching to the national parks, on the other hand, can be very difficult since most people either go on a tour or hire their own vehicle. Apart from that, once you get to the park lodges or camping areas, you will be entirely dependent on persuading other tourists with their own vehicles to take you out with them to view game since walking in the parks is forbidden.

Safaris

ORGANISED SAFARIS

There are essentially two types of organised safaris available – those where you camp at night and those where you stay in game lodges or luxury tented camps at night. Whichever you go on, they typically start and end in either Nairobi or Mombasa though there are a number of exceptions to this. Apart from transfer to and from Nairobi or Mombasa and driving from one park to another, once you're in a park you'll be taken on a number of game drives – usually two and sometimes three per day. Each drive typically lasts two to 2½ hours and the best (in terms of sighting animals) are those in the early morning and late afternoon when the animals are at their most active. The vehicles used for these drives are six to eight seater minibuses with roof hatches, Land Rovers or open-sided trucks.

As a general rule, you'll be left to your own devices between late morning and around 3 pm other than for lunch though, if you're on a camping safari, you may well be taken to a lodge in the early afternoon to relax over a cold beer or have a swim in the pool (if permitted – at some lodges the pool is for guests only). You may also be taken to a lodge after the late afternoon game drive for the same thing before returning to camp for dinner.

Kenyan National Parks
& Reserves

16 Aberdare National Park
20 Amboseli National Park
23 Arawale National Reserve
26 Boni National Reserve
2 Central Island National Park
25 Dodori National Reserve
30 Kisite & Mpunguti marine
   national parks
27 Kiunga Marine National Reserve
10 Lake Bogoria National Reserve &
   Lake Baringo
15 Lake Nakuru National Park
17 Longonot & Hell's Gate
   national parks
5 Losai National Reserve
28 Malindi Marine National
   Park & Reserve
4 Marsabit National Park
   & Reserve
18 Masai Mara National Reserve
12 Meru National Park, Bisanadi,
   Rahole, North Kitui &
   Kora national reserves
8 Mt Elgon National Park
13 Mt Kenya National Park
19 Nairobi National Park
7 Nasalot National Reserve

14 Ruma National Park
9 Saiwa Swamp National Park
11 Samburu, Buffalo Springs &
   Shaba national reserves
1 Sibiloi National Park
31 Shimba Hills National Reserve
3 South Island National Park
6 South Turkana National Reserve
24 Tana River Primate National
   Reserve
22 Tsavo East National Park
21 Tsavo West National Park
29 Watamu Marine National
   Reserve

Camping Safaris

Camping safaris cater for budget travellers, for the young (or young at heart) and for those who are prepared to put up with discomfort. They are no-frills safaris, there are none of life's little luxuries such as flush toilets, running water or iced drinks, they can be quite demanding depending on where you go, and you'll be expected to lend a hand. You'll end up sweaty and dusty and there may well be no showers available – even cold ones. On the other hand, you're in for an authentic adventure in the African bush with nothing between you and the animals at night except a sheet of canvas and the embers of a dying fire. It's not at all unusual for elephants or hippos to trundle through the camp at night, or even the occasional lion. No-one has so far been eaten or trampled on.

Another plus for these safaris is that you'll probably find yourself with travellers from the four corners of the earth. Those safaris which use trucks frequently have as many as half a dozen different nationalities on board.

The price of your safari will include three meals a day cooked by the camp's cook(s) though on some safaris you'll be expected to lend a hand in the preparation and cleanup. Food is of the 'plain but plenty' variety.

The price will also include all the necessary camping gear except a sleeping bag which you must provide or hire locally. The tents provided sleep two people as a rule and you'll be expected to erect and dismantle it yourself though there are some safaris where the camp is taken on ahead of you and the tents erected by the staff. Tents are invariably of the type which sleep two people and, if you're a single traveller, you'll be expected to share with someone else. If you don't want to do that then you'll be up for a 'single supplement' of between 15% to 20% on the price of the safari which will allow you to have a tent of your own. Mosquito nets are generally not provided so you'll have to hire one yourself or bring along insect repellent either in the form of coils or a skin cream.

You'll need to bring all your own clothing and footwear sufficient to cover you for hot days and cold nights but the amount of baggage which you'll be allowed to bring with you is limited. Excess gear can usually be stored at the safari company's offices. Don't forget to bring along a torch (flashlight) and penknife – the company will provide kerosene lanterns for the camp but they won't be left on all night.

There are also a number of somewhat more expensive camping safaris available which utilise permanent camp sites with pre-erected tents fitted with mosquito nets, beds and sheets and which have showers (though there's sometimes not enough water for everyone to have a shower).

Remember that at the end of one of these safaris your driver/guide and the cooks will expect a reasonable tip. This is only fair since wages are low and these people will have made a lot of effort to make your trip a memorable one. Be generous here. Other travellers are going to follow you and the last thing anyone wants to find themselves closeted with is a disgruntled driver/guide who couldn't care less whether you see game or not.

Lodge Safaris

The other type of safari is for those who want luxury at night and in between game drives. On these the accommodation is in game lodges or luxury tented camps. There are plenty of beautifully conceived and superbly sited lodges in the main national parks where you can expect a fully self-contained room or cottage, cuisine of an international standard, a terrace bar with ice-cold drinks, a swimming pool and videos and plenty of staff to cater for all your requirements. Many of these lodges overlook a watering hole or salt lick so you can sit on the viewing terrace and watch the animals from there. The watering hole or salt lick will usually be floodlit at night. Some of the lodges put out bait or salt to encourage certain animals to visit the spot and while this is often very contrived, it usually guarantees you a sighting of animals which you'd be very lucky to see otherwise.

There's obviously a considerable difference in price for these safaris as opposed to camping and most of the people who go on them are package tourists with expectations and attitudes of mind quite dissimilar to those who opt for a camping safari. Essentially for them, it's a holiday rather than in-depth involvement in Africa, its people and wildlife. It's the African bush at arm's length. On the other hand, if you have the money, it's worth staying at the occasional lodge just for the contrast.

Lodge safaris will cost you at least four times what a camping safari costs – and often considerably more. Luxury tented camps are no less expensive than lodges and the more exclusive ones cost up to four times the price of a lodge. They're for people to whom money is no object and who want to experience what it must have been like in the days of the big-game hunters except that it's cameras rather than guns which they tote these days.

Safari Options

There's a whole plethora of options available whether you take a camping safari or a lodge safari ranging from two days to 15 days and sometimes 25 days. If possible, it's best to go on a safari which lasts at least five days and preferably longer since otherwise a good deal of your time will be taken up driving to and from the national parks and Nairobi. You'll also see a great deal more on a longer safari and have a much better chance of catching sight of all the major animals. Remember that sightings of any particular animal cannot be guaranteed but the longer you spend looking, the better your chances are. A longer safari will also give you the opportunity of having some involvement with the local tribespeople.

A three day safari typically takes you either to Amboseli or Masai Mara. A four day safari would take you to Amboseli and Tsavo, to Masai Mara or to Samburu and Buffalo Springs. A five day safari would take you to Amboseli and Tsavo or to Masai Mara and Lake Nakuru whereas a six day safari would take you to lakes Nakuru, Bogoria and Baringo plus Masai Mara or to Lake Nakuru, Masai Mara and Amboseli. Going onto a seven day safari, you could expect to visit at least two of the Rift Valley lakes plus Masai Mara and Amboseli whereas on an 11 day safari you would take in one or more of the Rift Valley lakes plus Masai Mara, Amboseli and Tsavo or Mt Kenya, Samburu and Buffalo Springs, Meru, Lake Nakuru and Masai Mara.

Most of the safari companies cover the above standard routes but some also specialise in different routings designed to take you off the beaten track. There are, for instance, safaris which take in Masai Mara, Lake Victoria, Mt Elgon, Saiwa Swamp and Nakuru and others which take in Mt Kenya, Samburu and Buffalo Springs, Nyahururu, Lake Nakuru and Masai Mara. Other safaris visit Shaba, rather than Samburu and Buffalo Springs, where you'll hardly see another vehicle.

Most companies also offer safaris to Lake Turkana which range from seven days to 12 days. The shorter trips take one or other of the standard routes – Nairobi, Nakuru, Nyahururu, Maralal, Baragoi, South Horr and Loyangalani or Nairobi, Isiolo, Maralal, Baragoi, South Horr and Loyangalani. The longer trips detour from this route and take you to either or both of the Mathew's Range and the Ndoto Mountains. A full description of the options available can be found in the East of Turkana section in the Northern Kenya chapter.

Safari Costs

There's a lot of competition for the tourist dollar among the safari companies and prices for the same tour are very similar. Generally, the longer you go for, the less it costs per day.

For camping safaris you are looking at around KSh 1000 (US$48 to US$50) per day for three days, KSh 900 to KSh 920 (US$43 to US$45) per day for four days, KSh 860 to KSh 870 (US$40 to US$42) per day for five days, and KSh 775 (US$37) per day for seven or more days. The price per day for safaris over 11 days tends to rise somewhat since there's a lot more organisation involved and you'll be going to remote areas where there are no services available so everything has to be trucked in.

The prices for safaris which involve staying in lodges or tented camps will be at least four times the above daily rate.

Remember that if you're a single traveller and want a tent or room to yourself you'll have to multiply the above figures by a factor of 15% to 20%.

Prices include camping equipment or accommodation at a lodge, transport (including game drives), camp site and park entry fees and three cooked meals a day.

Frequency of Departures

This varies a lot from company to company and depends on the season. In the high season, many companies have daily or every second day departures to the most popular game parks – Amboseli, Masai Mara and Tsavo – since there's high demand. To the less frequented parks such as Samburu and Buffalo Springs, Shaba and Meru, they generally leave only once or twice per week. Safaris to Lake Turkana are usually only once weekly. In addition, most companies will leave for any of the most popular game parks at any time so long as you have a minimum number of people wanting to go – sometimes four, sometimes six. In the low season, there are fewer departures.

It obviously makes a lot of sense to either book ahead or to get a group together rather than just turn up and expect to leave the very next morning. Advance booking is essential for the Lake Turkana safaris since they're heavily subscribed. It's also essential for any of the 'Exotic Options' described below.

Which Safari Company?

There is no doubt that some safari companies are better than others. The main factors which make for the difference are the quality and type of vehicles used, the standard of the food and the skills and knowledge of the drivers/guides. It's equally true that any particular company can take a bunch of people on safari one week and bring them back fully satisfied and yet the following week take a different set of people on the same safari and end up with a virtual mutiny. That's an extreme example, but whether a company

gets praised or condemned can hinge on something as simple as a puncture which takes half a day to fix and for which there are no tools on board. Or a broken spring which involves having to wait around for most of the day whilst a replacement vehicle is sent out from Nairobi. There's obviously a lot which companies can do to head off breakdowns but a broken spring, for example, isn't reasonably one of them on a short safari though you would expect such spares to be on board for longer journeys and certainly on a safari to Lake Turkana.

The other major factor to take into consideration before you decide to go with any particular company is whether they actually operate their own safaris with their own vehicles or whether they are just agents for other safari companies. If they're just agents then obviously part of what you pay is their commission but the most important thing here is, if anything goes wrong or the itinerary is changed without your agreement, you have very little comeback and you'll be pushing shit uphill to get a refund. We get letters about this *all* the time from travellers to whom this happened.

Unfortunately, the situation isn't that easy to avoid. It's a minefield working out which are genuine safari companies and which are just agents. Go into any office in Nairobi and, naturally, they all have their own vehicles and, of course, they'll compensate you at the end of the safari if anything went seriously wrong. Not so if they're just agents. They will already have paid the lion's share of what you gave them to the company which actually provided the vehicles and staff so that gives them very little room for manoeuvre. Likewise, there's no way that the actual safari company is going to provide the agent with a refund.

It's perfectly obvious that quite a few so-called safari companies are merely agents. Simply pick up half a dozen leaflets from various companies and compare the wording on them. You'll find that quite a few are identical!

Another aspect of the safari business in Kenya is that there's a good deal of swapping of clients when one company's vehicle(s) are full for any particular safari and another's are not. This isn't philanthropy; it's pure business. In other words, you may find yourself on a certain company's safari which is not the one you booked through. The reputable companies won't do this without informing you but the agents certainly will.

Despite the pitfalls mentioned here, there are a number of reliable companies offering camping safaris which have their own vehicles and an excellent track record. Most of the people who run them paid their dues driving overland trucks around Africa for years so you can be sure they know the business back to front. They are:

Yare Safaris Ltd
1st floor, Union Towers, Mama Ngina St, PO Box 63006, Nairobi (tel 559313). This company specialises in safaris to Samburu Game Reserve (four days), Lake Turkana (eight days), Masai Mara and Nakuru (six days) and the gorilla sanctuaries/volcanos of Zaïre and the Serengeti (Tanzania) (25 days), plus they also offer the only genuine camel safari available in Kenya (five days).

In addition, they operate an excellent hostel/camp site at Maralal and, for those who intend to stay there or go on one of their safaris, there's a free transfer vehicle to and from Nairobi once a week. They're also willing to advise you even if you don't go on one of their safaris and they offer 8% discounts to IYHF members on the prices of all safaris booked either through their own offices or at the Youth Hostel in Nairobi.

Safari-Camp Services
Corner Koinange and Moktar Daddah streets, PO Box 44801, Nairobi (tel 330130, 28936). This company has been operating for years and has an excellent reputation. It offers both standard economy camping safaris plus what it calls 'lodge equivalent' camping safaris for those who prefer somewhat better facilities.

Its most popular safari is probably the Turkana Bus (seven days) but they also offer the Wildlife Bus (Samburu, Mt Kenya, Nyahururu, Lake Nakuru and Masai Mara – seven days), the Coast Bus (Nairobi-Mombasa via Amboseli and Tsavo – four days), the Hemingway (a 'lodge equivalent' safari to Samburu, Nyahururu, Lake Nakuru and Masai Mara – seven or 10 days) and Vanishing Africa (a 'lodge equivalent' safari to Masai Mara, lakes Nakuru, Bogoria and Baringo, Maralal, Lake Turkana, the Mathew's Range and Samburu – 14 days).

Gametrackers Camping Safaris
Finance House, Banda St between Koinange and Loita streets, PO Box 62042, Nairobi (tel 338927, 22703). This company offers safaris to Lake Turkana (eight days), Amboseli, Lake Nakuru and Masai Mara (seven days), Masai Mara and the Rift Valley lakes (six days), Amboseli (three days), and Lake Turkana plus a camel walk in Rendille country (10 days). They're highly recommended.

Special Camping Safaris Ltd
Gilfillan House, Kenyatta Ave, PO Box 51512, Nairobi (tel 338325, 20072). This is a small company operated by two people and their Kenyan staff and they pride themselves on personal service. They offer Lake Turkana, Samburu and Mt Kenya (10 days), Masai Mara (four days), Mt Kenya, Meru, Samburu, Maralal, lakes Baringo, Nakuru and Naivasha and Masai Mara (10 days), Amboseli, Tsavo and the coast (10 days) plus walking safaris in the Loita Hills (seven days) and horse-riding safaris on the Rift Valley escarpment (three days).

Bushbuck Adventures
3rd floor, Gilfillan House, Kenyatta Ave, PO Box 67449, Nairobi (tel 728737). To quote the company's leaflet, 'We do not offer safaris for those requiring all the comforts of home, nor do we offer rock bottom prices and comparable facilities. We specialise in safaris for (those) who want reasonable comfort while still feeling close to nature'. As a result, they're relatively expensive.

They offer Masai Mara (five days – US$710), Amboseli, Tsavo, Chyulu Hills (six days – US$845), Shaba, Mathew's Range, Ndoto Mountains, Lake Turkana, Maralal, Lake Bogoria (12 days – US$1550), Mt Kenya, Shaba and Meru (six days – US$845) and Masai Mara, Lake Victoria, Mt Elgon, Saiwa Swamp and Lake Nakuru (12 days – US$1550). Again, highly recommended.

Best Camping Tours
2nd floor, Nanak House, corner Kimathi and Banda streets, PO Box 40223, Nairobi (tel 29667, 29675). This is another company which offers budget camping safaris on all the main routes ranging from Amboseli and Tsavo (four days) right through to Masai Mara, Lake Nakuru, Amboseli and Tsavo (15 days).

This company has had a variable press over the last few years judging from the feedback which we've received – some abuse it virulently; others praise it. What seems to be happening is that they push their drivers too hard for too long (sometimes 20 days with no time off) so they get tired and bad tempered. There have also been complaints that the groups are too large and the food gets scarce towards the end of the trip. It's probably no worse than any other company in this respect.

Exotic Safaris

1st floor, South Wing, Uniafric House, Koinange St, PO Box 54483, Nairobi (tel 338811). We've had good reports of this company which offers a full range of safaris along the standard routes from Amboseli (three days) through lakes Nakuru, Bogoria and Baringo and Masai Mara (six days) to Mt Kenya, Samburu and Masai Mara (eight days) and Lake Turkana (eight days).

Centrex Tours & Travel

1st floor, Hughes Building, Muindi Mbingu St, PO Box 41830, Nairobi (tel 332267, 330539).

Farways Safaricentre Ltd

Opposite Castle Hotel, Moi Ave, PO Box 87815, Mombasa (tel 23307/9). This is a reputable company with its own vehicles and has a branch in Nairobi.

Safari Seekers

5th floor, Jubilee Insurance Exchange Building, Kaunda St, PO Box 23247, Nairobi (tel 26206).

Savuka Tours & Safaris

3rd floor, Pan Africa House, Kenyatta Ave, PO Box 20433, Nairobi (tel 725907, 25108).

Sunwise Travel Ltd

4th floor, Nanak House, corner Kimathi and Banda streets, PO Box 39073, Nairobi (tel 336777, 338715). Mainly luxury safaris.

Tete Travel Services Ltd

Corner Koinange and Moktar Daddah streets (above Goldstar Restaurant), PO Box 30729, Nairobi (tel 729461).

This is by no means an exhaustive list of companies which offer budget camping safaris nor is there necessarily any implication that others are unreliable (though some are). It's obvious, too, that if everyone who reads this book uses the companies listed above then they may get oversubscribed. On the other hand, we do get hundreds of letters from travellers every year describing their experiences with various safari companies. Some get consistently good reports and others get variable reports but there are some which get consistently bad reports. Regarding the latter category, we suggest you avoid:

Ebra Tours & Camping Safaris Ltd

4th floor, Standard Building, Standard St, PO Box 43457, Nairobi (tel 334937, 331494).

Massay Bush Safaris

3rd floor, Chester House, Koinange St, PO Box 74521, Nairobi (tel 727317)

Nutty Safaris

1st floor, Puri Building, Muindi Mbingu St, Nairobi (tel 21032, 26213)

There are also some lesser known safari companies which you should give a wide berth. They include Kiwa Safaris ('...a rip-off merchant well known to the police and the Ministry of Tourism...'), and Parrot Tours & Travels (tel 723796), Cambian Building, Moi Ave, PO Box 62951, Nairobi. Parrot Tours isn't even licensed and the owners are frequently in trouble with the authorities.

We've also had some bad reports and some very good reports about Nana Safaris (tel 21396), Chester House, PO Box 59603, Nairobi. On one of their safaris to Masai Mara and Lake Nakuru, the clients had to return to Nairobi by public bus from Nakuru and were only taken on three of the promised six game drives. On another, the group set off without a single tent! There was subsequently no compensation and a lot of aggro from the manager.

Similarly, Through the Lens Safaris, Jubilee House, Nairobi, came in for both good and bad reports. The complaints stemmed from lack of compensation and aggro from the management after a safari went seriously wrong (one group had been abandoned by their drunk driver in Tsavo!).

While many of these complaints are undoubtedly justified, it's only fair to say that some of the people who were caught out had been in too much of a hurry to go on a safari, hadn't done their homework, and had unrealistic expectations. Also, in some cases, it was just pure bad luck.

If you don't want to camp but prefer to stay in a lodge each night then check out:

African Tours & Hotels

Utalii House, Uhuru Highway, PO Box 30471, Nairobi (tel 336858)

Moi Ave, PO Box 90604, Mombasa (tel 23509)

Crossways Car Hire Tours & Travel

Banda St, Nairobi (tel 23949)

United Touring Company

International House, Mama Ngina St, PO Box 42196, Nairobi (tel 331960, 24847/8)

Moi Ave, PO Box 84782, Mombasa (tel 316333/4)

It's recommended that in this category you avoid Birds Paradise Tours & Travel (tel 22596, 722219), Standard St, PO Box 22121, Nairobi.

EXOTIC OPTIONS
Camel Safaris

There are only three companies which offer camel safaris at present and only one which is exclusively that. The other two are part of longer safaris to Lake Turkana by vehicle.

The first is that operated by Yare Safaris Ltd (tel 559313), 1st floor, Union Towers, Mama Ngina St, PO Box 63006, Nairobi, from their Maralal hostel. This is a five day trek along the Ewaso Nyiro River (which flows through Samburu and Buffalo Springs game reserves) and it leaves every Sunday.

On the first day you are transferred by vehicle to the camel base camp at Barsalinga bridge and from here you have the choice of riding the camels or walking alongside them for the next five days (it's up to you as the camels are not used for transporting food or equipment). You'll be accompanied the whole way by Samburu *morani* (warriors) and there's plenty of game to see in this unspoilt area. Your excess baggage and the camp is moved on ahead of you each day by support vehicle. The camps are equipped with two-person tents, mattresses and showers. The safari ends back at the Maralal hostel on Thursday. The cost is KSh 5500 (about US$262) which includes all transport, food, camping equipment (except sleeping bags) and transfer from Nairobi to Maralal and vice versa. There's an 8% discount on the cost of this safari for all IYHF members.

Gametrackers Camping Safaris (tel 338927), Finance House, Banda St (between Koinange and Loita streets), PO Box 62042, Nairobi, offer a partial four day walking/camel trek through the Ndoto Mountains, south-east of Lake Turkana, which is part of a 10 day safari to Lake Turkana but here the camels transport your food, water and equipment. You walk alongside them accompanied by Rendille guides. The cost of the safari is KSh 7000 (about US$333) which includes all transport, meals,

park entry fees, camp site fees and camping equipment (except sleeping bags). Departures depend on demand.

Bushbuck Adventures (tel 728737), 3rd floor, Gilfillan House, Kenyatta Ave, PO Box 67449, Nairobi, offer a 10 day camel trek once a year (in late October) which takes you to the Ndoto Mountains and Milgis Lugger or the Amaya River and Mt Silali depending on prevailing conditions. The camels are used for transportation of food and equipment – you walk. This trek costs US$1850.

The same company also offers a partial walking/camel trek through the Mathew's Range and the Ndoto Mountains which is part of a 12 day safari which also takes in Shaba National Reserve, Lake Turkana, Maralal and Lake Bogoria. Again, the camels are used for transporting food, water and equipment. The cost of this safari is US$1550 which includes all transport, food, camping equipment (except sleeping bags), park entry and camp site fees. Departures depend on demand.

Walking Safaris

Special Camping Safaris Ltd (tel 338325), Gilfillan House, Kenyatta Ave, PO Box 51512, Nairobi, offer a seven day walking safari in the Loita Hills including transfer to and from Nairobi. This trek takes you down the Nkuruman Escarpment into the Rift Valley accompanied by an experienced Maasai guide. You cover about 10 km (approximately five to six hours walk) per day and you're expected to carry food. At night you sleep in the open on groundsheets. As the company says, 'It's not suitable for vegetarians as a goat will be slaughtered for the farewell feast'. The trek costs KSh 5200 (about US$248). Departures depend on demand.

Horse-Riding Safaris

Special Camping Safaris Ltd (address above) also offer three day horse-riding safaris through the Ngong Hills and the Kitengela Reserve where you'll get beautiful views over the Rift Valley. Accommodation overnight is in tents and the cost of the safari is KSh 8100 (about US$386) which includes the horses, food, camping equipment (except sleeping bag) and other transport.

Flying Safaris

These safaris essentially cater only for the rich and those interested in big-game fishing. They centre around Rusinga Island in Lake Victoria. A light aircraft collects you from your nearest airstrip in the early morning and returns you in time for lunch or an afternoon game drive. In the meantime a motorboat takes you out on Lake Victoria where you can feed and photograph fish eagles and fish for Nile perch – the largest freshwater fish in the world. Angling gear is provided. Bookings can be made through Lonrho Hotels Kenya (tel 723776), PO Box 58581, Nairobi.

Balloon Safaris

For those with the money to spare, here is a unique experience to view the wildlife of Masai Mara Game Reserve from the air. These hot-air balloons depart daily from Keekorok Lodge just after dawn and return around mid-morning. The flight includes a champagne-style breakfast on the plains. The cost is KSh 4000 (about US$190). Bookings can be made through Block Hotels (tel 335807), PO Box 47557, Nairobi, or at Keekorok Lodge.

Further Afield

A few companies in Nairobi offer safaris to the Tanzanian game parks of Lake Manyara, Ngorongoro Crater and Serengeti but most of them are just agents for Tanzanian safari companies based in Arusha so you might as well go there yourself and organise things from there. It would certainly cost less doing it that way.

There is one outfit, however, which offers a superb 25 day safari from Nairobi all the way to Zaïre and back which takes in Uganda, Rwanda, the gorillas of Kahuzi Biega National Park (Zaïre), Lake Kivu (Zaïre), a chimpanzee sanctuary (Zaïre), Nyiragongo volcano (Zaïre), northern Tanzania, Serengeti National Park (Tanzania)

and Masai Mara Game Reserve (Kenya). For those with less time available, there's the option of joining the vehicle in Kigali (Rwanda) for 12 or 20 days of the Zaïre section only.

The people who operate this safari are all thoroughly experienced African overland hands and the company has its own well maintained 4WD trucks. It's a part camping and part budget hotel safari and it's excellent value at KSh 10,780 (about US$513) plus national park entry fees and budget hotel accommodation (US$100 for the gorillas, US$40 for the chimpanzees, US$30 for Nyiragongo (optional), US$42 for Serengeti) and US$45 for the food kitty. The food kitty is operated by the clients which allows greater flexibility in the choice of meals which are cooked by the camp's cook. Those joining this safari for only 12 or 20 days pay only US$25 or US$40 to the food kitty respectively. The price includes transport, camping equipment (except sleeping bags) and a camp cook. There's an 8% discount on these prices for all IYHF members.

For more details contact Yare Safaris Ltd (tel 559313), 1st floor, Union Towers, Mama Ngina St, PO Box 63006, Nairobi. Departures are usually once a month.

DO-IT-YOURSELF SAFARIS

This is a viable proposition in Kenya if you can get a group together to share the costs since you will have to rent a vehicle and camping equipment. The costs of renting a suitable vehicle can be found under 'Vehicle Hire' earlier on in this chapter.

Doing it yourself has several advantages over organised safaris. The main one is flexibility – you can go where you want, stop whenever you like and stay as long as you like. You don't have to follow the standard tourist routes. Another is that you can choose your travelling companions.

The main disadvantage is the extra effort you have to put in to organise the safari – hiring equipment, buying food and drink, cooking and agreeing among yourselves where you want to go and which route to take. It can also be a worry if none of you have mechanical skills and/or no tools and the vehicle breaks down. There's also the security of the vehicle and contents to think about if you want to leave it somewhere and go off walking. If you do this then you'll have to pay someone to guard it. Lastly, there's the question of maps especially if you intend to get right off the beaten track. Reasonably good large-scale maps are readily available in Kenya but the detailed ones are unavailable without going through a great deal of red tape. This means you could find yourself out in the middle of nowhere with not a clue where you're going and have to backtrack.

As far as costs go, it's probably true to say that organising your own safari is going to cost at least as much and usually more than going on a company organised safari. By how much more depends on a lot of factors but mainly the cost of hiring a vehicle and buying fuel. You'll have to sit down and work this out yourself.

Nairobi

Mark Knopfler could almost have been singing about Nairobi when he wrote *Telegraph Road*. Until the late 1800s there was nothing there. It was just a watering hole for the Maasai. Then came the Mombasa-Uganda railway, with its 32,000 indentured Indian labourers from Gujarat and Punjab, along with their British colonial overlords intent on beating the German colonial push for the Ugandan heartland. Being approximately halfway between Mombasa and Uganda and a convenient place to pause before the arduous climb into the highlands, it quickly became tent city.

Much of the area was still a foul-smelling swamp at this time and game roamed freely over the adjoining plains, yet by 1900 it had become a town of substantial buildings and five years later succeeded Mombasa as the capital of the British East Africa Protectorate. Since then it has gone from strength to strength and is now the largest city between Cairo and Johannesburg. The tower blocks of Nairobi can be seen for miles as you crest the hills which surround the plain on which it sits. Yet, in terms of the world's largest cities, Nairobi is still small with a population of about one million. You can walk from one end of the central business district to the other in 20 minutes. And where else in the world would you be able to see lion, cheetah, rhino and giraffe roaming free with the tower blocks of a city as a backdrop?

It's a very cosmopolitan place, lively, interesting, pleasantly landscaped and a good place to get essential business and bureaucratic matters sewn up. This is no Third World capital city though there are some very overcrowded shantytowns on the outskirts and even across the other side of the Nairobi River from Kirinyaga Rd. The latter are periodically bulldozed away and burnt down by the City Council's *askaris* (police) in the interests of hygiene but it takes only days for them to regenerate!

Like most cities, Nairobi has its crowded market and trading areas, its middle class/office workers' suburbs and its spacious mansions and beautiful flower-decked gardens for the rich and powerful. The first is an area full of local colour, energy, aspirations and opportunism where manual workers, exhausted matatu drivers, the unemployed, the devious, the down-and-out and the disoriented mingle with budget travellers, whores, shopkeepers, high school students, food stall vendors, drowsy security guards and those with life's little illicit goodies for sale. It's called River Rd – though, of course, it spans more than just this road itself. One of the funniest yet most poignant yarns I have ever read about an area such as this is to be found in a novel by Kenyan author Meja Mwangi called *Going Down River Road* (Heinemann: African Writers Series). I'd recommend this book to anyone and especially travellers passing through Nairobi. Even if you are not staying in this area you should make a point of getting down there one evening just to see how the other half lives on the wrong side of Tom Mboya St.

Elsewhere in Nairobi there are all the sort of things that you won't have seen for months if you've been hacking your way across the Central African Republic and Zaïre from West Africa or making do with the shortages in Zambia and Tanzania. Things like the latest films on big screens, bookshops, restaurants, cafés and bars full of travellers from all over the world, offices where you can get things done with the minimum of fuss, banks where you can change travellers' cheques in less than five minutes and a poste restante where you sort out your own letters from the pile so you don't end up with that feeling that letters have been put in the wrong pigeon hole. It's a great place to stay for a few days but if you stay too long it gets expensive because almost everyone you meet wants to do the same as you did when you first arrived –

splurge at the restaurants and drink your fill in the bars.

Orientation

The compact city centre is in the area bounded by Uhuru Highway, Haile Selassie Ave, Tom Mboya St and University Way. The main bus and train stations are within a few minutes walk of this area, while the main travellers' accommodation area is centred around Latema Rd, just east of Tom Mboya St on the fringe of the bustling and somewhat sleazy River Rd area.

To the west of the centre is one of the more enlightened bits of Nairobi town planning – Uhuru Park, although it will soon be overshadowed in the not too distant future by President Moi's shot at immortality – the 60-odd storey Times Media complex. The building of such a totally over-the-top skyscraper is Moi's bit of one-upmanship over Kenyatta (who has the conference centre) and over the rest of the continent – if it goes ahead it will be the tallest building in Africa. It's been a controversial project since the planning stages, but the only person with the courage to oppose it publicly, Professor Mathaai, found her attempted court injunction against the project unceremoniously tossed out on its ear along with an unbelievable amount of personal abuse and public harassment. It seems there's little room for legitimate opposition in Kenya – especially from a woman.

The park itself is a much needed lung for this increasingly crowded city and quite apart from the fact that a good quarter of it is going to disappear with the construction of the Times Media complex, the resulting traffic congestion is going to be horrendous. It's bad enough already at rush hours.

Directly west of Uhuru Park, and still within walking distance of the centre (although it's not advisable to try it at night), are some of the city's better mid and toprange hotels, the popular Youth Hostel, a number of government ministries and the hospitals. Beyond here are the sprawling upper middle class suburbs of Ngong and Hurlingham with their large detached houses

and carefully tended gardens surrounded by high fences, and guarded by askaris along with prominent signs warning that the premises are patrolled by 'Ultimate Security', 'Total Security', 'Securicor' and the like. These signs are surely one of the most enduring impressions of suburban Nairobi!

North of the centre is the University, the National Museum, the International Casino and one of Nairobi's original colonial hotels, the Norfolk. Beyond here is Westlands, another of Nairobi's upper middle class suburbs. North-east of the centre is Parklands, a slightly less desirable suburb which is home to many of Nairobi's Asian minority and where the Aga Khan Hospital is to be found. Close to the hospital is the popular Mrs Roche's guest house. Going east, there is the bustling and predominantly African suburb of Eastleigh along with the country bus station.

South of the city is Nairobi National Park, and to the park's north-east is Jomo Kenyatta International Airport which is connected to the city by an excellent dual carriageway.

Information

Tourist Office In a city the size of Nairobi, and in a country which relies so heavily on tourism, it seems inconceivable that there is no tourist office, but there isn't.

There is an 80 page leaflet called *Tourist's Kenya* (tel 337169, PO Box 40025) which is published every two weeks. It is free of charge and available from most large hotels – the Thorn Tree Café in the New Stanley Hotel is the most convenient place to find it. It contains most of what you'll need to know – hotels, restaurants, airlines, embassies, tour and safari operators – but it doesn't bend over backwards to keep its factual information up to date or even comprehensive.

Other similar free publications which you can pick up from hotels and bookstores are *What's On* (tel 728290/7, PO Box 49010), published by Nation Printers & Publishers, and *Tourist Index* (tel 26206, PO Box 9165). Both of these are published monthly.

Post The main post office is on Haile

Selassie Ave and is open Monday to Friday from 8 am to 5 pm and Saturday from 9 am to noon. The poste restante is well organised and they'll let you look through as many piles as you like plus there's no charge for letters collected. The only trouble is that the counter which deals with it is also one of the few which sells stamps, so the queues are often long.

With the huge volume of poste restante mail here it's not surprising that some letters get misfiled but, surprisingly, it doesn't happen too often. As a favour to other travellers you should pull out any letters you come across which are misfiled so the clerk can get them into the right pile.

This post office is also the best one from which to post parcels. The contents of all parcels sent overseas have to be inspected by the post office staff before being sealed so don't arrive with a sealed parcel or you'll have to pull it apart again. Bring all packing materials with you as there are none for sale at the post office. One of the cheapest places to buy good packing materials is at the supermarket on Posta Rd opposite where the old GPO used to stand (now demolished). Otherwise, try Biba on Kenyatta Ave at Muindi Mbingu St.

Telephone The Extelcoms office is on Haile Selassie Ave, almost opposite the post office. It is open from 8 am to midnight and you can make direct-dial calls yourself from here with a phonecard or go through the operator. They also have telex and fax facilities here.

The best place to make a call during normal business hours if you have to go through the operator is at the telephone exchange on the ground floor of the Kenyatta Conference Centre. If there is no conference in progress this office is much quieter than the Extelcoms office, and there are also two card phones here.

Banks At Jomo Kenyatta International Airport the branch of Barclays Bank is open 24 hours a day, seven days a week. In Nairobi, the bank's branch on the corner of

Kenyatta Ave and Wabera St is open Monday to Saturday from 9 am to 4.30 pm.

Foreign Embassies For a list of embassies in Nairobi, see the Visas section in the Facts for the Visitor chapter.

Airlines Airlines with offices in Nairobi include:

Aeroflot
    Corner House, Mama Ngina St (tel 20746)
Air Botswana
    Hilton Hotel (tel 338309)
Air France
    Hilton Hotel (tel 728910)
Air India
    Jeevan Bharati Building, Harambee Ave (tel 334788)
Air Madagascar
    Hilton Hotel (tel 25286)
Air Rwanda
    Mama Ngina St (tel 332225)
Air Mauritius
    Union Towers, Moi Ave (tel 29166)
Air Malawi
    680 Hotel, Muindi Mbingu St (tel 340212)
Air Zaïre
    Shretta House, Kimathi St (tel 25625)
Air Zimbabwe
    Chester House, Koinange St (tel 339522)
Alitalia
    Hilton Hotel (tel 24361)
British Airways
    International Life House, Mama Ngina St (tel 334362)
Cameroon Airlines
    HFCK Building, Kenyatta Ave (tel 337788)
EgyptAir
    Hilton Arcade (tel 26821)
Ethiopian Airlines
    Bruce House, Muindi Mbingu St (tel 330837)
Kenya Airways
    Koinange St (tel 29291)
KLM
    Fedha Towers, Muindi Mbingu St (tel 332673)
Pakistan International Airlines (PIA)
    ICEA Building, Banda St (tel 333900)
Pan Am
    Hilton Hotel (tel 23581)
Sabena
    International Life House, Mama Ngina St (tel 333284)
Somali Airlines
    Bruce House, Mama Ngina St (tel 335409)

■ PLACES TO STAY		● OTHER		42	Law Courts
				2	National Museum
1	Boulevard Hotel	12	Akamba Bus Terminal	36	Parliament House
30	Fairview Hotel	32	All Saints Cathedral	9	Police Station
22	Green View Lodge	45	American Embassy	41	Public Map Office
28	Grosvenor Hotel	46	Burundi Embassy	39	Railway Museum
47	Hermes Hotel	18	Barclays Bank	17	Rwandan & Somali
27	Heron Court Hotel	35	City Hall		Embassies
34	Intercontinental Hotel	11	City Market	3	Snake Park
26	Milimani Hotel	16	Country Bus Station	5	Spinners Web
8	Nairobi Safari Club	14	East African Road	21	Sudan & Zimbabwe
23	Nairobi Serena Hotel		Services		Embassies
6	Norfolk Hotel	24	Ethiopian Embassy	37	Tanzanian High
31	Panafric Hotel	44	Extelcoms		Commission
25	Sagret Hotel	13	Goldline/Coast-	15	Taxis to Namanga
7	YMCA		line/Mawingo	4	Text Book Centre
29	Youth Hostel		Bus Terminals	18	Ugandan High
20	YWCA	40	GPO		Commission
		33	Immigration (Nyayo	19	Zambian High
▼ PLACES TO EAT			House)		Commission
		10	Kenya Airways Terminal		
27	Buffalo Bill's	43	Kenyatta Conference		
38	Caboose Restaurant		Centre		

Sudan Airways
UTC Building, General Kago St (tel 21326)
Uganda Airlines
Uganda House, Kenyatta Ave (tel 21354)
Zambia Airways
Hamilton House, Kaunda St (tel 29908)

Travel Agents To get the best possible deal on an airline ticket, first make the rounds of the airline offices to ascertain the standard price and then make the rounds of the travel agents. Always get several quotes from the agents as things change constantly. It's sometimes, but not usually, possible to get as good a deal from the actual airline offices as it is from the agents. European and Asian destinations are the ones to which you'll find the best discounts. This is less so in the case of North American destinations and virtually impossible for Australasian destinations.

Most of the heavily discounted tickets will involve stopovers between connections – EgyptAir, Ethiopian Airlines and Sudan Airways, for example.

One of the most popular agents is Hanzuwan-el-Kindly Tours & Travel (tel 26810, 338729), Rajab Manzil Building (4th floor, room 3), Tom Mboya St. It used to be run by a man called Fehed A S H el-Kindly though he was known to everyone as Eddie. These days it's run by his brother Salim, and although most travellers speak well of the services provided, some recent reports suggest that he might be letting things slip. One traveller who had been assured that his bookings were confirmed later discovered he was No 146 on the waiting list! It's advisable to be cautious and not to hand over your money or passport until you actually see the ticket.

Also recommended are Prince Travel, Kenyatta Conference Centre (especially for flights to Cairo); Crocodile Travel, Tom Mboya St, in the same block as the Ambassadeur Hotel; and Falcon Travel, International House, Mama Ngina St. Banko Travel, Latema Rd, are also very friendly and offer similar deals. Others which are worth checking out are Let's Go Travel on Standard St close to the junction with Koinange St, Appel Travel, Tamana Tours and Kambo Travel.

Local expats speak highly of Molo Bay Tours, run by a Canadian woman and her Maasai husband.

Cultural Centres All the foreign cultural organisations have libraries which are open to the public and are free of charge except for the American Cultural Centre which is for members only. Both the French and German cultural centres welcome travellers. The addresses are:

Alliance Française
ICEA Building, ground floor, Kenyatta Ave (tel 340054). Open Monday to Friday from 10 am to 1 pm and 2 to 5.15 pm and on Saturday from 9.30 am to noon. There is a good French restaurant here, too, which is open in the evenings.
American Cultural Centre
National Bank Building, Harambee Ave (tel 337877). Open Monday to Friday from 10 am to 5 pm and on Saturday from 10 am to 1 pm.
British Council
ICEA Building, mezzanine floor, Kenyatta Ave (tel 334855). Open Monday to Friday from 10 am to 5 pm and on Saturday from 9 am to noon.
French Cultural Centre
Maison Francaise, corner Monrovia and Loita streets (tel 336263). Open Monday to Friday from 10 am to 5 pm and on Saturday from 10 am to 1 pm.
Goethe-Institut
Maendeleo House, corner Monrovia and Loita streets (tel 24640). Open Monday to Friday from 10 am to 6 pm.
Italian Cultural Institute
Prudential Building, Wabera St (tel 21615). Open Monday to Friday from 8.30 am to 1 pm and 2.30 to 5 pm.
Japan Information Centre
Matungulu House, Mamlaka Rd (tel 331196). Open Monday to Friday from 10 am to noon and 2.10 to 4.30 pm.

Bookshops The best selection of bookshops are along Kimathi St (Nation Bookshop – next to the New Stanley Hotel) and Mama Ngina St (Prestige Books – next to 20th Century Cinema). There are others but they don't carry the same range. The Text Book Centre on Kijabe Rd is not right in the centre and so the prices are a little lower.

For both new and second-hand books there are pavement bookstalls scattered throughout Tom Mboya St and Latema Rd.

Maps There are many maps of Nairobi available in the bookshops but probably the best

is the *City of Nairobi: Map & Guide* in English, French and German published by the Survey of Kenya in a red front cover with partially coloured photographs on the back cover. It covers the suburbs as well as having a detailed map of the central area. If you're going to be staying for a long time, however, the *A to Z: Guide to Nairobi* by D T Dobie (Kenway Publications) is worth buying.

Photography For passport-size photographs, the cheapest place to go is the machine under the yellow and black sign 'Photo Me', a few doors up Kenyatta Ave from the Nation Bookshop on the corner of Kimathi St. It costs KSh 25 for four prints and takes about three minutes. There's another machine on the corner of Tom Mboya St and Accra Rd. You can also get them from the photography shop in Kimathi House opposite the New Stanley Hotel but here they cost KSh 35 for three prints.

For camera repairs or equipment rental the Camera Maintenance Centre (tel 26920) in the Hilton Arcade is definitely not cheap. Make sure you get a quote beforehand as quite a few people have felt they've been ripped off here. Alternatively try Camera Experts (tel 337750) or Expo Cameras, both on Mama Ngina St.

Emergency If you need medical treatment try Dr Sheth on the 3rd floor of Bruce House on Standard St. This doctor has his own pathology laboratory if you need blood or stool tests. He charges KSh 300 per consultation plus laboratory fees. There is also a dentist on the same floor.

Otherwise go to the Nairobi Hospital which has the same scale of charges as Dr Seth. Avoid like the plague Kenyatta Hospital since, although it's free, treatment here is possibly worse than the ailment, according to local residents. The Aga Khan Hospital in Parklands opposite Mrs Roche's is also not a bad place.

Vaccinations You can get these at City Hall Clinic, Mama Ngina St. It is open for jabs from 8.30 to 11.30 am Monday to Friday.

Yellow fever shots cost KSh 250, cholera KSh 100, meningitis KSh 100, typhoid KSh 250 and tetanus KSh 100.

If you want a gamma globulin shot (for hepatitis) go to Dr Sheth, 3rd floor, Bruce House, Standard St.

Safety You may hear rumours about Nairobi being a dangerous city at night as far as robberies go. We've certainly had enough letters from people whom this has happened to but never once on any occasion that I've been to Nairobi have I felt uneasy or threatened walking back to my hotel. Perhaps I just look like I know where I'm going or pull out my wallet when someone asks me for a few shillings down a dark alley. And I don't walk across Uhuru Park at night.

The best thing that can be said is to be vigilant. It's no worse than many other cities around the world and there are plenty worse. You should definitely not walk from the centre to the Youth Hostel or through Uhuru Park or along Uhuru Highway/Waiyaki Way anywhere between Westlands and the roundabout with Haile Selassie Ave at night. You are asking for trouble. That taxi home may cost you KSh 60 but could save you a lot of money.

While we're on this subject, don't forget to read the stories in the Dangers & Annoyances section of the Facts for the Visitor chapter.

Left Luggage Many of the cheaper hotels, such as the Iqbal, the New Kenya Lodge and Mrs Roche's will store baggage for you, usually for a small daily charge. You're advised not to leave anything valuable with left luggage.

Nairobi railway station also has a left luggage office which is open daily from 8 am to noon and 1 to 6.30 pm. It costs KSh 12 per item.

Car Rental All the major companies, and many smaller ones have offices in the city centre, and the bigger ones such as Avis and Hertz have desks at the airport. A comprehensive description of car hire can be found in the Getting Around chapter.

Camping Equipment Hire If you want to hire anything from a sleeping bag to a folding toilet seat, tent or mosquito net, the best place to go to is Atul's (tel 25935, 28064), Biashara St. They have the lot and are open Monday to Friday from 8.30 am to 12.30 pm and 2 to 5.30 pm and on Saturday from 8.30 am to 12.30 pm and 2.30 to 4.30 pm. Hire charges have to be paid in full before commencement of hire as well as a deposit for each item. The deposits are refunded when hired items are returned in good condition. Identification is required (eg passport).

The items which they have for hire are far too numerous to mention here but they print a list which you can pick up for KSh 10. Advance booking is highly recommended and saves a lot of time. If you'd like a list before going to Kenya, write to PO Box 43202, Nairobi.

National Museum
The National Museum is on Museum Rd off Museum Hill which itself is off Uhuru Highway. The museum has a good exhibition on prehistoric people, an incredible collection of native birds, mammals and tribal crafts and a new section on the culture, history and crafts of the coastal Swahili people. It's just unfortunate that many of the displays are moth-eaten and tatty these days.

Opening hours are 9.30 am to 6 pm daily and admission is KSh 50.

Snake Park
Opposite the museum the Snake Park has living examples of most of the snake species found in East Africa – some of them are in glass cages, others in open pits. There are also tortoises and crocodiles. Hours and entry charges are the same as for the museum.

National Archives
Right opposite the Hilton Hotel on Moi Ave are the National Archives. They're regarded

by many as better value than the National Museum and entry is free. They don't just contain the sort of documents that you would expect in such a building but photographs of Mzee Kenyatta and Moi visiting different countries and exhibitions of handicrafts and paintings.

Railway Museum
The Railway Museum is on Station Rd – follow the railway tracks until you are almost at the bridge under Uhuru Highway or walk across the small piece of waste ground just next to the Uhuru Highway/Haile Selassie Ave roundabout.

In addition to old steam engines and rolling stock it will give you a good idea of Kenya's history since the beginning of the colonial period. There's also a scale model of the venerable MV *Liemba* which plies the waters of Lake Tanganyika between Mpulungu (Zambia) and Bujumbura (Burundi).

It's open daily from 8 am to 4.45 pm; entry is KSh 10, or KSh 5 for students.

Parliament House
Like to take a look at how democracy works in Kenya? If so, you can get a permit for a seat in the public gallery at Parliament House on Parliament Rd or, if Parliament is out of session, you can tour the buildings by arrangement with the Sergeant-at-Arms.

Art Galleries
There's not much in Nairobi in the way of art galleries. The only one is the Gallery Watatu in the ground floor of Bruce House on Standard St. This place usually has some interesting works by local artists and is worth a quick look.

Kenyatta Conference Centre
There is a viewing level on the 28th floor of the centre but the revolving restaurant no longer operates. If you'd like to go up there, you must request a guide at the information desk on the ground floor. He'll expect a tip but otherwise it's free. You're allowed to take photographs from the viewing level. Access

Kenyatta Conference Centre

is sometimes restricted when there's a conference in progress.

Places to Stay – bottom end
There is a very good selection of budget hotels in Nairobi and the majority of them, except for two very popular places outside of the city centre, are between Tom Mboya St and River Rd so if you find that one is full it's only a short walk to another.

In the Centre The *New Kenya Lodge* (tel 22202), River Rd at the junction with Latema Rd, is a legend among budget travellers and still one of the cheapest. There's always a wild and interesting bunch of people from all over the world staying here. Accommodation is basic but clean and there's hot water in the evenings. Rooms with shared bathroom facilities cost KSh 95/120/140 for singles/doubles/triples.

The same people who own this have also opened the *New Kenya Lodge Annex* just around the corner on Duruma Rd. Prices here are KSh 45 for a dorm bed plus KSh 95/120 for singles/doubles but there's cold water only and many travellers comment that the annexe doesn't have the same atmosphere as the old place and that some of the rooms don't even have windows! All the same, it's very popular, the staff are friendly, baggage is safe, and the notice board makes interesting reading. Baggage storage costs KSh 50 per week.

Sharing the legend is the *Iqbal Hotel* (tel 20914), Latema Rd, which has been popular for years. It is still very pleasant although recent price hikes mean it's not the bargain it once was. This place is so popular that it's unlikely you'll get a bed or room here after 9 am. The best plan is to turn up at 8 am and put your name on the waiting list. Checkout time is 10 am and the free beds are allocated then. Ali, the manager, is a friendly bloke who keeps a sense of humour in conditions which are sometimes trying. There's supposedly hot water available in the morning but you have to be up early to get it. Beds in three-bed rooms go for KSh 90, while double/triple rooms cost KSh 180/270, all with common facilities. Baggage is safe here and there's a store room where you can leave excess gear (KSh 5 per day) if you are going away for a while. The Iqbal's notice board is always a good place to look for just about anything.

If the above two are full there are three others on Dubois Rd, just off Latema Rd. The *Bujumbura Lodge* (tel 28078) is very basic but clean and quiet and very secure. The toilets and showers are clean and there is erratic hot water. It's not that friendly a place and we've had two complaints that some of the ceilings leak but it's OK for a short stay. Prices are KSh 85 a single (only two of these) and KSh 110/125 for doubles/triples. The *New Safe Life Lodging* is very similar and the staff are cheerful. The single rooms are overpriced at KSh 120 but the doubles for KSh 165 are not bad value. The *Nyandarwa Lodging* is very clean, quiet and comfortable and you can get a large double room for KSh 145. They also have single rooms but they're just glorified cupboards and not such good value for money at KSh 95.

Back on Latema Rd, the *Sunrise Hotel* is clean, secure and friendly and there's usually hot water in the mornings and evenings. Rooms here cost KSh 145/190 for singles/

doubles with shared bathroom facilities. The front two rooms overlooking the street are the largest and have a balcony but they are right next door to the Modern 24-Hour Green Bar which rages 24 hours a day, 365 days a year, so if you want a quiet room take one of those at the back of the hotel. If you're looking for material for a novel, on the other hand, then take one of these rooms.

Right at the bottom of the scale is the *Al Mansura Hotel* on Munyu Rd. It's basic and the rooms are clean enough but it's really only good for a night if you can't get in elsewhere. Women are likely to feel uncomfortable in this place. A bed in a shared room costs KSh 50; doubles are KSh 100.

Outside the Centre There are two very popular places away from the city centre. *Mrs Roche's*, 3rd Parklands Ave opposite the Aga Khan Hospital, is, like the New Kenya and the Iqbal, a legend. Mrs Roche has been making travellers welcome for almost 20 years and it's a favourite with campers and those with their own vehicle as well as those who don't particularly want a room in the city centre. There's always an amazing band of people here and the whole place has the general atmosphere of a gypsy camp – there's never a dull moment. It's situated in a very pleasant area amongst trees and flowering shrubs and is a very mellow place to stay. It's just a pity that some travellers with vehicles seem to disembowel them here and leave the discarded parts lying around for other travellers to camp amongst. Camping costs KSh 35 per night while a bed in a shared room costs KSh 60. Because it's so popular you may have to sleep on the floor for the first night until a bed is available.

This is another place with a good notice board. You can leave baggage for KSh 20. To get to Mrs Roche's, take a matatu (KSh 3) from the junction of Latema Rd and Tom Mboya St right outside the Odeon Cinema. They will have 'Aga Khan' in the front windscreen. Tell the driver you're heading for Mrs Roche's guest house. It's well known.

There are several places to eat cheaply in the immediate vicinity and the nearest bar (which also has an excellent barbecue) is the Everest Hotel just up the road. It's a lively place and I've met Mrs Roche there on several occasions!

The other very popular place is the *Youth Hostel* (tel 21789), Ralph Bunche Rd between Valley Rd and Ngong Rd. It's often very crowded here so it's a good place to meet other travellers. It's very clean, well run, stays open all day and there's always hot water in the showers. The wardens here are very friendly and will lock up gear safely for you for up to two weeks for KSh 10, then it's KSh 15 per day after that. On a day-to-day basis there are lockers to keep your gear in when you go out, but you must supply your own lock. The notice board here (for messages, things for sale, etc) is one of the best in Africa. A bed in a shared room costs KSh 70 but you must have a YHA membership card to stay. If not, you'll have to pay a temporary membership fee of KSh 30 per night or join the association for KSh 170 for a year.

Any matatu or bus which goes down either Valley Rd or Ngong Rd will drop you at Ralph Bunche Rd. The No 8 matatu which goes down Ngong Rd is probably the most convenient. You can pick it up either outside the Hilton Hotel or on Kenyatta Ave on the corner with Uhuru Highway. If you're returning to the Youth Hostel after dark don't be tempted to walk back from the centre of the city. Many people have been robbed. Always take a matatu or taxi.

The Ys There is both a *YMCA* (tel 337468) and *YWCA* (tel 338689) in Nairobi. The former is on State House Rd and the latter on Mamlaka Rd off Nyerere Rd. The YMCA costs KSh 180 per person for full board in a dormitory, KSh 210 per person in a shared room and KSh 230/420 for single/double rooms, all with communal facilities. Rooms with private bath are more expensive at around KSh 335/530. This place seems to have a semipermanent population of local students so could be an interesting place to stay.

The YWCA is reluctant to take short-term visitors. It prefers to take people who are going to stay at least one month and the room rates are geared towards this. It does, however, take couples as well as single women.

Camping Mrs Roche's is the only place to go if you want to camp. In the high season the limited garden space gets pretty cramped, not only with tents but also with vehicles. It costs KSh 35 per person to put up your tent.

Places to Stay – middle
In the Centre There are several mid-range hotels in the same area as the bulk of the budget hotels. One of the cheapest is the *Gloria Hotel* (tel 28916), Ronald Ngala St almost on the corner with Tom Mboya St. Rooms here are good value at KSh 190/215/360 for a single/double/triple. All rooms are with bath and hot water, and the price includes breakfast. The only problem here is that the rooms cop the noise from the street below. Just a couple of doors along is the *Terrace Hotel* (tel 21636) which has rooms with bath and hot water for KSh 180/215 including breakfast. It doesn't win any prizes for friendliness and some of the rooms are noisy, but overall it's not a bad place.

One of the best places in this category is the *Dolat Hotel* (tel 22797), Mfangano St, which is very quiet and friendly and costs KSh 172/253 for singles/doubles with bath and hot water. The sheets are changed daily and the rooms kept spotless. It's a good secure place and quite a few travellers stay here.

More expensive is the *Salama Hotel* (tel 25899), on the corner of Tom Mboya St and Luthuli Ave. It's a little on the pricey side at KSh 370/410/625 for a single/double/triple including breakfast and it's hard to see what the advantage is over places like the Gloria and the Terrace for around half the price, especially as the extra money doesn't buy you relief from the street noise. Similarly

Nairobi Centre

■	PLACES TO STAY	54	Terrace Hotel	39	The Pub
				29	Supermac
17	Africana Hotel	▼	PLACES TO EAT	11	Supreme
49	Ambassadeur Hotel				Restaurant
27	Al Mansura Hotel	37	African Heritage	47	Tamarind
18	Bujumbura Lodge		Café		Restaurant
53	Dolat Hotel	39	Akasaka Japanese	32	Thorn Tree Café
6	Embassy Hotel		Restaurant	45	Trattoria Restaurant
55	Gloria Hotel	41	Beneva Coffee-		
46	Hilton Hotel		House	●	OTHER
8	Hotel Pigale	34	Blukat Restaurant		
22	Iqbal Hotel	12	Bull Café	7	Atul's Camping
1	New Garden Hotel	43	The Coffee Bar		Equipment Hire
13	New Kenya Lodge	10	Dhaba Restaurant	47	American Cultural
14	New Kenya Lodge	42	Dragon Pearl		Centre
	Annexe		Restaurant	44	City Hall
15	New Safe Life	4	Goldstar	16	DPS & Wepesi taxis
	Lodging		Restaurant	29	Elite Camera
32	New Stanley Hotel	24	Growers Café		House
16	Nyandarwa	36	Harvest Restaurant	48	Florida 2000
	Lodging	28	The Honey Pot		Nightclub
30	Oakwood Hotel	33	Jacaranda Café	3	Kenya Airways
2	Parkside Hotel	31	Jax Restaurant		Terminal
51	Salama Hotel	9	Khyber Restaurant	40	Let's Go Travel
19	Sirikwa Lodge	26	Malindi Dishes	20	Modern 24-Hour
38	Sixeighty Hotel		Restaurant		Green Bar
52	Solace Hotel	11	Mayur Restaurant	50	National Archives
21	Sunrise Hotel	25	Nairobi Burgers	35	New Florida
5	Terminal Hotel	23	Panda Restaurant		Nightclub

overpriced is the *Solace Hotel* (tel 331277), Tom Mboya St, more or less opposite the Salama Hotel. Rooms here cost KSh 300/430 for singles/doubles including breakfast.

The *Sirikwa Lodge* (tel 26089) is another at the top of this bracket and is on the corner of Munyu and Accra roads. For KSh 314/374/575 you get a clean room with bath and hot water, breakfast is included and each room has a phone. Accra Rd is somewhat quieter than Tom Mboya St so this place is not a bad bet. Another quiet place is the *Africana Hotel* (tel 20654) on Dubois Rd between Accra and Latema roads. The rates are KSh 330/420/600 for rooms with bath, hot water and breakfast. It's good value and secure.

Further away from this area at the junction of Tom Mboya St and Haile Selassie Ave is the *Hermes Hotel* which has self-contained double rooms with breakfast for KSh 480.

The quietest rooms are at the back. The hotel has its own restaurant including an all-you-can-eat lunch. The food is good and the staff friendly.

Personally, I feel that the mid-range hotels in the vicinity of Jeevanjee Gardens and the central market are better value than those on the River Rd side of Moi Ave if only for the noise factor and the vehicle fumes but not everyone agrees.

Very popular (especially with US Peace Corps volunteers who get a 25% discount) is the *Hotel Pigale* (tel 331403), Moktar Daddah St facing Jeevanjee Gardens. Singles/doubles/triples here with bathroom, hot water, soap and towel cost KSh 210/265/380 including taxes. There are only 21 rooms so you need to get there early. There's a good notice board in the reception area which is worth checking out if you're looking for something.

Across the other side of Jeevanjee

Gardens are two other somewhat more expensive hotels, the *New Garden Hotel* and the *Parkside Hotel*. The New Garden is excellent value at KSh 265/310/470 for singles/doubles/triples with bathroom, hot water and breakfast. They also have doubles without shower for KSh 265. The Parkside has singles/doubles for KSh 277/385 with bathroom, hot water and breakfast. The staff are very friendly and the hotel has its own restaurant.

Opposite the Kenya Airways terminal is the *Terminal Hotel* (tel 28817), Moktar Daddah St, which is also popular with travellers. It offers rooms with bath, hot water, soap and towel and clean sheets for KSh 290/430/575 including taxes but without breakfast. Some of the rooms are getting a little tatty these days but the staff are friendly and honest and valuables left in the rooms are safe. There's a same-day laundry service on weekdays (but not at weekends).

Close by is the *Embassy Hotel* (tel 24087), Biashara St between Koinange St and Muindi Mbingu St. Rooms here, all with bathroom, hot water, soap and towel, cost KSh 360/515 for singles/doubles including taxes. They also have a number of smaller singles for KSh 300.

Outside the Centre Across the other side of Central Park, up a gravel track off Nyerere Rd at the back of the Minet ICDC House, is the *Green View Lodge* (tel 720908). It consists of several blocks of wooden huts in leafy surroundings with its own bar and restaurant. The rooms are reminiscent of a country cottage and are good value at KSh 145/240 for singles/doubles with shared bathroom facilities and KSh 478 for a double with private bathroom. All prices include breakfast.

Most of the other mid-range hotels are along Milimani Rd, Ralph Bunche Rd and Bishops Rd.

Very popular indeed with travellers and expatriates on contract work is the *Heron Court Hotel* (tel 720740, PO Box 41848), Milimani Rd. It's a large place and excellent value at KSh 420/540 for singles/doubles

with bathroom, hot water, soap and towels. They also have self-contained apartments with a double bedroom, separate lounge with balcony, bathroom and fully equipped kitchen for KSh 470/590 a single/double. Breakfast is not included in the room rates. The sheets and towels are changed daily in both types of room and the hotel facilities include a swimming pool, sauna, massage, guarded car park, shop and 24 hour laundry service. The staff here are friendly and helpful and security is excellent. At the front of the hotel is one of Nairobi's most popular bar/restaurants, Buffalo Bill's, which is open from early morning until around 11 pm daily.

Right at the top of Milimani Rd at the junction with Ralph Bunche Rd is the *Sagret Hotel* (tel 720933, PO Box 18324) which is of a somewhat higher standard than the Heron Court and offers singles/doubles with bathroom for KSh 520/835 including breakfast. The hotel has its own bar and restaurant.

Turning left up Ralph Bunche Rd brings you to the *Grosvenor Hotel* (tel 722080, Box 41038) which offers singles/doubles for KSh 460/595 including breakfast and all taxes. The hotel is divided up into several main buildings and cottages spread out over extensive wooded lawns and gardens and dates from the colonial era. It's getting a little tatty at the edges these days but has managed to preserve its olde-worlde charm and is popular with working expatriates and families since children can play in safety on the lawns and there are swings provided for them. There's also a swimming pool, bar and grill, an Ethiopian restaurant (which is excellent) and a Japanese restaurant.

On Bishops Rd at the back of the Panafric Hotel is the *Fairview Hotel* (tel 723211, PO Box 40842). Billed as 'the country hotel in the city' with some justification due to its pleasant garden and quiet location, it offers singles for KSh 430 to KSh 600, doubles for KSh 695 to KSh 900 and family units for KSh 900 to KSh 1440, all with bathroom, telephone, TV and video service, and including breakfast. Other meals average around KSh 120 but the food is said to be only average. The staff are friendly and helpful and it's a very popular place to stay for expatriates on contract work in Nairobi. Guests are entitled to use the swimming pool at the Panafric Hotel.

At the top end of this section is the *Oakwood Hotel* (tel 20592, PO Box 40683), Kimathi St, right opposite the New Stanley Hotel. This is a very pleasant place to stay and there are 23 self-contained rooms costing KSh 570/960/1170 a single/double/triple including breakfast and all taxes. There's constant hot water, a telephone and TV with in-house movies in every room and an overnight laundry service. Other hotel facilities include a private bar, restaurant and roof terrace.

Places to Stay – top end

In a city the size of Nairobi there are naturally many top-range hotels, some of them in the city centre and others outside this immediate area. If you are planning on staying in one it is worth booking through one of the travel agents in town instead of paying the so-called 'rack rates' as they can often get you a considerable discount. At the Serena, for example, it's possible to get a discount of nearly 40% by booking through UTC.

The *Ambassadeur Hotel* (tel 336803, PO Box 30399) on Moi Ave is right in the city centre and costs KSh 755/960/1250 for singles/doubles/triples. As with all hotels in this range, rooms are with bath and hot water. Somewhat more expensive but again right in the centre of town, on Muindi Mbingu St between Standard St and Kenyatta Ave, is the *Sixeighty Hotel* (tel 332680, PO Box 43436). This is a large modern hotel and good value at KSh 865/1320/1680 for singles/doubles/triples without breakfast. Even better value and less expensive is the *Boulevard Hotel* (tel 27567, PO Box 42831), Harry Thuku Rd, which offers rooms with bathroom, balcony, telephone and radio for KSh 720/900/1020 a single/double/triple including taxes but excluding breakfast. The hotel facilities include swimming pool, tennis court, restaurant, barbecue, bar and beer garden.

Similar in price to the above but up on Milimani Rd is the *Milimani Hotel* (tel 720760, PO Box 30715). This is a huge, rambling place popular with expatriates on contract and charges KSh 1080/1440/2015 for singles/doubles/triples including breakfast and taxes.

The *New Stanley Hotel* (tel 333233, PO Box 30680) on the corner of Kimathi St and Kenyatta Ave was built in 1907 and despite numerous subsequent renovations still has that old colonial charm. On the other hand, it's just about due for renovation again as it's definitely tatty around the edges these days and the staff can be decidedly unhelpful at times. Singles/doubles/triples here including taxes cost KSh 1680/2040/2650. The Thorn Tree Café at street level is a popular attraction here though the food is mediocre and service can be agonisingly slow.

The *Norfolk Hotel* (tel 3355422, PO Box 40064), Harry Thuku Rd, is even older than the New Stanley – it was built in 1904 – and was *the* place to stay in the old days. It's still extremely popular among those with the money to spend and a taste for nostalgia and is set in beautiful gardens. Singles and doubles in the main block range between KSh 2160 and KSh 2800 plus there are studio suites at KSh 3480 and luxury cottages from KSh 5040 to KSh 7200. The hotel has a popular terrace bar and restaurant.

Back in the city centre, the *Hilton Hotel* (tel 334000, PO Box 30624), Mama Ngina St at Moi Ave, has all the usual Hilton facilities including a rooftop swimming pool yet, despite the relatively high price, some of the rooms are surprisingly gloomy and tatty. Singles here go for KSh 1475 to KSh 1920, doubles for KSh 1850 to KSh 2400 and suites for KSh 3960 to KSh 9840. The *Intercontinental Hotel* (tel 335550, PO Box 30353), City Hall Way, is somewhat impersonal and a little frayed at the edges but certainly much more pleasant than the Hilton. Singles here cost KSh 1615 to KSh 1965, doubles KSh 1975 to KSh 2480 and suites KSh 3422 to KSh 6824.

Just outside the city centre, in the corner of Central Park between Kenyatta Ave and

Nyerere Rd, is the *Nairobi Serena Hotel* (tel 725111, PO Box 46302) which has to be one of the city's most pleasant hotels. Even Jimmy Carter stays here! It underwent a complete refit fairly recently and rooms now cost KSh 2220/2820/3480 for singles/doubles/triples without breakfast but including taxes. There are also suites for KSh 3480 a single, KSh 4200 a double and a 'state suite' for KSh 6000.

A little further up Kenyatta Ave where it turns into Valley Rd is the *Panafric Hotel* (tel 720822, PO Box 30486), a huge, multistorey modern hotel with all the facilities you'd expect. Rooms here cost KSh 1620/2160/3025 for singles/doubles/triples including breakfast and all taxes plus they have suites going for KSh 3600/3960 a single/double.

The most expensive hotel in Nairobi is the new *Nairobi Safari Club* (tel 330621, PO Box 43564), University Way at Koinange St. The cheapest rooms are KSh 3205/3565 for singles/doubles in 'executive suites', followed by 'panorama suites' at KSh 3815/4175 and 'penthouse luxury suites' at KSh 9815/13,550. To these prices you also have to add the cost of temporary membership.

Places to Eat

For most people with limited means, lunch is the main meal of the day and this is what the cheaper restaurants cater for. That doesn't mean that they're all closed in the evening (though quite a few are). It does mean, however, that what is available in the early evening is often what is left over from lunch time and the choice is limited. If you want a full meal in the evening it generally involves a splurge or eating from a barbecue attached to a bar.

Nairobi is replete with restaurants offering cuisines from all over the world – Italian, Spanish, Japanese, Chinese, Korean, Indian, Thai, Lebanese, steak houses, seafood specialists, etc – and at many the prices are surprisingly reasonable. For around US$8 per person you could eat well at quite a few of them. For US$10 to US$15 per person you could eat very well at almost all of them and

if you spent that much at some of them you'd hardly need to eat anything the next day.

Places to Eat – cheap

There are a lot of very cheap cafés and restaurants in the Latema Rd/River Rd area and at the top end of Tom Mboya St where you can pick up a very cheap, traditional African breakfast of mandazi and tea or coffee. Most of these places would also be able to fix you up with eggs and the like. Since many of them are Indian run, they also have traditional Indian breakfast foods like samosa and idli (rice dumplings) with a sauce.

For good local food the restaurant in the *Iqbal Hotel* is very popular and is something of a meeting place for travellers. The mkate mayai at KSh 21 here is excellent, although it does come served with a curious side plate of shredded lettuce with tomato sauce! One gets the feeling that the animals and birds used in the stews here died of plain old age, but the cabbage and potato stew is very good.

The *Malindi Dishes* restaurant in Gaborone Rd is well worth trying at least once. As the name suggests, the food here has the Swahili influence of the coast, and so coconut and spices are used to rev up what is otherwise pretty ordinary cuisine. Main dishes are in the KSh 40 to KSh 70 range, and they have excellent fruit shakes for KSh 18 as well as all the usual snacks and burgers.

For a good solid meal of a mixture of Western and local food, such as steak and matoke (mashed plantains and maize) or maharagwe (kidney beans), try the *Coffee Bar* on Mama Ngina St opposite City Hall. It's only open at lunch time and is popular with business people. Meals are priced at around KSh 40 to KSh 50 and are excellent value. Another place up at this end of town is the *Beneva Coffee House* on the corner of Standard and Koinange streets.

Another ultra-cheap café which is fairly popular is the *Bull Café* round the corner from the New Kenya Lodge on Ngariama Rd.

If staying at Mrs Roche's up in Parklands, the *Stop 'n Eat* offers ugali, ngombe (beef), etc for KSh 10 to KSh 18.

Very popular with the lunch time business crowd and said to be one of the cheapest in Nairobi for the quality of food it offers is the *Jacaranda Café* in the Phoenix House Arcade between Kenyatta Ave and Standard St. Hamburger, chips and salad cost just KSh 24! Similar are the row of ramshackle wooden eateries between the Railway Museum and Haile Selassie Ave which are jammed with local office workers in three-piece suits at lunch time. It's quite a sight!

Fast Food That well known English staple, fish & chips, has caught on in a big way in Nairobi and there are scores of places offering it. They're all cheap but the quality varies from grease ad nauseam to excellent.

My own recommendation for a lunch of fish & chips is *Supermac* on Kimathi St, directly opposite the Thorn Tree Café on the mezzanine floor of the shopping centre there. It's very popular at lunch time and deservedly so. They not only do some of the best fish & chips in Nairobi but also offer sausages, salads and fruit juices. Get there early if you don't want to queue.

Also recommended for this type of fast food is the *Prestige Restaurant*, Tsavo Lane off Latema Rd, which offers large servings of sausage, chips and salad for KSh 18. It's popular with local people.

The hamburger is all-conquering in Nairobi too, though, surprisingly, none of the American chains have got a foothold in Kenya yet. Too much Indian entrepreneurship perhaps? What has got a solid foothold is the *Wimpy* chain which has branches on Kenyatta Ave, Tom Mboya St and Mondolane St. They have the usual range of snacks and meals (burgers, sausages, eggs, fish, chicken, milkshakes, etc) costing up to KSh 60 and are open from 7.30 am to 9.30 pm. Another good café for a meal of burgers, fish or chicken with a mountain of chips and salad for around KSh 40 is *Nairobi Burgers* on Tom Mboya St right opposite the end of Latema Rd. They also serve sweets, soups and ice cream – it's a very popular place.

Good Breakfasts The *Growers Café* on

Tom Mboya St is deservedly popular with both local people and travellers and the prices are reasonable. They have such things as eggs (boiled or fried), sausages and other hot foods, fruit salads with or without yoghurt and good coffee. Another popular breakfast place is the *Honey Pot* on Moi Ave. Here a breakfast of eggs, sausages, juice, toast, jam and tea or coffee is KSh 34.

If you're staying over in the Koinange St area, the *Goldstar Restaurant* on the corner of Koinange and Moktar Daddah streets is a good place for breakfast. For KSh 40 you get juice, cornflakes, eggs, toast, jam and tea or coffee. For a little extra, they'll add on bacon and a sausage.

Big Lunches Kenya is the home of all-you-can-eat lunches at a set price and Nairobi has a wide choice of them, most offering Indian food. One of the best is the *Supreme Restaurant* on River Rd, which offers excellent Indian vegetarian food for KSh 65 to KSh 80 depending on whether you want the ordinary or the 'delux' lunch and whether you want dessert. It also has superb fruit juices.

Similar is the *Blukat Restaurant*, Muindi Mbingu St between Banda St and Kigali Rd. It offers both vegetarian and meat set lunches for around KSh 60. The day's specials are chalked up on a blackboard outside the restaurant. You'll see quite a few travellers eating here.

In the Harambee Plaza Building on the corner of Uhuru Highway and Haile Selassie Ave, the *Caboose Restaurant* does an 'African buffet' on Wednesdays from 12.30 to 3 pm for KSh 110, while on other weekdays the usual 'businessman's buffet' costs KSh 90.

The *African Heritage Café*, which you reach through the African Heritage shop on Kenyatta Ave or through a separate entrance on Banda St, is also highly recommended for lunch. There are actually two parts to the restaurant – the main room adjoining Banda St which tends to be somewhat gloomy and is more expensive and the much lighter barbecue grill in the centre of the building. The food in the barbecue section is excellent and there's a choice of meat, fish or chicken which comes complete with chips and salad for KSh 65 to KSh 80 depending on what you have. Get here early if you don't want to wait for a table as it's a popular place to eat.

The restaurant at *The Pub* underneath the Sixeighty Hotel, on Standard St between Muindi Mbingu St and Koinange St, offers similar barbecued fare to that of the African Heritage Café and the prices are much the same though some dishes cost up to KSh 100. The only trouble with this place is the variability of the meat dishes – sometimes the meat is beautiful and tender; other times it's tough as old boots. Lunch is served from 12 to 2 pm and dinner from 6 to 11 pm.

Another good place to go for lunch and well cooked, straightforward food is the *Harvest* on Kenyatta Ave between Koinange St and Loita St. It's a very pleasant spot to eat.

Jax Restaurant on the 1st floor of the Old Mutual Building, Kimathi St, is a very popular place for lunch. It offers a wide selection of beautifully prepared hot meals, a salad buffet and Goan specialities in various different dining areas, including open-air dining. There's a licensed bar and you can eat well for KSh 80 and up. It's open from 8 am to 5 pm Monday to Friday, 8 am to 5 pm on Saturday but closed on Sundays and public holidays.

Quite a few people eat at *Buffalo Bill's* in front of the Heron Court Hotel, Milimani Rd, and while the food is quite good it works out relatively expensive because of the hefty 15% service charges and tax which is added to the bill.

Out of the centre in Rhapta Rd, Westlands, is the *Kenya Continental Hotel*. The outdoor restaurant here serves mainly meat, and you order it by the kg! Chicken is KSh 115 a kg, meat KSh 65 and extras such as salads and chips are KSh 12 each. The atmosphere is lively and the jukebox loud – a good place but you'll probably have to get a taxi there as it's hard to find.

Places to Eat – more expensive

The choice here is legion and spans just about every cuisine in the world. If you're going to be spending any amount of time in Nairobi and want to explore the full range of possibilities then it's worth buying a copy of *Nairobi Eating Out Guide* by Alan Graham which lists more than 200 of these establishments. This booklet, which is sold by most bookshops in Nairobi, is actually an extract from the *Kenya Travel Handbook* by the same author (PO Box 11285, Nairobi).

Most of these restaurants are licensed and offer beer, wine and spirits but the major exceptions are the Indian vegetarian restaurants which usually offer only fruit juices and tea or coffee.

Virtually all these restaurants accept international credit cards but they don't all take the full range of them.

Good Breakfasts For a breakfast splurge, try one of the buffets at one of the major hotels. The *Illiki Café* on the ground floor of the Ambassadeur Hotel on Moi Ave is excellent value. Here you can make a total pig of yourself for KSh 100. They offer the works – a variety of juices, milk, yoghurt, cereals, porridge, eggs, bacon, beans, sausages, toast, fruits, cakes, you name it.

Most of the other top-end hotels also do buffet breakfasts, although all charge around KSh 120 to KSh 155. Those at the *Hilton* and the *Norfolk* are superb, the *Nairobi Serena* pretty good, the *Intercontinental* fair and the *New Stanley* extremely poor.

Indian Food By far the best place in Nairobi for North Indian tucker is the *Dhaba Restaurant* (tel 334862) up at the top end of Tom Mboya St. A lot of work and thought has gone into the decor here with some fine watercolour murals of Punjabi rural life and ceilings made of mangrove poles and plaster. It's very popular among Indian families which is a good indication of the quality of the food. The house speciality is the 'takataka' meat dishes, which take their name from the noise which comes from the tandoori kitchen as the chef prepares the meat with huge cleavers. Main dishes are in the range of KSh 83 to KSh 95, so expect a full meal to come to around KSh 145 per person with drinks.

The *Mayur Restaurant* (tel 331586), above the Supreme Restaurant (mentioned previously under 'Big Lunches') has been famous for superb Indian vegetarian food for years. It's not bad value at KSh 110 but the hushed atmosphere is a bit daunting. This place seems to have lost out badly to the newer and more gregarious Dhaba.

Also excellent is the *Minar Restaurant* (tel 29999), Banda St, which specialises in Mughlai dishes and offers buffet lunches and à la carte dinners. Expect to pay around KSh 180 for a three-course dinner including coffee. The restaurant is licensed, the service friendly and the restaurant is open from 12 to 2 pm and 7 to 10.30 pm daily.

At the Meridien Court Hotel on Murang'a Rd up near the top end of Moi Ave, the *Khyber Restaurant* (tel 25595) also specialises in Mughlai dishes and offers a buffet lunch. Dinner choices include tandoori chicken, lamb or fish (KSh 80 to KSh 100), other special lamb or chicken dishes (KSh 90 to KSh 140), seafood (KSh 115 to KSh 275), vegetarian dishes (KSh 35 to KSh 85) and the usual range of Indian breads and sweets. It's licensed and open from 12.30 to 2.30 pm and 7 to 10.30 pm daily including holidays.

If you're staying at the Milimani Rd/Ralph Bunche Rd end of town then you can't beat a meal at *The Golden Candle* (tel 720480), Ralph Bunche Rd, close to the Grosvenor Hotel. The food here really is good and some travellers rate it as the best Indian food in Nairobi. They specialise in North Indian and Mughlai dishes (KSh 55 to KSh 200) but also offer charcoal-grilled steaks and chops (KSh 90 to KSh 115), seafood (KSh 95 to KSh 240) and Indian vegetarian dishes (KSh 50 to KSh 80). It's licensed and open from 12.30 to 3 pm and 6.30 to 11 pm Tuesday to Sunday; closed Mondays.

Chinese Food Nairobi has a reasonable selection of Chinese restaurants although none of them are cheap. One of the best is

the *Panda Restaurant* on the corner of Tom Mboya and Cabral streets where the speciality is dishes from the Szechuan region of China. Similar is the *China Plate* (tel 20900), on the corner of Accra and Taveta roads, which also has Szechuan dishes in the range of KSh 90 to KSh 160. It's open daily from 12.30 to 2.30 pm and 7 to 10.30 pm.

Other places include: the *Dragon Pearl* (tel 340451), Bruce House, Standard St; the *Rickshaw Restaurant* (tel 23604) in Fedha Towers, Muindi Mbingu St at Kaunda St, which offers Mandarin, Cantonese and Szechuan dishes from KSh 180 and up; and the *Hong Kong Restaurant* (tel 28612) on Koinange St, which offers Cantonese dishes for KSh 145 to KSh 325. Most of the main dishes at the above Chinese restaurants are available in full or half portions.

Thai Food Nairobi's first Thai restaurant is in the Westlands shopping centre, just a few minutes north of the city centre along Uhuru Highway. The *Bangkok Restaurant* (tel 751311) has a good reputation and is in the Rank Xerox Building.

Italian Food For Italian food there is really only one place to go and that is the very popular *Trattoria* (tel 340855) on the corner of Wabera and Kaunda streets. It is open daily from 8.30 am to 11.30 pm and both the atmosphere and the food here are excellent. There's a wide choice on the menu but the attitude of the waiters can be decidedly supercilious and when the change comes you'd better take possession of it in a big hurry otherwise it will be snatched up at the speed of lightning regardless of the amount! A soup, main course, salad, dessert and a carafe or two of house chianti will relieve you of between US$10 to US$15. As you might expect, the ice cream here is superb.

Also good is the *Marino Restaurant* (tel 336210) on the 1st floor of the National Housing Corporation Building, Aga Khan Walk, just off Haile Selassie Ave. It has a spacious interior dining area as well as an open-air patio and is open from 9 am to 2 pm and 7 to 10 pm Monday to Saturday; closed on Sunday. There's a wide range of Italian and continental dishes with main courses priced from KSh 80 to KSh 155.

Outside of the city centre are two other Italian restaurants – the *Toona Tree* and *La Galleria* (tel 742600), both of them in the International Casino, Westlands Rd across from the National Museum. They offer a range of pizzas, seafood and charcoal-grilled meats from KSh 50 to KSh 195 and the Toona Tree has live bands on Tuesday, Thursday and Saturday evenings. The Toona Tree is open from 12.30 to 2 pm and 7.30 to 11 pm Tuesday to Saturday and 12.30 to 3 pm and 7.30 to 11 pm on Sunday but is closed on Monday. La Galleria is open from 12 to 2.30 pm Monday to Friday and 7 to 10.30 pm Monday to Saturday.

Japanese Food There's one Japanese restaurant in the city centre, the *Akasaka*, which you'll find next to The Pub on Standard St between Koinange and Muindi Mbingu streets. As you might expect, it's done out in traditional Japanese style and there's even a tatami room which you can reserve in advance though mostly it's table and chairs. They offer the full range of Japanese cuisine including tempura, teriyaki, sukiyaki, shabushabu and yosenabe as well as a full range of soups and appetisers. A full meal will cost KSh 100 to KSh 240 per person. It's licensed and open daily from 6 to 9 pm plus they're open for box lunches from 12.30 to 2 pm.

The only other Japanese restaurant in town is the *Shogun* (tel 720563) at the Grosvenor Hotel on Ralph Bunche Rd. It offers the same range of dishes as the Akasaka but there's a choice of eating at the sushi bar, at tables and chairs or cross-legged at low tables in tatami rooms. It's licensed and open daily but there's only a limited range of dishes available at lunch time.

Korean Food The only Korean restaurant in Nairobi is the *Restaurant Koreana* (tel 335544) on the 1st floor of Kenindia House, Loita St. Soups cost KSh 30 to KSh 60, starters KSh 60 to KSh 85, side dishes from

KSh 18, seafood KSh 85 to KSh 90 and main dishes KSh 60 to KSh 120. It's licensed and open from 11.45 am to 2.30 pm and 6.30 to 10.30 pm Monday to Saturday and closed Sunday.

Other Cuisines The only Spanish restaurant in town is *El Patio* (tel 340114) on the mezzanine floor of the Reinsurance Plaza Building, Taifa Rd at the junction with Aga Khan Walk. A meal here costs between KSh 95 and KSh 275 and the restaurant is open from 9.30 am to 10 pm Monday to Friday and 7 to 10 pm Saturday. It's closed on Sunday.

There's an excellent Ethiopian restaurant at the *Grosvenor Hotel*, Ralph Bunche Rd, which is well worth trying if you're staying in the area. Otherwise Ethiopian specialities are included in the dinner time menu at the African Heritage Café for around KSh 120.

Seafood & Steak The best seafood restaurant in Nairobi is the *Tamarind* (tel 338959) in the National Bank Building, Aga Khan Walk between Harambee Ave and Haile Selassie Ave. They offer a wide selection of exotic seafood dishes and culinary influences range from European to Asian to coastal Swahili. The cuisine is superb as are the surroundings which are decorated in a sumptuous Arabic-Moorish style. Eating here is definitely a major night out as most main courses are priced well over KSh 180 with crab and prawn dishes up to KSh 350 and lobster at KSh 60 per 100 g. There's also a special vegetarian menu. It's open for lunch Monday to Saturday from 12.30 to 1.45 pm and daily for dinner from 6.30 to 9.45 pm.

For steak eaters who haven't seen a decent doorstep since they left Argentina, Australia, Uruguay or America and are looking for a gut-busting extravaganza then there's no better place than the *Carnivore*, out at Langata just past Wilson Airport (bus Nos 14, 24 and 124). Tell the conductor where you are going and it's a one km signposted walk from where you are dropped off. It's easy to hitch back into the centre when you're ready to go. Otherwise, negotiate for

Creative Parking

Though the wildlife parks may be Kenya's premier tourist attraction, it's worth strolling around Kenya's other park – Nairobi's kerbsides – to observe the imaginative and often unbelievable way in which drivers utilise every inch of space to park their frequently scratched and battered vehicles.

It's virtually impossible to find a spot to park in central Nairobi any day during business hours except Sunday. So, if there's the slightest possibility of parking another vehicle between two others in any way whatsoever, then someone is going to do it! This is often at 90° to the adjoining cars with no thought about what happens to either the front or back ends. Neither pavements nor parking meters are any impediment to these people, nor the danger of having either end wiped out by harrassed pedestrians or kamikaze KBS bus drivers. If there's simply not an inch to spare that's just too bad and double parking becomes the order of the day. How you get a car out of this miasma is your problem – not that of the people who've boxed you in.

Parking wardens there certainly are, as well as fines for 'illegal' parking, but the deterrent effect of them is minimal and, in any case, always negotiable to a degree.

The best areas to view this spectacle are between Kenyatta Ave and University Way, and anywhere between Tom Mboya St and the Nairobi River. ■

Nairobi car parking (TW)

Tea Plantations

Tea workers, Kericho (HF)

Kenya is the world's third largest producer of tea and typically it accounts for 20% to 30% of the country's export income. Tea picking is obviously one of the main jobs in the area. A top tea picker can pick up to 100 kg per day, and they are paid at the rate of KSh 0.80 per kg. The bushes are picked every 17 days, and the same picker picks the same patches of the plantation each time. If you look closely at one of the fields of bushes you can see how one stalk of a bush is left to grow here and there; these are the markers by which workers identify their patch. The bushes are cut right back to about 50 cm high in January-March every four years, and after 90 days are ready for picking again. ■

Tea plantation, Kericho (HF)

a taxi. Whether it's lunch or dinner you take there's always beef, pork, lamb, ham, chicken, sausages and at least one game meat (often wildebeest or zebra). The roasts are barbecued on Maasai spears and the waiters carve off hunks onto your plate until you tell them it's enough. Prices include salads, bread, desserts and coffee. Meals here can be surprisingly cheap given the amount you receive and you're looking at KSh 180 and up which is great value.

Entertainment

Cinema Nairobi is a good place to take in a few films and at a price substantially lower than what you'd pay back home, but if you don't want scratched films then go to one of the better cinemas such as *The Nairobi* (behind The Kenya) and *20th Century*, Mama Ngina St. The cheaper ones (KSh 10 downstairs, KSh 15 in the upper circle) are on Latema Rd and include the *Odeon* and *Embassy*. There are also two good drive-ins if you have the transport, both have snack bars and bars. Nairobi is also a good place to see an Indian film. If you've never seen one of these then treat yourself one evening. If you have seen them before, you won't need persuading! Check with local papers to see what's on.

Theatre At the *Phoenix Theatre*, Parliament Rd, the auditorium is small and the acting professionally competent but it's quite expensive (around KSh 120). Check with local papers to see what's on.

Discos There's a good selection of discos in the centre of Nairobi. Single men may or may not find the attention of the many unattached women found in most of them to be exactly what they're looking for but there's never any pressure other than the occasional request for a drink. Perhaps the most popular in the centre of town is the *Florida 2000* on Moi Ave near City Hall Way. Entry costs KSh 100 for men and KSh 50 for women and it's open until 6 am. Also very popular is the *New Florida* (known to resident expatriates as the 'Mad House') on the corner of

Koinange and Banda streets which is a most unusually shaped building with a petrol station underneath it! Entry charges are the same as the Florida 2000 and it stays open until 5 am. There are floor shows at about 1 am at both discos but they're pretty kitsch and the dancers are obviously bored to tears.

Another popular disco in the centre is *Visions* on Kimathi St which is open daily except Monday from 9 pm.

Less popular but probably just as good is the *Hollywood* on Moktar Daddah St between Koinange and Muindi Mbingu streets where the entry charges are the same as the above.

Beer in all these places is reasonably priced but other drinks, especially imported liquors, are more expensive. Snacks are available at all of them.

There don't appear to be any rigid dress regulations at any of these discos. Joggers and jeans are quite acceptable as are clean T-shirts though it's probably true to say that most men wear open-necked shirts and a pair of slacks and the local women are always well turned out.

Further out of town is *Bubbles* alongside the International Casino, Westlands Rd, which costs KSh 100 for men and KSh 50 for women.

There's a live band/disco every night at the *Carnivore* in Langata but entry will cost you KSh 50 per person. There's usually a good crowd and it makes a refreshing change from the more enclosed and crowded space of the New Florida or the Florida 2000 in town.

Live Music The *African Heritage Café* on Banda St is a popular place to hear live bands every Saturday and Sunday afternoon between 2 and 5 pm. There's a cover charge of KSh 20.

Much further out of town, just below the roundabout at Dagoretti Corner on Ngong Rd, is the *Bombax Club* which has live bands every Thursday, Friday, Saturday and Sunday. Unlike many of the other discos and bars mentioned in this section, this one is frequented mainly by local Kenyans with only a sprinkling of Whites but the atmosphere is very friendly and convivial. There's a cover charge of KSh 20. To get there, take a minibus or matatu to Dagoretti Corner from Kenyatta Ave outside Nyayo House or share a taxi (KSh 95).

There are plenty of other bars which lay on live music but many of them are in Eastleigh and to find them you're going to need an African friend to show you where they are.

Bars The *Thorn Tree Café* in the New Stanley Hotel on the corner of Kimathi St and Kenyatta Ave is a bit passé these days but is still the place to be seen and is still something of a meeting place with travellers. The service is generally supercilious and lousy and a beer takes forever to arrive. Perhaps this is just a ploy by the management to discourage 'shabby' travellers who might lower the tone of the place. Whatever the case, if you sit down between 11 am and 2 pm and 5 and 7 pm you'll have to order something to eat as well. The best thing about the Thorn Tree is the notice board where you can leave personal messages (but not advertisements of any kind, such as things for sale, looking for people to join a safari, etc).

Another popular bar (where you don't have to buy a meal in order to have a beer) is *The Pub* on Standard St between Koinange and Muindi Mbingu streets. It's designed to resemble an English pub (in which it fails miserably) and is open daily from 11 am to 11 pm. It attracts a remarkable cross section of the population and is a good place to go if you're a single man looking for some action. It does vary from night to night but there are usually plenty of girls in this place but that doesn't mean it's solely a pick-up joint. The Pub is part of the Sixeighty Hotel which has another open-air bar, the *Terrace Bar*, on the 1st floor above the entrance lobby.

The liveliest bar in Nairobi by far, however, is *Buffalo Bill's* at the Heron Court Hotel, Milimani Rd, which even got a three

paragraph mention in the National Geographic magazine in May 1990 in an article describing the Rift Valley. Decked out with mock covered wagons (in denim!) complete with 'County Jail' surrounding a central bar and run by a resilient Korean woman, it's extremely popular with a wide variety of resident expatriates, tourists and local, unattached African women. It's *the* place to go if you're a single man but equally as much fun if you're a couple. While it's open all day, everyday, until around 11 pm, it only runs full-bore from about 5.30 pm onwards. Most of the women you see here migrate to the Florida 2000 once the bar closes. Meals and snacks are available throughout the day up until around 10.30 pm.

For an unparalleled spit-and-sawdust binge put aside a whole evening to join the beer swilling, garrulous hordes at the *Modern 24-Hour Green Bar*, Latema Rd next to the Sunrise Lodge. This place rages 24 hours a day, 365 days a year and the front door has never been closed since 1968 – except for one day in 1989 during a national census! All human life is here – teenage girls chewing *miraa* (stimulating leafy twigs and shoots), hustlers, whores, dope dealers and what one traveller once described as 'lowlife Whites'. The jukebox is always on full blast with screaming Indian vocalists or African reggae and the bar is completely encased in heavy duty wire mesh with a tiny hole through which money goes first and beer comes out afterwards. It's a great night out if you have the stamina but is definitely not for the squeamish.

Those looking for more genteel surroundings in which to sip their beer should try either the *Grosvenor Hotel*, Ralph Bunche Rd at the junction with Lenana Rd and close to the Youth Hostel, or the lawn of the *Fairview Hotel*, Bishops Rd close to 3rd Ngong Ave. For fading touches of the colonial era, try the terrace bar at the *Norfolk Hotel* which is open at lunch time and in the evening from 5 to 11 pm. Friday nights is when the young White population of Nairobi descends on this bar to drink itself legless. If you have transport, local residents also recommend the intimate atmosphere of the *Hurlingham Hotel*, Argwings Kodhek Rd about three km from the centre of town. They also offer very good, very cheap pub meals. You can eat lunch out in the garden.

Activities

Clubs & Societies For something with more intellectual and less alcoholic content there are a lot of specialist clubs and societies in Nairobi, many of which welcome visitors. Most of the foreign cultural organisations have film and lecture evenings (usually free of charge) at least once or twice a week. Give them a ring and see what they have organised. In addition to these, some local clubs you may be interested in contacting include:

Mountain Club of Kenya (MCK)
    PO Box 45741, Nairobi (tel 501747). The club meets every Tuesday at 8 pm at the clubhouse at Wilson Airport. Members frequently organise climbing weekends at various sites around the country. Information on climbing Mt Kenya and Kilimanjaro is available on the same evening.
East African Wildlife Society
    Nairobi Hilton, PO Box 20110, Nairobi (tel 27047). This society is in the forefront of conservation efforts in East Africa and it publishes an interesting monthly magazine. Membership costs KSh 190 but entitles you to certain reductions in the national parks.
Nairobi Chess Club
    PO Box 50443, Nairobi (tel 25007). The club meets every Thursday after 5.30 pm at the French Cultural Centre, on the corner of Monrovia and Loita streets.
Nairobi Photographic Society
    PO Box 49879, Nairobi (tel 891075). Members meet at 8.30 pm on the first and third Thursdays of each month at St John Ambulance Headquarters behind the Donovan Maule Theatre.

Sports For sporting facilities, contact one or other of the following: Impala Club (tel 568684), Ngong Rd; Nairobi Club (tel 725726), Ngong Rd; Nairobi Gymkhana (tel 742804), on corner of Rwathia and Forest roads; Parklands Sports Club (tel 742938), Ojijo Rd. They all offer facilities for tennis, squash, cricket and some of them also play football and hockey.

Swimming Pools Most of the international tourist hotels have swimming pools which can be used by nonresidents for a daily fee of KSh 40. The YMCA on State House Rd also has a large pool with spring board which you can use for KSh 20.

Things to Buy

Nairobi is a good place to pick up souvenirs although you do need to shop around. The City Market on Muindi Mbingu St has a good range of stuff, particularly kiondo baskets, and there's a whole gaggle of stalls in Kigali St behind the Jamia Mosque. It's all a bit of a tourist trap and you need to bargain fiercely.

Even though they originated in Tanzania (and they're still much cheaper there), makonde wood carvings have caught on in a big way in Nairobi and the shops are full of them. At the cheaper end of the market, however, it's worth looking at the examples which hawkers bring around to the bars where tourists congregate. Buffalo Bill's at the Heron Court Hotel is one of the best places. The quality of the carving varies a lot but if you're not in a hurry then you can find some really fine examples at bargain basement prices. Expect to pay around a half to two-thirds of the price first asked.

If you're not into bargaining or want top quality stuff, there are plenty of 'fixed price' souvenir shops around, although even at these they'll usually give you a 'special price' if you are obviously not a Hilton hopper. Two of the better ones are the one on the corner of Kaunda and Wabera streets, and another on Tubman Rd near the corner of Muindi Mbingu St.

If you want to get kitted out in the latest in designer 'White hunter' safari gear there are literally dozens of shops selling all the requisite stuff at outrageous prices.

The Spinners Web describes itself as a 'consignment handicraft shop' which sells goods made in workshops and by self-help groups around the country. They have some superb stuff, including hand-knitted jumpers, all sorts of fabrics and the huge

Turkana baskets. The shop is on Kijabe Rd, around the corner from the Norfolk Hotel.

For a much less touristed atmosphere try the Kariokor Market east of the centre on Racecourse Rd in Eastleigh. It's a few minutes by bus.

Getting There & Away

Air Kenya Airways is the main domestic carrier and has the following internal flights from Nairobi's Jomo Kenyatta International Airport:

To	Frequency
Kisumu	13 flights weekly
Malindi	10 flights weekly
Mombasa	4 flights daily

Make sure you reconfirm flights 48 hours before departure and remember that delays are frequent on Kenya Airways.

Air Kenya Aviation is one of many small operators and runs the following flights from Wilson Airport (prices quoted are one way; return fares are slightly less than double). As is the case with most of the smaller operators, baggage allowance is only 15 kg, and excess is charged at the rate of KSh 15 per kg.

To	Frequency	Fare
Nyeri	daily	KSh 1200
Nanyuki	daily	KSh 1200
Eldoret	2 weekly	KSh 1500
Masai Mara	2 daily	KSh 1585
Lamu	daily	KSh 2700
Amboseli	daily	KSh 1250
Lodwar	3 weekly	KSh 2880
Loyangalani	3 weekly	KSh 3360

Bus In Nairobi most long-distance bus offices are along Accra Rd near the junction with River Rd. For Mombasa there are numerous companies (such as Coast, Akamba, Mawingo, Goldline and Malaika) doing the run, both by day and night. The cost varies from KSh 165 (Mawingo) to KSh 190 (Coast) and the trip takes around eight hours with a meal break on the way.

The main country bus station is just off Landies Rd, about 15 minutes walk from the budget hotel area around Latema Rd. It's a huge but reasonably well organised place,

and all the buses have their destinations displayed in the window so it's just a matter of wandering around and finding the one you want. There is at least one daily departure and often more to virtually every main town in the country, and the buses leave when full.

There is one daily direct bus to Garissa with Garissa Express (except when flooding cuts the road) which leaves from outside the Munawar Hotel opposite the Kenya Bus Depot in Eastleigh. The fare is KSh 115 and the journey takes about eight hours. The depot is a 10 minute matatu ride from Ronald Ngala St (Route No 9).

Share-Taxi This is a good alternative to that dangerous and heart-stopping mode of transport – the matatu. Share-taxis are usually Peugeot 504 station wagons which take seven passengers and leave when full. They are much quicker than the matatus as they go point to point without stopping, and of course are more expensive. Again, most of the companies have their offices around the Accra Rd and River Rd area. DPS and Wepesi, in the same office on Dubois Rd, have daily Peugeots to Kisumu (KSh 215, four hours), Kakamega (KSh 250), Busia (KSh 300), Nakuru (KSh 205, two hours) and Kericho (KSh 205). These departures are only in the mornings so you need to be at the office by around 7 am.

For the Tanzanian border at Namanga the taxis leave from the top side of the service station on the corner of Ronald Ngala St and River Rd. They run throughout the day, take about two hours and cost KSh 120. Minibuses also run to Namanga from the same place, cost KSh 95 and take up to three hours.

Train Trains run from Nairobi to Mombasa every day in both directions at 5 and 7 pm and the journey takes about 13 hours. The fares are: KSh 420 in 1st class, KSh 197 in 2nd class and KSh 99 in 3rd class. This is a popular run so book your tickets as far in advance as possible, although you shouldn't have any trouble a day or two before. The fare to Voi is KSh 293/138/69 in 1st/2nd/3rd class.

To the Ugandan border at Malaba there are trains on Tuesday, Friday and Saturday at 3 pm arriving at 8.30 am the next day. In the opposite direction they depart Malaba on Wednesday, Saturday and Sunday at 4 pm and arrive at 9.30 am the next day. The fares are KSh 440 in 1st class, KSh 207 in 2nd class and KSh 103 in 3rd class. En route to Malaba these trains go through Naivasha (KSh 92/43/22), Nakuru (KSh 147/69/35), Eldoret (KSh 305/143/72) and Bungoma (KSh 400/188/94).

The Nairobi-Kisumu trains depart daily at 6 pm arriving at Kisumu at 8 am the next day. In the opposite direction they depart daily at 6.30 pm arriving at Nairobi at 7.35 am the next day. Depending on demand there is usually an additional train ('express') at 5.30 pm from Nairobi daily for the first week of every month (and sometimes for the second week too) which arrives at Kisumu at 6.40 am the next day. The fares are KSh 317 in 1st class, KSh 149 in 2nd class and KSh 75 in 3rd class. This is also a popular route and the train is often booked out weeks in advance. If that's the case you may have to rely on the extra coach which is added on the day of departure if demand warrants (it usually does). Many of the carriages used on the Kisumu run are older than those used on the Nairobi-Mombasa run and are not such good value.

Hitching For Mombasa, take bus Nos 13 or 109 as far as the airport turn-off and hitch from there. For Nakuru and Kisumu, take bus No 23 from the Hilton to the end of its route and hitch from there. Otherwise start from the junction of Waiyaki Rd and Chiromo Rd (the extension of Uhuru Highway) in Westlands. For Nanyuki and Nyeri take bus Nos 45 or No 145 from the central bus station up Thika Rd to the entrance to Kenyatta College and hitch from there. Make sure you get off the bus at the college entrance not the exit. It's very difficult to hitch from the latter. Otherwise, start

from the roundabout where Thika Rd meets Forest Rd and Muranga Rd.

Getting Around
Airport Transport The Jomo Kenyatta International Airport is 15 km out of town off the road to Mombasa. The cheapest way of getting into town is on the city bus No 34 *but* (and this is a big but) *you must keep your wits about you!* The number of people who get ripped off on this bus doesn't bear thinking about. The usual story is that an 'instant crowd' forms, you are jostled and before you know it your bag or money pouch has been slashed or ripped off. It's not much of an introduction to Kenya to lose your valuables on the first day so take the airline bus if you are at all hesitant. There is generally no problem when catching the bus from the city to the airport. The fare is KSh 6 and the trip takes about 45 minutes, more in peak periods.

A safer and far more pleasant way of getting into town is the Kenya Airways minibus. This leaves the airline's city terminus on Koinange St at 7, 8, 9, 10 and 11.30 am, and 2.30, 4.45, 6.30 and 8 pm. The trip takes about 30 minutes and costs KSh 70. When coming in from the airport this bus will drop you at any of the hotels in the centre, which is great if you're jetlagged.

The third way to or from the airport is by taxi, and this is really the only option if you have a dawn or late-night flight. The standard fare is KSh 300. If you want to share a taxi to the airport check out the notice boards at the Iqbal, the New Kenya Lodge and the Pigale.

To Wilson Airport (for small aircraft to Malindi, Lamu, etc) take bus Nos 14, 24 or 124 from in front of Development House, Moi Ave, and elsewhere. The fare is KSh 2.50 off-peak.

Bus Buses are the cheapest way of getting around Nairobi, but there is no great need to use them. The only ones you are likely to need are the No 34 to the airport and those mentioned in the Around Nairobi section.

Forget about them in rush hours if you have a backpack – you'll never get on and if by some Herculean feat you manage to do that, you'll never get off!

Taxi Taxis cannot usually be hailed on the street (because they don't cruise for passengers) but there are taxi ranks at the railway station, the museum and outside most of the main hotels. The cabs are not metered but the fares charged are remarkably standard and few cabbies attempt to overcharge. KSh 60 gets you just about anywhere within the city centre. The same would be true from Ralph Bunche Rd or Milimani Rd to the main post office though they sometimes ask for KSh 70 as it involves backtracking down the other side of Haile Selassie Ave.

Outside this immediate area, the fare generally goes up to KSh 95.

In addition to the usual saloon car taxis, there are now quite a lot of brand new London taxis which are rumoured to belong to a very prominent politician. These cost more – KSh 70 around the centre, KSh 120 outside it.

Around Nairobi

NAIROBI NATIONAL PARK
This park is the most accessible of all Kenya's game parks, being only a few km from the city centre. You should set aside a morning or an afternoon to see it. As in all the game parks, you must visit it in a vehicle; walking is prohibited. This means you will either have to arrange a lift at the entrance gate with other tourists, go on a tour, or hire a car. Entry to the park costs KSh 220 per person (Kenya residents KSh 50), plus KSh 50 for a vehicle.

Nairobi National Park is the oldest park in the country, having been gazetted in 1946. For a park so close to the city centre you can see an amazing variety of animals – with a backdrop of jumbo jets coming in to land at Jomo Kenyatta International Airport which is adjacent to the park! Gazelle, oryx, lion, zebra, giraffe, buffalo, cheetah and leopard are all seen regularly. Elephants are not found in this park as the habitat is unsuitable. However, it is in this park that you have one of the best chances for spotting a rhino – they are doing quite well here as the poachers prefer more remote areas.

The concentrations of game are higher in the dry season when water sources outside the park have dried up. Water is more plentiful inside the park as small dams have been built on the Mbagathi River which forms the southern boundary of the park.

The 'Animal Orphanage' by the main gate has a sign inside the gate which reads 'this is not a zoo' – it is. From time to time they do have young abandoned animals which are nursed through to good health and then released, but basically it is just a zoo, although it's been much improved by recent renovation and rebuilding of enclosures.

Getting There & Away
If you want to hitch a ride through the park from the main gate, city bus No 24 from Moi Ave goes right by it.

There are many companies offering tours of Nairobi National Park and there's probably not much to choose between them. They usually depart twice a day at 9.30 am and 2 pm for a four hour tour and cost from KSh 200. If you hang around in front of the Hilton Hotel at around 2 pm it is often possible to get a discounted seat on a tour at the last minute as they try to fill the van.

Most of the tour companies also offer a daylong combined tour of the national park with a visit to the Bomas of Kenya and including a gargantuan lunch at The Carnivore for KSh 600.

LANGATA GIRAFFE CENTRE
The Langata Giraffe Centre is on Gogo Falls Rd near the Hardy Estate Shopping Centre in Langata, about 18 km from Nairobi centre. Here you can observe and handfeed Rothschild giraffes from a raised circular wooden structure which also houses a display of information about giraffes. It's open during school terms from 4 to 5.30 pm Monday to

Nairobi National Park

Friday and 10 am to 5.30 pm on Saturday and Sunday. During school holidays and public holidays it's open from 11 am to 5.30 pm. Admission costs KSh 30 (free to children). To get there from the centre take bus No 24.

THE BOMAS OF KENYA

The Bomas of Kenya at Langata – a short way past the entrance to the national park on the right-hand side – is a cultural centre. Here you can see traditional dances and hear songs from the country's 16 ethnic groups amid authentically recreated surroundings though the dances are all done by one group of professionals rather than representatives of the tribes themselves. There is a daily performance at 2.30 pm (3.30 pm at weekends). Entry costs KSh 100 or KSh 50 for students. There's the usual clutter of souvenir shops around the site. If you are not on a tour, matatu No 24 from outside Development House, Moi Ave, will get you there in about half an hour.

KAREN BLIXEN MUSEUM

This is the farmhouse which was formerly the residence of Karen Blixen, author of *Out of Africa*, and was presented to the Kenyan government at independence by the Danish government along with the adjacent agricultural college. It's open daily from 9.30 am to 6 pm and entry costs KSh 50 or KSh 10 for students. It's right next door to the Karen College on Karen Rd between the residential areas of Karen and Langata.

Getting There & Away

Take public bus No 27 from Kenyatta Ave or from the corner of Ralph Bunche and Ngong roads, or No 24 from Moi Ave. Bus No 111 will also get you most of the way but you'll have to change to No 24 at the Karen Shopping Centre.

NGONG HILLS

Ngong and Karen, to the west of Nairobi, along with Limuru, to the north, were the sites where many White settlers set up farms and built their houses in the early colonial days. The transformation they wrought was

quite remarkable so that, even today, as you catch a glimpse of a half-timbered house through woodland or landscaped gardens full of flowering trees, you could imagine yourself to be in the Home Counties of England or some other European location. And, yes, the eucalypts which you see growing everywhere were an Australian import.

There are some excellent views over Nairobi and down into the Rift Valley from various points in the Ngong Hills, but it's unwise to go wandering around alone as people have been mugged here, especially at weekends. What you really need to get a feel for in these areas is your own car or, alternatively, that of a resident who is willing to drive you around the place.

LIMURU

Limuru is possibly even more 'European' in the feeling it leaves you than the Ngong Hills except that there are vast coffee and tea estates blanketing the rolling hills in between swathes of conifer and eucalypt forest. It's up here that you'll find *The Kentmere Club* (tel (0154) 41053, PO Box 39508, Nairobi), Limuru Rd, Tigoni. This is the quintessential White settlers' club – even more so than the Norfolk Hotel in Nairobi. It consists of a series of low, intimate wooden cottages with shingle roofs connected to each other by quaint walkways and bridges and a main block built in the same style which houses a restaurant and a superb re-creation of an English country pub with low ceilings, exposed beams and log-burning fireplaces. You wouldn't know the difference between this place and the Spaniard's Inn on Hampstead Heath if it weren't for the Tusker and White Cap instead of bar pumps and real ale.

The restaurant here is probably the best in Kenya. Certainly the spreads which I saw being laid out on Christmas Eve were absolutely superb. It would have to be *the* place to go for a Christmas banquet though it's naturally not cheap – KSh 600 for Christmas Eve or New Year's Eve dinner and KSh 360 for Christmas Day lunch. Advance booking is essential.

If you'd like to rent a cottage here then make enquiries over the phone. It's very peaceful.

Not far from the Kentmere Club is the *Waterfalls Inn* (tel (0154) 40672) with its picnic site, waterfalls, viewing point, restaurant and disco. Admission here costs KSh 95 per car including up to six passengers plus there's pony, horse and camel riding available at KSh 25 to KSh 60. To get there, turn off right from the Limuru Rd when you see the sign for Limuru Girls' School. The Waterfalls Inn (signposted) is 2½ km down the dirt road from the turn-off.

Another thing you can do at Limuru is to visit a tea farm. If you've never done this before then it's worth a day out. Visits are organised by Mitchell's Kiambethu Tea Farm (tel (0154) 40756) at Tigoni, about 35 km north-east of Nairobi. Here you'll be shown the whole process of tea production as well as taken on an accompanied walk into the forest to see the Colobus monkeys. Visits here come in a package which includes pre-lunch drinks and a three-course lunch, all for KSh 300 per person. Groups are preferred and visits are by prior arrangement only.

Getting There & Away
Public bus No 116 will take you fairly close to the farm. If you have your own transport then take the C62 Limuru Rd past City Park and turn left at Muthaiga roundabout. Seven km further on you reach Ruaka village where you turn right by the signpost for Nazareth Hospital and onto the D407 Limuru Rd (otherwise known as Banana Rd). Some 14½ km down this road you'll see a signpost for Limuru Girls' School where you turn right. Go down past the school and take the entrance on the left-hand side signposted 'L G Mitchell'.

The Coast

This cannot be less than natural beauty, the endless sand, the reefs, the lot, are completely unmatched in the world.

Ernst Hemingway

The coast of Kenya is one of the country's main attractions. It offers a combination of historical sites, trading ports with a strong Arab-Muslim influence, superb beaches and diving opportunities – an area not to be missed.

Mombasa is the coast capital, if you like, and is the first port of call for most people after leaving Nairobi. It is an old trading port with a history going back at least to the 12th century, and the old city here shows heavy influence of the town's previous rulers – the mosques and the Portuguese fort in particular. It has a steamy humid climate but is a pleasant place nonetheless. Unfortunately many people are in such a rush to get to the beach that they really only transit Mombasa, which is a pity as the city, particularly the old part, is well worth exploring.

South of Mombasa it's basically beaches all the way to the Tanzanian border at Lunga Lunga. Apart from the resort development at Diani Beach everything is pretty low-key and it's easy to while away a few days (or weeks) here.

To the north it's much the same story, with Malindi being the big coastal resort centre, but there's a couple of interesting attractions here as well – the historical site of Gedi just a short bus ride to the south, and the excellent diving on the coral reef in the offshore Malindi and Watamu marine national parks.

Head further north and you come to the island of Lamu – a beautiful Arab-influenced town which has been something of a travellers' Mecca for years and still draws visitors by the thousands. Despite that it retains the very distinctive personality which attracted people to it in the first place – an easy-going unhurried pace, traditional architecture and a unique culture which owes a

great deal to its Muslim roots but has evolved over the centuries.

The people of the coast are the Swahili, and it's here that KiSwahili – the lingua franca of the modern nation – evolved as a means of communication between the local inhabitants and the Arab traders who first began plying their dhows up and down this coast sometime before the 7th century. Other influences also shaped the language and there is a smattering of not only Arabic but also Portuguese, Hindi and English words.

History

The first traders here appear to have been Arabs from the Persian Gulf who sailed south along the coast during the north-east monsoon, sailing home north with the south-west monsoon. By the 12th century some substantial settlements had developed, mainly on islands, such as Lamu, Mandu, Pemba and Zanzibar, as these provided greater security than the coast itself. The main export trade in this early part was in ivory, tortoiseshell and leopard skins, while items such as glass beads from India and porcelain from as far afield as China were finding their way here.

From the 12th to the 15th centuries settlements grew and a dynasty was established at Kilwa (in present day Tanzania), and so by the end of this period Mombasa, Malindi and Paté (in the Lamu archipelago) were all substantial towns. The inhabitants were largely Arab but there was also substantial numbers of African labourers. Intermarriage was common and the settlements were far closer connected culturally with the Islamic Persian Gulf than they were with inland Kenya. Although all these city-states had this common heritage and cultural link, they were all virtually independent and were often vying for power against each other.

So preoccupied were they with their own internal struggles that the coastal centres were quite unprepared for the arrival of the

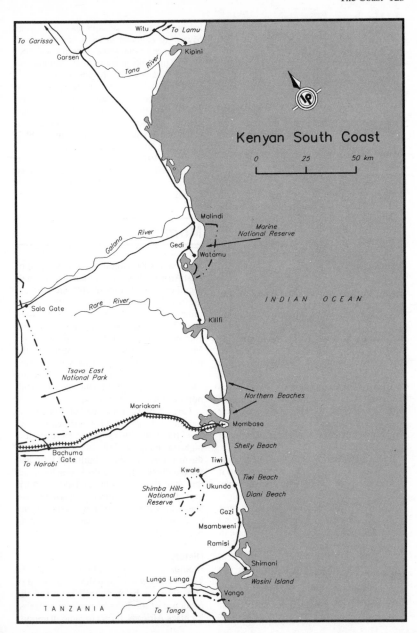

Kenyan South Coast

Portuguese in 1498. Before long they were paying tribute to the Portuguese and by 1506 the Portuguese had sacked and gained control of the entire coast. In the century which followed the Portuguese had raided Mombasa on two further occasions and built the beautiful defensive Fort Jesus in that city.

Trade was the main interest of the Portuguese and they concentrated their activities in that area. They did not exercise direct control over the administration of the coastal cities – just kept them in line and dependent.

Not all the locals were happy with this arrangement and the troubles started for the Portuguese with local uprisings in the 17th century. They were mainly inspired by the disaffected Sheikh Yusuf of Mombasa, who spent most of his time in conflict with the Portuguese, and in fact occupied Fort Jesus in Mombasa after murdering the Portuguese commandant there in 1631. With the help of the sultans of Oman, the Portuguese were defeated and Fort Jesus occupied by 1698.

The Omani dynasties flourished and Mombasa and Paté became the pre-eminent spots on the coast, although both were defeated by Lamu in 1810. The internecine struggles of the various Omani factions led to Zanzibar coming into ascendancy, which led the rulers of Mombasa to seek British assistance. The British, however, were reluctant to intervene and jeopardise their alliance with Seyyid Said, the Omani ruler, as their route to India passed close to Muscat. Before long the whole coast was under the control of the Omani ruler.

It was in this period of Omani rule that the slave trade flourished. Up until this time it had been carried out only on a small scale, but soon the newly established clove plantations on Zanzibar required labourers, and from there slaves were shipped to the Persian Gulf and beyond. It was also this increase in economic activity that brought the first Indian and European traders into the area. Trade agreements were made with the Americans (1833), the British (1839) and the French (1844), and exports to India also flourished – ivory, cloves, hides and coconut oil were all-important. This increase in trade

led Seyyid Said to transfer his capital from Muscat to Zanzibar in 1840, and decreased his reliance on the slave trade for revenue. He was thus able to sign a treaty banning the export of slaves to the Middle East.

Despite the fact that the British East Africa Company took over administration of the interior of the country, a 10-mile-wide coastal strip was recognised as the sultan's patch and it was leased from him in 1887, first for a 50 year period and then permanently. In 1920 the coastal strip became the British protectorate, the rest of the country having become a fully fledged British colony.

Mombasa

Mombasa is the largest port on the coast of East Africa. It has a population of nearly half a million of which about 70% are African, the rest being mainly Asian with a small minority of Europeans. Its docks not only serve Kenya, but also Uganda, Rwanda and Burundi. The bulk of the town sprawls over Mombasa Island which is connected to the mainland by an artificial causeway which carries the rail and road links. In recent years Mombasa has spread onto the mainland both north and south of the island.

Large Mombasa may be but, like Dar es Salaam to the south, it has retained its low-level traditional character and there are few high-rise buildings. The old town between the massive, Portuguese-built Fort Jesus and the old dhow careening dock remains much the same as it was in the mid-19th century, asphalt streets and craft shops apart. It's a hot and steamy town, as you might expect being so close to the equator, but an interesting place to visit.

History
Mombasa's history goes back to at least the 12th century when it was described by Arab chroniclers as being a small town and the residence of the King of the Zenj – Arabic for black Africans. It later became an import-

ant settlement for the Shirazis and remained so until the arrival of the Portuguese in the early 16th century. Determined to destroy the Arab monopoly over maritime trade in the Indian Ocean, especially with regard to spices, the Portuguese, under Dom Francisco de Almeida, attacked Mombasa with a fleet of 16 ships in 1505. After a day and a half it was all over and the town was burnt to the ground. So great was the quantity of loot that much of it had to be left behind, for fear of overloading the ships, when the fleet sailed for India.

The town was quickly rebuilt and it wasn't long before it regained its commanding position over trade in the area, but peace didn't last long. In 1528, another Portuguese fleet under Nuña da Cunha arrived on the East African coast too late to catch the south-western monsoon which would take them to India, so they were forced to look around for temporary quarters. Naturally, Mombasa was in no mood to welcome them but, unfortunately, Mombasa was at that time engaged in bitter disputes with the kings of Malindi, Pemba and Zanzibar. An alliance was patched together and the Portuguese were again able to take Mombasa, but sickness and constant skirmishing over many months eventually decided the outcome. The city was again burnt to the ground and the Portuguese sailed for India.

The Portuguese finally made a bid for permanency in 1593 when the construction of Fort Jesus was begun, but in 1631 they were massacred to the last person in an uprising by the townspeople. The following year a Portuguese fleet was sent from Goa and Muscat to avenge the killings but was unable to retake the town. By this time, however, the Mombasan ruler had decided that further resistance was useless and, having reduced the town to rubble and cut down all the fruit trees and palms, he withdrew to the mainland. It was reoccupied without a fight by the Portuguese the following year.

Portuguese hegemony of the Indian Ocean was on the wane by this time, not only because of corruption and nepotism within their own ranks, but because of Dutch,

French and English activity in India and South-East Asia. The 17th century also saw the rise of Oman as a naval power and it was the Omanis who, in 1698, were the next to drive the Portuguese from Mombasa, after a 33 month siege in which all the defenders were slaughtered. Even this disaster wasn't enough to convince the Portuguese that their days were over. Mombasa was reoccupied yet again but the end finally came in 1729 following an invasion by an Arab fleet, a general uprising of the population in which Portuguese settlers were slaughtered and an abortive counteroffensive which involved the entire military resources of the Viceroyalty of Goa.

In 1832 the Sultan of Oman moved his capital from Muscat to Zanzibar and from then until Kenya's independence in 1963 the red flag of Zanzibar fluttered over Fort Jesus. Meanwhile, the British became active along the East African coast. In their attempts to suppress the slave trade, they interfered increasingly in the affairs of Zanzibar until, in 1895, the British East Africa Protectorate was set up with Mombasa as the capital (until it was moved to Nairobi) and the Sultan of Oman's possessions were administered as a part of it. When independence came, the Sultan's coastal possessions were attached to the new republic.

During the protectorate years the British confirmed Mombasa's status as East Africa's most important port by constructing a railway from Mombasa to Uganda. It was completed in 1901, using indentured labourers from Gujarat and Punjab in India – hence the origin of Kenya's (and Uganda's and Tanzania's) Asian population.

Information & Orientation
Tourist Office The regional tourist office (tel 311231) is just past the famous tusks on Moi Ave and is open Monday to Friday from 8 am to noon and 2 to 4.30 pm, and on Saturdays from 8 am to noon. They have a good map of Mombasa for sale but otherwise they're geared to high spenders – mainly those who want to stay at a beach resort hotel – so they're of little help to budget travellers.

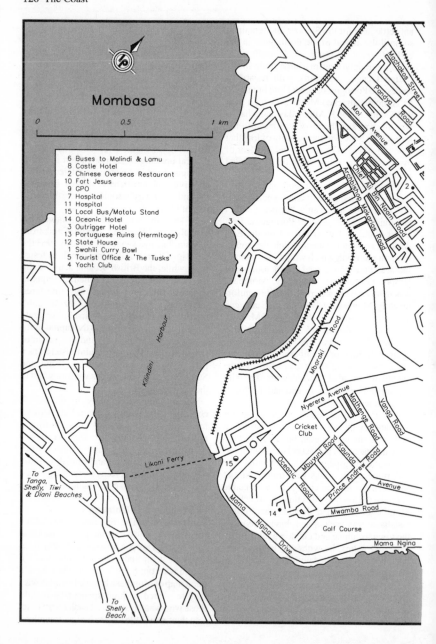

Mombasa

0   0.5   1 km

6 Buses to Malindi & Lamu
8 Castle Hotel
2 Chinese Overseas Restaurant
10 Fort Jesus
9 GPO
7 Hospital
11 Hospital
15 Local Bus/Matatu Stand
14 Oceanic Hotel
3 Outrigger Hotel
13 Portuguese Ruins (Hermitage)
12 State House
1 Swahili Curry Bowl
5 Tourist Office & 'The Tusks'
4 Yacht Club

You can also buy the local guide books to Fort Jesus and Mombasa Old Town here.

Post The GPO is on Digo Rd and is open Monday to Friday from 8 am to 4.30 pm and on Saturday from 8 am to noon. There is one international card phone in the bank of phones outside the post office, or you can make calls through the operator.

Bank The branch of Barclays Bank on Moi Ave, just up the road from the Castle Hotel, is open Monday to Friday from 8.30 am to 4.30 pm, and on Saturday from 8.30 am to 12.30 pm and 2 to 4.30 pm. Outside these hours you can change travellers' cheques at the Castle Hotel, or at any of the beach resort hotels north and south of Mombasa, although a commission may be charged.

Consulates The following countries have diplomatic representation in Mombasa:

Austria
    Raili House, Nyerere Ave (tel 313386)
Belgium
    Mitchell Cotts Building, Moi Ave (tel 20231)
Denmark
    Liwatoni Bay (tel 311826)
France
    Southern House, Moi Ave (tel 20501)
India
    Bank of India Building, Nkrumah Rd (tel 24433)
Netherlands
    ABN Bank Building, Nkrumah Rd (tel 311043)
Sweden
    Southern House, Moi Ave (tel 20501)

Books If you'd like more details about Mombasa's stirring history, the best account is to be found in *The Portuguese Period in East Africa* by Justus Strandes (East African Literature Bureau, 1971) which can be bought in most good bookshops in Nairobi and Mombasa.

Before you set off on a tour of the old town of Mombasa get a copy of the booklet *The Old Town Mombasa: A Historical Guide* by Judy Aldrick & Rosemary Macdonald, published by the Friends of Fort Jesus. It can be bought from either the tourist office or at Fort Jesus for KSh 50. This excellent guide is an essential companion for an exploration of this part of town and has photographs, drawings and a map.

Also well worth buying is *Fort Jesus* by James Kirkman, which gives a detailed account of the history of the Fort, as well as pointing out the salient features. It is available from the fort (KSh 20) or the tourist office (KSh 30).

Maps The best map you can buy of Mombasa is the Survey of Kenya's *Mombasa Island & Environs*, last published in 1977. Many of the street names have changed, but little else.

Left Luggage The left luggage service at the railway station costs KSh 12 per item per day. It is open from 8 am to noon and 2 to 6.30 pm Monday to Saturday, and from 7.30 to 10 am and 2 to 6.30 pm on Sunday.

Car Rental All the major companies and many of the smaller outfits have offices here as well as in Nairobi. Details can be found under Vehicle Hire in the Getting Around chapter.

Motoring Organisations The Automobile Association of Kenya (tel 26778) has its office just north of the tourist office on the road which connects Aga Khan Rd with the railway station. They have a few road maps and may be of use if you have specific questions about roads or traffic conditions.

Fort Jesus
The old town's biggest attraction dominates the harbour entrance. Begun in 1593 by the Portuguese, it changed hands nine times between 1631 and 1875. These days it's a museum and is open daily from 8.30 am to 6 pm. Entry costs KSh 50 (KSh 5 for Kenyan residents). There are no student reductions. It's well worth a visit and it's easy to pass a couple of hours here. Early morning is the best time as the air is still cool and the rest of the tourists are still in bed. The guidebook, *Fort Jesus*, by James Kirkman is useful for

a full description of the history and finer points of the fort.

The fort was designed by an Italian architect, Joao Batista Cairato, who had done a lot of work for the Portuguese in Goa. He incorporated some ingenious elements into the design, such as the angular configuration of the walls, making it impossible for would-be invaders to lay siege to one wall without being sitting ducks for soldiers in one of the other walls.

The most interesting features today include the Omani house in the San Felipe bastion in the north-west corner of the fort. Built in the late 18th century it has served different purposes as the purpose of the fort changed – it was the Chief Warder's House when the fort was a prison in the early 20th century. The view of the old town from the roof here is excellent.

The museum along the southern wall is built over what was the barracks rooms for the garrison. The exhibits are mostly ceramics but include other interesting odds and ends and have either been donated from private collections or dug up from various sites along the coast. The origins of many of the pieces are a reflection of the variety of cultures which have influenced the coastal culture – Chinese, Indian, Portuguese and Persian. Also displayed in the museum are finds from the Portuguese frigate *Santo António de Tanná* which sank off the Fort during the siege in 1697.

The western (seaward) wall of the fort is probably the most interesting and includes an Omani audience hall (now covered by a second storey but still complete with official inscriptions – and unofficial graffiti) and the Passage of the Arches – a passage cut through the coral giving access to the outer part of the fort, although it was later blocked off.

The Old Town

The old town isn't as immediately interesting as the Fort, but it's still a fascinating area to wander around in. Early morning or late afternoon is the best time to walk around; there's more activity then, and it's very quiet in the middle of the day.

Though its history goes back centuries, most of the houses in the old town are no more than 100 years old but you'll come across the occasional one which dates back to the first half of the 19th century. They represent a combination of styles and traditions which include the long-established coastal Swahili architecture commonly found in Lamu, various late 19th century Indian styles and British colonial architecture with its broad, shady verandahs and glazed and shuttered windows.

There are very few houses constructed entirely of coral rag, however. Most are of wattle and daub though they may include coral here and there. Most of the old palm thatch or tile roofing has been replaced with corrugated iron as well. What does remain are many examples of the massive, intricately carved doors and door frames characteristic of Swahili houses in Lamu and Zanzibar. It seems that when anyone of importance moved from these towns to Mombasa they brought their doors with them or had them newly made up to reflect their financial status. Of course, they're not as numerous as they used to be, either because of the ravages of time, or because they have been bought by collectors and shipped abroad. There is now a preservation order on those remaining so further losses should hopefully be prevented.

It's not just carved doors that you should look out for, though. Almost as much effort was put into the construction of balconies, their support brackets and enclosures. Fine fret work and lattice work are a feature of the enclosures, reflecting the Muslim need for women's privacy. Sadly, quite a few of these were damaged or destroyed along Mbarak Hinawy Rd in the days when oversized trucks used the road for access to the old port.

By 1900, most of the houses in the main streets were owned by Indian business people and traders whilst Mbarak Hinawy Rd (previously called Vasco da Gama St) and Government Square had become the centre for colonial government offices, banks, con-

Mombasa Old Town

34 Ali's Curio Market
31 Ali's Curio Shop
33 Anils Arcade
32 Arcaf House
5 Badala Mosque
7 Badri Mosque
12 Bohra Mosque
39 Bank of India
29 Cemetery
21 'The Club'
41 Commercial Bank
24 Criterion
17 Customs
30 Dalal House

11 First Public Library
14 Former Italian Consulate
37 Fort Jesus
4 Glen's Building
16 Government Square
19 Hansing & Co
9 Ithna Asheri Mosque
2 Jama Khana
35 Jubilee Hall
8 Kitovuni–Pillar House
10 Leven House Customs
25 Mandhry Mosque
6 Memon Mosque
1 Mkanyagenyi Mosque

36 Mombasa Club
28 Old Edward St Rose
38 Old Law Courts
18 Old Post Office
26 Old Standard Book
15 Old Treasury
3 Pigott Place
20 Recoda Restaurant
13 Scent Emporium
40 Standard Bank
22 Swahili Bakery
23 Whitehouse
27 Whiteways

sulates and business or living quarters for colonial officials. Ndia Kuu housed immigrant entrepreneurs from India, Goa and Europe. The colonial headquarters at this time were situated in Leven House on the waterfront overlooking the old harbour, but shortly afterwards they were moved to Government Square and, in 1910, moved again up the hill to Treasury Square above Fort Jesus.

In later years as Mombasa expanded along what are today the main roads, many of the businesses which had shops and offices in the old town gradually moved out, leaving behind ornate signs, etched glass windows and other relics of former times. Their exact location is described in *The Old Town Mombasa: A Historical Guide*.

You can start your exploration of the old town anywhere you like but the main points of interest are marked on the street map. There is a notice in Government Square saying that photography of the old harbour area (but not the buildings) is prohibited. I don't know how serious the authorities are about this since I can't imagine what is so sensitive about the place, but if you want pictures of it there are plenty of narrow streets leading off to the waterfront between the square and the Leven Steps where no-one will bother you.

Places to Stay

There's a lot of choice for budget travellers and for those who want something slightly better, both in the centre of the city and on the mainland to the north and south. Accommodation up and down the coast from Mombasa Island itself is dealt with separately.

Places to Stay – bottom end

One of the best value for money places in this category is the *Mvita Hotel*, on the corner of Hospital and Turkana streets. The entrance is on the first alley on the left-hand side on Turkana St or through the bar on the ground floor on Hospital St. It's Indian run, very

clean and quiet, secure, friendly, all the rooms have fans and a hand basin and the beds are comfortable. Even toilet paper is provided. The showers and toilets are scrubbed out daily. It costs KSh 145/180 for double/triple rooms but is often full as it's only a small place. There's a lively bar downstairs (which you can't hear in the rooms upstairs) and at lunch and dinner times barbecued meat and other snacks are available in the back yard.

Equally good value and popular with travellers is the *Cosy Guest House* (tel 313064), Haile Selassie Rd, which costs KSh 90 a single, KSh 120 a double and KSh 180 a triple, all with common facilities. All the rooms have fans but due to chronic water problems the toilets can stink. It will most likely be full if you get there late in the day. On the opposite side of the road from the Cozy Guest House is the *Midnight Guest House* (tel 26725) which is not all that friendly but would do if you're stuck. It costs KSh 90 a single and KSh 145 a double with common showers and toilets.

Just around the corner on Shibu Rd is the friendly *New Al Jazira Hotel* which has double/triple rooms with balcony and common bath and toilets for KSh 95/145. As is the case with many Mombasa hotels, there are no single rooms.

If all these places are full then you could try the *Balgis Hotel* (tel 313358), Digo Rd, which is very friendly. It's about the cheapest in Mombasa with dorm beds for KSh 40 and single/double rooms for 85/110 with common bath. The rooms only have internal windows which makes them pretty hot, except the dorm which has windows overlooking the noisy Digo Rd. Another real cheapie which is habitable is the *Down Town Lodge* on Hospital St for KSh 85/110, but the rooms here don't have fans.

Heading towards the northern end of town, the *Al Nasser Lodging* (tel 313032) on Abdel Nasser Rd is good value at KSh 70/145 for single/double rooms with shower.

Another budget hotel in this area, and one which has been popular for years, is the *New People's Hotel* (tel 312831), Abdel Nasser

Rd right next to where the buses leave for Malindi and Lamu. Some travellers rate this place very highly and it certainly compares very well in price with the others but it is a little tatty and the rooms which face onto the main road are very noisy and the air stinks of diesel fumes. This is mainly because of the bus drivers who seem to have a fetish about revving their engines for anything up to an hour before they actually leave. The management are friendly and gear left in the rooms is safe. It costs KSh 70/120/140 a single/double/triple for a room with common showers and toilets, and KSh 100/205/310 with bathroom. All the rooms have fans, the sheets are clean and the water in the showers is generally lukewarm. It's a large place and is rarely full. There's a good, cheap restaurant downstairs.

Another place which has been a popular budget hotel for years is the *Hydro Hotel* (tel 23784), on Digo Rd at the junction with Kenyatta Ave. It's a bit shabby these days but is undeniably cheap at KSh 50 for a dorm bed, and KSh 85/165 for slightly cramped single/double rooms with fan. There is also one room with four beds for KSh 190. The restaurant on the 1st floor is not bad and serves some Swahili dishes.

The *New Britania Boarding & Lodging* on Gusii St is yet another popular place. The hotel entrance is through the downstairs bar and then up the stairs. The bar itself is a lively and friendly place. The rooms are clean and good value at KSh 120, and if the place is full you can sleep an extra person or two on the floor.

Up the scale a bit is the *ABC Lodge* near the Glory Guest House on Shibu Rd. The rooms are a good size and have their own bath and fan. At KSh 110/210 they're not bad value.

Somewhat more expensive than the above (but not necessarily better value) is the *Hotel Fortuna*, Haile Selassie Rd, which costs KSh 180 a single and KSh 240 a double, both with private showers and toilets. The *Hotel Fortuna Annex* across the road shares the same reception but is cheaper at KSh 120/155 for rooms with common bath.

Places to Stay – middle

One of the best in this range is the friendly *Hotel Relax* (tel 311346), Meru Rd, which is clean and good value at KSh 335 a double including shower, toilet and breakfast. Soap and towels are also provided, all the rooms have fans and are cleaned daily. There are also a couple of rooms with common facilities and these are excellent value at KSh 185 including breakfast. It's also possible to store luggage here if you're heading up or down the coast; there's no charge for this.

On the next block is the *Hotel Splendid* (tel 20967), a huge place which is rarely full. It is much more expensive at KSh 455 for a double with bathroom and breakfast. It's a very clean and modern place and there's a popular rooftop restaurant which gets sea breezes in the evenings. The hotel has an annexe on Meru Rd between Digo Rd and Msanifu Kombo St and rooms here go for KSh 305 for a double with breakfast.

Better value perhaps is the *Continental Guest House* (tel 315916) on Haile Selassie Rd near the Hotel Fortuna. Double rooms (no singles) go for KSh 240 with bath and breakfast. This is a new place which usually fills up early. Close by is the *Visitor's Inn* on the corner of Shibu Rd. It's not a bad place at KSh 130/210 with bath and breakfast although some of the rooms overlook Haile Selassie Rd and so cop the noise. The entrance is on Shibu Rd and is easy to miss.

Another new place is the *Glory Guest House* (tel 314557) on Shibu Rd. The rooms are a bit on the small side but are spotlessly clean and well maintained. The charge is KSh 270/380 for singles/doubles with bath and hot water. Air-con doubles cost KSh 450.

The best place to stay in this range is the beautiful *New Palm Tree Hotel* (tel 312167), Nkrumah Rd, which I'd rate as being very similar in quality to the much more expensive Castle Hotel. A very comfortable room here costs KSh 290 a single and KSh 430 a double with a shower and toilet and including breakfast. The hotel has its own bar and restaurant.

The most expensive place in this category is the *Hotel Hermes* (tel 313599) on Msanifu

Kombo St near the Sheik Jundoni Mosque. You could hardly call it a friendly place but the rooms are pleasant, if a little dingy, and the tariff of KSh 385/480 includes bath and breakfast.

Places to Stay – top end

In the centre of town the very popular *Castle Hotel* (tel 21683), Moi Ave, costs KSh 870 a single and KSh 1380 a double, including breakfast. The hotel has a coffee shop and a good restaurant, and the terrace bar is the Mombasa equivalent of the Thorn Tree Café in Nairobi. You'll find all the comforts and facilities you would expect of a top-end place.

The older, colonial style *Manor Hotel* (tel 31643), Nyerere Ave, with a wide verandah and surrounding garden, is cheaper at KSh 540 to KSh 660 a single and KSh 840 to KSh 960 a double with bath and breakfast. It's a very pleasant place with a bar and restaurant.

At Ras Liwatoni, the *New Outrigger Hotel* (tel 20822) is at the very top of the range. It's a Belgian-managed resort type place right on the beach, but also has a swimming pool if you can't stagger that far. All rooms are air-conditioned, have a private bath and a balcony facing the sea. The tariff is KSh 835/1075 for a single/double with breakfast.

Places to Eat

Mombasa has a good range of restaurants. If you are putting your own food together, or want to stock up with goodies to take down the coast, the Fort Supermarket on Nyerere Ave is well stocked, and there's a wide variety of fruit and vegies in the market on Digo Rd next to the Hydro Hotel.

Places to Eat – cheap

If you are just looking for fish or chicken with chips try the *Blue Fin Restaurant*, on the corner of Meru Rd and Msanifu Kombo St. There's very little variety but it's not a bad place. There's a better choice at the *Blue Room Restaurant* on Haile Selassie Rd. They have excellent burgers for KSh 20 to KSh 35, depending on what you have with it, and the

fish & chips and Indian snacks are also worth a try.

The *Pan Coffee House* near the GPO on Digo Rd is another place doing standard food which is worth trying. The *Masumin Restaurant*, opposite the GPO on Digo Rd, does a good full breakfast for KSh 35, and at other times has various curries with rice for KSh 30, as well as steaks and cheap juices.

The *Kenya Coffee House* on Moi Ave is a good place for fresh coffee and snacks, and you can also buy coffee beans here.

Indian Food Since many of the restaurants in Mombasa are Indian owned you can find excellent curries and thalis and at lunch time (12.30 to around 3 pm) there is often a cheap, substantial set meal available. One which you'll hear nothing but praise for is the *Geetanjalee*, Msanifu Kombo St, which offers a 'deluxe' thali for KSh 55. Both the food and service are excellent.

Similar is the *New Chetna Restaurant*, Haile Selassie Rd directly under the Cosy Guest House. Here it's South Indian vegetarian food (masala dosa, idli, etc) and sweets, plus they offer an all-you-can-eat set vegetarian lunch for KSh 55. It's a very popular restaurant.

Excellent tandoori specialities can be found at the very popular *Splendid View Restaurant*, opposite, but not part of, the Hotel Splendid. They have things like chicken, lamb, fruit juices and lassis and you can eat well here for around KSh 60. There are tables outside and inside.

Swahili Food For coastal Swahili dishes made with coconut and coconut milk, the *Swahili Curry Bowl*, Tangana Rd off Moi Ave, is recommended. Prices are reasonable. It's also one of *the* places for coffee and ice cream. Don't bother trekking out here on a Sunday as it's closed then.

Another excellent place, and one you should try at least once, is the *Recoda Restaurant* on Nyeri St in the old town. It's a hugely popular place amongst the locals and the tables are set up along the footpath. The atmosphere is great and the waiters are keen

Mombasa Centre

■ PLACES TO STAY

3   Al Nasser Lodging
15 Balgis Hotel
38 Castle Hotel
20 Continental Guest House
18 Cosy Guest House
12 Down Town Lodge
30 Glory Guest House
21 Hotel Fortuna
23 Hotel Hermes
29 Hotel Relax
31 Hotel Splendid
11 Hydro Hotel
41 Manor Hotel
17 Midnight Guest House
13 Mvita Hotel
16 New Al Jazira Hotel
24 New Britania Boarding & Lodging
44 New Palm Tree Hotel
1   New People's Hotel
19 Visitor's Inn

▼ PLACES TO EAT

32 Blue Fin Restaurant
22 Blue Room Restaurant
39 Fontanella Restaurant
14 Geetanjalee Restaurant
34 Kenya Coffee House
25 Masumin Restaurant
18 New Chetna Restaurant
33 Pistacchio Ice Cream & Coffee Bar
28 Splendid View Restaurant

● OTHER

8   Akamba Bus
43 American Express
36 Barclays Bank
5   Bus Station
2   Buses to Malindi & Lamu
6   Cat Bus
4   Coast Bus
42 Executive Air Services
40 Fort Supermarket
26 GPO
37 Istanbul Bar
9   Malindi Taxi Bus
10 Market
7   Mawingo Buses
35 Rainbow House Night Club
27 Sheik Jundoni Mosque

to explain what is available that day – usually dishes such as beans in coconut, grilled fish (KSh 50), meat, superb chapatis and salad. You may well find yourself coming back here each night (it's not open at lunch time).

The restaurant in the *Hydro Hotel* also has some Swahili dishes but certainly lacks the atmosphere of the Recoda.

Places to Eat – more expensive

Going up in price, the rooftop restaurant in the *Hotel Splendid* catches the breeze in the evenings and has surprisingly moderate prices, although the food is only mediocre; KSh 40 to KSh 70 for a main meal, KSh 55 for steak with chips and vegetables. Don't come here with any ideas of having a quick meal, as the service is hardly lightning fast.

The *Pistacchio Ice Cream & Coffee Bar* is a small café near the Hotel Splendid. Not only does it have excellent ice cream, but the fruit shakes (expensive at KSh 19) are great. The buffet lunch or dinner for KSh 80 is not bad value although the selection is limited. They also serve à la carte dishes such as spaghetti.

For Chinese tucker you could try the *Chinese Overseas Restaurant* on Moi Ave, just north of the tusks. It's not cheap, however, as dishes are priced in the range of KSh 80 to KSh 150.

The *Fontanella Restaurant* is in a shady courtyard on the corner of Digo Rd and Moi Ave. The extensive menu runs the whole gamut from fish & chips (KSh 40) through steaks (KSh 90) to lobster thermidor (KSh 300) – great for a splurge or just a quiet beer or snack.

Entertainment

For an ice-cold beer in the heat of the day many people go to the terrace of the *Castle Hotel* which overlooks Moi Ave. It's the nearest thing you'll find to the Thorn Tree Café in Nairobi but the comparison isn't really valid. If you prefer more local colour and a livelier place then try the *Istanbul Bar* also on Moi Ave, on the opposite side of the road from the Castle Hotel towards the tusks. It's primarily a pick-up joint but attractively set under *makuti* (plaited palm leaf) roofs and has an atmosphere not unlike that of the Modern 24-Hour Green Bar in Nairobi.

For a night out the *Rainbow House Night Club*, on the corner of Meru Rd and Moi Ave, is perhaps a little less daunting than some of the others and is a popular disco and African reggae club. It's always filled with local ragers, sailors, whores and travellers. There are plenty of other excellent reggae clubs in the suburbs which are very cheap and good fun – ask around.

Things to Buy

Mombasa isn't the craft entrepôt you might expect it to be, but it's not too bad either. The trouble is that there are a lot of tourists and sailors who pass through this port with lots of dollars to shed in a hurry. Bargains, therefore, can take a long time to negotiate. There are a lot of craft stalls along Msanifu Kombo St near the junction with Moi Ave; along Moi Ave itself from the Castle Hotel down to the roundabout with Nyerere Ave; along Jomo Kenyatta Ave close to the junction with Digo Rd; and a few in the old town close to Fort Jesus.

Have a look around – you might find something. Makonde wood carvings, stone chess sets and animal or human figurines, basketwork, drums and other musical instruments and paintings are the sorts of things that are sold.

Biashara St west of Digo Rd is the centre for fabrics and *kangas,* those colourful, beautifully patterned, wraparound skirts complete with Swahili proverbs, which most East African women wear (other than Hindus) even if they wear it under a *bui bui* (black wraparound skirt). You may need to bargain a little over the price (but not too much). What you get is generally what you pay for and, as a rule, they cost around KSh 150 a pair (they are not sold singly). Assuming you are willing to bargain, the price you pay for one will reflect the quality of the cloth. Buy them in Mombasa if possible. You can sometimes get them as cheaply in Nairobi but elsewhere prices escalate rapidly.

Getting There & Away

Air Four companies operate flights from Mombasa to Malindi and Lamu. They are Eagle Aviation Ltd (tel 316054), Prestige Air Services Ltd (tel 21443), Skyways Airlines (tel 432167) and Equator Airlines.

They all have two flights per day in either direction between Mombasa, Malindi and Lamu. Flights from Mombasa depart at 8.30 am and 2.15 pm and arrive Malindi 30 minutes later. The fare to Malindi is KSh 900 one way and KSh 1800 return. Children over two years old pay full fare. Check-in time is 30 minutes before departure and the baggage allowance is 10 kg per person. Most of the time they don't hassle if your baggage is over 10 kg but, even if they do, excess charges are minimal. The airport departure tax is KSh 50 at Malindi and Mombasa but there's no charge at Lamu.

Kenya Airways also flies Mombasa-Malindi-Nairobi in either direction once daily except on Saturday, using F50 propeller planes. If you're relying on these flights to get back to Nairobi to connect with an international flight, then make absolutely sure you have a confirmed booking or, preferably, go back a day before. Don't join the legion of people who are left on the tarmac tearing out their hair because they didn't reconfirm and the flight was full.

There is a KSh 50 departure tax payable on all flights out of Mombasa.

Bus & Matatu In Mombasa bus offices are mainly along Jomo Kenyatta Ave. For Nairobi buses there are many departures daily in either direction (mostly in the early morning and late evening) by, among others, Coast, Cat, Mawingo, Malaika and Akamba. The fare ranges from KSh 165 to KSh 190 and the trip takes seven to eight hours including a meal break about halfway.

To Malindi there are also many departures daily in either direction from early morning until late afternoon by several bus companies and matatus. Buses take up to three hours; matatus about two hours. In Mombasa they all depart from outside the New People's Hotel, Abdel Nasser Rd. See the Malindi section for more details and for the alternative of hiring a share-taxi.

It's possible to go straight through from Mombasa to Lamu but most travellers stop en route at Malindi.

For Tanga and Dar es Salaam in Tanzania, Cat Bus has departures on Monday, Wednesday and Friday at 4 pm. The journey to Tanga takes about eight hours (KSh 145) and all the way to Dar es Salaam about 20 hours (KSh 360).

For buses and matatus to the south of Mombasa you first need to get off the island via the Likoni ferry (see below).

Train Trains to or from Nairobi operate in either direction at 5 and 7 pm, arriving at 8 and 8.30 am respectively. There's nothing to choose between the two trains, except that on the 5 pm train you get to see a bit more of the countryside before it gets dark. The fares in KSh are:

Destination	1st class	2nd class	3rd class
Voi	155	74	35
Tsavo	205	95	50
Nairobi	505	236	118

You should make a reservation as far in advance as possible as demand sometimes exceeds supply. The booking office at the station in Mombasa is open daily from 8 am to noon and 2 to 6.30 pm.

Boat Depending on the season, it's possible to get a ride on a dhow to Pemba, Zanzibar or Dar es Salaam in Tanzania. It's hard to pin them down as to what day they are likely to depart, let alone what time, so you need to be persistent. Hang around at the dhow dock in the old town and ask a lot of questions. Once you find a boat, make sure you are well stocked as the trip takes anything up to 36 hours to Dar es Salaam (if it goes via Zanzibar) and you get zilch in the way of food or facilities. The toilet is a long-drop perched out over the back of the boat. Expect to pay around KSh 240 to Dar es Salaam.

If you're interested in yachts or boats to India or the Seychelles it's worth getting out to Kilibi Creek. Most of the people with yachts moor at Kilibi Creek because mooring berths at the Mombasa Yacht Club are very expensive. If you want to make enquiries you can get to Kilibi by going to Tom's Beach, about 1½ km out of Mombasa centre, near the Seahorse Hotel.

Getting Around
Airport Transport There's a regular public bus which goes to the airport and costs KSh 3.50. Any 'Port Reitz' matatu will take you past the airport turn-off (ask to be dropped off) from where it's about a 10 minute walk. The standard taxi fare is KSh 190.

Likoni Ferry This ferry connects Mombasa Island with the southern mainland and runs at frequent intervals throughout the night and day. There's a crossing every 20 minutes on average between 5 and 12.30 am; less frequently between 12.30 and 5 am. It's free to pedestrians. To get to the ferry from the centre of town take a Likoni matatu from outside the GPO on Digo Rd.

Taxi Mombasa's superbly beaten up old taxis are not metered so make sure you agree on a fare before stepping in.

Harbour Cruises Cruises around the old harbour and Kilindini Harbour – the modern harbour where container ships and the like dock – are available through the Castle Hotel, Moi Ave. There is a four hour lunch cruise at 10.30 am which includes lunch, live music and swimming but it's not cheap at KSh 840. The evening cruise departs at 6.30 pm and costs KSh 1080. For information or bookings phone 315569. It may well be possible to find cheaper cruises if you ask around.

South of Mombasa

The real attractions of the coast south of Mombasa are the beaches, and although it is

The Swahili People

Although the people of the coast do not have a common heritage, they do have a linguistic link which unites them – KiSwahili (commonly referred to as Swahili), a Bantu-based language which evolved as a means of communication between Africans and foreign traders such as Arabs, Persians and the Portuguese. As might be expected with such diverse inputs, the Swahili language borrows words from Arabic, Hindi, Portuguese and even English. The word *swahili* is a derivative of the Arabic word for coast – *sahel.*

Arab traders first started plying the coast in their sailing dhows sometime before the 7th century, arriving with the north-east monsoon and sailing home on the south-west monsoon. The main exports were ivory, tortoiseshell and leopard skins, while items such as glass beads from India and porcelain from as far afield as China found their way here.

After the 7th century Islam became a strong influence as traders began settling along the coast. Today the majority of the coastal people are Muslims, although it's a world away from the stricter forms of Islam which prevail in some places in the Middle East.

Swahili subgroups include Bajun, Siyu, Pate, Mvita, Fundi, Shela, Ozi, Vumba and Amu (residents of Lamu). ■

Typical Swahili house on the coast of Kenya

Siwa instrument

basically all resort hotels, there are a few options for the budget traveller – at Tiwi and Diani beaches.

All the beaches are white coral sand and are protected by a coral reef so there is no danger from sharks when you go swimming. Tiwi is probably the best beach – at Diani all the sand has washed away in places leaving just a coral bed.

SHELLY BEACH

Shelly Beach is the closest beach to Mombasa and as such, is not a bad place to swim if you just want to day-trip from Mombasa. There is no budget accommodation available here, nor any restaurants, so forget it for a long stay unless you want an expensive resort.

Places to Stay

The only place here is the *Shelly Beach Hotel* (tel 451001), about three km from the Likoni ferry. As far as resort hotels go it's not a bad place, and seems to be popular with British tour groups. Most people seem to prefer swimming in the pool than in the sea just a few metres away. Half board rates are KSh 710/1080 for single/double rooms, or KSh 920/1680 with air-con. In the off season it may be possible to get a reduction on these rates, but don't expect too much.

Getting There & Away

From the Likoni ferry, take the first turn to the left after the bus stand. From here it's a 30 minute walk and there are occasional matatus and enough traffic to make hitching possible.

TIWI BEACH

Next along the coast is Tiwi Beach, and it too is about three km off the main coast road, along a dirt track which winds its way through the coastal scrub. This is the best beach to head for if you have your own camping gear, and it's also probably the least developed of all the beaches so you need to be fairly self-sufficient.

The beach itself is a lot wider than at Shelly Beach.

Places to Stay & Eat

The only relatively cheap place is the very popular *Twiga Lodge* (tel (0127) 4061). It is certainly *the* place to camp along the coast as you can pitch your tent just a few metres from the water, there's plenty of shade and if you have a vehicle there's room for it too. The cost is KSh 35 per person to camp, and KSh 35 to rent a tent, although they only have a couple of these so don't rely on one being available. Single/double rooms go for KSh 240/430 with breakfast, while the cheapest *bandas* (circular, grass-thatched traditional-style houses) cost KSh 430 for four people. The restaurant does good meals for around KSh 60 to KSh 95, and also serves snacks and drinks. It's a good place to stay as there's usually an interesting mix of people here.

Right next door to the Twiga Lodge are the *Coral Cove Sea Cottages* (tel (0127) 4164). The bandas here range in price and facilities from KSh 110 for a basic double with no facilities to KSh 190 for a double with bath and cooking gear. It's a very pleasant place to stay and popular with young expatriate workers.

If you are putting your own food together the Twiga Lodge has a basic provision store which has a limited range of tinned and fresh foods. About 500 metres back along the track towards the main road there's a small fruit and vegie stall which also has limited stocks of varying quality.

Getting There & Away

The buses and matatus drop you at the start of the dirt access road, from where it's a three km or 45 minute walk. This road used to be notorious for muggings but these days there are plainclothes police 'patrolling' (read: sitting under a tree) the road and it is supposedly safe. Certainly if there are a few (or more) of you it should be no problem, but solo travellers are still better off waiting for a lift. There's a few trucks and cars going in and out so you shouldn't have to wait long.

DIANI BEACH

Diani is *the* typical 'tropical paradise' beach:

coconut palms, dazzling white sand and clear blue water. It's also the most developed – virtually the whole beach front is taken up with resorts ranging from expensive upwards, although it must be said that most of these resorts are not too intrusive as they have low lines and local materials are often incorporated.

The Diani Beach road runs parallel to the coast about 100 metres inland, so the resorts are well shielded from the outside world.

Information & Orientation

Just south of the T-junction where the road from the main Mombasa-Tanzania highway joins the smaller beach road is a shopping centre which seems to expand by the month to cash in on the package tourists with bulging wallets. Not only are there a couple of expensive souvenir shops and boutiques, but more usefully there is a couple of fairly well stocked supermarkets where you can stock up with goodies, two banks, a petrol station and a couple of car hire places. The branch of Barclays Bank is open Monday to Friday from 10 am to 3 pm.

Also here is the rather unusual South Coast Fitness Centre where you can hire go-karts to zip around the track they have there. You can also rent bicycles but these are such dreadful old clunkers that it's hard to imagine going any distance on one. They cost KSh 40 for half a day or KSh 80 for a full day, and there's a KSh 200 deposit.

Back up on the main road is the village of Ukunda, and it's here that you find the nearest post office and basic lodges to Diani. It's a few km and it's advisable not to walk – this road is also notorious for people getting mugged. It's not a problem as there are plenty of matatus (and KBS buses) running backwards and forwards all day on their way to or from Likoni.

Places to Stay – bottom end

The only cheap place is *Dan Trench's*, behind the Trade Winds Hotel. It's not well signposted but is the place on the right, directly behind the Trade Winds. Unfortunately, this place, like Dan himself, is on the

Beaches South of Mombasa

way down which is a real shame as it's been a travellers' haven for years. The camping is the best bet at KSh 35 per person but the site is not all that wonderful and as it's not securely fenced, theft is a real problem. The small dorm here has just four beds at KSh 60 each. There's just one very small double banda, the thatch roof of which would be an entomologist's delight. If you're staying here you can use the beach and bar at the Trade Winds Hotel.

It's also possible to camp at the *Diani Beachalets* (see below) for KSh 50 per person, with use of the communal cooking facilities included. It's far safer than at Dan's as there is an askari on duty at night.

In Ukunda, the village up on the main road, the *Sunset Lodge* charges KSh 60 for a double but as the whole idea of coming to Diani is to stay at the beach there seems little point in staying at Ukunda.

Places to Stay – middle

There's only one place in this category, and that's the *Diani Beachalets* (tel (01261) 2180) at the southern end of the beach, a couple of hundred metres past the end of the bitumen, where the buses and matatus stop and turn around. The site itself is quite pleasant, the only problem being that at this end of the beach there's no sand – it's just a flat coral bed. This may just be a seasonal phenomenon but certainly didn't look like it. Unlike the up-market resorts, there's no pool, restaurant or bar, although there is a tennis court which you can use for a small fee.

There is a range of bandas available; the cheapest ones have their own fridge but communal cooking and washing facilities. For KSh 180 for two they are pretty good value, although you need to bring all your own food or be prepared to go to the Diani shopping centre as nothing is sold on site. The more expensive rooms and cottages are fully self-contained and range in price from KSh 235 for a double room up to KSh 565 for a six bed cottage. These rates increase by 50% in the high seasons (July to September, December to February).

The next cheapest option are the *Four Twenty South* beach cottages, right at the southern end of the bitumen road. These are fully self-contained, sleep four people and cost from KSh 505 to KSh 790 depending on the season. You need to supply your own bed linen and food.

Places to Stay – top end

The other hotels along this beach cost from KSh 540 per person per day including breakfast in the off season up to around KSh 2400 for a double with full board in the high season. They all offer much the same – air-con rooms, swimming pool, bars, restaurant and have water sports equipment for hire. The better ones, such as the Trade Winds, have been designed with the environment in mind and are fairly unobtrusive; others, such as the Golden Beach, are something of an eyesore.

From north to south along the strip the hotels are:

Golden Beach Hotel, from KSh 560 per person with breakfast

Diani Reef Hotel (tel (01261) 2175), KSh 2160/2400 a single/double with breakfast, up to KSh 2400/2880 for full board

Leisure Lodge (tel (01261) 2011), KSh 1620/2160 for full board

Leopard Beach Hotel (tel (01261) 2111), KSh 805/1265 for half board

Trade Winds Hotel (tel (01261) 2016), KSh 1500/1980 for full board

Diani Sea Lodge (tel (01261) 2114), KSh 1390/1860 for full board

Two Fishes Hotel (tel (01261) 2101), KSh 1680/2280 for full board

Jadini Beach Hotel (tel (01261) 2021), KSh 1740/2665 with breakfast

Nomad Beach Bandas (tel (01261) 2155), KSh 1105/2185 with breakfast

Safari Beach Hotel (tel (01261) 2088), KSh 1980/2940 with breakfast

Robinson Baobab Hotel (tel (01261) 2026), KSh 2160/3120 for full board

Diani Beach Cottages, KSh 1080/2160 for half board

Places to Eat

If you are staying at Dan Trench's or Diani Beachalets and want to put your own food together the supermarkets at the Diani shopping centre are pretty well stocked. For fresh fruit and seafood buy from the hawkers who come around to these places on a bicycle with baskets laden.

For a regular meal, the restaurant in the *South Coast Fitness Centre* does a reasonable fish, chips and salad for KSh 80. Also in the shopping centre is the *Cheers* restaurant but it is more expensive.

If you feel like lashing out, the *Trade Winds Hotel* has a huge buffet lunch for KSh 155 or dinner for KSh 180. The other resorts no doubt have similar deals.

Ali Barbour's is an expensive seafood restaurant set in a coral cave between the Trade Winds Hotel and the Diani Sea Lodge. Don't expect to have any change out of KSh 720 for two people. Opposite the Two Fishes Hotel is the *Bush Baby Restaurant*, an open-air restaurant and night club and not a bad place for a bop.

Entertainment

Apart from the hotel bars and fairly sterile and contrived discos, there's not much to do at night. There is a troupe of local dancers who do the rounds of the resorts to give the resort guests their dash of local colour but that's about the limit of it.

Getting There & Away

Diani is the most accessible beach if you are dependent on public transport. From the Likoni ferry there are KBS buses (No 32) every 20 minutes or so from early morning until around 7 pm. The fare is KSh 9.50 and the trip takes about 30 minutes.

There are also plenty of matatus doing the Likoni-Diani trip. They do the journey slightly faster and cost KSh 8.50.

When the buses and matatus get to Diani they first head north along the Diani road then turn around and go to the southern end of the bitumen where they turn again and head for Likoni. Just tell the driver where you want to get off.

SHIMONI

Shimoni is right out at the end of a small peninsula 76 km south of Likoni, and not far from the Tanzanian border. Apart from a couple of expensive lodges catering to game fishers, there's very little in Shimoni apart from a couple of coral caves which are worth exploring.

Offshore lies Wasini Island which is well worth a visit.

Places to Stay

The *Pemba Channel Fishing Club* (tel Msambweni 5Y2) and the *Shimoni Reef Fishing Club* (tel Msambweni 5Y9) both charge around KSh 1320/1920 for full board.

If you have your own gear it should be possible to camp on Wasini Island.

Getting There & Away

There are a couple of direct buses and matatus daily to and from Likoni.

WASINI ISLAND

Wasini is a small unspoilt island off the Shimoni peninsula. The peace and quiet found here is very soothing – there are no cars, roads, running water and the only electricity comes from generators. It's a great place to relax, experience the undiluted Swahili culture and organise a visit to the Kisiti/Mpungutu Marine National Park.

On a wander around you can come across Muslim ruins, local women weaving mats, men preparing for fishing by mending nets and making fish traps, the coral garden with its odd-shaped stands of old coral that you can walk through and beautiful pools.

Snorkelling

Masood Abdullah, who runs the Mpunguti Restaurant, can arrange trips to the marine park to see some of the best fish and coral in Kenya. His dhow will take you for KSh 250 per person to the park, plus KSh 20 per person for snorkel and mask. It's also possible to hire a dugout canoe and do it yourself for KSh 100.

Places to Stay & Eat

The *Mpunguti Restaurant* has the only accommodation on the island. Camping is possible on the grass for KSh 35 per person, or else you can pay KSh 360 for a small cottage including three excellent meals a day. If you are camping bring supplies from Mombasa; there's fish, coconuts, maize flour and rice for sale on the island but very little else.

Getting There & Away
From Likoni take a taxi to Shimoni for KSh 480, or one of the few KBS buses for KSh 35. You could also take a Lunga Lunga matatu but would then have to hitch the 14 km from the main road to Shimoni.

Once at Shimoni take a matatu boat for the 10 minute ride to Wasini for KSh 40 return. Alternatively, the dhow from the Mpunguti Restaurant on the island runs if there are five or more people (KSh 50 per person).

SHIMBA HILLS NATIONAL RESERVE
This national reserve is in the hills behind the coast south of Mombasa, directly inland from Diani Beach. The forest setting is beautiful but the game is not prolific. There is a baited water hole at the Shimba Hills Lodge, and so it's possible you'll see leopards and plenty of elephants but not much else. Other animals which frequent the reserve include the rare sable antelope – a tall and compact animal with beautifully curved horns on both the male and female. The adult bull is a dark brown on the upper body and white below, while the female is a lighter brown. The animals are, unfortunately, often killed by poachers for meat, and this is the only park or reserve where they are found.

Places to Stay
The *camp site* has a superb location on the edge of the range with views right down to Diani Beach. It's about three km from the main gate, which itself is about three km from the village of Kwale.

The only alternative to camping is the *Shimba Hills Lodge* (tel Nairobi 335807) where single/double rooms cost KSh 1535/4200 with half board. For some curious reason children under seven years old are not admitted to this lodge. The water hole here is baited to attract a few animals and is floodlit at night.

Getting There & Away
There are KBS buses to Kwale, from where it shouldn't be too difficult to hitch to the park entrance. Once there, however, you may have a long wait for a vehicle. The road from Kwale to Kinango, the next inland town, actually passes through the northern part of the park and there's a chance of seeing animals from the KBS buses. The No 34 bus goes from Likoni to Kwale.

North of Mombasa

MOMBASA TO KILIFI
Like the coast south of Mombasa, the north coast has been well developed almost two-thirds of the way up to Kilifi with resort complexes which take up much of the beach frontage. Most of them cater to package tourists on two to three week holidays from Europe but there is scope for individual initiative here and there although only the 'youth hostel' at Kanamai and Jauss Farm at Vipingo genuinely fall into the budget accommodation bracket.

As with Shelly and much of Tiwi beaches south of Mombasa, the northern beaches are plagued with seaweed which clogs them and makes swimming an often unpleasant experience. Only at the expensive resort hotels are people employed to minimise this inconvenience by raking it into piles and either burning it or burying it. Elsewhere you literally have to jump into the soup.

Going north from Mombasa the names of the beaches are Nyali, Bamburi, Shanzu, Kikambala and Vipingo.

Mamba Village
Mamba Village (tel 472709) is north of Mombasa on the mainland opposite Nyali Golf Club in the Nyali Estate. It's a crocodile farm set amongst streams, waterfalls and wooden bridges. If you've never seen a crocodile farm with reptiles ranging from the newly born to the full grown, here's your chance. Personally, I've seen a lot of these farms in the past and I don't find them that

Dhows

Dhows have been sailing along the coast of East Africa for centuries and, until fairly recently, were the principal trading vessels used between the eastern coast of the continent and the Persian Gulf and India. They once numbered in the thousands but, since the turn of the century, they have declined rapidly in the face of competition from steamships. These days only a few make the journey to the Gulf. Those that remain confine themselves to sailing between the mainland and the offshore islands and between the islands themselves, and even then only in certain areas. Their romantic appeal, nevertheless, remains and a dhow trip around the Lamu archipelago is an extremely popular activity amongst travellers.

Essentially, all dhows are wooden vessels, either planked or dug out, along with a rudder, mast and lateen (triangular) sail. Like all sail boats unless motorised, they're completely dependent on the wind but, unlike boats with only square sails, they're capable of tacking into the wind.

Dhows are differentiated by size and shape. The largest are known as *jahazi*, which are planked, ocean-going vessels with broad hulls and ruggedly designed to be capable of withstanding constant bumping along rocky shores and submerged coral reefs. They can have either one or two lateen sails. Most have woven coconut fibre matting fixed to their sides to reduce splash and a wooden 'eye' attached to each side of the bow below a decorated or carved tailboard. Dhows of this type built in the Lamu archipelago often have a perpendicular bow whereas those from Zanzibar have sloping bows. A jahazi often has a toilet hanging off the stern of the boat.

Motorised versions of the jahazi are known as *mtaboti* or *mchaboti*. The only difference is that these have an inboard motor instead of a sail.

Smaller craft go under the generic name of *mashua* and there are many different types. Around Lamu they're usually known as *kijahazi*. These dhows differ from the jahazi in being smaller, much narrower in the hull and having only one sail. They can be remarkably fast given a favourable wind and are the ones you're most likely to utilise for trips around Lamu.

Another common type of dhow, smaller still, is the *dau la mwao* – a sort of dugout canoe with a narrow hull, small mast and no keel which sits low in the water and is frequently used for transporting soil, sand and coral-rag building blocks. Most do not have a square stern. A variation of this type from the Kizingitini area is the *mtori* which is somewhat smaller and faster and fitted with a keel. Decoration on the mwao and the mtori is restrained. It's interesting to note that the mwao is the nearest surviving relative to the *dau la utango* which was the most common type of dhow found along the coast during the 19th century.

There are excellent models of the various types of dhow in the Lamu Museum. ■

A (GC)
B (TW)
C (HF)
D (TW)
E (GC)
F (TW)

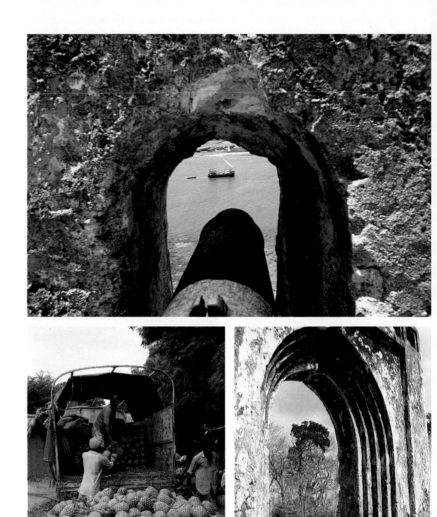

Top: Fort Jesus, Mombasa (GP)
Bottom Left: Malindi market (TW)
Bottom Right: Omani ruins, Malindi (GC)

interesting. They're often just a collection of concrete and wire-mesh cages with thousands of young crocodiles up to five years old and a few token, full grown adults to pull in the punters. You pay through the nose to see them, too, even though the owners of the farms are making megabucks selling skins to Gucci and the like.

Bamburi Quarry Nature Trail

Further up the coast this nature trail (tel 485729) has been created on reclaimed and reforested areas damaged by cement production activities which ceased in 1971. Once the forest was established, the area was restocked with plants and animals in an attempt to create a mini replica of the wildlife parks of Kenya. At present, animal species represented include eland, oryx, waterbuck, buffalo, wart hog, bush pig, various monkeys and many different varieties of birds. There's also what the owners claim to be an 'orphan' hippo which was introduced as a baby from Naivasha and which has remained bottle-fed ever since. A likely story!

The complex also includes a fish farm, crocodile farm, reptile pit and plant nursery. The centre is open daily from 2 to 5.30 pm. Feeding time is at 4 pm. To get there take a public bus to Bamburi Quarry Nature Trail stop (signposted) on the main Mombasa-Malindi road.

Places to Stay – bottom end

There are very few cheap places to stay on the beaches north of Mombasa. Even places way back from the beach with nothing special going for them can be remarkably expensive.

One of the few genuine cheapies is the *Kanamai Conference Centre* (tel Kikambala 46, PO Box 46) at Kikambala Beach which was previously a youth hostel but is no longer affiliated to the IYHF. Here they have dormitory beds for KSh 40 to KSh 50 (depending on the number of bunks per room) and one, two and three bedroom self-contained cottages which cost KSh 360/470/660 in the low season and KSh 420/550/780

Beaches North of Mombasa

To Malindi Lamu & Garissa

Seahorse Hotel

Kilifi

Mnarani Club
Dhows Inn

Takaungu

0   5   10 km

Tropicana Beach Hotel

Kurwitu

Jauss Farm

Vipingo

Sun 'n' Sand Beach Hotel

Whispering Palms Hotel

Kanamai Conference Centre
Continental Beach Cottages

Majengo

Dolphin Hotel
Intercontinental Hotel
Serena Beach Hotel

Fisherman's Inn
Neptune Beach Hotel
Severin Sea Lodge
Plaza Beach Hotel

Shimo

Kenya Beach Hotel
Bamburi Beach Hotel
Whitesands Hotel
Ocean View Beach Hotel

Bamburi
Quarry
Nature
Trail

Reef Hotel
Mombasa Beach Hotel
Silver Beach Hotel

Nyali Beach Hotel

Mamba Crocodile Village

Mombasa

in the high season respectively. You can also camp for KSh 35 per person per night. Meals are available for KSh 50 (breakfast) and KSh 70 (lunch and dinner) – expensive for what is basically ugali and chicken stew. There's also a laundry service.

The trouble with this place is getting there! First you have to take a matatu to Majengo on the Mombasa-Kilifi road (from near the New People's Hotel in Mombasa). Get off when you see a yellow sign saying 'Camping Kanamai'. Go down the dirt track by this sign for about 300 metres and then turn left at the fork. Continue for about three km and you'll find it on the left-hand side by the beach. It's a long, hot walk and lifts are few and far between. With a backpack it's a major effort.

Close by are the *Continental Beach Cottages* which are described by people who have stayed there as 'a bargain' at KSh 480 for a bungalow with bedroom, lounge, kitchen, bathroom and air-con but which are very run-down and infested with ants and termites. On the other hand, you may be the only guests there and there's a good swimming pool, bar and restaurant and a pleasant beach. Cheap meals (omelette and chips and curries) are available for around KSh 50. As with the Conference Centre, the only problem about this place is getting there from the main road. Taxis are expensive.

If you're staying at either of the above places and want a change of scene or a cold beer, the Whispering Palms Hotel is about 15 minutes walk north along the beach. Breakfasts here cost KSh 50 and you can use their swimming pool for KSh 60 per day.

Further up the coast at Vipingo, about 40 km north of Mombasa, there is *Jauss Farm* (tel (01251) 2218) which consists of a camp site, a number of budget chalets as well as luxury farm houses on 85 hectares of a dairy and tropical fruit farm with its own quiet and unspoiled silver sand beach. The camp site is equipped with showers and toilets and costs KSh 60 per person per night. Tents, which sleep two to three people, can be rented for KSh 90 per night. The budget chalets are fairly basic twin rooms with clean beds and mattresses, and toilets and showers have to be shared with those occupying the camp site. The chalets are lockable and cost KSh 120 per person per night.

The luxury farm houses are fully furnished and include the use of lounge, verandah, bathroom, shower and fully equipped kitchen. They cost KSh 1020 for one with a double bedroom and KSh 1800 for one with four double bedrooms.

Breakfasts can be ordered for KSh 60 and evening meals for KSh 120 plus there's an on-site shop which sells meat, fruit and vegetables as well as canned goods. Other facilities include a swimming pool, full workshop facilities including the services of an expert mechanic, a video lounge, snorkel and scuba gear rental and 24 hour Masai security staff.

Bookings can be made by telephoning the above number but you are welcome to simply turn up and take pot luck. The place is managed by British-based Into Africa Safaris (tel (0883) 347784), 143 Stafford Rd, Caterham CR3 6JH, UK. They can arrange budget camping safaris from Jauss Farm and many tours leave from the camp site.

There are interesting Arab ruins and slave trading caves nearby.

It's much easier to get to Jauss Farm than to the Kanamai 'youth hostel' since it's only one km from the main Mombasa-Malindi road. To get there, take a bus or matatu from Mombasa and get off two km north of Vipingo where there's a sign for Jauss Farm. It's about 15 minutes walk from there towards the beach to the farm (again signposted). Alternatively, get off in Vipingo village and telephone the farm from the post office. They'll come and collect you free of charge most of the time.

Places to Stay – top end

Virtually all the other hotels along this stretch of the East African coast before you arrive at Kilifi are resort complexes and cater largely for package tourists from Europe. Most of them are so self-contained that many of those staying there hardly ever see anything of Africa other than Mombasa airport, the inside of minibuses, the hotel itself and Black Kenyan waiters. As at the hotels south of Mombasa and at Malindi, many cater almost exclusively for one specific European nationality whether they be British, German or Italian (French people don't feature prominently in East African tourism). There's precious little intermingling.

All the hotels compete furiously with each other to provide the utmost in creature comforts, mellow surroundings, day trips and sports facilities and there's little to choose between them though it's generally true to say that the further you get from Mombasa, the cheaper and less ritzy they become.

Down at Nyali Beach – the closest to Mombasa – even places which don't face the sea and are in no way hotel resorts, and which you might imagine should be fairly cheap given the facilities they offer, can be surprisingly expensive. The *Bamburi Chalets*, for example, which offers self-contained cottages with two bunk beds, two normal beds, shower, cooking facilities, gas stove and refrigerator and use of swimming pool cost between KSh 1440 and KSh 3000 per night depending on the season. Likewise, the *Fishermen's Inn*, further up the coast, charges KSh 720/960 for singles/doubles with breakfast in the low season and KSh 960/1200 in the high season. Meals at the Fishermen's will cost you between KSh 180 and KSh 300.

It's unlikely that if you intend to stay at any of the genuine resort complexes that you'll be reading this book since you'd have reserved your hotel via an agent and your air fares would be included in a package deal. Should you wish to make your own arrangements for staying at any of the resort complexes, however, here's a selection of the hotels.

Nyali Beach The following resorts are at Nyali Beach:

Mombasa Beach Hotel (five star) PO Box 90414, Mombasa (tel 471861). Singles/doubles/triples for KSh 1620/2160/3025 with breakfast

Nyali Beach Hotel (five star) PO Box 90414,

Mombasa. Singles/doubles for KSh 2580/3360 with breakfast and KSh 2750/3695 for full board

Reef Hotel (four star) PO Box 82234, Mombasa (tel 471771). Singles/doubles/triples for KSh 2480/3455/4735 with breakfast and KSh 2670/3840/5310 for full board

Silver Beach Hotel (four star) PO Box 81443, Mombasa. Singles/doubles for KSh 1105/1680 with full board

Kenyatta-Bamburi Beach Further north are the following hotels:

Bamburi Beach Hotel (three star) PO Box 83966, Mombasa (tel 485611). Singles/doubles/triples for KSh 1045/1370/1720 with breakfast and KSh 1080/1440/1830 for half board

Kenya Beach Hotel (three star) PO Box 95748, Mombasa. Singles/doubles for KSh 1315/1980 for full board

Neptune Beach Hotel (three star) PO Box 83125, Mombasa (tel 485701). Singles/doubles/ for KSh 1250/1765 with breakfast and KSh 1320/1910 for full board

Ocean View Beach Hotel (four star) PO Box 81127, Mombasa. Singles/doubles for KSh 1105/1470 for full board

Plaza Beach Hotel (four star) PO Box 88299, Mombasa. Singles/doubles for KSh 1200/1705 with breakfast and KSh 1550/2630 for full board

Severin Sea Lodge (five star) PO Box 82169, Mombasa (tel 485001). Singles/doubles/triples for KSh 1550/1775/3325 with breakfast and KSh 1740/2160/3900 for full board

Whitesands Hotel (four star) PO Box 90173, Mombasa (tel 485926). Singles/doubles/triples for KSh 1705/2330/2990 with breakfast and KSh 1800/2520/3275 for full board

Shanzu Beach At Shanzu Beach there are the following resorts:

Dolphin Hotel (five star) PO Box 81443, Mombasa. Singles/doubles for KSh 1140/1740 for full board

Intercontinental Hotel (five star) PO Box 83492, Mombasa (tel 485811). Singles/doubles/triples for KSh 2285/2900/3560 with breakfast and KSh 2635/3655/4735 for full board

Serena Beach Hotel (five star) PO Box 90352, Mombasa (tel 485721). Singles/doubles at KSh 2640/3360 for half board plus KSh 145 supplement per person for full board

Kikambala Beach Finally, Kikambala Beach offers the following:

Whispering Palms Hotel (three star) PO Box 5,

Kikambala (tel Kikambala 3, 4, 5, 6). Singles/doubles/triples for KSh 1380/1860/2605 for full board

Sun 'n' Sand Beach Hotel (four star) PO Box 2, Kikambala (tel Kikambala 8). Singles/doubles for KSh 1645/2195 with breakfast and KSh 1740/2390 for full board

Takaungu

Right up at the top end of this long line of beaches close to Kilifi is the village of Takaungu. It's supposedly the oldest slave port on the Kenyan coast – Zanzibar is the oldest. It's worth a visit if you have the time. The local people are very superstitious and no-one goes down to the beach at night except the fishers. If you can speak Swahili you'll hear many weird stories going around which date back to the slaving days. It's an interesting place right off the beaten track where you won't meet any other travellers.

Places to Stay Rooms can be rented in private houses in Takaungu for around KSh 35 per night. Ask around in the tea shops.

KILIFI

Other than Mtwapa Creek, just north of Mombasa, Kilifi is the first major break in the coastline between Mombasa and Malindi and there is still no bridge across the creek, though this will soon change with the completion of the Japanese-funded suspension bridge. Once this happens, the ferries which transport all vehicles from one side to the other will be made redundant and a colourful era of Kenyan coastal history will come to an end. So too, perhaps, will the livelihoods of those who presently sell packets of roasted cashew nuts (the cheapest in Kenya) and fruit juices to travellers waiting for the arrival of the ferries on either side of the creek.

Kilifi has been a backwater for many years, ignored by developers yet coveted by discerning White Kenyans, artists, writers and adventurers from various parts of the world who have gradually bought up most of the land overlooking the wide creek and the ocean and built, in many cases, some quite stunning and imaginative houses. They form a sort of society within a society and keep largely to themselves. Without an introduction, it's unlikely you'll meet them though sailing a yacht into the creek would probably secure you an invitation! Kilifi Creek is a popular anchorage spot for yachties in this part of the world and you can meet them in the evening at the Seahorse Hotel off to the left of the main road on the northern side of the creek.

So why stop off in Kilifi? The answer to this is mainly for the contrast it offers to Mombasa and Malindi and for the Mnarani Ruins on a bluff overlooking the creek on the Mombasa side. Very few travellers ever see these ruins yet they're well preserved and just as interesting as those at Gedi though not as extensive. The beach, too, on either side of the creek is very pleasant and doesn't suffer from the seaweed problem which plagues the beaches further south. The only problem is access which is mostly through private property though you can walk along it from the ferry landing at low tide.

The present district centre of Kilifi is on the northern bank of the creek.

Information

Kilifi consists of the small village of Mnarani (or Manarani) on the southern bank of the creek and Kilifi itself on the northern bank. It's a small town which you can walk around within minutes.

There's a good variety of shops (including a small bookshop), a lively open-air market and an enclosed fruit and vegetable market, a post office, a number of basic hotels and two banks.

Barclays Bank is open Monday to Friday from 8.30 am to 1 pm and on Saturday from 8.30 to 11 am. The Kenya Commercial Bank keeps the same hours.

Azzura Tours (tel 2385, PO Box 2, Kilifi) on Kilifi's main street can organise car rental, boat trips and safaris and is an agent for Garissa Express buses.

Mnarani Ruins

Mnarani, on the southern bank of Kilifi Creek overlooking the ferry landing, was once one of the string of Swahili city-states

4 Barclays Bank
2 Bookshop
12 Bus Station
15 Dhows Inn
9 Fruit & vegetable market
6 Hotel '36'
1 Jay's Coffee House
5 Kenya Commercial Bank
7 Kilifi Cafeteria
10 Kilifi Hotel
14 Mnarani Club
3 New Mwangea Lodge
8 Post Office
13 Top Life Boarding & Lodging
11 Tushaurine Boarding & Lodging

To Malindi

Mnarani Ruins

Ferry

Bridge under construction

Kilifi Creek

Bars

Bars

Mnarani Village

To Mombasa

Kilifi

0   100   200 m

Note: map to scale except Kilifi Creek which is considerably wider than indicated

which dotted the East African coast. Excavations carried out in 1954 showed that the site was occupied from the end of the 14th century to around the first half of the 17th century after which it was destroyed by marauding Galla tribespeople. The principal ruins here include the Great Mosque with its finely carved inscription around the mihrab (niche in mosque showing direction of Mecca), a group of tombs to the north (including one pillar tomb), a small mosque dating from the 16th century, and parts of the town wall and a gate. There's also a large and forbiddingly deep well whose shaft must go down at least as far as the low tide level of the creek.

Mnarani was associated with Kioni, at the mouth of Kilifi Creek on the same side, and with Kitoka, about 3½ km south of here on the northern bank of Takaungu Creek. A carved stone with an interlaced ornament, probably from a mihrab, was found at Kioni on the cliff above the creek and is presently in the Fort Jesus museum at Mombasa. The ruins at Kitoka include a mosque similar to the small mosque at Mnarani along with a few houses. All these settlements were subject to Mombasa.

The Mnarani ruins are just above the southern ferry landing stage and the path to them (about 300 metres) is prominently signposted on the main road. Entry costs KSh 30 but there's often no-one there to collect the fee.

Places to Stay – bottom end

There are a number of cheap places to stay at in Kilifi including the *Top Life Boarding & Lodging* (hardboard cubicles), the *Kilifi Hotel*, the *Hotel '36'* and the *New Mwangea Lodge* but probably the best place to stay is the *Tushaurine Boarding & Lodging* between the bus station and the open-air market. This is a recently constructed hotel, several storeys high, which offers good, clean, simple rooms with mosquito nets and shared bathroom facilities for KSh 70 a single and KSh 145 a double.

Places to Stay – middle

There's only one mid-range hotel in Kilifi and that is the *Dhows Inn* at the back of Mnarani village on the southern side of Kilifi Creek. It's a fairly small place with a number of double rooms surrounding a well kept garden, and a lively and quite popular bar and restaurant though the owner could do with replacing the sound system and definitely retiring some of the tapes his employees attempt to play. A room here with mosquito nets and bathroom will cost you KSh 300 though the price is negotiable. When the new bridge over Kilifi Creek opens, the Dhows Inn will be right on the southern access road.

Places to Stay – top end

The large resort complex at Kilifi is the somewhat exclusive *Mnarani Club* on the southern side of Kilifi Creek and quite close to the Dhows Inn. It caters largely to package tourists from Germany and Switzerland and it's these people who keep the craft shop owners of Mnarani village smiling. Despite its size, the Mnarani Club is hardly visible from the main road or even from a boat on the creek since it's constructed of local materials including some enormous makuti roofs

and surrounded by beautifully landscaped gardens full of flowering trees.

The other top-range hotel is the *Seahorse Hotel* off to the left of the main Mombasa-Malindi road on the northern side of the creek. It's patronised mainly by White Kenyans and yachties of various nationalities.

Places to Eat

A cheap and very popular place to eat both for lunch and dinner is the *Kilifi Hotel* at the bus station (actually just a patch of dirt). They offer standard Indo-African fare and you can eat well here for around KSh 30. Another popular place, especially at lunch time, is the *Kilifi Cafeteria* though prices here are somewhat higher.

Across the other side of the creek, you can eat at the *Dhows Inn* which has a limited menu of meat and seafood dishes. The only trouble with eating here is that food takes forever to arrive and the quality is variable: sometimes it's good, sometimes it's almost inedible. The average price of a main course would be between KSh 70 and KSh 85.

For a splurge, go for a meal at the *Mnarani Club* where both the cuisine and the service are excellent and the surroundings superb. It's a good idea to book in advance if you want to eat here. Expect to pay around KSh 145 for main courses.

Entertainment

For a spit-and-sawdust evening on Tusker or White Cap you can't beat the bars in Mnarani village of which there are several, but the amount of action in any of them depends largely on how many tourists brave the 200 metres or so of dirt road between the Mnarani Club and the village. Don't expect cold beers at any of these places.

The bar at the *Dhows Inn* is usually pretty lively and you can be assured of cold beer – ice-cold if you get there early.

The *Mnarani Club* has a nightly floor show – usually of tribal dancing – followed by a live African band which plays till late. The residents can be quite shy about dancing so don't expect too much action. On the other hand, this means you have the floor to yourself. Entry to the show and dance costs KSh 100 unless you ate dinner there or the manager takes a liking to you. Nonresidents can rent windsurfing equipment from this hotel during the day for KSh 100 per hour.

Other travellers have recommended the far more informal *Kilifi Club* directly opposite the Mnarani Club on the northern side of the creek.

Getting There & Away

All the buses and matatus which ply between Mombasa and Malindi stop at Kilifi but getting on a bus at Kilifi to go to either Mombasa or Malindi can be problematical since they're often full. Matatus are a much better bet.

The Tara Bus company also run buses between Kilifi and Nairobi twice daily. They depart Kilifi at 7.40 am and 7.40 pm and arrive in Nairobi at 4.30 pm and 4.30 am respectively.

MALINDI

Malindi was an important Swahili settlement as far back as the 14th century and often rivalled Mombasa and Paté for control of this part of the East African coast. It was also one of the very few places where the early Portuguese mariners found a sympathetic welcome, and today you can still see the cross which Vasco da Gama erected as a navigational aid.

These days, on account of its excellent beaches, it has experienced a tourist boom similar to that north and south of Mombasa and resort hotels are strung out all the way along the coast. On the other hand, it still retains a recognisable African centre where commerce, business and everyday activities, which aren't necessarily connected with the tourist trade, continue. Cotton growing and processing, sisal production and fishing are still major income earners. It isn't, however, a Lamu or Zanzibar. The streets here are relatively wide and straight and there are few buildings more than a century old.

It's a popular port of call for travellers heading north from Mombasa or south from Lamu, and the beaches here have one major advantage over those close to Mombasa and that is the absence of seaweed. There's a break in the coral reef at this point along the coast and this prevents the build up of seaweed which often chokes the beaches around Mombasa and makes swimming unpleasant. It also means that the surf is able to make it right through to the shore. Sharks are no problem either. The only drawback to Malindi is the brown silt which flows down the Galana River at the northern end of the bay during the rainy season which makes the sea very muddy. For the rest of the year it's perfect and even during the rainy season you can largely avoid the muddy waters by going to the beaches south of town.

Information

Tourist Office There is a tourist office next door to Kenya Airways opposite the shopping centre on the Lamu road. The staff are helpful and enthusiastic and they have a lot of information about the area, particularly accommodation.

Bank Barclays Bank is open Monday to Friday from 8.30 am to 1 pm and 2.30 to 5 pm and on Saturday from 8.30 am to noon. In the low season it's often closed on Saturdays. The Standard Chartered Bank has much the same hours of opening.

Immigration There is an office next to the Juma Mosque and pillar tombs on the waterfront (see street map for location).

Railway Bookings Travel agents in Malindi can make you bookings on the Mombasa-Nairobi railway but will charge you KSh 50 for the service. Save money and make your own booking by making a KSh 5 telephone call to (011) 312221.

A Warning

Don't walk back to your hotel along the beach at night. Many people have been mugged at knife point. Go back along the main road (which has street lighting) or take a taxi. You also need to exercise caution if returning from the Baobab Café to the Youth Hostel late at night – people have even been mugged along that short stretch of road, although you're probably safe if you're part of a group.

Malindi Town

Malindi has a pedigree going back to the 12th century and was one of the ports visited by the Chinese junks of Cheng Ho between 1417 and 1419, before the emperor of China prohibited further overseas voyages. It was one of the few places on the coast to offer a friendly welcome to the early Portuguese mariners and to this day the pillar erected by Vasco da Gama as a navigational aid still stands on the promontory at the southern end of the bay. The cross which surmounts this pillar is of Lisbon stone (and therefore original) but the supporting pillar is of local coral.

There's also the partial remains of a Portuguese church, which is undoubtedly the one which St Francis Xavier visited on his way to India. A painting of the crucifixion is still faintly visible. Not far to the north are a number of pillar tombs and the remains of a mosque and a palace. Other than this, however, little remains of the old town. The nearest substantial ruins from pre-Portuguese days are at Gedi, south of Malindi.

Malindi Marine National Park

The most popular excursion from Malindi is to the Marine National Park to the south of town past Silver Sands. Here you can rent a glass-bottomed boat to take you out to the coral reef. Snorkelling gear is provided though there generally aren't enough sets for everyone at the same time. The variety and colours of the coral and the fish are simply amazing and you'll be surprised how close you can get to the fish without alarming them. On the other hand, the area is getting a little overused and there's been quite a lot of damage to the coral. Shell collectors have also degraded the area.

The best time to go is at low tide and, preferably, on a calm day when the water will

be clear. It's advisable to wear a pair of canvas shoes or thongs for wading across the coral to where the boats are moored in case you step on a sea urchin or a stone fish. These fish are extremely well camouflaged and can inflict a very painful sting. The boat trips generally last an hour.

You can arrange these trips in Malindi – people come round the hotels to ask if you are interested in going. The usual price is KSh 145 per person which includes a taxi to take you to and from your hotel, hire of the boat and the park entry fee. You may be able to get it for less if you bargain hard but you won't be able to knock too much off this price.

Scuba Diving

If you'd like to go scuba diving you can do this from the Driftwood Club at Silver Sands. A dive costs KSh 400 (KSh 450 if they do it at Watamu including the cost of transport). They also have a diving school here for those who wish to learn but it's not cheap at KSh 2500.

Places to Stay – bottom end

There are a number of cheap, basic lodges in the centre of town, but they're usually fairly noisy at night and you don't get the benefit of sea breezes or instant access to the beach. Most travellers prefer to stay in one of the hotels on the beach.

In Town If you do want to stay in the centre of town there are several places where you can get a single room for around KSh 55 and a double for KSh 70 to KSh 95 with shared bathroom facilities. They include the *New Safari Hotel* (KSh 40 for a dormitory bed and KSh 95 for a double room), the *Malindi Rest House* (KSh 95 a double) and the *Lamu Hotel*. Also here is the *Tana Hotel* which has been thoroughly renovated, is very clean and comfortable and costs KSh 120/180 for singles/doubles with shared bathroom or KSh 240 for a self-contained double.

Closer to the beach is *La Fortuna Hotel,* which changes its name to the 'Lucky

Lodge' according to the particular tourist season. It is fairly basic but provides mosquito nets and costs KSh 95 a double with shared bathroom.

Right over the other side of town and not far from the beach is the very clean *Youth Hostel* (tel 20531) which is popular with those who are quite happy with a dormitory bed. There's a fridge for use by residents but mosquito nets are not provided. Each room has six beds at a cost of KSh 40 per person. No membership card is required to stay here.

On the Beach The main area for budget hotels in this position is close to the fishing jetty. Probably the best value for money is the *Travellers' Inn* which is very pleasant and clean, has excellent showers and mosquito netting on the windows. It costs KSh 145/180/240 for singles/doubles/triples between September and April and a little less during the rest of the year. The staff are very friendly and soft drinks and food are available. It's very popular so you may find it's full during the high season.

Also quite popular is the *Metro Hotel*, although it's hard to see why since all but one of the rooms (a triple at KSh 212 which overlooks the ocean and gets the sea breezes) are dingy, hardboard-partitioned cells. The other rooms cost KSh 70 a single and KSh 140 a double with mosquito coils and towels provided. The showers are hopeless and the water supply is totally inadequate. It's run by Mary Wanini who's very friendly and helpful. The beer garden at the front of the property, which used to be a very lively place, is currently closed but may reopen.

The other similarly priced place to stay here is *Gilani's Hotel* next door to the Metro, but many travellers who have stayed here have described the place as 'a dump'.

About 1½ km south of the above hotels along the coast road is the very popular *Silver Sands Camp Site* (tel 236), which is used by long-distance overland safari trucks whenever they come through. It costs KSh 50 per person to camp here (less in the low season) and there are good toilets and saltwater showers as well as freshwater taps but very

little shade. Those without tents can rent one for KSh 90. There are also two types of banda for rent. The so-called 'green' bandas, of which there are three, are actually tents under a makuti roof and cost KSh 160/300/450 for singles/doubles/triples (less in the low season) and have mosquito nets, own shower and toilet and electric lights. The 'white' bandas are actually huts and have two single beds, mosquito nets, screened windows, electric lights and lockable doors but common shower and toilet facilities. They cost KSh 205/385/540 for singles/doubles/triples (less in the low season). Bicycles can be rented for KSh 45 per day.

The beach here is excellent and is protected by a coral reef. At the far end of the camp site there's a snack bar with a large shady terrace which offers cold drinks and snacks such as hamburgers and a shop selling everything from suntan lotion to biscuits. They also offer breakfast for KSh 40 and dinners from KSh 40 and up.

The only other cheap place to stay is the *Lutheran Guest House* (tel 21098) at the opposite end of town off the Lamu road. This is excellent value and very popular. It offers singles/doubles without bathroom for KSh 95/180 and self-contained singles/doubles at KSh 130/240. They also have a bungalow which is fully equipped and which has two bedrooms for KSh 360 per night, KSh 1200 per week or KSh 4200 per month.

Places to Stay – middle
There are few places to stay in this price range and their tariffs vary considerably from one month to another. The cheapest is *Ozi's Bed & Breakfast* (tel 20218, PO Box 60, Malindi), overlooking the beach near the fishing jetty. Singles/doubles/triples cost KSh 180/265/395 with breakfast in the low season (May to July) and KSh 240/480/720 in the high season (16 December to 9 January). For the rest of the year it is KSh 190/300/450 (4 September to 10 November and 10 January to 30 April) and KSh 215/395/595 (29 July to 3 September and 11 November to 15 December).

Half-board rates are available for KSh 90/180/270 extra for singles/doubles/triples. All prices are inclusive of government taxes. Checkout time is 10 am and children between the ages of three and 10 are given a 50% discount.

More expensive are *Malindi Cottages/Robinson Island* (tel 20304, 21071; PO Box 992, Malindi), out on the Lamu road and close to the Eden Roc Hotel. This place consists of several fully furnished and self-contained cottages surrounding a swimming pool each with two bedrooms, a sitting room, kitchen and verandah. Facilities include a refrigerator, gas cooker, mosquito nets and fans. Each cottage sleeps up to five adults and costs KSh 480 during May and June, KSh 720 during August. For the rest of the year they cost KSh 575.

The owners of this place also run the *Sultan's Cottages* further up the Lamu road where they have one self-contained cottage which sleeps two people for KSh 360 per day. Reservations can also be made in Nairobi (tel 743414/5, PO Box 14960) and Mombasa (Farways Safari Centre Ltd, tel 23307/9, PO Box 87815).

More expensive still are the *African Dream Cottages* (tel 21296, PO Box 939, Malindi), on the Lamu road. All the units here are self-contained (though a cooker costs an extra KSh 120 per day) and have four beds. There's a swimming pool and private beach. In the low season (30 April to 16 July and 27 August to 8 October) the units cost KSh 540 per day, KSh 2880 a week or KSh 4800 a fortnight. In the high season (1 January to 26 February and 30 July to 27 August) they cost KSh 1080 per day, KSh 6000 a week or KSh 10,800 a fortnight. Intermediate prices prevail for the rest of the year. A bar and restaurant are in the planning stages.

Just beyond the Eden Roc Hotel on the Lamu road are *Sea View Lodges* which consist of a number of round makuti-roofed cottages divided in half to form two double rooms each with its own shower and toilet. The prices here are much the same as at African Dream Cottages but the place is

■ PLACES TO STAY		49	Silver Sands Camp Site	41	Fish Market

considerably run-down, breakfasts take forever to arrive, the swimming pool resembles an algal broth and the bar is moribund. A substantial discount on the posted tariff can be expected if you look like you're about to go elsewhere.

Places to Stay – top end

Malindi's top-range hotels are strung out along the beach front both north and south of the town centre and more are being built each year. Some are very imaginatively designed and consist of clusters of makuti-roofed cottages in beautifully landscaped gardens full of flowering trees. Others are fairly standard beach hotels. All of them have swimming pools and other sporting facilities and many have a discotheque. They cater mostly, but not exclusively, to package tourists from Europe on two to three week holidays and they all seem to pitch their business at a specific nationality – British, German or Italian. Very little intermingling seems to take place and you can definitely feel you've

come to the wrong spot in some hotels if you don't belong to the dominant nationality. It's a common trait with package tourism anywhere in the world.

Most of the hotels impose a supplement over the Christmas and New Year periods which can be quite considerable (KSh 360, for example), so bear this in mind if you intend to stay at this time of the year.

Closest to town on the Lamu road are *Lawford's Hotel* (tel 20440/1, PO Box 20, Malindi), and *Blue Marlin Hotel* (tel 20440/1, PO Box 54, Malindi). Both cater largely to German tourists and there's even a German consulate in the Blue Marlin Hotel! Lawford's is the cheaper of the two and in the low season it offers bungalows for KSh 600 and KSh 720 for singles and KSh 840 and KSh 960 for doubles. Rooms in the main building are KSh 840/1080/1510 for singles/doubles/triples. For the rest of the year the bungalows are KSh 840 to KSh 960 for singles and KSh 1130 to KSh 1270 a double. Rooms in the main building at this time are KSh 1055/1405/1970 for singles/ doubles/triples. All prices are for half board and include taxes.

The Blue Marlin offers a somewhat higher class of accommodation with superb facilities and costs KSh 810/1080/1510 for singles/doubles/triples in the low season and KSh 950/1250/1765 in the high season. There are also rooms with four beds for KSh 1945/2270 in the low/high seasons. All prices are for half board and include taxes. Full board costs an extra KSh 70 per person per day.

Both Lawford's and the Blue Marlin offer discounts to Kenyan residents.

Further up the Lamu road is the *Eden Roc Hotel* (tel 20480/1/2, PO Box 350, Malindi), one of the few hotels which seems to have a mixed clientele. It's also one of the few places with tennis courts though these are not open to nonresidents. The hotel has three seasons: 1 December to 15 April (high), 16 April to 30 June (shoulder) and 1 July to 30 November (low). Standard rooms (fan, shower, toilet and balcony) cost KSh 490/575/685 for breakfast/half board/full board per person in the high season and KSh 295/380/480 in the low season. Deluxe rooms (air-con, shower, toilet and balcony) cost KSh 530/610/730 per person in the high season and KSh 330/420/530 in the low season. There's also a somewhat cheaper bungalow with shower, fan and toilet as well as more expensive double suites. All prices include taxes and service charge. The hotel has a swimming pool and a popular discotheque which goes until dawn every night.

South of town, the top-range hotels stretch all the way from the path leading to the Vasco da Gama monument down to Casuarina Beach and the Malindi Marine National Park.

First is the *Sailfish Club* (tel 20016, PO Box 243), which is a very intimate hotel with only nine rooms all of them self-contained and air-conditioned. It's essentially for those interested in big-game fishing and caters largely for charters.

Opposite is *Scorpio Villas* (tel 20194, 20892; PO Box 368, Malindi) which has 17 cottages spread over some 1½ hectares of beautiful tropical gardens with three swimming pools and just 50 metres from Silver Sands beach. All the cottages are fully furnished in Lamu style and come complete with your own cook/house steward. There's an excellent restaurant and bar within the complex. It's Italian owned and Italians form the bulk of the clientele. B&B charges are KSh 840 for a double cottage, KSh 1560 for a cottage with four beds and KSh 2160 for a cottage with six beds. Half board costs a further KSh 300 per person per day and full board KSh 480 per person per day.

Further down the beach beyond the Silver Sands Camp Site is the *Driftwood Club* (tel 20155, PO Box 63, Malindi). This was one of the first beach resorts to be built at Malindi and it's different from the other hotels as it's used more by individual travellers rather than package groups. Although it gets more of a mixture of nationalities, the clientele is mainly British and White Kenyan. The club offers a variety of rooms from just KSh 550/755 for singles/doubles with shared bathroom facilities to luxury cottages with two bedrooms, two bathrooms, living room, verandah, air-con and use of private swimming pool for KSh 4800. Singles/doubles/ triples in the main building cost KSh 790/1055/1475 with fan and bathroom and KSh 1030/1295/1715 with air-con and bathroom. There are also more expensive rooms with air-con and bath for KSh 1270/1535/ 1955. These prices include breakfast and all taxes and service charge. The bar, restaurant and other facilities are open to nonresidents on payment of a temporary membership fee of KSh 10 per day.

Next down the beach is *Coconut Village* (tel 20928, 20252; PO Box 868, Malindi), where the clientele is mainly Italian. Double rooms with full board here cost between KSh 720 and KSh 1920 per person per day depending on the time of year (and there are no less than eight 'seasons'!). Single occupancy rates are plus 50% of the above prices. Children under two years old are free of charge and those under 12 years old pay 50% of the above rates. Half board prices are KSh

100 less per day and with breakfast only they're KSh 200 less per day. All prices include taxes and service charge. The hotel has a popular open-air, makuti-roofed discotheque which overlooks the beach.

Next door is the *Tropical Village* (tel 20256) where, again, the clientele is mainly Italian. Rooms here in the high season cost KSh 1320 to KSh 2040 a single for half board and KSh 1440 to KSh 2280 a double for full board.

Next on down is the *African Dream Village* (tel 20442/3/4) which is owned by the same people who run the African Dream Cottages on the Lamu road. Unlike the cottages, this is a fully fledged beach resort which has double rooms with shower, toilet, verandah, air-con and telephone, and a range of facilities which include swimming pool, sports centre, bars and restaurant. Full board rates in the high season are KSh 2250/3000/3240 for singles/doubles/triples and KSh 1140/1680/1620 in the low season. There are two shoulder periods where the rates are intermediate.

Beyond the above is the *Silver Sands Villas* (tel 20842, PO Box 91, Malindi) which consists of a main building with single and double rooms and a number of two and four person self-contained villas. Half board in the main building costs KSh 2510/3815 for singles/doubles in the high season and KSh 1465/2225 in the low season. A two person villa in the high season costs KSh 4610 and KSh 2690 in the low season. Four person villas cost KSh 7630 to KSh 8700 in the high season and KSh 2690 to KSh 5075 in the low season. All prices include taxes and service charges.

Further down the beach still are three other resort hotels – the *White Elephant, Jambo Club* and *Kivolini Hotel*.

Places to Eat – cheap

There's not a lot of choice in this range as many of the cafés which travellers used to use in the past have closed down. Two which have survived the tourist boom and which remain popular are the *Travellers' Café* and the *Baobab Café – Pint Pot*, both very close

to each other near the Portuguese Church. The Travellers' Café offers Western and African-style meals for between KSh 30 and KSh 55. The Baobab is a full-on Western-style restaurant with a good selection of dishes, including seafood, ranging from KSh 50 to KSh 65, fruit juices from KSh 14 to KSh 18 and breakfasts from KSh 18 and up. Part of the premises is a bar where you can get ice-cold beers at normal prices.

Other cheap meals can be found in the restaurants at the hotels in the centre of town. The fare is standard Indo-African. The *Bahari Restaurant* offers much the same sort of thing plus seafood and very good milk shakes. Also worth visiting for its excellent milk shakes and fruit juices is the *Malindi Fruit Juice Garden* in the market. Further afield, it's worth trying the *Urafiki Bar & Restaurant* on Kenyatta Rd which offers ugali and meat stew for around KSh 30. The bar here gets very lively later on in the evening and the jukebox knows no other setting than full bore.

Slightly more expensive but excellent value is the *Palm Garden* on Lamu road opposite the petrol station. They do very tasty food here at prices similar to those at the Baobab Café. The menu is mainly seafoods and curries. Make sure you eat in the main part of the restaurant under the makuti-roofed shelters at the back rather than in the part which fronts onto the street as here they only do snacks, fruit juices and the like.

Ozi's Bed & Breakfast is also worth checking out for reasonably priced curries (around KSh 70) though they do have more expensive seafood dishes such as prawns and lobster.

It's also possible to eat German-style food relatively cheaply at the *Beer Garden* on the Lamu road if you choose the simple dishes such as wurst and potato salad or something similar but most of the dishes here will be at least KSh 120.

Places to Eat – more expensive

For a splurge it's worth trying the *Driftwood Club* where you have to pay KSh 10 per day for temporary membership. This entitles you to the use of the swimming pool, hot showers, bar and restaurant. The prices are very reasonable – lunch for KSh 65, dinner for KSh 80, good snacks for KSh 21 and up (smoked sailfish and prawn sandwiches, etc), and à la carte seafood main dishes for KSh 40 to KSh 80. It's especially convenient if you are staying at the Silver Sands Camp Site.

At the *Eden Roc Hotel*, simply brave the *haute couture* and the Ambre Soleil and have one of their set meals in the dining room. It's open to nonresidents. For KSh 85 you get soup, avocado vinaigrette and a self-service buffet consisting of a choice of some 10 different salads, pepper steak, vegetables and three sweets plus coffee.

I Love Pizza in front of the fishing jetty and close to the Metro Hotel is a popular place for a splurge. As you might expect, it serves Italian food (pizzas and pastas for around KSh 80) but also such things as chicken casserole and seafood dishes though these will cost you KSh 145 and up. It's open from 11 am to 11 pm daily.

Recently opened and an excellent place to while away a long lunch hour or a whole evening is *Eddie's* (tel 20283) which is probably one of the best seafood restaurants in Malindi as well as having a tastefully intimate atmosphere. It's open from 12 to 2.30 pm and 7.30 to 10.30 pm and there's a swimming pool which you can cool off in before eating your meal. Expect to pay KSh 120 and up.

Entertainment

Because Malindi is a holiday resort there are a lot of lively bars and discos to visit in the evening, some of which rock away until dawn. The most famous of them is the *Stardust Club* which generally doesn't get started until late (10 or 11 pm) and costs KSh 50 entry. You can also get a meal here. The *Tropicana Club 28* is similar but can get very hot and sweaty as it's quite a small place and is often packed out. Entry costs KSh 100.

There's also a disco at least once a week – usually on Wednesdays – at *Coconut Village* past the Driftwood Club and, if you get there

early enough, you won't have to pay the entry charge. It's a pleasant place to dance away the evening and you won't drown in perspiration as it's open-air under makuti roofs right on the beach. The bar is incredible and is worth a visit just to see it. It's built around a living tree with one of the branches as the bar top!

Another place which is worth checking out if you want to catch a film is the *Malindi Fishing Club*, right next to the Metro Hotel. It's a very attractive, traditionally constructed building with a makuti roof. There's a bar and snacks are available. The clientele, mainly British, are friendly, although some of the videos they show are decidedly daggy.

The two liveliest tourist bars are the *Beer Garden* and the *Baobab Café* though the tape collection at the Beer Garden is positively antediluvian. Bring your own. The beers are ice-cold at both of them. One of the liveliest African bars is the *Urafiki Bar & Restaurant* with its deafening jukebox that seems to play Franco nonstop. It closes by 11.30 pm and the beers are often lukewarm but, somehow, you don't notice the Arctic fetish of ice-cold beer.

Things to Buy

A few years ago there were many craft shops lining both sides of the road between Uhuru Park and the post office but major drainage works forced them to relocate onto the beach below Gilani's Hotel and the Metro. This has made it much more of a sellers' market since why else would you go there. All the same, prices are reasonable (though you must, of course, bargain) and the quality is high. They offer makonde carvings, wooden animal carvings, soapstone and wooden chess sets, basketware and the like. If you have unwanted or excess gear (T-shirts, jeans, cameras) you can often do a part-exchange deal with these people.

Getting There & Away

Air Four companies operate flights to Malindi from Mombasa and Lamu. They are Eagle Aviation Ltd (tel Malindi 21258, Mombasa 316054, Lamu 3119), Prestige Air

Services Ltd (tel Malindi 20860/1, Mombasa 21443), Skyways Airlines (tel Malindi 21260, Mombasa 432167, Lamu 3226), and Equator Airlines (tel Malindi 2053). All these companies have their offices on the Lamu road in Malindi though they are more spread out in Mombasa.

They all have two flights per day in either direction between Mombasa and Malindi and between Lamu and Malindi. Flights from Mombasa depart at 8.30 am and 2.15 pm and arrive in Malindi 30 minutes later. From Lamu they depart at either 10 or 11 am and 4 pm and arrive in Malindi 40 minutes later. The fare from Lamu to Malindi is KSh 900 one way and KSh 1800 return. Children over two years old pay full fare. Check-in time is 30 minutes before departure and the baggage allowance is 10 kg per person. Most of time they don't hassle if your baggage is over 10 kg but, even if they do, excess charges are minimal. The airport departure tax is KSh 50 at Malindi and Mombasa but there's no charge at Lamu.

Kenya Airways also flies Nairobi-Malindi-Mombasa in either direction once daily except on Saturday using F50 propeller planes. If you're relying on these flights to get back to Mombasa or Nairobi to connect with an international flight then make absolutely sure you have a confirmed booking or, preferably, go back a day before.

Bus & Matatu Three bus companies operate between Mombasa, Malindi and Lamu on a daily basis. They are Malindi Bus Service, Tana River Bus Service and Garissa Express and they all have offices in Mombasa, Malindi and Lamu. There are several departures daily in either direction between Mombasa and Malindi which take about 2½ hours and cost KSh 55. There are also matatus which do this run taking about two hours and costing KSh 70. There's no need to book in advance from Mombasa if you turn up early enough in the morning. In Mombasa the buses leave from outside the New People's Hotel early in the morning. Matatus leave from the same place all day until late afternoon and go when full.

Both the buses and matatus literally *fly* up and down this coast road as though they were being pursued by a marauding army of *shifta* (bandits) in high-speed Land Cruisers, and they pack in as many punters as they possibly can. I counted 138 people on one such bus and that didn't include the driver and his mate!

At present, there's a ferry crossing between Mombasa and Malindi over Kilifi Creek (about halfway) but a Japanese company is busy building a huge suspension bridge and approach roads and, when finished, this will cut the journey time between Mombasa and Malindi by about half an hour. In the meantime, on arrival at Kilifi, you have to get off your bus or matatu, walk onto the ferry, and reboard on the other side.

Buses from Lamu to Malindi leave from the mainland between 7 and 7.30 am. The fare from Lamu to Malindi is KSh 120 and the journey takes about five hours. You must book tickets in advance for this journey as there's heavy demand for tickets.

Share-Taxi It's also possible to find Peugeot 504 station wagons which do the journey between Mombasa and Malindi. They go when full (seven passengers) and cost KSh 60 per person. You'll find them at the bus station in Malindi but only in the mornings. Commissioning a normal taxi to take you between Mombasa and Malindi will cost you far more.

Train You can make advance reservations for Kenyan Railways at most of the large hotels in Malindi but they'll charge you KSh 50 for the service. All they do for this is make a telephone call to Mombasa railway station. You can do it yourself for a fraction of the cost.

Getting Around
Bicycle Rental You can rent bicycles from the Silver Sands Camp Site and from outside the Tropicana Club 28 at KSh 45 per day. This is probably the best way to get around town unless you prefer to walk.

Dhow Trips Dhow trips around the area can be arranged at Nelson Safaris which have a small office on the beach front between Gilani's Hotel and the Metro Hotel. The average cost would be KSh 300 per person per day including food.

WATAMU

About 24 km south of Malindi, Watamu is a smaller beach resort development with its own marine national park – part of the Marine National Reserve which stretches south from Malindi. The coral reef here is even more spectacular than at Malindi since it has been much less exploited and poached by shell hunters. In addition, underwater visibility is not affected by silt brought down into the sea by the Galana River.

The coast at Watamu is broken up into three separate coves divided by craggy and eroded headlands and there are a number of similarly eroded islands just offshore. The coral sand is a dazzling white and although there is some shade from coconut palms, you'll probably have to retreat to the cooler confines of a hotel bar or restaurant in the middle of the day. The most southerly cove is fronted entirely by extensive beach resorts and exclusive private houses as is much of the central cove, though less so. The northern cove and part of the headland is covered by the rambling Watamu Beach Hotel at the back of which is the actual village of Watamu.

Before tourist development got underway here, Watamu was a mellow little fishing village of makuti-roofed cottages nestled beneath coconut palms and it still retains much of that atmosphere despite the intrusion of souvenir shops, bars, restaurants and night clubs catering for the tourist hordes. A lot of development has taken place on the outskirts of the village and seems destined to continue.

Information

There is a branch of Barclays Bank in the village of Watamu which is open from 9 am to noon on Monday, Wednesday and Friday.

Watamu Marine National Park

The actual coral reef lies between one and two km offshore and to get to it you'll have to hire a glass-bottomed boat. These can be arranged at any of the large hotels or, alternatively, at the marine park entrance which is at the end of the peninsula just south of the Turtle Bay Beach Hotel. Expect to pay KSh 220 per person. It's worth every cent!

There are also boat trips to a group of caves at the entrance to Mida Creek which are home to a school of giant rock cod many of which are up to two metres long. Diving equipment is usually necessary to get down to their level since, most of the time, they remain stationary on the bottom.

Places to Stay – bottom end

Budget accommodation has always been something of a problem in Watamu but the choice is getting better. The best deals are probably to be found by asking around among the local people for a room in a private house. Most of the people who offer such rooms specifically request not to be included in a guide book so it's fair to respect their wishes. Until you find a private room, the cheapest places to stay are the *Nyambene Lodge* and the *Blue Lodge* in the village. They're both basic lodges with simple rooms and shared bathroom facilities.

Better is the *Villa Veronica Mwikali Lodge* (PO Box 57, Watamu), opposite the Hotel Dante Bar & Restaurant. This is a very friendly and secure place which offers spotlessly clean rooms with fan, mosquito nets, shower and toilet for KSh 300 a double including breakfast. Close by is the *Iritoni Hotel* which costs KSh 180 a double without breakfast but has only two rooms.

On the main road leaving the village is the *Watamu Paradise Restaurant & Cottages* (tel 32062, PO Box 249, Watamu) which has a number of cottages each containing three double bedrooms with fan, mosquito nets and bathroom. A double here costs KSh 300. It's a very pleasant place to stay and there's a swimming pool in the complex.

Considerably further out of the village, not far from the junction of the road to Gedi,

9	Barclays Bank
12	Barracuda Inn
4	Bicycle Hire
15	Blue Bay Village
3	Blue Lodge
7	Come Back Club/Mustafa's Restaurant
10	Happy Night Bar & Restaurant
18	Hemmingways
11	Hotel Dante Bar & Restaurant
5	La Bamba Country Lodge & American Bar
2	Nyambene Lodge
16	Ocean Sports
17	Seafarers
13	Seventh Day Adventist Youth Camp
19	Turtle Bay Beach Hotel
8	Villa Veronica, Mwikali Lodge
1	Watamu Beach Hotel
14	Watamu Cottages
6	Watamu Paradise Restaurant & Cottages

are the *Watamu Cottages*. While they're one of the best deals in Watamu at KSh 145 per person with breakfast, they're often full for obvious reasons but worth trying to get into. There's a swimming pool in the compound.

It may occasionally be possible to get a cheap room at the *Seventh Day Adventist Youth Camp* if there's no group there but don't count on it. You can also camp here if you have your own tent but the facilities are minimal though there is a gas cooker which you can use.

Places to Stay – top end

Top-end hotels take up much of the beach frontage along each of the three coves. As at Malindi, they're mostly resort-type hotels which cater to package tourists' every need and are quite specific as to the European nationality which they appeal to – German, British or Italian.

At the northern end and next to Watamu village is the rambling *Watamu Beach Hotel* (tel 32001, 32010), where most of the German tourists stay. Full board here costs KSh 1175/1650/2295 for singles/doubles/triples and KSh 1245/1790/2435 with air-con. It has all the usual facilities including a swimming pool, open-air and covered bars, a huge restaurant and a plethora of boats waiting to take residents out to the reef or wherever else they want to go.

At the northern end of the central cove is the spectacular and only recently completed *Barracuda Inn* (tel 61, 70, 74; PO Box 59, Watamu). This amazing and traditionally built structure with its soaring makuti roofs and associated individual rustic cottages would have to qualify as one of the most imaginatively conceived hotels in the world and must surely have been designed by a film set director rather than an architect. Once the landscaped gardens have matured it will be even more superb. Yet, despite the grandeur of its conception, the atmosphere here is languidly informal.

The cottages are double storeyed: upstairs there's a double bed but no air-con, and downstairs are two separate beds and air-con. Each room has its own bathroom and toilet, refrigerator, stereo system, table and chairs and verandah. Full board costs KSh 1440 a double in the upstairs rooms and KSh 1165/2880 a single/double downstairs. The cuisine is excellent and facilities include a swimming pool, tennis and squash courts, horse riding, boating, bars and a disco-theque. It's Italian owned and the clientele is mainly Italian though not exclusively so.

The southern cove sports five hotels which, in order of appearance from north to south, are *Blue Bay Village* (tel 32626, PO Box 162, Watamu), *Ocean Sports, Seafarers*, *Hemingways* (tel 32624, PO Box 267, Watamu), and *Turtle Bay Beach Hotel* (tel 32622, PO Box 457, Watamu).

The Blue Bay Village caters mostly to Italians and full board singles/doubles vary according to the season from KSh 1115/1750 in the low season to KSh 1620/2640 in the high season, including all taxes and service charges. There's a Christmas and New Year supplement of KSh 540 per person per day. Children between the ages of three and 12 years are charged at half the adult rate.

Ocean Sports and Seafarers are mainly for those interested in big-game fishing and are only relatively small hotels.

Hemingways is a relatively new place and caters predominantly to British tourists and White Kenyans. High season half board rates are KSh 2575/3960 for singles/doubles (KSh 1920/2880 for Kenyan residents) and low season rates are KSh 1190 per person. The full board supplement is KSh 180 per person at any time of year plus there is an additional supplement of KSh 360 per person per day between 20 December and 1 January. All prices include taxes and service charges. Malindi airport transfers are available for KSh 180 each way. The hotel has its own deep-sea fishing boats.

At the far end of the cove is the Turtle Bay Beach Hotel which caters to a mixture of nationalities – mainly British and German. Like the Watamu Beach Hotel, it's a huge, rambling place with all the usual facilities and water sports equipment. Prices vary according to the season and the standard of room. In the low season, full board in a standard twin room costs KSh 630/1250 for singles/doubles and, in the high season, KSh 1185/1580. 'Superior' twin rooms in the low season cost KSh 810/1440 and, in the high season, KSh 1365/1760. Deluxe twin rooms in the low season cost KSh 990/1620 and, in the high season, KSh 1545/1940. All 'superior' and deluxe twin rooms have air-con and a sea view.

Places to Eat

Budget eating facilities are at a premium in Watamu though it is possible to get simple meals at one or other of the local bars in the village.

More expensive but excellent value are the meals at the *Watamu Paradise Restaurant & Cottages* which offers both meat and seafood dishes. The food here is very tasty and pleasantly presented and you can eat well for around KSh 70 so long as you don't go for such things as lobster. The menu, on the other hand, requires a high degree of imaginative interpretation since it sports such bizarre concoctions as 'Onion omqiiate', 'Thaliathel', 'Paper steak', 'Loabster, and 'Crubs'! Not far away and very similar in quality is the *Come Back Club/Mustafa's Restaurant*. It is open all night and has loud music.

Diagonally opposite Mustafa's is the *Hotel Dante Bar & Restaurant* (tel 32243) which offers good Italian fare. The *Happy Night Bar & Restaurant* has ice-cold beers and European-style food, all at Kenyan (rather than lodge) prices. It often has live music or disco nights.

Apart from the places which are just restaurants as such, you can use the facilities at any of the large hotels even if you're not a resident – most of them have a bar, restaurant, swimming pool and disco. It's also possible to utilise their water sport facilities though there will be a charge for this. Scuba diving at the Seafarer Hotel is quite expensive. It's wise to book in advance if you want a meal at any of these hotels.

In addition to the restaurants and hotels at Watamu, there's the *La Bamba Country Lodge, Coco Grill Bar & Restaurant* and the *American Bar* opposite the main entrance to the Watamu Beach Hotel which are worth checking out.

Getting There & Away

There are plenty of matatus from the bus station in Malindi to Watamu throughout the day. They cost KSh 12 and take about 30 minutes. Most of these first go down to the Turtle Bay Beach Hotel after which they turn around and go to Watamu village. On the return journey they generally go direct from Watamu village to Malindi without first going down to the Turtle Bay Beach Hotel.

Getting Around

Bicycles can be hired for KSh 20 per hour or KSh 100 per day from a place next door to the Nyambene Lodge in Watamu village.

GEDI

Some three to four km from Watamu, just off the main Malindi-Mombasa road, are the famous Gedi ruins, one of the principal historical monuments on the coast. Though the ruins are extensive, this Arab-Swahili town

is something of a mystery since it's not mentioned in any of the Portuguese or Arab chronicles of the time.

Excavations, which have uncovered such things as Ming Chinese porcelain and glass and glazed earthenware from Persia, have indicated the 13th century as the time of its foundation, but it was inexplicably abandoned in the 17th or 18th century, possibly because the sea receded and left the town high and dry, or because of marauding Galla tribespeople from the north. The forest took over and the site was not rediscovered until the 1920s. Even if you only have a passing interest in archaeology it's worth a visit.

Entry costs KSh 50 (KSh 20 for student card holders). A good guidebook with map is for sale at the entrance.

The site is surprisingly large and surrounded by two walls, the inner one of which was possibly built to enclose a smaller area after the city was temporarily abandoned in the 15th to 16th centuries. In places it actually incorporates earlier houses into its structure. The site is lush and green with numerous baobab trees. Monkeys chatter in the tree tops, lizards rustle in the undergrowth and large, colourful butterflies flutter among the ruins.

The buildings were constructed of coral rag, coral lime and earth and some have pictures incised into the plaster finish of their walls, though many of these have deteriorated in recent years. The toilet facilities in the houses are particularly impressive, generally in a double-cubicle style with a squat toilet in one and a wash stand in the other where a bowl would have been used. Fancier versions even have double 'washbasins' with a bidet between them.

The other notable feature of the site is the great number of wells, many of them of remarkable depth!

Most of the interesting excavated buildings are concentrated in a dense cluster near the entrance gate. There are several other scattered around the site within the inner wall and even between the inner and outer walls. Outside the site, by the car park, there's a small museum with some items found on the site. Other items are exhibited in Fort Jesus in Mombasa.

The Tombs

On your right as you enter the site is the Dated Tomb, so called because the Muslim date corresponding to 1399 has been deciphered. This tomb has provided a reference point for dating other buildings within the complex. Next to it is the Tomb of the Fluted Pillar which is characteristic of such pillar designs found up and down the East African coast. There's another good example of this kind of pillar in Lamu.

The Great Mosque

The Great Mosque originally dates from the mid-15th century but was rebuilt a century later, possibly as a result of damage sustained at the time of Gedi's first abandonment. The mosque is of typical East African design with a mihrab facing towards Mecca. You can see where porcelain bowls were once mounted in the walls flanking the mihrab.

The Palace

Behind the mosque are the ruins of the extensive palace which is entered through an arched door. Once through the doorway, you enter a reception court and then a large audience hall while to the left of this are numerous smaller rooms. Look for the many 'bathrooms' and the room flanking the audience hall with its square niches in the walls intended for lamps. Behind that room is another one with no doorway at all which would probably have been used to store valuables. Entry was by ladder through a small hatch high up in the wall. Beyond this is a kitchen area with a small but still very deep well.

The palace also has a particularly fine pillar tomb while to the right is the Annexe with four individual apartments, each with its own courtyard.

The Houses

In all, 14 houses have been excavated at Gedi, 10 of which are in a compact group beside the Great Mosque and the Palace. They're named after particular features of their design or after objects found in them by archaeologists. They include the House of the Cowrie, House of the Cistern and House of the Porcelain Bowl.

Other Buildings

Follow the signposted path from the Tomb of the Fluted Pillar to the adjoining House of the Dhow and House of the Double Court with a nearby tomb. There are pictures in the wall plaster in these houses. A path follows close to the inner city wall from here to the Mosque of the Three Aisles where you will also find the largest well in Gedi. Beside it is the inner wall of the East Gate from where a path leads to the Mosque Between the Walls; a path cuts back to the car park from here.

Alternatively, from the East Gate you can follow another path right around the inner circuit of the inner wall or divert to the Mosque on the Wall at the southern extremity of the outer wall. The House on the West Wall actually comprises several adjoining houses of typical design while at the northern end of the town there is the more complex North Gate.

Getting There & Away

Take the same matatu as you would to go to Watamu but get off at Gedi village, where the matatu turns off from the main Malindi-Mombasa road. From there it's about a one km signposted walk to the monument along a gravel road.

It's also possible to get a taxi to take you on a round trip from Malindi for about KSh 360 with an hour or more to look around the site. Could be worth it if your time is limited and there's a small group to share costs.

Lamu

In the early 1970s Lamu acquired a reputation as the Kathmandu of Africa – a place of fantasy and other-worldliness wrapped in a cloak of mediaeval romance. It drew all self-respecting seekers of the miraculous, globetrotters, and that much maligned bunch of people called hippies. The attraction was obvious. Both Kathmandu and Lamu were remote, unique and fascinating self-contained societies which had somehow escaped the depredations of the 20th century with their culture, their centuries-old way of life and their architecture intact.

Though Kathmandu is now overrun with well heeled tourists and the hippies have retired to their rural communes or into business as purveyors of the world's handicrafts, Lamu remains much the same as it has always been – to a degree.

With an almost exclusively Muslim population, it is Kenya's oldest living town and has changed little in appearance or character over the centuries. Access is still exclusively by diesel-powered launch from the mainland (though there's an airstrip on Manda Island) and the only motor-powered vehicle on the island is that owned by the District Commissioner. The streets are far too narrow and winding to accommodate anything other than pedestrians or donkeys. Men still wear the full length white robes known as *khanzus* and the *kofia* caps, and women cover themselves with the black wraparound bui bui as they do in other Islamic cultures, although here it's a liberalised version which often hugs their bodies, falls short of the ankles and dispenses completely with the dehumanising veil in front of the face.

There are probably more dhows to be seen here than anywhere else along the East African coast and local festivals still take place with complete disregard for cameratoting tourists. The beach at Shela is still magnificent and uncluttered and nothing happens in a hurry. It's one of the most relaxing places you'll ever have the pleasure to visit.

At least, that was the story until the late 1980s. Since then a number of pressures have been threatening to undermine the fabric of this unique Swahili settlement. The most important is tourism. In the high season several hundred tourists visit Lamu every day, either by air or overland by bus and launch, and Kenyan Airways is reportedly planning to introduce a DC-9 jet on the route. One of the spin-offs of this influx is that many of the houses at Shela have been bought up by foreigners. As a result, local newspapers (particularly *Mvita*, published in Mombasa) have begun running scare articles with headlines such as 'Lamu Under Siege', and suggesting that tourism is gradually destroying the culture and even physical fabric of Lamu. It's a moot point but neither entirely right or wrong.

The other major pressure is population increase. It's expected that the town's current population of some 12,000 will increase to 30,000 by the end of the century. To accommodate and provide services for all those extra people is going to take some very sensitive planning.

Tourism certainly distorts centuries-old cultural values and economic patterns and can even destroy them but Lamu urgently needs an injection of cash for preservation, restoration, creation of employment, schools and for a cleanup – particularly of the open drainage system. Tourism could be the source of that cash and, to a large extent, is already. And it's hardly fair to blame tourism for corrugated iron replacing traditional wall and roofing materials. Most tourists would much prefer to see traditional materials used.

There was also a spate of overzealousness by the police where local young men seen in the company of *wazungu* (White people) were arrested and accused of illegal currency dealings, selling drugs or some other trumped-up charge. Appeals on their behalf apparently fell on deaf ears and cast a shadow over relationships between residents and visitors. This sort of harassment appears now to have stopped.

What perhaps poses the biggest threat to Lamu – if the rumour is true (and officials are very tight-lipped about this) – is the construction of a US military base on neighbouring Manda Island. Dredgers were already at work in late 1989 in the channel separating the two islands but it wasn't for the benefit of Lamu's tiny harbour since the dredgers were far too close to Manda. Let's all hope it is just a rumour and the dredging was for some other purpose.

History

The 20th century may have brought Lamu a measure of peace and tranquillity but it has not always been that way. The town was only of minor importance in the string of Swahili settlements which stretched from Somalia to Mozambique. Although it was a thriving port by the early 1500s, it surrendered without a fight to the early Portuguese mariners and was generally politically dependent on the more important Sultanate of Paté which, at the time, was the most important island port in the archipelago. It did manage to avoid, until the late 1700s, the frequent wars between the sultanates of Paté, Mombasa and Malindi following the decline of Portuguese influence in the area.

After that there followed many years of internecine strife between the various island city-states of Lamu, Paté, Faza and Siyu, which only ended in 1813 when Lamu defeated the forces of Paté in a battle at Shela. Shortly afterwards Lamu became subject to the Sultanate of Zanzibar which nominally controlled the whole of the coastal strip from Kilwa to the Somali border (under a British Protectorate from 1890) until Kenya became independent in 1963.

In common with all the other Swahili coastal city-states, Lamu had a slave-based economy until the turn of the 20th century when the British forced the Sultan of Zanzibar to sign an antislaving agreement and subsequently intercepted dhows carrying slaves north from that island. All that cheap labour fuelled a period of economic growth for Lamu and traders grew rich by exporting ivory, cowries, tortoiseshell, mangrove poles, oil seeds and grains, and importing oriental linen, silks, spices and porcelain. When it came to an end in 1907 with the abolition of slavery, the economy of the island rapidly went into decline and stayed that way until very recently when increased receipts from tourism gave it a new lease of life. That decline, and its strong sense of tradition, is what has preserved the Lamu you see today. No other Swahili town, other than Zanzibar, can offer you such a cultural feast and an undisturbed traditional style of architecture.

Information & Orientation

Tourist Office The office is on the waterfront next to the Standard Chartered Bank and staffed by enthusiastic people but it's of limited use. They don't even know the schedules of the ferries to the outlying islands. The office also purports to offer a railway and air ticket booking service for KSh 30 and KSh 40 respectively but save your money because there'll be no ticket waiting for you on arrival. I learnt this from personal experience at Mombasa railway station.

Bank The Standard Chartered Bank on the harbour front is the only bank in Lamu. It's open Monday to Friday from 8.30 am to 1 pm and Saturday from 8.30 to 11 am. In the low season, cashing a cheque can take as little as half an hour but in the high season it can take considerably longer. Get there early.

Books There are some excellent books about Lamu and the Swahili civilisation if you are interested in digging deeper into this fascinating period of East African history and culture. The best general account is *The Portuguese Period in East Africa* by Justus Strandes (East African Literature Bureau, Nairobi, 1971). This is a translation of a book originally published in German in 1899 with up-to-date notes and appendices detailing recent archaeological findings, some of which contradict Strandes' opinions. It's very readable.

Lamu: A Study of the Swahili Town by Usam Ghaidan (East African Literature Bureau, Nairobi, 1975), is a very detailed study of Lamu by an Iraqi who was formerly a Lecturer in Architecture at the University of Nairobi and has since devoted his time to research into the Swahili architecture of the north Kenyan coast. You can find both of the above books in most good bookshops in

To Malindi

Swamp

Mokowe

Swamp

Manda
Ruins

Airstrip

Swamp

Manda Island

Matondoni

Lamu

Lamu Island

Takwa
Ruins

Shela

Pepani's
Hotel

Ras Kitau
Hotel

Shela Beach

Coral Reef

Around Lamu Island

0   2.5   5 km

Nairobi or Mombasa and the latter at the museum in Lamu.

If you're going to stay long in Lamu the leaflet-map *Lamu: Map & Guide to the Archipelago, the Island & the Town* is worth buying at the museum bookshop.

Bookshops Apart from the museum, the Lamu Book Centre, next door to the Garissa Express office, has a small but reasonable selection of English-language novels and other books. It's also the only place where you can buy local newspapers and international news magazines (*Time, Newsweek,*

etc). It's open from 6.30 am to 12.30 pm and 2.30 to 9 pm.

Dhow Trips See the Islands Around Lamu section later in this chapter for details about dhow trips.

Lamu Town
The town dates back to at least the late 14th century when the Pwani Mosque was built. Most buildings date from the 18th century, but the lower parts and basements are often considerably older. The streets are narrow,

cool and quiet and there are many small courtyards and intimate spaces enclosed by high walls. Traditionally, buildings were constructed entirely out of local materials – faced coral-rag blocks for the walls, wooden floors supported by mangrove poles, makuti roofs and intricately carved shutters for windows. This is changing gradually with the increasing use of imported materials and is one of the factors of great concern to conservationists.

One of the most outstanding features of the houses here, as in old Zanzibar, is the intricately carved doors and lintels which have kept generations of carpenters busy. Sadly, many of them have disappeared in recent years but the skill has not been lost. Walk down to the far end of the harbour front in the opposite direction to Shela and you'll see them being made.

Only a few of the mosques have minarets and even these are small affairs. This, combined with the fact that there's little outward decoration and few doors and windows opening onto the street, make them hard to distinguish from domestic buildings.

There is pressure from private developers for permission to build modern hotels on the island but, so far, this has been blocked by the National Museums of Kenya. Nevertheless, you will come across the occasional modern building on the outskirts of town which sticks out like a sore thumb.

Lamu Museum
A couple of hours spent in the Lamu Museum, on the waterfront next to Petley's Inn, is an excellent introduction to the culture and history of Lamu. It's one of the most interesting small museums in Kenya. There's a reconstruction of a traditional Swahili house, charts, maps, ethnological displays, models of the various types of dhow and two examples of the remarkable and ornately carved ivory *siwa* – a wind instrument peculiar to the coastal region which is often used as a fanfare at weddings. There's a good slide show available at the museum – ask to see it. Entry costs KSh 30 (KSh 10 for residents)

and the museum is open daily from 8 am to 6 pm.

The museum has a good bookshop specialising in books on Lamu and the Swahili culture.

Swahili House Museum
If the museum stokes your interest in Swahili culture then you should also visit this museum tucked away off to the side of Yumbe House (a hotel). It's a beautifully restored traditional house with furniture and other house wares as well as a pleasant courtyard. Entry costs KSh 30 (KSh 10 for residents) and it's open at the same times as the main museum.

Lamu Fort
The building of this massive structure was begun by the Sultan Paté in 1810 and completed in 1823. From 1910 right up to 1984 it was used as a prison. There are now ambitious plans to convert it into an aquarium, maritime history and natural history museum with a restaurant and other amenities. Progress has been slow but is going ahead. At the time of writing it was closed to the public.

Dhow Building & Repairing
You'll see many dhows anchored in the harbour at the southern end of town but if you want to see them being built or repaired you can do this at Shela or Matondoni villages. The latter is perhaps the best place to see this and you have a choice of walking there (about two hours), hiring a donkey, or hiring a dhow and sailing there. If you choose the dhow it will cost about KSh 240 for the boat (so you need a small group together to share the cost) but it usually includes a barbecued fish lunch.

To walk there, leave the main street of Lamu up the alleyway by the side of Kenya Cold Drinks and continue in as straight a line as possible to the back end of town. From here a well defined track leads out into the country. You pass a football pitch on the right-hand side after 100 metres. Follow the touch line of the pitch and continue in the same direction past the paddock/garden on the left-hand side and then turn left onto another track. This is the one to Matondoni. The football pitch has telephone wires running above it. These go to Matondoni and they're almost always visible from the track so if you follow them you can't go wrong. If you don't cut across the football pitch you'll head off into the middle of nowhere and probably get lost – although this can be interesting (old houses, wells, goats, etc).

Set off early if you are walking. It gets very hot later on in the day. There's a small café in the village where you can get fish and rice for around KSh 18 as well as fruit juice. There are no guest houses in the village but a bed or floor space can usually be arranged in a private house if you ask around. An impromptu group of travellers generally collects later in the afternoon so you can all share a ride in a dhow back to Lamu.

One traveller also recommended a visit to Kipongani village where local people make straw mats, baskets and hats. It's a friendly place and tea and snacks can be arranged plus there's a beautiful empty beach nearby with waves.

Donkey Sanctuary

One of the most unexpected sights on Lamu is the Donkey Sanctuary which is run by the International Donkey Protection Trust of Sidmouth, Devon, UK. Injured, sick or worn-out donkeys are brought here to find rest and protection. As in most societies where they're used as beasts of burden, donkeys are regularly abused or get injured so it's good to see something positive being done for their welfare. The sanctuary is right on the waterfront.

Shela Village & The Beach

The most popular beach is just past Shela village, a 40 minute walk from Lamu. To get there, follow the harbour-front road till it ends and then follow the shore line. You will pass the new hospital built by the Saudi Arabian government and a ginning factory before you get to Shela. If the tide is out, you can walk along the beach most of the way. When it's in, you may well have to do a

considerable amount of wading up to your thighs and deeper. If that doesn't appeal, there is a track all the way from Lamu to Shela but there are many turn-offs so stay with the ones which run closest to the shore (you may find yourself in a few cul-de-sacs doing this as a number of turn-offs to the left run to private houses and end there).

A popular alternative to walking there is to take a dhow. This should cost KSh 12 per person. There's also a motor boat operated by Peponi's Hotel which costs KSh 70 shared between however many of you there are.

The best part of the beach if you want waves is well past Peponi's Hotel – there's no surf at Peponi's because you're still in the channel between Lamu and Manda islands. There was a spate of robberies and a couple of rapes way out along this beach several years ago but there's been no repeat of that following a big police crackdown at the time, so it's probably safe to go as far along the beach as you like. It's possible to hire wind surfing equipment at Peponi's.

Shela itself is a very pleasant little village and well worth a wander around. The ancestors of the people here came from Takwa when that settlement was abandoned in the late 17th century and they still speak a dialect of Swahili which is distinct from that of Lamu. Many have migrated to Malindi in recent years. Don't miss the famous mosque with its characteristic minaret at the back of Peponi's. Many of the houses in this village have been bought up and restored by foreigners in the last few years so it has a surprising air of affluence about it yet the languorous atmosphere remains unspoiled. Quite a few travellers prefer to stay in Shela rather than in Lamu town.

Places to Stay – bottom end

Lamu has been catering for budget travellers for well over a decade but, in the last few years, budget hotels have mushroomed to cater for the hordes of travellers who come to stay here. As a result, there's a bewildering choice of simple, rustic lodges, rooftops and whole houses to rent. Don't believe a word anyone tells you about there being running water 24 hours a day at any of these places. There often isn't. Water is not an abundant commodity on Lamu and restrictions are in force most of the year. It's usually only available early in the morning and early in the evening which, in most cases, means bucket showers only and somewhat smelly toilets.

Prices are remarkably consistent because there's a lot of competition though you obviously get what you pay for both in terms of facilities and position. A dormitory bed or space on the floor of a rooftop would be around KSh 60, a single room between KSh 95 and KSh 120, and a double room KSh 120 to KSh 240. Almost all of these would involve sharing bathroom facilities but some of the higher priced doubles might have their own bathroom. Prices rise in the high season (August-September) by a factor of up to 50%.

If a lodge is full when you arrive but you like it a lot and want to be first in line for a room, they'll usually let you sleep on the roof or elsewhere until the following morning.

Where you stay initially will probably depend largely on what sort of room you are offered, what's available and who meets you getting off the ferry from the mainland. Most of the young men who meet the ferries have no connection with any of the lodges other than the hope of a tip (from travellers) or a small commission (from the hotel management). Some of them can be very insistent. Those who board the ferry from the airstrip on Manda Island for the trip across the channel are very insistent indeed and incredibly difficult to shake off.

If you plan on staying in Lamu for a while it's worth making enquiries about renting a house, so long as there's a group of you to share the cost. On a daily basis it won't be much cheaper (if at all) than staying at a lodge but on a monthly basis you're looking at a considerable saving. You can share them with as many people as you feel comfortable with or have space for and prices usually include a houseboy. Some of the simpler houses can be very cheap indeed and include a refrigerator and cooking facilities. They're

available in Lamu town itself but also at Shela and between Lamu and Shela. Some of them can be excellent value and very spacious. You need to ask around and see what is available. It's possible to find some remarkably luxurious places especially around Shela.

Lamu Town It's virtually impossible to arrange budget hotels in any order of preference since there are so many and conditions and facilities vary so much. This selection has been done on the basis of the cheapest available beds or rooms but implies no preference – hotel owners please note!

On the waterfront, close to the jetty, is the *New Shamuty Lodge* which is friendly, relaxed and has a large rooftop with mattresses and chairs. Doubles cost KSh 50 with shared bathroom facilities. Also on the waterfront at the far end of town is the *Kisiwani Lodge* which has singles/doubles for KSh 60/95 in the low season and KSh 120/145 in the high season, all with shared bathroom facilities. It's very basic, there's no toilet paper and the sheets have been described as 'near rags' but it's a popular place to stay. High season prices are a rip-off. Attached to the lodge is the Lick 'n Smile Restaurant which is equally basic and has a very limited range of food. We have had many complaints from travellers who have stayed at this hotel about theft and the lack of cooperation from the owner, Ali Banana.

On the first street parallel to the waterfront is the *Kenya Lodge* which is equally basic and costs KSh 50 a single. It's fairly clean and has mosquito nets and cold bucket showers. Next to the fort is the *New Castle Lodge* which overlooks the main square and picks up sea breezes since it's fairly high up. It has a rooftop dormitory for KSh 50 per bed and doubles at KSh 180 with shared bathroom facilities. There's an amusing notice in the reception which lets you know that 'Drugs and spirits are prohibited. Prostitutes, beach boys and homosexuals are not allowed in your rooms. Hotel nakedness and public exposure of yourselves is not permitted on the roof terrace. Love and fun affairs with the staff of this hotel is not allowed'!

Also in this range is the *Saiga Lodge* which is very basic but friendly and has rooms for KSh 60 on the roof, and the *Rainbow Guest House* at the back of the Dhow Lodge which has doubles for KSh 95.

Kadara's Lodge, at the Shela end of town, is airy and pleasant with a courtyard and has doubles with shared bathroom facilities for KSh 85. Doubles with private bathroom and sea views cost KSh 120. Close to the post office is the *Dhow Lodge* which only has a few rooms, some of them scruffy, others reasonable. The rooms are high and airy with string beds and thin mattresses. Doubles/triples with shared bathroom cost KSh 120/180. The lodge has its own well.

The *Salama Guest House* at the other end of town is very popular and well run and, as a result, often full. The downstairs rooms cost KSh 120/180 for doubles/triples with shared bathroom and the upstairs rooms cost KSh 85/180/240 for singles/doubles/triples with own bathroom. There are also rooms with four beds for KSh 300. Discounts of 20% are available if you stay more than just a few days. It's worth trying to get in here.

Behind this area is the equally popular *Jambo Guest House* though it only has four double rooms at KSh 240 (negotiable if you stay for a week) including breakfast. Fans and mosquito nets are provided and there's use of a refrigerator and gas stove. There's also a large rooftop area. The *Lala Salama Guest House* is similar and has doubles with shared bathroom for KSh 180. Right opposite the Jambo Guest House is the similarly priced *Karibuni Guest House.*

The *Sanaa Guest House* is a very pleasant little place which offers doubles with bathroom for KSh 240 and a choice of double beds or two single beds. They're not keen on alcoholic beverages here as the notice, 'No Beer', implies.

Very good value, clean and simple, is the *Lamu Guest House* at the back of the Lamu Museum. There's a choice of different rooms here but the best are probably those on the top floor which cost KSh 180 for a double

and a bathroom shared with one other room. There are no fans but the sea breezes and sea views adequately compensate for this. Lower down there are doubles with bathroom and fan for KSh 360 and smaller doubles with the same facilities for KSh 240. All the rooms can be occupied singly for about two-thirds of the above prices.

Back on the waterfront and close to the jetty is the popular *Full Moon Guest House* which is very friendly and has an excellent 1st floor balcony but only has four rooms. It costs KSh 215 for either a double or a single with shared bathroom facilities. It does have a lot of charm but the doubles are perhaps not worth the price whereas the triple room is. If you're staying for a week or more then the price is KSh 155.

Right out at the back of town (10 minutes walk) is the *Peace Guest House* which is clean, provides mosquito nets and morning tea and costs KSh 85 for a dormitory bed and KSh 180 to KSh 360 for a double. It's a wooden building surrounded by gardens. You can also camp here for KSh 50. Facilities include two showers and access to the kitchen. This place has been highly recommended by everyone who has stayed there. If you're heading there, enquire first at the Jambo Café close to the Yoghurt Inn on the street parallel to the waterfront.

Another place well worth considering if there's a group of you is the *Shuweri Guest House* just below the Swahili House Museum. You may need to ask where it is as it only has a tiny sign. You're looking at a whole house here, albeit small, with six beds in one large room (partially divided into two), an upstairs, open-air, makuti-roofed 'lounge', refrigerator, cooking facilities and a very helpful houseboy. It's a bargain at KSh 360 if staying long term.

The *Bahati Lodge*, off to the right of the fort as you face it, has an excellent position with the top rooms overlooking the harbour and catching the sea breezes but it's very primitive. That doesn't seem to stop people staying here if they can get one of the bedrooms on the top floor but the rooms on the ground floor are Dickensian and a rip-off.

Lamu

To Matondoni

Fort

Jetty

Dhow
Moorings

To Shela
Beach

0   50   100 m.

Singles/doubles/triples cost KSh 90/145/215 with shared bathroom facilities. Mosquito nets are provided.

More expensive but right on the waterfront is the *Casuarina Rest House* which was formerly the police headquarters. It offers large, airy rooms with good views and it's clean, well maintained and scrubbed down daily. It's excellent value at KSh 300 to KSh 360 a double depending on how long you intend to stay. There's access to a large flat roof area.

The Kisiwani Lodge also appears to be moving into the whole-house rental business. They're setting up the *Sanctuary Guest House* which will cost KSh 2400 per day for a house with three self-contained suites, two other suites with one double room each and a further suite with two double bedrooms. Facilities include a garden, refrigerator,

kitchen and rooftop area. That's a good deal if you're a large group.

Similar is *Suli Suli House* next to the Pole Pole Guest House. Those who have stayed there describe this place as 'an amazing eight bedroom house with courtyard'. It's very clean and the caretaker, Tabu, is an excellent cook. Rates vary from KSh 360 to KSh 720 depending on how long you intend to stay.

My good friend and fellow globetrotter, Tony Wheeler, who spent some time in Lamu during 1989 along with his wife Maureen and their two kids, recommended the *Mlangilangi House*, behind the fort. It's a very pleasant old house and has rooms for KSh 240 plus use of kitchen facilities. He also recommended the *Pool House* near the Swahili House Museum – so called because it has a swimming pool – which has four double rooms around the pool all with bathrooms and mosquito nets for KSh 300 (less if staying a few nights).

Finally, but also top of the range in this section, are the *Mtamwini Guest House*, which offers singles/doubles for KSh 240/360 with bathroom, and *Dudu's Guest House*, up behind the fort, which is a beautiful old house with terrace offering large rooms with fan, mosquito nets, bathrooms and use of kitchen for KSh 360.

Shela Quite a few travellers, especially beach lovers, prefer to stay at Shela village rather than in Lamu itself.

If you're going to stay here for a while – and it seems most of the people who stay here do – then it's best to ask around for a house to rent and have a small group together to share the cost. Many of the houses here are owned by expatriate foreigners (especially Italians) who have poured vast amounts of money into them but only live here for part of the year. Most of them have been very sensitively upgraded and some are stunning. Quite a lot of them can be rented out so talk to the caretakers.

In the meantime, stay at the *Samahane Guest House* (tel 3100) which has double rooms with twin beds, table and chair and shared bathrooms for KSh 240. It's simple, clean and catches the sea breezes.

Cheap, simple rooms with no frills and shared bathroom facilities can also be found at the *Stop Over Restaurant* right on the beach.

The other former guest house – the *Shela Rest House* – was being converted into self-contained apartments at the end of 1989 and is destined to become a mid to top-end hotel.

Other places worth trying here are *Akasimani House*, close to the Samahane, and *Giovanna's House*. The latter costs KSh 1200 per night but sleeps four people on two floors and has a garden, kitchen and pergola. Ask for Omari, the caretaker, if you want to rent it.

Places to Stay – middle

The most beautiful place by far to stay in this range is *Yumbe House* (tel (0121) 3101, PO Box 81, Lamu), adjacent to the Swahili House Museum. If any hotel exposes the lie about 'tourism eating into the fabric of Lamu' this is it! Here is a four storey traditional house surrounding a central courtyard which has been superbly and sensitively converted into a hotel with airy terraces and makuti roofs. All rooms are self-contained, it's spotlessly clean, towels and soap are provided and there are mosquito nets. It's excellent value at KSh 430/650 for singles/doubles including breakfast. It's simply the best!

Also very good but nowhere near as attractive is *Hal-Udy Guest House* which has four self-contained suites (bedroom and sitting room plus terrace) with refrigerators and cooking facilities for KSh 300/480 a single/double in the low season and KSh 480/720 in the high season (less if you stay for a week or longer). Mosquito nets are provided and there's a houseboy. It's very popular with slightly older couples with children who prefer to do their own cooking (or, at least, some of it).

Far less attractive than the above two and nowhere near the same value is the *New Mahrus Hotel* (tel 3001, PO Box 25, Lamu), adjacent to the square in front of the fort. This hotel has been going for years and is long overdue for a complete rehabilitation – many of the rooms are no better than anything you'd find at a third of the price. It would also benefit if half the staff were sacked tomorrow and replaced by new blood. The level of indifference here is staggering. I can't recommend it but die-hards do stay here. The worst rooms ('3rd class') cost KSh 205/360 a single/double. Better rooms ('2nd class') cost KSh 300/480 and the best rooms ('1st class') cost KSh 480/600. All prices include breakfast.

Other mid-range hotels which are worth checking out if the Yumbe and Hal-Udy are full are the *Darini Guest House* (KSh 480 for an apartment including breakfast) and *Jannat House* (KSh 480 per room – five rooms in total).

Places to Stay – top end

Lamu Town The only top-range hotel in Lamu itself is *Petley's Inn* (tel 48, PO Box 4, Lamu) right on the harbour front next to the Lamu Museum. It was originally set up in the late 19th century by Percy Petley – a somewhat eccentric English colonist who ran plantations on the mainland at Witu until he retired to Lamu. It has been renovated since then, of course, but in traditional style with the addition of a swimming pool, (occasional) disco and two restaurants (neither of which are anything special). It also has the only hotel bar in Lamu (there are two other non-hotel bars).

Full board at Petley's is KSh 2040/2760 for singles/doubles or KSh 2280/3000 for a sea-facing room with private shower and balcony. Half board rates are KSh 1800/2400 for singles/doubles or KSh 1920/2640 for a sea-facing room. Children between the ages of three and 12 pay 50%.

Shela At the far end of Shela village and right on the beach is *Peponi's Hotel* (tel 29, PO Box 24, Lamu) which is *the* place to stay if you want a top-range hotel on Lamu. It consists of self-contained, whitewashed cottages with their own verandahs facing the channel between Lamu and Manda islands and is reckoned to be one of the best hotels in the world, both in terms of its position and the quality of the cuisine. It's run by young Danish people and up-market informality is the name of the game here. The rates for full board are KSh 3460/4655 a single/double. Children sharing the same accommodation are charged KSh 530 (one to three years), KSh 1060 (four to 10 years) and KSh 1875 (over 10 years). The hotel has its own restaurant (residents only) plus a grill and bar which are open to both residents and nonresidents. There's a full range of water sports facilities. Advance booking is essential and the hotel is closed during May and June.

Diagonally opposite Peponi's, across the channel on Manda Island, is another top-range hotel, the *Ras Kitau Hotel* – or at least it used to be top range. Recent reports indicate that it has gone downhill rapidly and that there are management disputes which have yet to be resolved. It's been impossible to ascertain current rates.

Places to Eat – cheap

One of the cheapest places to eat in Lamu is the *New Star Restaurant*. You certainly won't beat the prices and some people recommend it highly, but others visit once and never return. Service is certainly slow (depending on what you order and the time of day) and the menu is often an unbridled act of creativity. I thought the food was average but nothing special. They also have good yoghurt. Similar in price is the *Sabrina Restaurant* which serves mainly Indian food for main courses and Western breakfasts but they do offer very reasonably priced lobster, prawn and crab dishes. Again, the food is only average. For standard African fare, the *Jambo Café* just before the Yoghurt Inn has become popular of late. It's used a lot by local people so guaranteed to be cheap.

For consistently reliable good food at a reasonable price there are four very popular restaurants. The first is the *Sindbad Restaurant* on the waterfront overlooking the dhow moorings. Here you can get pancakes with various fillings, grilled fish and salad for KSh 30 or a full lunch or dinner of soup, main course and fruit juice for KSh 55.

The *Yoghurt Inn* has also been popular for years and has an attractive garden with individual outside tables each with a grass roof. It offers banana pancakes with honey for just KSh 12, grilled fish for KSh 45, crab for KSh 50, yoghurt for KSh 5.50 and lassi for KSh 16. There are also daily 'specials' such as crab with avocado salad for KSh 85. The food is generally very good and well presented but they brew up foul tea. It's open daily from 7 am to 9.30 pm except on Fridays when it's open from 7 am to noon and 4 to 9.30 pm.

Somewhat more expensive but very popular is *Bush Gardens* on the waterfront, next door to the Hapahapa Restaurant. It's run by the very personable and energetic

'Bush Baby' who personally supervises the cooking which sometimes makes for slow service but guarantees you an excellent meal. Fish dishes (barracuda, tuna, snapper or shark) cost KSh 50 to KSh 60, crab KSh 95, prawns KSh 115 and lobster KSh 130, all served with chips or coconut rice and salad. Fruit juices are also available. While it stays open all day, you can only get a meal here at lunch time or dinner time as, in the afternoon, 'Bush Baby' is out catching the fish. It's arguably the best seafood restaurant in Lamu.

Next door is the *Hapahapa Restaurant* which is also very good and offers a similar range of dishes, including seafood and possibly the best fruit juices and milkshakes in town (KSh 12 for half a pint and KSh 18 for a full pint). Prices are similar to those at Bush Gardens.

Most travellers come across a man popularly called 'Ali Hippy' who, for several years now, has been offering travellers meals at his house for between KSh 95 and KSh 120. The meal usually includes lobster, crab, fish, coconut rice and vegetable stew and the whole family entertains you while you eat. Most people come away quite satisfied (it's definitely an unusual evening out) but others have complained that KSh 120 is a lot to pay for heaps of rice and very little fish or that the meal is rushed and there's no time to relax, so it appears that what he lays on varies a lot.

At Shela, the *Stop Over Restaurant* right on the beach is a popular place to eat or drink and prices are very reasonable though they only offer simple meals.

Places to Eat – more expensive

For a splurge there are several places you can try. Probably the best for a night out is the *Equator Restaurant* which is open from 12 to 2 pm and 6 to 9 pm. The atmosphere here is very relaxing (classical music and oldies) and many people rate it as the best restaurant in Lamu though they tend to overcook the lobster. At the bottom of the range you can get a meal for KSh 65 to KSh 80 plus they have crab (very popular) for KSh 95, a three-course dinner with pineapple steak for KSh 110 and lobster for KSh 155. It's a good place but it's *very* popular so book a table in advance if possible. It can be more expensive than Ghai's but it's well worth the little extra.

Equally popular is *Ghai's*, on the waterfront next to the donkey sanctuary. Ghai may be somewhat eccentric but he considers himself to be the best seafood cook on the island. This is usually the case but not always – a friend who ate there recently described the meal he got in these terms: 'fish curry and grilled whole fish both mediocre, fish tough and flavourless, rice blah, salad poor'. Prices are almost identical to those at the Equator.

A meal at *Petley's Inn* – either in the restaurant itself or in the adjacent barbecue garden – also used to be a popular splurge but these days the food is only mediocre and you'll see very few people eating here. Most meals are priced between KSh 180 and KSh 210 and there's nothing under KSh 120. The ice cream, on the other hand, is very good.

The rooftop restaurant at the *New Mahrus Hotel* touts itself as a classy restaurant but the food is only average and the hygiene suspect.

For a splurge at Shela the *Barbecue Grill* at Peponi's offers delicious food and is open to nonresidents. There's a choice of both barbecued fish and meat and a superb range of salads. Expect to pay around KSh 80 to KSh 90 for a meal.

Places to Drink

Fruit Juices Two of the best places for fruit juices are the *Sindbad Restaurant*, on the waterfront, and the *Hapahapa Restaurant*.

Kenya Cold Drinks used to be another very popular place for fruit juices but a lot of travellers have complained recently of watered-down juices and the fact that they're often out of most of the things on the menu. There were certainly not many people in there every time I passed it.

Beer & Spirits There are three places where you can get a beer in Lamu itself but only one which has cold beers. This is the bar at *Petley's Inn* which is an English-style pub,

Top: Mosque, Lamu (GP)
Bottom Left: Lamu street (GP)
Bottom Right: Lamu market (TW)

Top: Waterfront street, Lamu (GC)
Bottom: Waterfront, Lamu (GP)

the entrance to which is in the alley between the hotel and the barbecue garden opposite. It's the most popular watering hole on the island and is open to nonresidents. The only trouble with this bar is that the beer is always 'running out' – usually by 8 pm but sometimes even earlier – and after that they'll only sell you spirits. The beer doesn't actually 'run out' at all – it's just the hotel's way of making it plain that you're not staying there. The bar is open at lunch times from 12 to around 2 pm and in the evening from 5 pm to around 9.30 pm (though it often closes earlier).

One bar which never 'runs out' of beer is that at the *Police Club* but they are always warm so you have to be slightly desperate to drink here. It's open in the evenings until fairly late and you don't have to be in the police to get in. Ask directions when you get to the Garissa Express bus office.

There's another bar at the *Civil Servants' Club* which has a disco on Friday and Saturday nights. Entry costs KSh 20 and it's a good night out.

Out at Shela, *Peponi's* is a mandatory watering hole and the beers here are always ice-cold and never 'run out'. The bar is on the verandah overlooking the channel and beach. It's open all day until late at night.

Getting There & Away

Air Four companies operate flights to Lamu from Mombasa and Malindi. They are Eagle Aviation Ltd (tel Mombasa 316054, Malindi 21258, Lamu 3119), Prestige Air Services Ltd (tel Mombasa 21443, Malindi 20860/1), Skyways Airlines (tel Mombasa 432167, Malindi 21260, Lamu 3226) and Equator Airlines (tel Malindi 2053).

They all have two flights per day in either direction between Mombasa and Lamu and Malindi and Lamu. Flights from Mombasa depart at 8.30 am and 2.15 pm and arrive in Lamu an hour and 10 minutes later. From Malindi they depart at 9 am and 3 pm and arrive 40 minutes later. In the opposite direction, they depart Lamu at 10 am and 4 pm for both Mombasa and Malindi. The fares are KSh 1680 (Mombasa-Lamu) and KSh 1020

(Malindi-Lamu) one way. Return fares are double. Children over two years old pay full fare. Check-in time is 30 minutes before departure and the baggage allowance is 10 kg per person. Most of the time they don't hassle if your baggage is over 10 kg but, even if they do, excess charges are minimal. The airport departure tax is KSh 50 at Malindi but there's no charge at Lamu.

The airport at Lamu is on Manda Island and the ferry across the channel to Lamu costs KSh 12. Hotel touts will be waiting for you at the airport and will pursue you all the way. They're very persistent and hard to shake off.

Bus Three bus companies operate between Mombasa, Malindi and Lamu on a daily basis. They are Malindi Bus Service, Tana River Bus Service and Garissa Express and they all have offices in Mombasa, Malindi and Lamu. The fare from Malindi to Lamu is KSh 120 and the journey takes about five hours. Buses leave in either direction at 7 or 8 am depending on the company. The buses from Mombasa to Lamu arrive in Malindi around 8.30 am and leave around 9.30 am so there's a choice of departure times from Malindi if seats are available. It's wise to book in advance as there's heavy demand for tickets. Garissa Express also operate a daily service between Garissa and Lamu which costs KSh 180 and takes eight to 10 hours.

The buses terminate at the ferry jetty on the mainland not far from Mokowe. From here you take a motorised ferry to Lamu which costs KSh 12.

Dhow Other than trips around the Lamu archipelago, you can also find dhows sailing to Mombasa. The journey takes two days on average and prices are negotiable. Before you set off you need to get permission from the District Commissioner. His office is on the harbour front close to the post office and opposite the main quay. It's best if you can persuade the captain of the dhow to take you along here and guide you through the formalities. It shouldn't take more than 1½ hours in that case. Usually they will do this without charging you money but be prepared to pay if the captain is unwilling.

Getting Around

Boat There are frequent ferries between Lamu and the bus terminus on the mainland (near Mokowe). The fare is KSh 6. Ferries between the airstrip on Manda Island and Lamu cost KSh 12.

There are also regular ferries between Lamu and Paté Island – see below for details.

Islands Around Lamu

A popular activity while you're in Lamu is to take a dhow trip to one of the neighbouring islands. You need a small group (six to eight people) to share costs if you're going to do this but it's very easy to put a group like that together in Lamu. Just ask around in the restaurants or budget hotels.

Since taking tourists around the archipelago is one of the easiest ways of making money for dhow owners in Lamu, there's a lot of competition and you'll be asked constantly by different people if you want to go on a trip. You'll also see many notices advertising trips in the restaurants. Negotiation over the price and what is included in it is essential both to avoid misunderstandings and being overcharged. The price of day trips is usually settled quickly because a lot of travellers will have been on them and the cost will be well known.

Dhow trips are usually superb whoever you go with so it's unfair to recommend any particular dhow or captain but, if you're going on a long trip – say, three days – then it's a very good idea to check out both the dhow and the crew before committing yourself. Don't hand over any money until the day of departure except, perhaps, a float for food for a long trip. Also, on long trips, it's probably best to organise your own beer and soft drink supplies. And remember that the person who touts for your business is often not the captain of the boat but an intermediary who takes a commission for finding you.

Dhows without an outboard motor are naturally entirely dependent on wind to get them anywhere though poling – or even pushing – the boat is fairly common along narrow creeks and channels. If you have to pole the boat or you get becalmed out in the channels between the islands, there's no point in remonstrating with the captain. He's not God and there's nothing he can do about it yet it's surprising how many people imagine otherwise. With that in mind, never go on a long trip if you have a deadline to meet. A three day trip can occasionally turn into five, though not usually.

Likewise, dhows are dependent on the tides. You can't sail up creeks if the tide is out and there's not enough depth of water to float the boat. This will be the main factor determining departure and return times.

To give you some idea of what a longer dhow trip involves, a brief description of the one which I took with five others at the end of 1989 follows:

After discussions with three different middlemen in Lamu about trips to Kiwayu we made our choice and arranged to meet outside the Kisiwani Lodge at 6 am the next morning. The price was fixed at KSh 4000 for a three day trip or around KSh 180 to KSh 200 per person per day including food. Meanwhile we purchased beers and soft drinks from the Kenya Breweries depot and dropped them off at the Kisiwani (the crews will generally do this for you but it will cost more).

Next morning the dhow finally turned up at 7.30 am along with a crew of four and we set off in the direction of the channel between Manda Island and the mainland. Since the wind wasn't in the right direction, the dhow had to tack all the way to the channel by which time it was low tide. There was sufficient water in the channel to keep the boat afloat – but only just – but the wind had dropped completely. There was no alternative but to pole and push the dhow all the way to the end of the channel and naturally we all lent a hand. It took hours.

Once out in the open sea again, the wind picked up and we were able to get close to Paté Island but then again the wind dropped and the clouds burst. It looked very much like we and all our gear were about to get a soaking so it was with considerable relief that we discovered the crew had brought along an enormous sheet of plastic.

After the storm, the wind picked up again and we reached Mtangawanda by about 3.30 pm where we got off the boat and had a late lunch cooked by the crew. Despite only having one charcoal burner, they did an excellent job of this and the food was delicious.

We set off again about 4.30 pm and headed for Faza with a stiff side wind which enabled us to make good progress for the next two hours. After that it died completely and darkness fell. By 10 pm, it was obvious we were going nowhere that night so the anchor was dropped and a meal prepared (by torch light!). By now we were all getting to know each other very well and there was a good rapport between crew and passengers. The tranquillity and beauty of a becalmed night at sea added immensely to this. After the meal, we all bedded down as best we could for a night of 14th century discomfort.

By first light we discovered that seepage through the hull of the boat had brought the water level to well above the toe-boards so it was all hands on deck and bail out with anything to hand. Shortly after this, the wind picked up and we sped our way across the channel between Paté Island and Kiwayu, arriving about 11 am off the tip of the island. At this point, all the passengers and one of the crew got off the dhow and went snorkelling among the reefs on the eastern side. The dhow, meanwhile, sailed on to Kiwayu village.

We caught up with the dhow again around 3 pm after walking along the beach and climbing over the ridge. Lunch was prepared by the crew (again delicious) and we settled down to an afternoon and evening of relaxation – sunbathing, fishing and exploring the village. Those with tents camped on the beach and the others took a banda at the camp site.

Next morning brought heavy rain but by 11 am we were on our way back to Lamu with a strong tail wind and making excellent progress. Just off Faza, however, the wind died again and the captain (rightly) predicted there'd be no more that day so it was Faza for the night at his family's house. But it wasn't that simple getting off the boat! The tide was out and we couldn't sail up the creek to the town. It didn't look like a particularly feasible idea from the relative 'comfort' of the boat but, after some persuasion, we all jumped overboard with our packs on our heads and headed for the shore in thigh-deep water. There were no mishaps but a lot of jokes and laughter. Half an hour later we reached Faza.

The dhow was brought up at high tide and we were given three bedrooms to share at the family house. That evening a superb meal was prepared for us by the captain's family which we ate in the company of what must have been a good proportion of the town's younger children, all fascinated by this strange collection of wazungu that had turned up in town. Though we did offer, the family refused to take any money for the meal and the accommodation.

After the meal, the captain gave us his prediction about the winds next day – pretty pessimistic – and advised us to take the motor launch back to Lamu. The food was at an end, the last beers had been consumed with the meal that night and so, in the end, we all opted for the motor launch rather than another possible two days and a night back to Lamu. He did, on the other hand, firmly offer to take any or all of us back to Lamu on the dhow if that's what we preferred at no further cost.

All things considered, an excellent trip, superb value, great company, quite an adventure and I'd do it again.

In addition to dhows there are a number of regular motorised ferries which connect Lamu with various towns on the islands.

MANDA ISLAND

This is the easiest of the islands to get to since it's just across the channel from Lamu and almost everyone takes a half-day trip to the Takwa ruins at the head of the creek which almost bisects the island. The average cost of a dhow to this place is around KSh 360 shared by however many people you can put together. Sometimes this includes a barbecued fresh fish lunch but not always so settle this issue before you leave.

The extensive Takwa ruins are what remains of an old Swahili city which flourished between the 15th and 17th centuries and which attained a peak population of some 2500. It was abandoned for reasons unknown when the townspeople moved to Shela. The ruins consist of the remains of about 100 limestone and coral houses, all aligned towards Mecca as well as a mosque and tomb dated 1683 (1094 by the Islamic calendar). The settlement is surrounded by the remains of a wall and huge baobab trees dot the site. It's maintained by the National Museums of Kenya and entry costs KSh 30.

There's a *camp site* adjacent to the ruins for those who wish to stay overnight.

Just off the north-east coast of Manda is Manda Toto Island which offers some of the best snorkelling possibilities in the archipelago. The reefs here are excellent and there are also good beaches. The only way to get here is by dhow.

Getting There & Away

The trip across to Manda takes about 1½

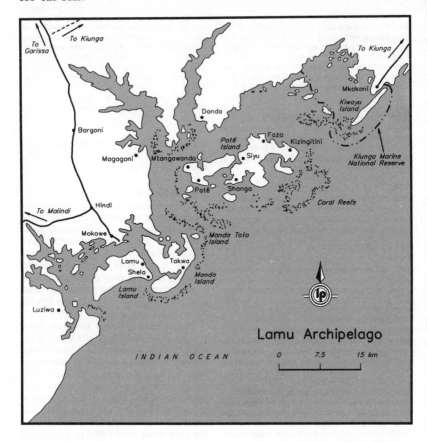

Lamu Archipelago

hours and can only be done at high tide as it's reached by a long mangrove-fringed inlet which is too shallow at low tide. You may well have to wade up the final stretch so wear shorts. Since you have to catch the outgoing tide, your time at the site will probably not be more than 45 minutes.

It's possible to walk to the Takwa ruins from either the airstrip or Ras Kitau but it's quite a long way and the paths are not too clear.

PATÉ ISLAND

There are a number of historical sites on Paté Island including Paté the town, Siyu, Mtangawanda and Faza. All are still inhabited – mainly by fishers and mangrove pole cutters – but very little effort has been put into preserving or clearing the remains of the once powerful Swahili city-states and that's not likely to happen until tourist receipts warrant the expense. Indeed, the only foreigners who come to this island are those on dhow trips and the occasional archaeologist so you can expect to be a novelty and treated with friendly curiosity especially by the children.

Accommodation and food on the island is

easy to arrange with local families. The cost is negotiable but very reasonable. There are no guest houses as such except at Faza but there's generally one or two simple restaurants which offer basic meals like bean or meat stews and tea.

Partly because the island is so low lying, mosquitos are a real pest and you're going to need insect repellent. Mosquito coils are for sale in the island's shops.

Paté

The origins of Paté are disputed. There are claims that it was founded in the 8th century by immigrants from Arabia, but recent excavations have produced nothing earlier than the 13th century when another group of Arabs, the Nabahani, arrived and gradually came to exert considerable influence over the other semiautonomous settlements along the coast.

By the time the Portuguese arrived in the early 16th century, Paté's fortunes were on the decline but were given a shot in the arm by the European mariners' interest in the silk cloth for which the town was famous and the introduction by the Portuguese of gunpowder. A number of Portuguese merchants reputedly settled here but their welcome was relatively short-lived and by the mid-17th century their descendants had withdrawn to Mombasa following a series of uprisings by the Patéans against taxes imposed by the Portuguese authorities.

For the next half century or so, Paté regained some of its former importance and successfully fought off attempts by the Omani Arabs to take it over. Paté's harbour, however, had long been silting up and the city-state was eventually forced into using that of Lamu. The dependency created frequent tensions particularly as Paté claimed sovereignty over Lamu and the two were frequently at war. The final crunch came in 1812 when a Patéan army was soundly defeated at Shela. Thereafter, Paté faded into insignificance and lost all importance after the ruling family were driven out by Seyyid Majid in 1865 and were forced to set up the short-lived Sultanate of Witu on the mainland.

Today, Paté resembles a down-at-heel Lamu. The narrow, winding streets and high-walled houses are there but the streets are earthen and the coral rag walls unplastered. Its one redeeming feature is the Nabahani ruins just outside of town. These are quite extensive and include walls, tombs, mosques and houses. They're worth exploring but they've never been seriously excavated or cleared so it can be difficult to get around because of the tangle of vegetation. In addition, local farmers plant their tobacco crops among the ruins and have demolished substantial sections of the walls.

Getting There & Away There is a motor launch which leaves Lamu for Mtangawanda (about two hours) and Faza (about four hours) three times a week on Monday, Wednesday and Friday (Tuesday, Thursday and Saturday in the opposite direction). The fare is KSh 30.

From Mtangawanda it's about an hour's walk to Paté town along a narrow footpath through thick bush and across tidal flats but you're unlikely to get lost as the path is easy to follow and you'll probably be walking it together with local people who get off the launch.

The launch doesn't always call at Mtangawanda on the return trip from Faza to Lamu, so it's best to walk across to Faza and take it from there, paying a visit to Siyu on the way.

Siyu

Founded in the 15th century, Siyu was famous not for commerce or military opportunism but as a centre of Islamic scholarship and crafts, particularly between the 17th and 19th centuries. In its heyday it boasted some 30,000 inhabitants and was the largest settlement on the island though, today, less than 4000 people live here and there are few signs of its former cultural and religious influence.

Though one of the last upholders of coastal independence, Siyu's demise came in 1847 when it was occupied by the Sultan of

Zanzibar's troops. The huge fort outside town dates from this period and is one of the largest buildings on the island. It's well worth a visit to this fort which, unlike many other Swahili relics, has undergone considerable renovation.

The modern village displays little of Siyu's former glory and consists essentially of a sprawl of simple mud-walled and makuti-roofed houses.

Getting There & Away The mangrove-lined channel leading up to Siyu is too shallow and silted up to allow the passage of anything but the smallest boats and so cannot be reached directly from the sea by dhow or motor launch. The only feasible access is on foot either from Paté or Faza.

From Paté it's about eight km to Siyu along an earth track through the bush. The first part is tricky since there are turn-offs which are easy to miss so it's a good idea to take a guide with you as far as the tidal inlet. From here on it's easy as the path bears left and then continues straight through to Siyu. This last leg should take you about one hour.

Faza

Faza has had a chequered history. It was destroyed by Paté in the 13th century and refounded in the 16th century only to be destroyed again by the Portuguese in 1586 as a result of its collaboration with the Turkish fleet of Amir Ali Bey. It was subsequently rebuilt and switched its allegiances to the Portuguese during their attempts to subdue Paté in the 17th century but declined into insignificance during the 18th and 19th centuries. These days it has regained some of its former importance as a result of being chosen as the district headquarters for Paté Island which includes part of the Kenya mainland to the north.

Faza has very little to offer in the way of interesting ruins. About the only thing there is in the town itself are the remains of the Kunjanja Mosque right on the creek front next to the district headquarters where the ferries anchor. Even so, most of it is just a roofless pile of rubble though there's a beau-

tifully carved mihrab and some fine Arabic inscriptions above the doorway. Outside town is the tomb of Amir Hamad, commander of the Sultan of Zanzibar's forces, who was killed here in 1844 whilst campaigning against Siyu and Paté.

The modern town is quite extensive and includes a post office, telephone exchange, the district headquarters, a simple restaurant, two general stores (including one owned by Bwana Mzee Saad) and two guest houses – *Lamu House* and *Shela House*. These two houses are essentially family residences but they're more than willing to turn over one or more bedrooms for your use and cook you a delicious evening meal if you need somewhere to stay. The price is negotiable but the family is very friendly. The simple *restaurant* mentioned above offers bean stews, tea and mandazi for just a few cents and is a popular meeting place for the men of the town. It's an interesting place to wander around and easy to strike up conversations with just about anyone – men, women or children. Most of the houses here are mud-walled or coral-rag walled with makuti roofs though concrete and corrugated iron have made their appearance too.

Getting There & Away The inlet leading up to Faza from the main channel is deep enough at high tide to allow the passage of dhows and motor launches (though at low tide you'll have to walk in over the mud and sand banks from the main channel).

There's a regular motor launch which connects Lamu with Faza via Mtangawanda three times a week on Monday, Wednesday and Friday (Tuesday, Thursday and Saturday in the opposite direction). The fare is KSh 30 and the journey takes four hours. From Faza to Lamu, the launch leaves at about 6 am but you need to be down by the district headquarters about half an hour before that as you have to ferried out to the launch in small boats (costs KSh 1.50).

Getting to Siyu from Faza involves a two hour walk through shambas and thick bush along an earth track. The first hour's walk as far as the disused airstrip involves no problems and there are generally people to ask direction of if you're unsure. The second half is more confusing and you may need a guide so it might be best in the long run to take a guide with you all the way from Faza.

KIWAYU ISLAND

Kiwayu Island is at the far north-east of the Lamu archipelago and is included in the Kiunga Marine National Reserve. It acquired a reputation some years ago as an exclusive hideaway for rock stars and various other members of the glitterati, both local and foreign. It's unlikely you'll be rubbing shoulders with these people. The main reason for coming here is to explore the coral reefs off the eastern side of the island which the tourist literature rates as some of the best along the Kenyan coast. Personally, I think it's somewhat overrated (Watamu was better) but the dhow trip there was definitely one of the highlights of my last trip to Lamu and I can highly recommend it.

The village on the western side of the island where the dhows drop anchor is quite small but it does have a general store with a limited range of basics. The place to stay here is the *Kiwayu Camping Site* run by a friendly man named Kasim. There are several beautifully conceived bandas to stay in, all constructed out of wooden poles and makuti including one on stilts and another built over a tree. The cost varies between KSh 240 and KSh 360 depending on which one you take, but they'll all sleep up to three people. Clean sheets, pillows and mattresses are provided as well as a kerosene lantern and mosquito

coil. There are good toilet and shower facilities. Campers can erect their tents here for KSh 30 including use of showers and toilets. You'll pay the same charge even if you camp on the beach below the site since this is also apparently owned by Kasim. There's a covered dining and cooking area for the use of both campers and banda dwellers.

Way up above the village on the crest of the hill are a series of much larger, white-washed bandas and a partly stone-built dining hall and bar. They're apparently owned by a Nakuru man who keeps them solely for his own use and those of his friends but they look partly derelict and there was no caretaker to be seen anywhere.

Further up the coast across from Kiwayu on the mainland is the *Mkokoni* luxury lodge which is where the glitterati stay. The cost of a night here is KSh 6240 with full board. There's a speed launch to it from Lamu which takes less than an hour or charter flights by African Express Airways (Lamu) in six-seater planes for KSh 8400 return. You can forget about going up there for a cold beer if you're staying at the camp site as there's no transport across the channel between the island and the mainland.

Getting There & Away

Virtually the only way to get to Kiwayu is by dhow and, for most people, this would be part of a longer trip from Lamu with stop-overs elsewhere. If there's sufficient wind, the return trip to Kiwayu from Lamu takes three days and two nights.

The Rift Valley

In Kenya the Rift Valley comes down through Lake Turkana, the Cherangani Hills, lakes Baringo, Bogoria, Nakuru and Naivasha then exits south through the plains to Tanzania. Together these areas make up some of Kenya's most interesting places to visit. Lake Turkana (dealt with in the Northern Kenya chapter) is a huge lake in the semidesert north, home to nomadic pastoralists and a world away from the tourist minibuses and fancy hotels of the south. The Cherangani Hills provide some excellent walking opportunities and brilliant scenery – and hair-raising roads. More accessible are the central lakes which attract literally hundreds of species of birds and many animals alike – they're a naturalist's dream and a visit to at least one of them is a must.

Volcanic activity is usually an accompaniment to rift valleys, and Kenya has Mt Longonot – accessible, easy to climb and certainly the most dominant feature of the landscape as you enter the Rift Valley from Nairobi, and Mt Kenya – at 5200 metres it's a challenging climb, although Point Lenana at 4985 metres can be reached without specialist equipment. Further south of course you have the vast plains, home of the Maasai, and also home to a profusion of wildlife that you're not likely to come across anywhere else in the world – not to be missed.

What is the Rift Valley?

What is known as the Rift Valley in Kenya is in fact part of the Afro-Arabian rift system which stretches some 6000 km from the Dead Sea in the Middle East, south through the Red Sea, Ethiopia, Kenya, Tanzania and Malawi to Mozambique. There's a western branch of the system which forms the string of lakes in the centre of the African continent – Mobutu Sese Seko (formerly Albert) and Rutanzige (formerly Edward) forming part of the Uganda-Zaïre border, Kivu on the Zaïre-Rwanda border and Tanganyika on the Tanzania-Zaire border. This western arm joins up with the main system at the northern tip of Lake Malawi.

Soda Lakes

Because the shoulders of the rift slope directly away from the valley, the drainage system in the valley is generally poor, and this has resulted in the shallow lakes along the valley floor in Kenya, some of which have no outlet. Due to high evaporation, the waters have become extremely concentrated and the high alkalinity from the volcanic deposits around makes the perfect environment for microscopic blue-green algae and diatoms, which in turn provide food for tiny crustaceans and insect larvae. These in turn are eaten by certain species of soda-resistant fish.

The water of these soda lakes (Nakuru, Bogoria and Magadi in Kenya, Lake Natron in Tanzania) may feel a little strange to the touch (it's soapy) and often doesn't smell too pleasant (though this is mostly due to the bird shit). What's all this about soapy water and bird shit got to do with me, you might ask. Well, the fact is it's simply heaven to many species of water bird and they flock here in their millions – it's a twitcher's paradise!

Foremost among the birds is the deep pink lesser flamingo (*Phoeniconaias minor*), which feeds on the blue-green algae, and the pale pink greater flamingo (*Phoenicopterus ruber*), which feeds on the tiny crustaceans and insect larvae. Also numerous are various species of duck, pelican, cormorant and stork. The highest concentrations of these birds are found where food is most abundant and this can vary from year to year and lake to lake. Another curious feature of the uplifting of the valley shoulders is the effect it has had on existing drainage patterns, although this of course happened in the last couple of millions years. In Uganda it caused the White Nile to form a pond (Lake Nyoga) after it left Lake Victoria, flow up what was previously a tributary, and into the northern

Rift Valley

0   50   100 km

Approximate Scale

end of Lake Albert via a circuitous route. Prior to the uplift the river had flowed direct from Lake Victoria into the southern end of Lake Albert.

Views

The best place to view the escarpments of the Rift Valley is from the viewpoints along the Nairobi-Naivasha road, just past Limuru. Here the road descends into the valley and the views are stunning. Mt Longonot is directly in front while the plains of the Maasai sweep away to the south. Predictably there are souvenir stalls at the viewpoints

(signposted) but the stuff for sale is some of the worst I saw in the whole country.

The old road to Naivasha also descends into the rift in this area, and it's the route to take if you are heading for Mt Longonot or Masai Mara, as the new road runs direct to Naivasha. It's also the road used by the heavy vehicles and is in a diabolical state. This road was originally built by Italian POWs in WW II, and there is a chapel at the bottom of the scarp.

Getting There & Around

Lakes Naivasha, Nakuru, Elmenteita and, to

a lesser extent, Baringo are readily accessible to independent travellers without their own vehicle. There are plenty of buses and matatus and a rail link between Nairobi, Naivasha and Nakuru and less frequent buses and matatus between Nakuru and Marigat (for Lake Baringo). The other lakes, however, are more remote and there's no public transport. Hitching is very difficult and can be impossible. There's also the problem that both lakes Nakuru and Bogoria are in national parks, which you are not allowed to walk in – you must tour them in a vehicle.

Renting a vehicle may be expensive for budget travellers but it would certainly work out cheaper for four people to hire a vehicle to visit Naivasha, Nakuru, Bogoria and Baringo than for them all to pay individually for safari company tours. A one day tour of Lake Nakuru starting from Nairobi goes for around US$40. A two day tour of lakes Nakuru, Bogoria and Baringo costs about US$150 per person. A car hired for several days and shared between four people would cost considerably less than the total cost of a two day tour for four people.

MT LONGONOT NATIONAL PARK

Hill climbers and view seekers should not miss the opportunity of climbing to the rim of dormant Longonot (2886 metres), a fairly young volcano which still retains the typical shape of these mountains, although it's far from being a perfect conical shape.

As this is gazetted a national park there is an entrance fee of KSh 220. The scramble up to the rim takes about 45 minutes from the parking area, and to do the circuit of the rim a further 2½ to three hours is needed. If you're feeling game there's a track leading down inside the crater to the bottom. If you want to do this it's worth hiring a local guide before you set off.

Places to Stay

There's no accommodation in the park or immediate vicinity, but it is possible to camp at the *ranger's station* at the foot of the mountain. If you are just on a day trip you

can leave your gear at the Longonot railway or police station.

Getting There & Away

If you don't have your own transport it's a long walk from Longonot railway station on the old road to Naivasha. It's about seven km into the track head, and even if you have your own car it's wise to pay someone to keep an eye on it, or leave it at the Longonot railway station.

LAKE ELMENTEITA

Like Lake Nakuru, Elmenteita is a shallow, soda lake with a similar ecology. Flamingos live here too, but in nowhere near the same numbers as at Nakuru. It does have the advantage, though, that it's not a national park so you can walk around it and you don't have to pay to get in. The easiest way to get there is to take a matatu along the Naivasha-Nakuru road and get off at one of the viewpoints (signposted) on the escarpment above the lake. Walk down from there or hitch a ride if there's anything going.

NAIVASHA

There's very little of interest in the town of Naivasha itself. It's just a small service centre for the surrounding agricultural district. Most travellers just pass through here on the way to or from Mt Longonot, Lake Naivasha, Hells' Gate National Park and Nakuru. The main road actually skirts the town so if you're just going direct from Nairobi to Nakuru you don't actually pass through Naivasha. It's a good place to stock up with supplies if you're planning a sojourn by the lake as there are very limited stocks in the dukas dotted along the lake shore road.

The area around Naivasha was actually one of the first settled by wazungu and the Delamere Estates, originally owned by Lord Delamere, surround the town and stretch away to the west towards Nakuru. Many of the plots around Naivasha are still European owned – hardly surprising as this was one of the stamping grounds of the Happy Valley set of the 1930s.

The town is basically just a couple of

The Rift Valley

The Rift Valley system consists of a series of troughs and areas of uplift known as swells. The troughs, generally 40 km to 55 km wide, are along parallel fault lines and are formed by blocks dropping down in relation to the rest of the land. They account for most of the lakes and escarpments in East Africa. The swells are the land on either side of the troughs, and it's on these that you find two of Africa's mightiest peaks, Kilimanjaro (5895 metres) and Mt Kenya (5199 metres), and lesser peaks such as Mt Elgon (4321 metres) – all extinct volcanoes. The floor of the Rift Valley is still dropping, although at the rate of a few mm per year you are hardly likely to notice anything!

The Rift Valley is certainly not one long well formed valley with huge escarpments either side, although this does occur in places (the Rift Valley Province is one such place). Sometimes there is just a single scarp on one side (such as the Nkuruman Escarpment east of Masai Mara) or just a series of small scarps. In some cases uplift has occurred between parallel fault lines and this has led to the formation of often spectacular mountain ranges, such as the Ruwenzoris on the Uganda-Zaire border. ■

streets, and everything is within walking distance.

Places to Stay – bottom end
If you need to stay overnight in Naivasha there's a good range of budget hotels. The *Naivasha Super Lodge* has no doubles but the single beds are large enough for a couple. At KSh 60 it's not bad value. For something a little less cosy try the *Olenkipai Boarding & Lodging* or the *Heshima Bar Boarding & Lodging*, both of which are adequate and charge around KSh 70 for a double.

There are plenty of other cheap places along Kariuki Chotara Rd.

Places to Stay – middle
For more salubrious lodgings the *Naivasha Silver Hotel* on Kenyatta Ave is a new place with clean rooms complete with bath, hot water and telephone for KSh 180/240 a single/double. It seems a trifle out of place in this small rural town.

More upmarket still is the *La Belle Inn* (tel (0311) 20116) on Moi Ave, which has a certain faded charm. Rooms cost KSh 205/385 including a light breakfast.

Places to Eat
For a breakfast lash-out you can't beat the *La Belle Inn*. For KSh 95 you get fresh juice, croissant with butter and home-made jam, toast, eggs, bacon, sausage, tomato and tea or coffee – worth its weight in cholesterol! The outdoor terrace is also a pleasant place to have a beer or a light meal, and is a popular watering hole with people on their way through town; it is closed on Tuesdays.

The *Jolly Cafe* next to the Silver Hotel on Kenyatta Ave is slightly less extravagant and has decent food. For good old no-frills African stodge try the *Sun Set Restaurant* on the corner of Kenyatta Ave and Kariuki Chotara Rd.

Getting There & Away
Bus & Matatu The bus and matatu station is on Kariuki Chotara Rd. There are frequent buses and matatus to Nairobi, Nakuru and all

Naivasha

0   100   200 m

~ 2 km

2 Barclays Bank
3 Heshima Bar Boarding & Lodging
5 La Belle Inn
8 Matatus to Kongoni (South Lake Rd)
9 Naivasha Silver Hotel, Jolly Cafe
4 Naivasha Super Lodge
7 Olenkipai Boarding & Lodging
1 Post Office
6 Sun Set Restaurant

points further west. There are also departures for Nyahururu and Narok.

Train Travel from Naivasha to Nairobi by train is inconvenient as all the trains pass through in the early hours of the morning. The trains to Kisumu and Malaba pass through in the late afternoon. Unless you are prepared to travel 3rd class, make a booking in Nairobi before arriving in Naivasha.

Hitching It's useless trying to hitch out of Naivasha town to Nairobi without first getting onto the main (new) road. The accepted point for hitching, and where the main road passes closest to the town, is about 500 metres east of the bus station. It's about one km to the main road in either the Nakuru or Nairobi direction.

LAKE NAIVASHA

Naivasha is one of the Rift Valley's fresh-water lakes and its ecology is quite different from that of the soda lakes. It's home to an incredible variety of bird species and one of the main focuses of conservation efforts in Kenya. Not everyone supports these efforts, however, and the ecology of the lake has been interfered with on a number of occasions, the most notable introductions being sport fish, commercial fish, the North American red swamp crayfish, the South American coypu or nutria (an escapee from a fur farm) and various aquatic plants including *salvinia* which is a menace on Lake Kariba in southern Africa.

The lake has ebbed and flowed over the years as half-submerged fencing posts indicate. Early in the 1890s it dried up almost completely but then it rose a phenomenal 15 metres and inundated a far larger area than it presently occupies. It has receded since then and currently covers about 170 square km.

Since it's a freshwater lake which can be used for irrigation purposes, the surrounding countryside is a major production area of fresh fruit and vegetables as well as beef cattle both for domestic consumption and export. There's even a fledgeling vineyard on the eastern shore.

On the western side of Lake Naivasha, past the village of Kongoni, there is a crater lake with lush vegetation at the bottom of a beautiful but small volcanic crater. If you have transport it's worth visiting. You have to cross private land for about 500 metres in order to get there, so close all gates behind you or ask permission if necessary. South of the lake is the Hell's Gate National Park which is well worth exploring.

Almost opposite Hippo Point, a couple of km past Fisherman's Camp, is Elsamere, the former home of the late Joy Adamson of *Born Free* fame. She bought the house in 1967 with the view that she and her husband, George might retire there. She did much of her writing from Elsamere right up until her murder in 1980. It seems George never spent much time there. It is now a small museum and for KSh 50 someone will show you around, and you get an excellent afternoon tea with mountains of home-made cakes and biscuits! It's open daily between 3 and 5 pm.

Between 1937 and 1950 Lake Naivasha was Nairobi's airport! Imperial Airways and then BOAC flew Empire and Solent flying boats here on the four day journey from Southampton. Passengers came ashore at the Lake Naivasha Hotel where buses would be waiting to shuttle them to Nairobi. The lake also featured strongly with the decadent Happy Valley settler crowd in the '30s. The mansion known as Oserian (or the Djinn Palace) which features in the book (and the dreadful movie) *White Mischief* is on the southern shore of the lake. It's privately owned and is not open to the public. For a full account of the history of European activity in the area, get hold of a copy of *Naivasha & the Lake Hotel* by Jan Hemsing, available from the Lake Naivasha Hotel for KSh 60.

Places to Stay – bottom end

There's a couple of budget accommodation possibilities on the lake shore. The most popular place is *Fisherman's Camp* on the southern shore of the lake. You can camp here for KSh 50 with your own tent or rent one for KSh 50 per person, although there's only a couple of these. There's firewood for

Lake Naivasha

0   2.5   5 km

To Gilgil & Nakuru

Masai Gorge

North Lake Road

To Nairobi (new route)

Naivasha

Lake Naivasha

Crater Lake

Crescent Island

Hippo Point

'Elsamere'

Lake Naivasha Hotel

Kongoni

South Lake Road

Fisherman's Camp

dukas

Safariland Lodge

YMCA

Ol Karia Gate

Hell's Gate

Elsa Gate

To Langonot & Nairobi (old route)

Ol Karia Geothermal Station

Fischer's Tower

sale for KSh 20 per bundle, as well as basic groceries, food and beer (of course) from a small group of dukas about 500 metres away back towards the YMCA. Rowing boats are available free to campers. There are a few four-bed bandas for rent for KSh 180 per person with bath. It's a very pleasant site with grass and shady acacia trees. At the time of writing they were in the process of building a youth hostel here, so hopefully this will be finished by now and will ｣ ｣vide cheap beds for those without camping equipment.

The other choice is the *YMCA*, a couple of km back towards Naivasha town. The problem with this place is that it's not possible to get down to the lake shore. You can rent a bed in a shabby concrete banda here for KSh 80 per night plus KSh 5 for temporary membership of the YMCA. Camping is also possible for KSh 50 but it's not the best site. The bandas have kitchens but no firewood or charcoal although you can buy this for KSh 4. Cooking utensils are provided free of charge. The office here has a limited supply of canned and packaged foods (corned beef, biscuits, soft drinks and the like). Look out for the sign on the right-hand side.

It's also possible to camp at the *Safariland Lodge* (tel (0311) 20241), but at KSh 120 per person it's a blatant rip-off, and that doesn't even include use of the swimming pool (KSh 30, free to other guests)!

Places to Stay – top end

The *Safariland Lodge* (tel (0311) 20241) is a top-range hotel with all the facilities you might expect. A room costs KSh 2345 a single and KSh 2795 a double with full board. Bookings can be made through UTC Safari Trail in Nairobi (tel 331960, PO Box 42196). Facilities are free to residents but campers and nonresidents must pay a daily fee of KSh 30 to use the horse-riding, tennis, archery and indoor sports facilities.

The *Lake Naivasha Hotel* (tel Naivasha 13) is very similar and can be booked through New Stanley House Arcade (tel Nairobi 335807), Standard St, PO Box 47557, Nairobi. Rooms cost KSh 2215 a

single and KSh 2940 a double with full board.

Getting There & Away

The usual access to Lake Naivasha is along South Lake Rd. This also goes past the turn-off to Hells' Gate National Park. There are fairly frequent matatus between Naivasha town and Kongoni on the western side of the lake. It's 17 km from the turn-off to Fisherman's Camp and costs KSh 8.50 from Naivasha. This road has to be one of the worst in Kenya! It was originally built by the Germans before WW II and was surfaced all the way to the Safariland Lodge. These days the bitumen has broken up so badly that you have to drive on either side of it. It's also extremely dusty in the dry season.

Getting Around

Boats for game viewing can be hired from the Safariland Lodge for KSh 320 per hour for four people and KSh 560 for seven people. The Lake Naivasha Hotel also offers trips to Crescent Island (a game sanctuary) for KSh 80 per person, plus a charge of KSh 50 per person if you wish to get off there for a while. It also runs other boat trips at KSh 350 per hour shared by up to eight people.

HELL'S GATE NATIONAL PARK

This park is a recent creation and it is one of only two parks in the country which you can walk through (the other is Saiwa Swamp near Kitale). The looming cliffs and the Hell's Gate gorge itself are home to a wide variety of bird and animal life. On a walk through the park it is possible to see zebra, Thomson's gazelle, antelope, baboon and even the occasional cheetah or leopard. Ostriches and the rare lammergeyer are also sighted on occasion.

The usual access point is through the main gate, Elsa Gate, two km from South Lake Rd. From here the road takes you past Fischer's Tower, a 25 metre high column of volcanic rock named after Gustav Fischer, a German explorer who reached here in 1883. He had been commissioned by the Hamburg Geographical Society to find a route from

Mombasa to Lake Victoria but this was about as far as he got, largely because he was unable to get on to good terms with the hostile Maasai.

The road then continues through the steep-sided gorge and emerges at the Ol Karia Geothermal Project – a power project which is utilising one of the hottest sources in the world. From the plant the track heads back to the lake shore via the Ol Karia Gate, and emerges in the vicinity of Oserian farm (now a large supplier of cut flowers, fruit and vegetables to the European market) and Elsamere.

The entire walk from the lake road turn-off via Elsa Gate and Ol Karia Gate to the lake shore is 22 km. The distance between the two gates via the lake road is nine km. If you intend walking the whole way through the park (and it is well worth doing so), allow a full day, and take along some drinking water and something to eat. The usual park entry fees apply.

If you want to take a tour through the park there's a guy called Thomas who hangs around Fisherman's Camp on the weekends. He works on the geothermal project and organises tours on the weekends.

KARIANDUSI PREHISTORIC SITE

The Kariandusi site is signposted off to the right of the main road on the way from Naivasha to Nakuru. There's not much to see as the only excavation was carried out by Louis Leakey in the 1920s, although the small museum is worth a look.

NAKURU

Kenya's fourth largest town is the centre of a rich farming area about halfway between Nairobi and Kisumu on the main road and railway line to Uganda. It's here that the railway forks, one branch going to Kisumu on Lake Victoria and the other to Malaba on the Ugandan border.

It's a pleasant town with a population of 75,000 but it's of interest mainly to those who work and farm in the area. The big draw for travellers is the nearby Lake Nakuru National Park with its prolific bird life. The Menengai Crater and Hyrax Hill Prehistoric Site in the immediate area are both worth a visit (see later in this chapter).

Places to Stay – bottom end

The *Amigos Guest House* on Gusil Rd is a friendly place to stay and is the best value in Nakuru. Rooms cost KSh 70/120/180 a single/double/triple with common bath. Don't confuse this place with the other Amigos at the junction of Kenyatta Ave and Bondoni Rd. The other one isn't anywhere near as good and can be very noisy because of the upstairs bar.

Another good place is the *Tropical Lodge* on Moi Rd. It's clean and friendly and charges KSh 85/120 for singles/doubles.

Places to Stay – middle

Going up in price, the *Mukoh Hotel* on the corner of Mosque and Gusil roads is very clean, quiet and comfortable. It costs KSh 95/145 a single/double without bathroom and KSh 120/190 with bathroom. Soap and towels are provided and there is erratic hot water.

A new place in the centre of the town is the *Shik Parkview Hotel* (tel 45330) on the corner of Kenyatta Ave and Bondoni Rd. It's not that chic and at KSh 120/215 with common bath and breakfast is somewhat overpriced. A single with bathroom and breakfast is KSh 180. The rooms overlooking Kenyatta Ave are noisy. The best thing about this place is its proximity to the bus and railway stations.

The *Shiriksho High Life Hotel* on Mosque Rd is conveniently close to the bus and matatu stand but otherwise is not a great bargain. Rooms with common bath go for KSh 120/215.

Places to Stay – top end

There's a choice of two top-end places in Nakuru. The old-established *Midland Hotel* (tel 43954) on Kamati Rd is a rambling old place with rooms for KSh 335/605 with bath, hot water and breakfast. A very pleasant alternative is the newly constructed *Waterbuck Hotel* (tel 40081, 44122) on the corner

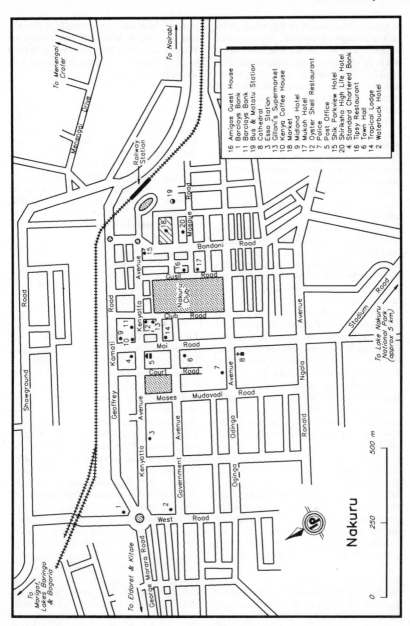

Nakuru

16 Amigos Guest House
1 Barclays Bank
11 Barclays Bank
19 Bus & Matatu Station
8 Cathedral
3 Esso Station
13 Gillani's Supermarket
10 Kenya Coffee House
18 Market
9 Midland Hotel
17 Mukoh Hotel
12 Oyster Shell Restaurant
7 Police
5 Post Office
15 Shik Parkview Hotel
20 Shiriksho High Life Hotel
4 Standard Chartered Bank
16 Tipsy Restaurant
6 Town Hall
14 Tropical Lodge
2 Waterbuck Hotel

of Kenyatta Ave and West Rd, which offers very pleasantly decorated, self-contained rooms all with balcony for KSh 420 a single and KSh 600 a double including a substantial breakfast. The hotel has its own bar, restaurant and barbecue bar and the staff are very friendly. Vehicles can be parked safely in the hotel compound which is guarded 24 hours a day.

Places to Eat
For the price and quality of food, the best place to eat is the *Tipsy Restaurant* on Gusil Rd. It's very popular with local people especially at lunch time. They offer Indian curries, Western food and lake fish. It's very tasty food.

The restaurant on the ground floor of the *Mukoh Hotel* is a good place for breakfast and also serves good meals and snacks. For just a coffee and a snack try the *Kenya Coffee House* on the corner of Moi Rd and Kenyatta Ave. You can also buy roasted coffee beans here.

The town's flashiest restaurant is probably the *Oyster Shell Restaurant*, upstairs on Kenyatta Ave near the corner of Club Rd. The menu is extensive and the focus is on Western food, but expect to spend around KSh 120 per person on a meal here.

You could also try the restaurant in the *Midland Hotel*. It's large and not that popular so you may feel a little lost in the cavernous room. Main dishes are in the KSh 60 to KSh 120 range, and they also do a KSh 130 four-course curry set meal.

If you like eating alfresco then head off to the barbecue bar at the *Hotel Waterbuck* (at the back of the hotel) where there's an excellent range of delicious food priced from KSh 40 to KSh 70 and where you can eat under makuti-roofed gazebos by candlelight. If you like a game of darts, this is the place! The local players are very keen and very hard to beat. Get there early if you want to eat.

Getting There & Away
Road The bus and matatu station is right in the thick of things at the eastern edge of town, near the railway line. It's a pretty chaotic place although generally it doesn't take too long to locate the bus, matatu or Peugeot you want. There are regular departures for Naivasha, Nairobi, Nyahururu and all points west.

Train As is the case with Naivasha, trains often come through here in the middle of the night so you're better off going by road. The Kisumu and Nairobi trains come through daily (nightly?) at 12.30 am and 2.25 am respectively, while the Malaba trains are on Tuesday, Friday and Saturday at 8.45 pm. Also like Naivasha, you need to make an advance reservation in Nairobi if you're heading west and want to travel in 1st or 2nd class. The fares in KSh are:

Destination	1st class	2nd class	3rd class
Nairobi	176	83	40
Kisumu	210	98	49
Eldoret	195	92	45
Malaba	356	165	85

LAKE NAKURU NATIONAL PARK
Created in 1961, the park has since been considerably increased in size and now covers an area of some 200 square km. Like most of the other Rift Valley lakes, it is a shallow soda lake. Some years ago the level of the lake rose and this resulted in a mass migration of the flamingos to other Rift Valley lakes, principally Bogoria, Magadi and Natron. What had been dubbed 'the world's greatest ornithological spectacle' suddenly wasn't anywhere near as spectacular. Since then the lake has receded and the flamingos have returned. Once again you have the opportunity of seeing up to two million flamingos along with tens of thousands of other birds. It's an ornithologists' paradise and one of the world's most magnificent sights. Those of you who have seen the film, *Out of Africa*, and remember the footage of the flight over the vast flocks of flamingos, are in for a very similar treat. Simply go up to the lookout on the top of Baboon Cliffs on the western side of the lake

and feast your eyes on the endless pink masses which fringe the lake.

Don't blame us, though, if the birds are not there in such profusion or even if the lake dries up! The flamingos migrate from time to time if food gets scarce and there's a better supply elsewhere – usually to Lake Bogoria further north or to lakes Magadi and Natron further south.

The lake is very shallow and fluctuates by up to four metres annually. When the water is low the soda crystallises out along the shoreline as a blinding white band of powder which is going to severely test your skills as a photographer. Lake Nakuru last dried up in the late 1950s and, at that time, soda dust storms and dust devils whipped up by high winds made life unbearable for people in the town and surrounding area. In the dry season you'll see these dust devils (like tiny tornadoes) whipping up soda into the air as they course along the shoreline.

Since the park also has areas of grassland, bush, forest and rocky cliffs there are many other animals to be seen apart from birds. One species you'll see plenty of are wart hogs with their amusing way of running with their tails erect. Right by the water you'll come across waterbuck and buffalo, while further into the bush are Thomson's gazelle and reedbuck – there's even the occasional leopard. Around the cliffs you may catch sight of hyrax and birds of prey. There's even a small herd of hippos which generally lives along the northern shore of the lake.

The national park entrance is about six km from the centre of Nakuru. Entry costs KSh 220 per person plus KSh 50 per vehicle. As in most national parks, you must be in a vehicle. Walking is not permitted so you will either have to hitch a ride with other tourists, rent your own vehicle or go on a tour.

You can get out of your vehicle on the lake shore and at certain viewpoints – but only there. It's a memorable experience being in the proximity of several hundred thousand flamingos feeding, preening, grunting and honking and even more memorable when several thousand of them decide that you're a little too close for comfort and they take off

to find a more congenial spot. Don't drive too close to the water's edge, the mud is very soft! Take your cue from the tracks of other vehicles.

Places to Stay – bottom end

There is a good camping site, known as the *Backpackers' Campsite* just inside the park gate which costs KSh 60 per person per night. Fresh water is available and there's a couple of long-drop toilets but you need to bring all your own food. Make sure tents are securely zipped up when you're away from them otherwise the vervet monkeys will steal everything inside them. If you are backpacking and trying to hitch a ride, the rangers at the gate will let you camp here without paying the park entry until you are successful.

If you have no camping equipment there's the very basic *Florida Day & Night Club* about half a km before the entrance gate.

A km or so further into the park is the *Njoro Campsite* and this is the one to head for if you have a vehicle. It's a beautiful grassy site under acacia trees, there's firewood around, water on tap and the usual long-drop toilets.

Places to Stay – top end

For those with the shillings to spend there are two fine lodges within the park. The *Sarova Lion Hill Lodge* (tel Nairobi 333233) is up on the edge of a rise on the eastern side of the park and the views are excellent. It's beautifully laid out and has everything you could possibly need. Rooms go for KSh 2160/2580 a single/double with full board.

The *Lake Nakuru Lodge* (tel Nairobi 20225) is further south on the same side of the lake. It too has excellent views and all the facilities you'd expect in a place like this. The room rates are KSh 1800/2400 for a single/double with full board.

Getting There & Away

From Nakuru the only way in is by taxi if you don't have your own vehicle. You can hire a taxi in Nakuru to take you round the park for

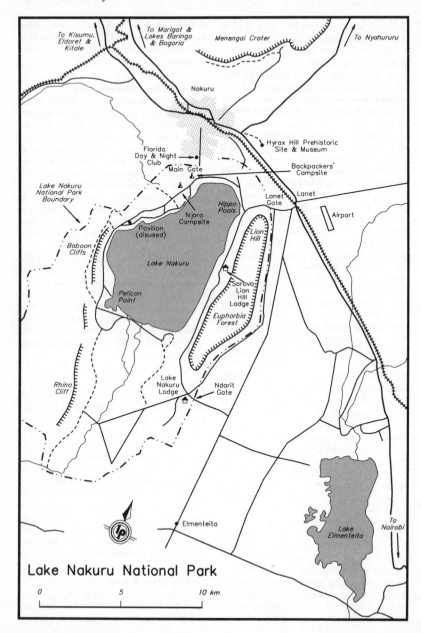

To Kisumu, Eldoret & Kitale

To Marigat & Lakes Baringo & Bogoria

Menengai Crater

To Nyahururu

Nakuru

Florida Day & Night Club

Main Gate

Hyrax Hill Prehistoric Site & Museum

Backpackers' Campsite

Lake Nakuru National Park Boundary

Lanet Gate

Lanet

Airport

Njoro Campsite

Hippo Pools

Pavilion (disused)

Baboon Cliffs

Lion Hill

Lake Nakuru

Pelican Point

Sarova Lion Hill Lodge

Euphorbia Forest

Rhino Cliff

Lake Nakuru Lodge

Ndarit Gate

Elmenteita

Lake Elmenteita

To Nairobi

Lake Nakuru National Park

0   5   10 km

around three hours for about KSh 540 though the starting price will no doubt be a lot more.

If you are driving there's access from the main gate at Nakuru, from Lanet just a few km along the Nairobi road, and from around the southern end of Lake Elmenteita.

MENENGAI CRATER

Rising up on the northern side of Nakuru is the Menengai Crater, an extinct 2490 metre high volcano. The crater itself descends to a maximum depth of 483 metres below the rim. You can drive right up to the edge, where there's one of those totally trivial signs telling you that you're five million km from some city halfway across the world and six squillion km from somewhere equally irrelevant.

To walk up there takes a solid couple of hours, and it's *up*, but still a very pleasant walk. The views back over Lake Nakuru are excellent, as are the views north towards Lake Bogoria once you reach the top. About three-quarters of the way along there is a small group of dukas where you can get basic meals, sodas and, of course, the all-conquering amber fluid.

HYRAX HILL PREHISTORIC SITE

Just outside Nakuru on the Nairobi road there's a small museum at this prehistoric site. The site is open daily from 9 am to 6 pm and admission is KSh 15. The small booklet, *Visitor's Guide to the Hyrax Hill Site*, is available from the museum there.

Archaeological excavations were first conducted here in 1937 although the significance of the site had been suspected by Louis Leakey since 1926. Further excavations have been conducted periodically, right up into the 1980s.

The finds at the site indicate that three settlements were made here, the earliest possibly 3000 years ago, the most recent only 200 to 300 years ago. From the museum at the northern end of the site you can take a short stroll around the site, starting with the North-East Village where 13 enclosures or pits were excavated. Only Pit D, investigated in 1865, is still open; the others have grown

over. The North-East Village is believed to be about 400 years old, dated by comparison with the nearby Lanet site. A great number of potsherds were found on the site, some of which have been pieced together into complete jars and are displayed in the museum.

From the village the trail climbs to the scant remains of the stone-walled hill fort near the top of Hyrax Hill, which gave the site its name. You can continue up to the peak of the hill from where there is a fine view of flamingo-lined Lake Nakuru.

Descending the hill on the other side you come to the Iron Age Settlement where the position of Hut B and Hut C is clearly visible. Just north of these huts was found a series of burial pits containing 19 skeletons. Since they were mostly male and a number of them had been decapitated it's possible they were killed in some sort of fighting.

Virtually underneath the Iron Age site a Neolithic site was discovered. The Iron Age burial pits actually topped a Neolithic burial mound and a second Neolithic burial mound was found nearby. This mound is fenced off as a display. Between the burial mound and the Nairobi road are more Iron Age pits, excavated in 1974. The large collection of items found in these pits included a real puzzle – six Indian coins, one of them 500 years old, two of them dating from 1918 and 1919!

Finally, following the path back to the museum, there's a *bau* board in a large rock. This popular game is played throughout East Africa.

LAKE BOGORIA

The two completely dissimilar lakes Bogoria and Baringo are north of Nakuru off the B4 highway to Marigat and Lodwar. Lake Bogoria is a shallow soda lake while Lake Baringo is a deeper freshwater lake. They're connected to Nakuru by the B4 road which is a superb, sealed highway the whole way. Bogoria is a national park so there's an entry fee of KSh 220 per person plus KSh 50 per vehicle.

Most of the bird life on Bogoria has migrated to the (presently) richer pastures of

Lake Nakuru but the stalwarts (of all species) remain. It's a very peaceful area but it doesn't currently compare with the ornithological spectacle of Nakuru. There are, however, the hot springs and geysers about three-quarters of the way down the lake going south. They're not comparable with those at Rotorua in New Zealand but if you've never seen geysers before then this is the place. The springs are boiling hot so don't put your bare foot or hand into them unless you want to nurse scalds for the next week.

The land to the west of the lake is a hot and relatively barren wilderness of rocks and scrub, and animals are rare though you may be lucky to catch sight of a greater kudu, impala and klipspringer. The eastern side of the lake is dominated by the sheer face of the northern extremities of the Aberdares.

Places to Stay

There are two camp sites at the southern end of the lake – *Acacia* and *Riverside* – but there are no facilities whatsoever and the lake water is totally unpalatable. Bring all water and food with you if you are intending to stay at either site. Otherwise, the camp sites are shady and very pleasant.

There's another *camp site* just outside the northern entrance gate (Loboi). Drinking water is available here and there's a small shop nearby which sells basic supplies (canned food, jam, biscuits, washing powder, soft drinks, etc). A top-range lodge has also been built near the entrance but few people seem to stay there.

Getting There & Away

There are two entrance gates to Lake Bogoria – one from the south (Mogotio) and another from the north (Loboi). You'll see the sign-post for the southern entrance on the B4 about 38 km past Nakuru heading north but, if you take it, you'll probably regret it! Most of this road is good smooth dust or gravel but there is about five km of it which leads down to the southern park entrance which will certainly rip apart any tyres and destroy any vehicle driven at more than a few km per hour. Without 4WD you'd be wasting your

time. These razor-sharp lava beds don't end once you reach the park gate but continue for at least as far on the other side. In addition, signposting along the route from the turn-off is almost nonexistent.

A far better entry to the park is from the Loboi Gate just a few km before you reach Marigat on the B4. It's also signposted. From the turn-off, it's a good 15 km to the actual park entry gate but the road is now sealed the whole way.

Whichever gate you enter through, you're going to need your own vehicle since hitching is well-nigh impossible. Very few people visit Bogoria and those who do are usually in tourist minibuses so they won't pick you up unless you're booked with them. It *may* be possible to walk into the park since there are no large predators living here (with the possible exception of the occasional leopard) but don't count on it. Officially, you're supposed to tour the park in a vehicle.

LAKE BARINGO

Some 15 km north of the town of Marigat you come to the village of Kampi-ya-Samaki which is the centre for exploring Lake Baringo. This lake, like Naivasha, is a fresh-water lake with a very different ecology from Lake Bogoria. It supports many different species of aquatic and bird life as well as crocodiles and herds of hippos which invade the grassy shore every evening to browse on the vegetation. You'll hear their characteristic grunt as you walk back to your tent or banda after dark or settle down for the night. They might even decide to crop the grass right next to your tent. If they do, stay where you are. They're not aggressive animals – they don't need to be with a bulk and jaws like that! – but if you frighten them or annoy them they might go for you. And, despite all appearances, they can *move*!

Crocodiles and hippos apart, Lake Baringo's main attraction is the bird life and the lake is the bird-watching centre of Kenya. People come here to engage in this activity from all over the world. Kenya has over 1200 different species of birds and over 450 of them have been sighted at Lake

Rhino Rescue

Many of Africa's animals are threatened by the loss of their habitat due to human overpopulation or by poachers, and it's the poor rhino which is in the greatest danger. The rhino's horn, its trademark cause the problem – plenty of people covet them and this only serves to push the price up as they become increasingly rare.

The stark statistics are horrific. In 1970, it is estimated that Kenya had about 20,000 black rhinos. By 1985, that number had dwindled to just 425 and rhinos were so few and so scattered that it was becoming increasingly difficult for a lady rhino to meet a compatible gentleman rhino, object baby rhinos. With this huge fall in the numbers, the price of rhino horn on the black market had soared from US$35 per kg to over US$30,000 per kg – and is still rising. Elsewhere in Africa, the fall in rhino numbers has been equally dramatic.

Rhino horn is a popular ingredient in many Chinese traditional medicines and we all know of the supposed effects of rhino horn on one's libido. But the major market for rhino horn is, of all places, North Yemen, where Djambia daggers with rhino horn handles are worth over US$15,000. These fantastic prices are inspiring ruthless tactics from poachers who tote modern weapons and are as likely to shoot as run when confronted by rangers. In 1990, their brazenness reached new heights when they shot not only Kenya's only five white rhinos (in Meru National Park), but also shot the armed guards first in order to do so!

The only solution is felt to be small parks where rhinos can be carefully watched and protected. Funded by Rhino Rescue, an organisation set up in 1986 specifically to save the rhino, the Nakuru National Park was selected as the first manageable rhino sanctuary. The park is now protected by a 74 km electric fence with manned guard posts every 15 km. The construction involved over 11,000 fence posts and 880 km of high tensile wire. An initial group of 19 rhino was established and there are plans to increase this number, possibly to as many as 60.

Additional sanctuaries are planned but saving the rhino isn't going to come cheap. Donations can be sent to:

Rhino Rescue,
PO Box 1
Saxmundham
Suffolk, IP17 3JT
UK

Baringo. Some bird-watchers are so keen they're known as 'twitchers' since their primary concern seems to be to rack up sightings of as many different bird species as possible. It's a serious business and the Lake Baringo Club even has a 'resident ornithologist' who leads bird-watching walks and gives advice to guests. A few years ago he set a world record for the number of species seen in one 24 hour period – over 300!

There's a constant twittering, chirping and cooing of birds in the trees around the lake, in the rushes on the lake and even on the steep face of the nearby escarpment. Even if you've had no previous interest in bird watching, it's hard to resist setting off on the dawn bird walk and the highlight of the morning is likely to be a sighting of hornbills or the magnificent eagles which live almost exclusively on rock hyrax.

Places to Stay – bottom end

There's a superb place to stay just before the village called *Robert's Camp* (tel Kampi-ya-Samaki 3 – through the operator) where you can camp for KSh 60 per person per night with bundles of firewood for KSh 25. Facilities include clean showers and toilets. There are also three double bandas available with use of cooking facilities for KSh 120 per person plus 18% tax. I'd strongly recommend the bandas if there is one available but demand is heavy and it would be wise to book one in advance (through David Roberts Wildlife, PO Box 1051, Nakuru). They are beautiful, circular, grass-thatched traditionally styled houses which are clean as a new pin and furnished with comfortable beds, table and chairs and mosquito netting at the windows. Showers and toilets are separate and cooking facilities are available for a small extra charge. They are superb value. The people here are very friendly and there's a huge land tortoise which ambles around the grounds and appears to be used to the attention it receives.

If you're camping here then you need to exercise some common sense regarding the hippos. Although hippos may graze within just a metre of your tent at night, you should not approach nearer than 20 metres to them. It's dangerous to go nearer especially if they have young ones. Don't frighten them in any way with headlights, torches (flashlights) or loud noises and don't use flash photography. No-one's ever been hurt by a hippo in over 10 years but they are wild animals and should be treated with respect.

If this place is full or you have no camping equipment then try the *Bahari Lodge* in Kampi-ya-Samaki which costs KSh 35 a single and KSh 60 a double. It's basic. This village is also the only place you will find beer apart from the lodge next door to the Robert's and the bar on the main road above the Robert's site. There's a lively bar at the end of the road facing you as you enter the village. The beer is cheap but lukewarm and the clientele isn't used to seeing wazungu but it's a good crowd. It's also one of the few places with electric lights.

You can also check out some of the other similarly priced hotels in Kampi-ya-Samaki.

There are also places to stay in Marigat if you prefer though it's quite a way from the lake shore and it's not the world's most interesting place. At the crossroads of the B4 and the village is the *Wananchi Lodge* which costs KSh 60 a double and is basic but provides towels, soap and mosquito nets. More expensive is the *Marigat Inn* about 1½ km from the main road turn-off (where there's a sign for it). It costs KSh 85 a double and is very pleasant with its own bar and restaurant.

Places to Stay – top end

Right next door to the Robert's Camp is the *Lake Baringo Club*, one of the Block Hotels chain (reservations through Nairobi, tel 335807 or telex 22146; PO Box 47557). Singles/doubles here cost KSh 1855/2275 for half board and KSh 1950/2465 for full board. There's a considerable discount in the low season (1 April to 30 June) when the rates are KSh 870 per person for half board and KSh 965 per person for full board. Children under 12 years old sharing a room with adults are free apart from being charged 50% of the adult meal prices. Facilities at the Club include a swimming pool, darts, table tennis, badminton, a library and a whole range of local excursions including boat trips and bird-watching trips accompanied by an expert.

Scheduled one hour boat trips cost KSh 180 per person (minimum three people), other boat trips KSh 600 per boat per hour (minimum eight people), bird walks KSh 60 per person (or KSh 90 including transport) and camel rides KSh 40 per half-hour. They also offer trips to Lake Bogoria for KSh 530 per person (minimum three people) and to a nearby Njemps village for KSh 75 per person (minimum three people). The Njemps are the local tribespeople who live in villages around the lake shore and practice a mixture of pastoralism and fishing. The club has an arrangement with the headman of the village which they take you to so you're allowed to walk around freely and to take photographs though you'll probably be hassled to buy some of the handicrafts which they produce.

The club also offers trips to what it calls a 'snake park' but you'd be wasting your time since there are no snakes there any longer.

The facilities at the club are open to non-residents on payment of KSh 50 per person per day temporary membership unless you're eating either lunch or dinner there in which case it's free. Use of the swimming pool costs KSh 50 per person per day regardless of whether you eat meals here. If you drive in, on the other hand, you probably won't be asked for the fee.

The other top-end hotel is *Island Camp* which is also part of the Block Hotels chain. This is a luxury tented lodge which is rated highly by those who have stayed there but is even more expensive. There are 25 double tents each with their own shower and toilet, two bars, a swimming pool and water sports facilities. Singles/doubles cost KSh 2305/2930 for half board and KSh 2400/3120 for full board. In the low season (1 April to 30 June) the charges are KSh 1045 per person for half board and KSh 1140 per person for full board.

The prices of various activities here include water-skiing (KSh 1300 per hour),

windsurfing (KSh 175 per hour), boat trips (KSh 600 per hour), bird walks on the island (KSh 30 per person) and a Njemps dancing performance (KSh 550 shared between those who watch).

Boat transfers from the mainland to the island cost KSh 210 return and car transfers from the airstrip on the mainland to the boat jetty are KSh 210 each way.

Places to Eat
If you're camping at Robert's Camp and want to keep costs down then you'll have to bring your own food with you as well as cooking facilities and equipment (unless you want to cook over a wood fire). Only very basic foodstuffs are available in the village of Kampi-ya-Samaki, and a slightly better choice in Marigat, so bring what you will need from Nakuru.

Travellers have reported that in Kampi-ya-Samaki, Moses at the Lake View Hotel will provide meals on request for KSh 50. Some hotels also serve fried fish for just KSh 4 to KSh 5.

Those who want to splurge can eat at the *Lake Baringo Club*. As you might expect, the meals here are very good but will cost you KSh 130 for breakfast and KSh 240 for either lunch or dinner. The club is also the only place where you will be able to find a cold beer as well as the only place where you can buy petrol and diesel between Marigat and Maralal.

Getting There & Away
There are frequent matatus between Nakuru and Marigat but they don't all continue on to Kampi-ya-Samaki, so you may have to hitch from Marigat or take another of the infrequent matatus which go to the village. In the opposite direction, there's a minibus from Kampi-ya-Samaki at about 7 am which goes to Nakuru and another which comes through later from Loruk at the top end of the lake.

It's an interesting journey between Nakuru and Baringo since the country remains relatively lush and green until you pass the equator where it almost immediately becomes drier and dustier and continues to get more barren and forbidding the further north you go. As you near Marigat there are spectacular mountains, ridges and escarpments.

A gravel track connects Loruk at the top end of the lake with the Nyahururu-Maralal road. It's in good shape if you have your own transport and are contemplating doing the trip. There's no public transport along this road and hitching is extremely difficult.

LAKE MAGADI

Lake Magadi is the most southerly of the Rift Valley lakes in Kenya and is very rarely visited by tourists because of its remoteness. Like most of the Rift Valley lakes, it is a soda lake and supports many flamingos and other water birds. It also has a soda extraction factory, hence the railway line here. A few years ago it was the site of a major rescue

operation of young flamingos when drought threatened hundreds of thousands of them because of soda encrustation on their feathers – this doesn't affect the adults.

Magadi is quite different from the lakes to the north as it lies in semidesert. Temperatures hover around the 38°C mark during the day and much of the lake is a semisolid sludge of water and soda salts. There is a series of hot springs around the periphery of the lake.

Getting There & Away

There is a rail link to the lake shore which branches off from the main Nairobi-Mombasa line but there are no passenger services along it. There's also a minor road from Nairobi (the C58) but there's no public transport along it so you will either have to hitch or have your own vehicle.

The Central Highlands

The Kenyan central highlands comprise the Aberdares, which begin around Limuru just north-west of Nairobi and continue on up to Maralal, plus the massif of Mt Kenya itself. They form the eastern wall of the Rift Valley and are the heartland of the Kikuyu people. Within the main area are two national parks, Aberdare and Mt Kenya.

It's a very fertile region, well watered, intensively cultivated and thickly forested. The climate, likewise, is excellent. Given these qualities, it's not surprising that the land was coveted by the White settlers who began arriving in ever increasing numbers once the Mombasa-Uganda railway was completed. Here they could grow anything year-round and particularly cash crops in demand in Europe. It's also not surprising

Central Highlands

0   25   50 km

that the Kikuyu eventually became so disenchanted with the alienation of their best land that war erupted between the two groups in the form of the Mau Mau Rebellion. Probably no other event was of more importance than this in forcing the British colonial authorities to reassess their position and ultimately to grant independence to the country.

While White Kenyan farmers still exist in considerable numbers in the area, their holdings have been reduced and much of the land parcelled out among the Kikuyu but it's anyone's guess how much longer this subdivision and further encroachment on the forest can continue, given the current level of population growth, before the environment is seriously threatened. Soil erosion is a serious problem and plots too small to support a family are common. It's true there's still a great deal of forest remaining but with pressure on it for construction material and firewood (the most common form of fuel for cooking and heating) there are limits to the expansion of agricultural land. It's wise to remember that much of Kenya is scrub and desert.

The Aberdares

Known to the Kikuyu as *nyandarua*, 'drying hide', the Aberdares were named after the president of the Royal Geographical Society by the explorer Thomson in 1884. With peaks of up to 4000 metres and covered in dense forests and bamboo thickets, the lower eastern slopes were long cultivated by the Kikuyu while the higher regions were left to the leopard, buffalo, lion and elephant. The arrival of the Europeans saw the establishment of coffee and tea plantations on the eastern side and wheat and pyrethrum farms on the western slopes. Most of this land has now been returned to the Kikuyu. Not all of the higher reaches of the Aberdares, however, are dense forest. There are also extensive areas of mist-covered moors along the ridges and a good swathe of forest out of

which the Aberdare National Park was created in 1950.

ABERDARE NATIONAL PARK

This park essentially encloses the moorland and high forest of the Kinangop plateau – around 60 km long – along with an eastern salient reaching down to the lower slopes in the vicinity of Nyeri. Only rarely does this park feature in the itineraries of safari companies and it's even less visited by individual travellers. There are various reasons for this. The main one is perhaps the weather. As on Mt Kenya, rain can be expected at any time and when it arrives, it's heavy. Roads turn into mud slides and 4WD is absolutely essential. The park is often closed during the wet season as a result.

Another drawback (though the wild game would no doubt describe it as a plus) is the difficulty of seeing animals because of the dense forest. This is not savannah like Amboseli and Masai Mara so you have to take your time and stay a few nights which brings us to the third drawback – where to stay? There are indeed three camp sites within the park but facilities are minimal and you're going to need a good tent and warm sleeping gear. Add to that the fact that there's no public transport whatsoever, hitching is virtually impossible and that, as elsewhere, walking isn't permitted without special permission. That essentially puts them out of reach for anyone without their own transport. The only other accommodation possibilities are the two very expensive lodges – The Ark and Treetops – which you are not allowed to drive to in your own vehicle. You must make advance reservations for both and be driven there in the lodges' transport.

In the dry season it may be possible to walk over the high moorland between the four main peaks if the weather is favourable but you can't do this without the express permission of the game warden at Mweiga north of Nyeri (tel Mweiga 24). If this is what you want to do then it's best to first contact the Kenya Mountain Club in Nairobi before setting out. They may be planning such a trip.

These sorts of difficulties and/or the expense involved put off most independent travellers but if you're determined to go then the rewards can well justify the effort.

The park does offer a variety of fauna, flora and scenery which you won't find elsewhere except, perhaps, on Mt Kenya. There's also the dramatic Gura Waterfall which drops a full 300 metres, thick forest, alpine moorland and a good chance of seeing the elusive bongo, a black leopard, elephants, hundreds of species of birds and even a rhino. The major plus about this park is that you'll never feel part of the safari bus gravy train as you can often do in Masai Mara, Amboseli or Nairobi national parks.

Places to Stay

If you wish to camp in the park, reservations have to be made at the Park Headquarters at Mweiga (tel Mweiga 24), about 12 km north of Nyeri. The charges are standard.

Both of the lodges are built beside water holes and animals – especially elephant and buffalo – are lured to them by salt which is spread below the viewing platforms each day. This is obviously a contrived way of getting the animals to turn up but it pulls in the well heeled punters and they, in turn, keep Lonrho, Block Hotels, Kodak and Nikon in business. What it doesn't do is anything positive to the immediate environment. Elephants eat a prodigious amount of herbage each day and trample down even more. Buffaloes aren't exactly light on the hoof either. The two combined make sure that the area in front of the viewing platforms resembles a matatu stand which, in turn, makes the smaller and more timid animals reluctant to approach because of lack of cover. I suppose if you pay big bucks the video has to be good even if it's thin on authenticity.

On the other hand, *Treetops* isn't exactly a 'luxury' lodge with its trestle tables, creaking floorboards, shoe-box sized rooms and shared bathroom facilities, though it does have that yuppie appeal of knowing that you've stayed under the same roof as various crowned heads of Europe and presidents of state – there are even faded mug-shots of the *nomenclatura* on the walls.

Full board including transfer from Nyeri but excluding park entry fees at Treetops costs KSh 2010 (ordinary room) and KSh 3150 (suite) per person between 1 July and 31 March, and KSh 1075 per person the rest of the year. Children under seven years old are not admitted. You must book in advance through Block Hotels (tel 335807, PO Box 47557), Central Reservation Office, Rehema House, Standard Street, Nairobi. Having booked, you must turn up at the Outspan Hotel in Nyeri not later than 12.30 pm. Here you'll be served with lunch and then driven to the lodge. It isn't necessary to stay at the Outspan the previous night unless you particularly want to.

The Ark is somewhat better appointed than Treetops and is further into the park but it costs much more, too. Full board here including transfer from Mweiga but excluding park entry fees costs KSh 2605 a single and KSh 4585 a double, plus there are 'staterooms' for KSh 4540 a single and KSh 5430 a double. These prices apply year-round. As at Treetops, children under seven years old are not admitted.

You must book in advance through Lonrho Hotels Kenya (tel 723776, PO Box 58581), 5th floor, Bruce House, Standard St, Nairobi. Having booked you must turn up at the Aberdare Country Club at Mweiga, north of Nyeri, on the appointed day and you'll be driven to the lodge.

You can also arrange game drives in the park from The Ark at KSh 1980 (half day) and KSh 3960 (full day) per vehicle.

Other Options If you can't afford the above overnight charges at the lodges there is a somewhat cheaper option and that is to go on a game drive organised by the Outspan Hotel in Nyeri. You can do this into the eastern salient for KSh 350 per person (minimum three people) or anywhere in the park for KSh 515 per person, all excluding park entry fees. You can also rent self-drive vehicles from here for KSh 1200 (salient only) and KSh 1620 (whole park).

To Ndaragwa
& Nyahururu

Rhino
Gate

To Nyahururu
& Gilgil

Shamata
Gate

Chebuswa
3364m

Ongobit River

Engare River

Road under
construction

To Nyahururu

Aberdare Country
Club

Wanderis
Gate

To
Nanyuki

Amboni River

Oldonyo Lesatima
4001m

The Ark

Aberdare
National Park
Headquarters

Table Mountain
3791m

River

Thaara River

Treetops

To
Nanyuki

Honi

Ruhuruini
Gate

Maratini Hill
3698 m

Chania
Falls

Chania River

Nyeri

Kiandongoro Gate

Outspan
Hotel

To Naivasha
& Gilgil

Self
Help
Fishing
Lodge

Gura River

To Nairobi

Mutubio West Gate

Karuru
Falls

Karuru River

Gura
Falls

Gura River

Nyandarua
3906m

Aberdare National Park

0   3   6 km

NYERI

Nyeri is one of the largest towns in the central highlands, the administrative headquarters of Central Province, and the usual gateway to Aberdare National Park. It's a lively place with an extensive market, several banks, hardware stores, vehicle repair shops, bookshops and a plethora of other stores selling everything under the sun. It also has a good choice of hotels and restaurants.

It started out life as a garrison town back in the early days of colonialism but quickly became transformed into a trading and social centre for White settlers ranching cattle or growing coffee and wheat. Their watering holes, in the form of the White Rhino Hotel in town and the Aberdare Country Club out at Mweiga are nostalgic reminders of their proclivities though the White Rhino appears to have accepted inevitable decline.

It's a very green area and intensively cultivated for all manner of vegetables, sugar cane, citrus fruits, bananas, tea, coffee and even that Australian import – macadamia nuts! On a clear day, too (usually early mornings), you can see Mt Kenya in all its snow-capped glory over in the distance. Apart from these virtues, however, it's hardly the most magnetic town in Kenya and few travellers stay more than a couple of nights.

Places to Stay – bottom end

If you're down and out, there are some real dives to stay at here such as the *New Alaska Hotel* and the *South Tetu Hotel* but they can't be recommended. One of the best in this range and one which travellers have recommended in the past is the *Bahati Boarding & Lodging* at the front of the upper bus and matatu stand. It's simple and clean and offers rooms for KSh 92 a double without bathroom and KSh 145 a double with bathroom. There's hot water in the mornings. The hotel has its own bar and restaurant. It's a convenient place to stay if you're taking an early bus. If it's full (unlikely), then try the *New 7 Star Boarding & Lodging* across the other

side of the road. You can also check out the *Ibis Hotel* or the slightly better *Cedar Tree Boarding & Lodging*.

Places to Stay – middle

The best and most economical place to stay in this range is the *New Thingira Guest House* (tel 4769, PO Box 221, Nyeri) which you get to by turning left and going downhill just after the mosque coming in on the Nairobi-Karatina road. It's a new place and, though it has pretensions of becoming a 'conference centre', the staff are friendly (in fact, almost obsequious) and it's very clean but the architect ought to be shot (or the institute where they trained closed down abruptly)! Badly designed it may be but it's good value at KSh 215 a single and KSh 325 a double with bathroom and hot water. Breakfast costs KSh 35 and lunch or dinner KSh 60. It's wise to order dinner in advance if you intend to eat here. An askari is employed to guard the car park overnight.

Slightly more expensive is the equally modern *Central Hotel* at the top end of town which is less pretentious in its aspirations. Singles/doubles here with bathroom and hot water cost KSh 300/420. The hotel has its own bar and restaurant and there's a disco on Friday and Saturday nights.

For a touch of olde-worlde charm at about the same price, though you pay more for nostalgia than the facilities which it offers, there's the old White settlers' watering hole, the *White Rhino Hotel*. It's a popular place to stay, has a terrace bar, lounge, garden and quite a cheap restaurant and offers rooms for KSh 300 a single and KSh 480 a double.

Top of the range is the *Green Hills Hotel* (tel 2017, PO Box 313, Nyeri) which sits on the crest of the hill across the narrow valley opposite the White Rhino. It's a large place set amongst rolling lawns and has 124 double rooms (though it's not high-rise). It costs KSh 382.50 a single and KSh 589 a double including taxes. Children up to 12 years old occupying the same room are free. There are two restaurants, a bar, sauna, massage facilities, children's playground, swimming pool and guarded parking facilities. Average meal prices are KSh 60 for breakfast, KSh 90 for lunch and KSh 100 for dinner. Checkout time is 10 am. The staff are friendly and the rooms very pleasantly decorated and furnished.

Places to Stay – top end

There's only one top-range hotel in Nyeri itself and that is the *Outspan Hotel*, one of the Block Hotels chain (tel 335807, PO Box 47557, Nairobi). This is the place you have to check in at before being driven to Treetops lodge in the Aberdare National Park. It's sited in beautifully landscaped gardens opposite the golf course and has all the facilities you would expect from a top-range country hotel except that the Mt Kenya Bar has, in fact, no view of Mt Kenya at all – surely a major planning balls-up. Prices depend on the season and the type of accommodation which you take. In the high season (16 December to 31 March and 1 July to 31 August) B&B costs KSh 1870/2100 for singles/doubles and KSh 3070 for a twin

To Nanyuki,
Aberdare Country Club,
The Ark &
Aberdares National Park

To Aberdare
National Park

Golf
Course

Park

13 Bahati Boarding & Lodging
7 Barclays Bank
19 Barclays Bank
24 Cedar Tree Boarding & Lodging
4 Central Hotel
15 City Hall
20 Clock Tower
8 Cousin Café Bar & Restaurant
2 Green Hills Hotel
9 Ibis Hotel
11 Kenya Commercial Bank
18 Library
22 Lower Bus & Matatu Stand
16 Mosque
21 Municipal Market
14 New 7 Star Boarding & Lodging
17 New Thingira Guest House
1 Outspan Hotel
10 The People's Café
6 Post Office
23 Post Office
3 Standard Chartered Bank
12 Upper Bus & Matatu Stand
5 White Rhino Hotel

Nyeri

0   100   200 m

Playing
Field

To Nairobi
& Karatina

Top: Hot springs, Lake Bogoria National Park (GC)
Bottom: Flamingoes, Lake Nakuru National Park (HF)

Top: Cliffs around Lake Baringo (TW)
Bottom Left: Thomson's Falls, Nyahururu (TW)
Bottom Right: Sisal plantation, Nakuru (GC)

cottage. In the low season (1 September to 15 December) the same costs KSh 1680/1860 for singles/doubles and KSh 2770 for a twin cottage. For the rest of the year the prices are KSh 960 for a single room and KSh 1410 for a double. Children under 12 years old are free if sharing the same room with adults.

Self-drive cars can be hired from the hotel to visit Aberdare National Park (see Other Options earlier).

The only other place in this price range is the *Aberdare Country Club* (tel Mweiga 17, PO Box 449, Nyeri), about 12 km north of Nyeri, which is now part of the Lonrho Hotels Kenya group (tel 723776, PO Box 58581), 5th floor, Bruce House, Standard St, Nairobi. Like the Kentmere Club at Limuru and the Norfolk Hotel in Nairobi (also owned by Lonrho), this was once one of the quintessential White planters' watering holes and social foci except that these days it caters for the international leisure set and those with the money to burn on a night or two at The Ark. Full board inclusive of temporary membership costs KSh 2080 a single and KSh 2700 a double.

Self-drive vehicles can be rented from the club for touring Aberdare National Park.

Places to Eat

The most reliable places for a meal are the *White Rhino Hotel* and the *Central Hotel* where you can eat well and relatively cheaply. Forget the *New Thingira Guest House* for a while until they get their cooking act together – there's a menu but rarely is anything available.

The *Cousin Café Bar & Restaurant* is worth a visit if you want cheap, tasty, no-frills food. They have a good range of European and African food here such as ugali with stew for KSh 24, chicken and chips for KSh 40, meat and potatoes for KSh 43, sandwiches for KSh 12 and breakfasts for KSh 35.

Another cheap place for snacks and coffee is the *People's Café* near the post office.

NYAHURURU (THOMSON'S FALLS)

Nyahururu, or 'T Falls' as virtually everyone calls it, was one of the last White settler towns to be established in the colonial era and didn't really take off until the arrival of the railway spur from Gilgil (on the main Nairobi-Malaba-Kisumu line) in 1929. The railway still operates but these days carries only freight. It's one of the highest towns in Kenya (2360 metres) and the climate is cool and invigorating. The surrounding undulating plateau is intensively cultivated for maize, beans and sweet potatoes and well forested, mainly with conifers. The most interesting approach to the town is probably along the newly surfaced road from Nakuru which snakes up hill and down dale through farmlands and forests and offers some spectacular views over the Aberdares.

The falls, on the outskirts of town, are named after Joseph Thomson who was the first European to walk from Mombasa to Lake Victoria in the early 1880s. They're a popular stopover for safari companies en route to Maralal and points further north and well worth a visit. Formed by the waters of the Ewaso Narok River, the falls plummet over 72 metres into a ravine and the resulting spray bathes the dense forest below in a perpetual mist. A series of stone steps leads down to the bottom of the ravine and is the only safe access. Don't attempt to go down any other way as the rocks on the side of the ravine are often very loose. Up above the falls and partially overlooking them (though the view is obscured by a row of ugly souvenir shacks) is the old colonial watering hole, Thomson's Falls Lodge, which has retained much of its quaint atmosphere and is still the most interesting place to stay.

Places to Stay – bottom end

The best place to stay if you have camping equipment is the camp site at *Thomson's Falls Lodge* which is very pleasant and costs KSh 50 per person per night with as much firewood as you need. Campers are entitled to use all the facilities at the Lodge including hot showers and toilets with toilet paper.

For those without camping equipment

■ PLACES TO STAY

21 Baron Hotel
24 Cyrus Lodge
 3 Good Shepherd's Lodge
17 Muronje Family Boarding
   & Lodging
23 Nyahururu Boarding & Lodging
 7 Nyandarua County Council
   Headquarters
16 Stadium Lodging
 1 Thomson's Falls Lodge

▼ PLACES TO EAT

24 Arafa Restaurant
20 Tropical Bar & Restaurant

♦ OTHER

10 Barclays Bank
14 BP station
22 Bus & Matatu Station
 2 Catholic Church
18 Clock Tower
13 Covered market
 5 Esso station
 4 Hospital
 6 Kenya Commercial Bank
 8 Kenya Commercial Bank
19 Mosque
15 Open air market
12 Police
 9 Post Office
11 Town Hall

Nyahururu

0   125   250 m

The Falls

To Rumuruti
& Maralal

To Nyeri
& Nanyuki

To Nakuru

Railway Station
(goods only)

Stadium

To Gilgil

there are several budget hotels available in town. Cheapest are the *Muronje Family Boarding & Lodging* and the *Nyahururu Boarding & Lodging* where you can get a room with shared bathroom facilities (cold water only) for KSh 55, but they're both very basic and you shouldn't expect too much. Far better value is the *Good Shepherd's Lodge* which offers self-contained rooms with towel and soap provided for just KSh 60 (one or two people).

It's also sometimes possible to get a room at the *Nyandarua County Council Headquarters*, next to the post office, which has self-contained rooms with soap, towel and toilet paper provided. They're supposedly single rooms but have double beds and will allow two people to share.

Going up in price, the *Stadium Lodging* is excellent value at KSh 95/165 for singles/doubles with bathroom and hot water. There's a large grille across the entrance so you need have no worries about theft. Similar is the *Cyrus Lodge/Arafa Restaurant* (tel 22190) opposite the bus station.

Places to Stay – middle
The place to stay in this category if you have

the money is *Thomson's Falls Lodge* (tel 22006) overlooking the falls. Though it's no longer frequented by White planters, it exudes nostalgia and olde-worlde charm with its polished wooden floorboards and log fires. Accommodation is available either in the main building with its bar, lounge and dining room or in separate cottages scattered over the well maintained lawns. Rooms here are self-contained with hot water and your own log fire and cost KSh 300/420 for singles/doubles though there is scope for negotiation.

If you prefer modernity and a place in the centre then *Baron Hotel* is the choice. It's clean, well organised and self-contained rooms with hot water go for KSh 180/300 a single/double. The hotel has its own restaurant and the food is good with a choice of three dishes each day – fish, meat or chicken. Prices are very reasonable.

Places to Eat

Most of the budget hotels and many of the bars have a restaurant where you can get standard African food for between KSh 24 and KSh 50, depending on what you order. Meals at the *Baron Hotel* are also excellent value.

For local colour and a barbecued meal, try the *Tropical Bar & Restaurant* round the corner from the Baron Hotel.

For a minor splurge – or if you're staying there – eat at *Thomsons' Falls Lodge*. They do breakfast, lunch and dinner but you need to let them know you intend to eat there if you're taking your meal in the main dining room. A full English-style breakfast will cost you about KSh 65. Three-course lunches or dinners with dessert and tea or coffee cost KSh 120. There's also an open-air grill which operates at lunch time and offers a variety of dishes including soups and various types of nyama choma (barbecued meat). A meat dish will cost you about KSh 50. The Lodge also has the most interesting and one of the liveliest bars in town with deep comfortable armchairs and blazing log fires. All the facilities are open to nonresidents including campers.

For those who want to put their own food together, there's an excellent choice of fruit, vegetables and meat in the covered market.

Entertainment

The *Baron Hotel* has a discotheque every Friday and Saturday night.

Getting There & Away

There are plenty of buses and matatus throughout the day until late afternoon in either direction between Nakuru and Nyeri and Nyahururu. The best bus to take is the once daily OTC bus which runs between Nairobi and Nakuru via Nyeri and Nyahururu. Both roads are in excellent shape and surfaced.

There's also one minibus per day in either direction between Maralal and Nyahururu which leaves early in the morning and costs KSh 85. Get there early if you want a seat. For the rest of the day, hitching is feasible but not easy. The road is surfaced as far as Rumuruti after which it's gravel or *murram* (dirt). Parts of this gravel road are in bad shape but it improves considerably the nearer you get to Maralal.

Mt Kenya & Around

Although a distinctly separate massif from the Aberdares, Mt Kenya also forms part of the central highlands. Africa's second highest mountain at 5199 metres, its gleaming and eroded snow-covered peaks can be seen for miles until the late morning clouds obscure the view. Its lower slopes, like those of the Aberdares, are intensively cultivated by the Kikuyu and the closely related Embu and Meru peoples, along with the descendants of the White settlers who grow mainly wheat on the grassy and largely treeless plains on the northern side. So vast is this mountain that it's not hard to understand why the Kikuyu deified it, why their houses are built with the doors facing the peak and why it was probably never scaled until the arrival of European explorers.

These days it's every traveller's dream to get to the top and take home with them a memory which money cannot buy.

The mountain is circled by an excellent tarmac road along which are the area's main towns – Naro Moru, Nanyuki, Meru and Embu, along with Isiolo at the extreme north-eastern end. We deal first with the towns along this road and then with Mt Kenya itself since the towns are the jumping off points for climbing the mountain.

NARO MORU

The village of Naro Moru on the western side of the mountain consists of little more than a string of small shops and houses, a couple of very basic hotels, agricultural warehouses and the famous Naro Moru River Lodge but it's the most popular starting point for climbing Mt Kenya. There's a post office here but no banks (the nearest are at Nanyuki and Nyeri). The other important thing to bear in mind is that the River Lodge has acquired an exclusive franchise on the mountain huts along the Naro Moru Trail including those at the Meteorological Station so you have to go to this lodge to make bookings. It's all been carefully calculated to sew up the market on this trail but that doesn't prevent you from climbing independently so long as you're prepared to camp and have the appropriate equipment.

Places to Stay

There is just one very basic lodge in the village, the *Naro Moru 82 Bar & Restaurant*, but hardly anyone stays there because it really is the pits and the mattresses stink of urine. Most people head off to the *Naro Moru River Lodge* (tel (0176) 22018, PO Box 18, Naro Moru) which is about 1½ km off to the left down a gravel track from the main Nairobi-Nanyuki road. It's essentially a top-range hotel set in landscaped gardens alongside the Naro Moru River but it does have a well equipped camp site with hot showers and toilets for KSh 50 per person per night. Campers are entitled to use all the hotel facilities.

Those seeking a degree of luxury either before or after climbing the mountain have the option of self-contained cottages for KSh 1225 a single and KSh 1895 a double including breakfast. The hotel has a swimming pool, restaurant and a cosy bar complete with log-burning fireplace and decked out with autographed T-shirts of various groups from all over the world who have climbed the mountain at one time or another. Lunch in the restaurant costs KSh 270 and dinner KSh 240 but if you want dinner and are not staying in a cottage then book in advance or you may go hungry. American Express and Visa cards are accepted.

The main reason for coming to this lodge if you're an independent traveller is that it's here you must book and pay for any of the mountain huts which you want to stay at along the Naro Moru Trail. Those at the Meteorological Station cost KSh 165 per person (Kenyan residents KSh 110) and the ones at Mackinder's Camp KSh 275 per person (Kenyan residents KSh 200). You can also pay for the camp sites here which cost KSh 18 per person (no charge for guides or porters). Members of the Mountain Club of Kenya are entitled to a 25% discount on these

prices and the accommodation charges at the lodge.

The other reason for coming to this lodge if you don't have a tent, cooking equipment or appropriate clothing is that it runs a comprehensive hire service which is open daily from 7 am to 1 pm and 2 to 8 pm. The charges are similar to those at Atul's in Nairobi and are detailed under the description of climbing the mountain.

There's also an excess baggage store which costs KSh 20 per piece. You can use this service whether you're a guest or not.

The only other place to stay in the vicinity is the *Mt Kenya Hostel*, about 12 km up the road towards the mountain, off the main road to the right. This is a very popular place with budget travellers and campers and it's run by a very friendly and helpful man named Joseph. At one time, there used to be a substantial brick hostel here which was affiliated to the IYHF but it burnt down in 1988. Rebuilding is scheduled to start in early 1990 but meanwhile there are a number of rustic huts to stay in and facilities include hot water showers and cooking facilities. The huts cost KSh 50 per bed and you can camp for KSh 30 (own tent) or KSh 35 (rented tent). The hostel is signposted on the main road up to the mountain. The advantage of staying here is that it's only some four km to the park entrance gate.

Places to Eat

There are no restaurants at Naro Moru so you'll either have to cook your own food or eat at the *Naro Moru River Lodge*. There's very little choice of food available at the shops in Naro Moru so bring your own or, if you have transport, go to Nanyuki to buy it.

Getting There & Away

There are plenty of buses and matatus from Nairobi and Nyeri to Nanyuki and Isiolo which will drop you off in Naro Moru.

The Naro Moru River Lodge also operates a shuttle bus between the lodge and Nairobi on a daily basis. It departs from the lodge at 9 am and from Nairobi at 2.30 pm and costs KSh 600 one way and KSh 1080 return (not

The Kikuyu

The Kikuyu number more than three million and their heartland is the area around Mt Kenya. The original Kikuyu are thought to have migrated to the area from the east and north-east of Africa over a period of two hundred years from the 16th century, and were actually part of the group known as Meru. They overran the original occupants of the area such as the Athi and the Gumba, although intermarriage and trading did take place.

The Kikuyu's new land was bordered by the Maasai and, although there were periods of calm between the two groups, there were also times when raids were carried out against each other's property and cattle. Both groups placed a high value on cattle. Intermarriage was not uncommon between them and there are a number of similarities – particularly in dress, weaponry, and dancing – shared by both as a result of their intermingling.

The administration of the clans (mwaki), made up of many family groups (nyumba), was originally taken care of by a council of elders, with a good deal of importance being placed on the role of the witch doctor, medicine man and the blacksmith. Traditionally the Kikuyu God (Ngai) is believed to reside on Mt Kenya (kirinyaga – variously 'mountain of brightness', 'mountain of whiteness' and even 'the black and white peak spotted like ostrich feathers') which accounts for the practice of orientating Kikuyu homes with the door facing Mt Kenya.

Initiation rites for both boys and girls are important ceremonies and consist of circumcision in boys and clitoridectomy in girls (the latter now rarely practiced), accompanied by elaborate preparations and rituals. Each group of youths of the same age belong to an age-set (riika) and pass through the various stages of life (with associated rituals) together.

Subgroups of the Kikuyu include the Embu, Ndia and Mbeere. ■

cheap!). In Nairobi you have to book the bus on the 1st floor of College House, University Way – ask for Stanley Matiba or ring 337501/8. In Naro Moru, book at the lodge.

NANYUKI

Nanyuki is a typical small country town about halfway along the northern section of the Mt Kenya ring road and a popular base from which to climb the mountain via either the Burguret or Sirimon trails. It was founded by White settlers in 1907 in the days when game roamed freely and in large numbers over the surrounding grassy plains. The game has almost disappeared – shot by the settlers for meat and to protect their crops from damage by foragers – but the descendants of the settlers remain and the town has also become a Kenyan Air Force base as well as a British Army base for the joint manoeuvres conducted by the two armies each year. It's a fairly pleasant town and still has a faint ring of the colonial era to it. There's all the usual facilities here including banks, a post office and a good range of well stocked stores.

Places to Stay – bottom end

The cheapest place to stay is the *Youth Hostel* (tel 2112) at the Emmanuel Parish Centre, Market Rd, which is pretty basic but has beds for KSh 40 per night. The showers have only cold water. Only slightly more expensive are a number of simple lodges which include the *Silent Guest House* and the *Juba Boarding & Lodging*.

More expensive but a popular place to stay is the *Josaki Hotel* (tel 2181) which has singles/doubles with bathroom for KSh 70/145. There's a bar and restaurant on the ground floor. Equally popular is the *Sirimon Guest House* (tel 22243) fronting the park which offers self-contained rooms with hot water for KSh 100/130 a single/double. Parking is available here. Similar is the *Nyakio Boarding & Lodging* across the other side of the park and the nearby *Landview Boarding & Lodging*.

Further afield up the Nyahururu road is the *Nanyuki Guest House* which is basic but

clean and offers self-contained singles (there are no double rooms) for KSh 72. Vehicles can be parked in the hotel compound. Another place which has cheap singles – but only two of them – is the *Simba Lodge* not far from the Catholic church off the road heading to Isiolo at the top end of town. A single here costs KSh 50 or KSh 120 with breakfast. All the other rooms are doubles which go for KSh 300 including breakfast. Vehicles can be parked in the hotel compound and are guarded by an askari.

Places to Stay – middle

One of the nicest places to stay in this range is the *Sportsman's Arms Hotel* (tel 22598), across the other side of the river from the main road. Run by an Asian lady, Mrs Dia, this was once the White settlers' watering hole as the style of the building and the extensive surrounding lawns indicate. It offers self-contained rooms with hot water and breakfast for KSh 310 a single and KSh 540 a double. It used to be possible to camp on the lawns but this is no longer allowed.

At the opposite end of town on the right-hand side just before you enter Nanyuki is the *New Silverbeck Hotel* (tel 2740). It consists of a main block with bar and restaurant and a collection of wooden cottages which were obviously once very pleasant but are now quite decrepit and in need of major renovation. Part of the reason is that the shower water falls directly onto the wooden floors with just a hole in the boards as a waste outlet (surely the plumbing must have been better than this in the past!?). There are also four new rooms available in a modern concrete block though they're devoid of character. Bucket hot water showers are available ('problems with the water tank' I was told) and you can have a wood fire in the cottages in the evening. All in all, it's not exceptional value at KSh 505 a single and KSh 790 a double. The Sportsman's Arms is much better value. Also in the hotel compound is a row of souvenir shops and a third (!) Equator sign – the other two are on the main road. Package tourists are traipsed through here by the bus load.

To Nyahururu

Nanyuki

0   75   150 m

13 Barclays Bank
20 Catholic Church
14 Clock Tower
16 Josaki Hotel
7 Juba Boarding & Lodging
19 Kenya Commercial Bank
3 Landview Boarding & Lodging
11 Marina Bar & Restaurant
2 Market
6 Matatu Stand
1 Nanyuki Guest House
21 Nanyuki Sports Club
4 Nyakio Boarding & Lodging
12 Post Office
8 Prison
10 Silent Guest House
5 Simba Lodge
17 Sirimon Guest House
22 Sportsman's Arms Hotel
18 Standard Chartered Bank
15 United Stores
9 Youth Hostel

Park

To Isiolo & Meru

To Naro Moru,
Nairobi &
New Silverbeck
Hotel

Outside of Nanyuki itself, about two-thirds of the way to Naro Moru, is *Bantu's Mt Kenya Leisure Lodge* (tel (0176) 22787, PO Box 333, Nanyuki) which is tucked away in wooded surroundings just less than a km from the main road. It offers pleasant self-contained cottages with hot showers and fireplaces for KSh 390 a single and KSh 660 a double including breakfast. Half board rates are KSh 535/950 and full board rates KSh 700/1285 respectively. There's also a well equipped camp site with hot and cold water, toilets, cooking facilities, electricity and ample firewood for KSh 95 per person

per night. All prices are inclusive of taxes and service charges. The main block consists of a spacious dining room, bar, lounge and makuti-roofed terrace. The hotel accepts credit cards.

Horse-riding (KSh 150 per hour), trout fishing (KSh 100 per hour including fishing rod and licence) and bird-watching (KSh 100 per person including guide) are some of the activities which the lodge caters for plus there are traditional dances performed each evening from 8.30 pm (KSh 100 per person). The main reason for coming here, however, is to take one of their guided treks to the summit of Mt Kenya via the Naro Moru, Burguret or Sirimon trails. There are a whole range of these to choose from depending on where you want to go and how long you wish to take. The full range of possibilities are outlined in the section dealing with climbing Mt Kenya.

Bantu's Mt Kenya Leisure Lodge is easy to locate on the main Naro Moru to Nanyuki road.

Places to Eat

There are very few restaurants in Nanyuki which are not attached to hotels so take your pick. The *Marina Bar & Restaurant* is a reasonable place to eat in the centre of town and an expats' watering hole. For a splurge, have lunch or dinner at either the *Sportsman's Arms* or the *New Silverbeck Hotel*.

Getting There & Away

There are daily buses from Nairobi and Isiolo to Nanyuki as well as minibuses and matatus from Nyeri and Nyahururu which run throughout the day.

ISIOLO

Isiolo, where the tarmac ends, is the frontier town for north-eastern Kenya – a vast area of forested and barren mountains, deserts, scrub, Lake Turkana and home to the wild and colourful Samburu, Rendille, Boran and Turkana peoples. It's a lively town with a good market and all the usual facilities including petrol stations, a bank, a post office and a good choice of hotels and restaurants. There are also bus connections to places north, east and south of here. The resident population is largely Somali in origin as a result of the resettlement here of Somali ex-soldiers following WW I. It ought, in addition, to be famous for the number of 'rumble strips' (or speed bumps) which force traffic to a snail's pace on the way into town from the south. There are no less than 21 of these and more still at the northern edge of town!

Information

Isiolo is the last place going north which has a bank (Barclays) until you get to either Maralal or Marsabit. There are no banks on the way to or at Lake Turkana (assuming you bypass Maralal).

Likewise, there are no petrol stations north of here until you reach Maralal or Marsabit except at the Samburu Lodge (in Samburu National Park). This doesn't mean that petrol or diesel is totally unobtainable since you can buy it in Baragoi (with ease) and possibly at Christian mission stations elsewhere (with difficulty or not at all if they're low on stock) but you will pay well over the odds for it due to transport costs and irregularity of supply. Stock up in Isiolo!

Travellers about to go to the national parks north of here or to Lake Turkana and who intend to do their own cooking should stock up on food and drink in Isiolo as there's very little available beyond here except at Maralal, Marsabit and (less so) Wamba. There's a very good market in Isiolo adjacent to the mosque for fresh fruit, vegetables and meat. The general stores, too, have a good range of canned food and other items.

Places to Stay – bottom end

There are a number of fairly primitive lodging houses available for those tight on funds which include the *Maendeleo Hotel, Farmers Boarding & Lodging, Savannah Inn, Tawakal Boarding & Lodging, Frontier Lodge, Coffee Tree Hotel* and the *National Hotel*, all offering rooms with shared bathroom facilities (cold water only) starting from KSh 55 a single and KSh 70 a double. The downstairs area of the Frontier Lodge is taken up by a lively bar which sometimes puts on live bands. The Tawakal Boarding & Lodging also has a bar which is open 24 hours a day.

The best place to stay, however, is the *Jamhuri Guest House* which is excellent value and has been popular with travellers for a number of years. It's run by Ibrahim and Arden who are both very friendly and will go out of their way to be helpful. The rooms are very clean and pleasant, mosquito nets

To Marsabit,
Maralal,
Wamba
& Wajir

Isiolo

0   100   200 m

To Nanyuki,
Meru & Nairobi

11 Barclays Bank
8 Bomen Hotel
17 Coffee Tree Hotel
14 Farmers Boarding & Lodging
10 Jamhuri Guest House
5 Maendeleo Hotel
19 Market
16 Mosque
12 Mwingi Bus Office
13 National Hotel
18 Pasoda Lodge
4 Petrol Station
6 Petrol Station
1 Police Checkpoint
2 Post Office
7 Savannah Inn
9 Silent Inn
3 Talent Lodge
15 Tawakal Boarding & Lodging
& OTC Office

are provided and the communal showers
have hot water in the mornings. It costs KSh
60 a single and KSh 85 a double. Belongings
left in the rooms are quite safe.

Next door to it and similar in price and
quality is the *Silent Inn*.

Also good is the *Talent Lodge* on the way
to the post office which offers rooms with
shared bathroom facilities for KSh 40 a
single and KSh 90 a double. There is supposedly hot water all day in the showers (or so
the management will assure you). The centre
of the hotel and the terrace overlooking the
street are taken up by a bar so it's not as quiet
as the Jamhuri Guest House.

Going up in the price, there is the *Pasoda
Lodge* which is clean and quiet and offers
doubles with bathrooms for KSh 130. There
are no singles. The hotel has its own restaurant.

Places to Stay – middle
There's only one mid-range hotel in Isiolo
and that is the newly constructed *Bomen
Hotel* (tel (0165) 2225, PO Box 67, Isiolo).
This three storey hotel has a total of 40
spacious rooms, tastefully decorated and furnished and complete with bathrooms and hot
water. B&B costs KSh 275 a single and KSh
375 a double plus KSh 104 for an extra
person in a double room including taxes and
service charges. Children under 12 years old
are charged 30% of the single rate when
sharing a room. The hotel has its own bar
(with ice-cold beers!) and restaurant which
serves excellent food at very reasonable
prices. Meal times are 7 to 9.30 am (breakfast), 12 to 2.30 pm (lunch) and 7.30 to 10
pm (dinner). Guarded parking is available in
the hotel compound.

This is an excellent place to stay if you
want to visit the nearby Samburu National
Park or Buffalo Springs Game Reserve but
can't afford the charges at the lodges inside
the parks or don't want to camp.

Places to Eat
Most of the simple boarding houses also
have restaurants where you can eat typical

African-style meals for less than KSh 50. For a minor splurge, go for lunch or dinner at the *Bomen Hotel*.

Things to Buy

A good proportion of the young men who hang around on the main street of Isiolo are salespeople for the brass, copper and aluminium/steel bracelets which you'll already have come across elsewhere except that the craft here is particularly fine. If you're one of those people who like decking out your forearms with as many of these bracelets as you can get on them, then this is the place to buy them. They're much cheaper here than anywhere else though haggling is, of course, obligatory. The same people also sell daggers in leather scabbards but the craft in these is generally unremarkable.

If you're simply *walking* around Isiolo then these salespeople will hardly ever bother you but if you're *driving* around and especially if you're filling up with petrol at a station then expect a real hassle. Their wares will be thrust in front of your face from both sides and you'll be hard pressed to drive away.

Getting There & Away

Both OTC and Mwingi operate buses to Nairobi which take about seven hours. OTC has daily buses at 7 and 7.30 am and 7 pm which cost KSh 115. The Mwingi buses leave daily at 7 am and 7.30 pm. Mwingi has its own little office on the top side of the main street. The OTC booking office is part of the Tawakal Boarding & Lodging on the same side of the main street.

Mwingi also runs buses to Marsabit and Moyale on Tuesday, Thursday and Saturday, which take about six hours to Marsabit and the same, on the following day, to Moyale. The fare for each stage of the journey is KSh 180. These buses only go when full and, consequently, departures are frequently delayed by up to a day. There's no alternative except to simply hang around and wait, or either negotiate a ride on a truck (relatively easy and usually somewhat less than the bus fare) or walk out to the police checkpoint

north of town where the tarmac ends and hitch a ride with tourists (not so easy).

To Wajir and Mandera, north-east of Isiolo, Mwingi operate buses three times a week usually on Wednesday, Friday and Sunday. Each stage of the journey takes about nine hours (considerably longer if there are punctures or mechanical problems) and costs KSh 180. Hitching a ride along this route is considerably more difficult than to Marsabit.

Mwingi also operate buses to Maralal every second day (depending on demand) which cost KSh 180.

MERU

Up at the north-eastern end of the ring road around the southern side of Mt Kenya, Meru is an important town which services the intensively cultivated and forested highlands in this part of Central Province. It's quite a climb up to Meru from either Isiolo or Embu and, in the rainy season, you'll find yourself in the clouds up here along with dense forest which frequently reaches right down to the roadside. When the weather is clear there are superb views for miles over the surrounding lowlands. Views of the peaks of Mt Kenya, on the other hand, are hard to come by due mostly to the forest cover.

Although there's a small centre of sorts, Meru is essentially just a built-up area along the main road and, as far as travellers' interests go, there's precious little reason to stay for the night here. It's certainly much too far away from any of the trail heads leading to the peaks of Mt Kenya to be a suitable base to take off from. The nearest of these begins at Chogoria, about halfway between Meru and Embu.

The main thing that Meru is famous for is the quality of its miraa – those bundles of leafy twigs and shoots which you'll see people all over Kenya (and particularly Somalia and Ethiopia) chewing for its stimulant and appetite suppression properties. While it still grows wild here, much of it is now cultivated and it's become a major source of (legal) income for the cultivators and harvesters who supply both the internal

The Meru

The Meru arrived in the area north-east of Mt Kenya from the coast sometime around the 14th century following invasions of that area by Somalis from the north. The group was led by a chief known as the *mogwe* up until 1974 when the incumbent converted to Christianity and denied his son inheriting the role. A group of tribal elders *(njuuri)* were all powerful, and along with the mogwe and witch doctor would administer justice as they saw fit – which often consisted of giving poison-laced beer to an accused person. Other curious practices included holding a newly born child to face Mt Kenya and then blessing it by spitting on it, and witch doctors who might eliminate one of their rival's sons by putting poison on the circumcision blade.

Subgroups of the Meru include the Chuka, Igembe, Igoji, Tharaka, Muthambi, Tigania and Imenti. ■

Meru woman

To Isiolo & Nanyuki

To Meru National Park

To Meru National Park

To Embu & Nairobi

Meru

0   250   500 m

16 Barclays Bank
11 Bus & Matatu Stand
 7 Castella Bar & Hotel
15 Continental Hotel
 5 County Hotel
12 Kenya Commercial Bank
 1 Market
17 Market
 9 Matatu Stand for Embu
 6 Meru National Museum
13 Miraa Market
14 Mosque
 2 New Milimani Hotel
 8 OTC Booking Office
 4 Post Office
10 Standard Bank
 3 Stansted Hotel

market and also export it to neighbouring countries. No doubt the marijuana growers are livid with envy!

Meru National Museum

This small museum just off the main road is worth calling at if you're staying here or passing through. It has the usual display of exhibits detailing the progress of evolution along with stuffed birds, animals and mounted insects, but also a small and informative section concerning the agricultural and initiation practices of the Meru people and their clothing and weapons. Out at the back of the building are a number of appallingly small and sordid cages containing obviously neurotic and pathetically bored specimens of baboon, vervet monkeys and a caracal cat which someone ought to liberate immediately as an act of sheer pity if not humaneness. There's also a reptile pit with a notice advising visitors that 'Trespassers will be bitten'.

The museum is open daily from 9.30 am to 6 pm except on Sundays and holidays when it's open from 11 am to 6 pm and 1 to 6 pm respectively. Entrance costs KSh 10 (KSh 5 for children) and KSh 5 for Kenyan residents (KSh 2 for children).

Places to Stay

Two of the cheapest places to stay here are the *Castella Bar & Hotel* and the *Continental Hotel* in the town 'centre'. They're basic and neither is particularly special. Much better value is the *Stansted Hotel* (tel 20360) on the main road past the post office which is clean, quiet and offers self-contained rooms at KSh 75 a single and KSh 100 a double. The hotel has its own bar and restaurant.

Also good value is the *New Milimani Hotel* further up the hill from the Stansted which offers good self-contained rooms with bath and hot water for KSh 100 a double. Vehicles can be parked safely in the hotel compound and, at weekends, there's a disco.

The best mid-range hotel here is probably the *County Hotel*, again on the main road and close to the turn-off for the museum. It's clean, comfortable, has its own restaurant and lively bar and secure parking. Rooms here cost KSh 320 a double with breakfast.

Those with their own transport might like to check out the *Rocky Hill Inn*, about eight km out of town to the north, which is essentially a barbecue and bar but has basic chalets for rent, or the *Forest Lodge* even further out which has a swimming pool, pretensions to being a sort of country club along with expensive chalets.

Getting There & Away

The best way of getting to Meru is by OTC bus from either Isiolo or Nairobi. There is a booking office on the main road at the top of the town 'centre'. Other buses also service this town and have their booking offices in the same central area. The matatu park for transport to Embu can be found on the main road next to the OTC booking office.

EMBU

On the south-eastern slopes of Mt Kenya, Embu is an important provincial centre but spread out over many km along the main road. It has a famous school and hotel and is set in a very hilly area which is intensively cultivated. It's also the provincial headquarters of the Eastern Province though it's on the extreme eastern edge of this and can only have been chosen because of its agreeable climate. Not many travellers stay here overnight and with good reason since there's nothing much to see or do and it's a long way from the only feasible eastern route up Mt Kenya (the Chogoria Trail).

Places to Stay & Eat

There are quite a few cheap hotels spread out along the main road but most of them are very basic and can't be recommended. Right opposite the bus and matatu park is the *New White Rembo Hotel* which offers self-contained rooms for KSh 80 a single, KSh 100 a double and KSh 145 a triple. There's a good restaurant here which serves tasty, reason-

ably priced food. Similar is the *Al-Aswad Hotel* just a little further up the road which also has a good restaurant where you can eat for just KSh 30. The *Kubukubu Lodge*, further down the hill from the New White Rembo Hotel, is another reasonable choice.

At the top end of this range is the *Valley View Hotel* (tel 20147) where self-contained rooms with hot water cost KSh 165 a single and KSh 300 a double. It's clean and tidy and soap and towel are provided, plus the staff are friendly and helpful. The hotel has its

To Meru &
Isaak Walton
Inn (1.5 km)

Embu

0   50   100 m

To Kitui

To Nairobi

6 Al–Aswad Hotel
5 Barclays Bank
8 Bus & Matatu stand
10 Kubukubu Lodge
2 Library
9 New White Rembo Hotel
7 OTC Booking Office
1 Post Office
4 Taxis
3 Valley View Hotel

own bar and restaurant. It's also much quieter than the hotels around the bus stand.

If you'd like to splurge then consider a night at the *Izaak Walton Inn* (tel 20128/9) about two km up the main road towards Meru from the town centre. It's right out of the colonial era and set in extensive lawns and gardens with a good restaurant and cosy bar – both with log-burning fireplaces. There's even a yellowing notice in the bar detailing appropriate 'rules' of conduct by inebriated and amorous 'gentlemen' towards 'ladies' though it's couched in bar humour and obviously not meant to be taken seriously. Originally a farmhouse and set in 3.4 hectares, it has 42 double rooms (described as 'specious' in the promotional leaflet though they no doubt meant 'spacious'!) each with bathroom and hot water plus a balcony which cost KSh 448 a single, KSh 560 a double and KSh 700 a triple including breakfast. The staff are friendly and helpful and it's definitely *the* place to stay if you have the money.

Even if you don't stay here it's definitely worth turning up for a beer or meal.

Getting There & Away

There are daily OTC buses between Nairobi and Embu and this is the safest way to travel between the two places. The booking office is on the top side of the bus and matatu stand. Matatus also offer the same service but they are invariably overcrowded – often dangerously so – and the drivers are like maniacs. 'Accidents' are frequent and often result in everyone on board being killed. This happens on average about once a fortnight so, if you value your life, *don't do this trip by matatu*. It's not that the road is in bad shape – it's an excellent road – but its sweeping curves, high bridges and constant up-hill-down-dale progression seems to encourage total recklessness among drivers. The fare to Nairobi on the matatus is KSh 60 and they terminate on Accra Rd (if you're fortunate to get that far).

The alternative to the buses and matatus is a shared Peugeot taxi. You can find these on the main road at the turn-off for the Valley View Hotel.

The matatus to Meru are not quite the same hair-raising and dangerous prospect since there's not the same pressure on drivers but they're no joy ride either. Take the OTC bus or a Peugeot taxi in preference.

MT KENYA

Africa's second highest mountain at 5199 metres, Mt Kenya was formed between 2½ and three million years ago as a result of successive eruptions of the volcano. It has a diameter at its base of about 120 km. It's probable that when first formed it was over 6000 metres in height and had a summit crater much like that on Kilimanjaro. Intensive erosion, however, principally by glacial ice, has worn away the cone and left a series of jagged peaks, U-shaped valleys and depressions containing glacial lakes or tarns.

In many of these valleys you will come across terminal moraines (curved ridges of boulders and stones carried down by the glaciers) whose position – some as low as 3000 metres – indicates that during the Ice Ages the glaciers must have been far more extensive than they are today. They began retreating rapidly about 150,000 years ago as the climate changed and the process is still going on today. Since records first began to be kept back in 1893, already seven of the glaciers have disappeared leaving only the current 11 remaining and even these are getting quite thin. It's estimated that if the present trend continues there could be no permanent ice left on the mountain in 25 years.

The volcanic soil and the many rivers which radiate out from the central cone have created a very fertile environment and especially so on the southern and eastern sides which receive the most rain. Human agricultural activity currently extends up to around 1900 metres in what used to be rainforest but which is still well wooded even today in many parts. Above this zone, except where logging takes place, stretches the untouched rainforest characterised by an abundance of different species, particularly the giant camphors, along with vines, ferns, orchids and other epiphytes. This forest zone is not quite so dense on the northern and eastern sides since the climate here is drier and the predominant tree species are conifers. Vines, likewise, are absent.

The forest supports a rich variety of wildlife and it's quite common to come across elephant, buffalo and various species of monkey on the forest tracks. Rhino, numerous varieties of antelope, the giant forest hog and lion also live here but are usually only seen in the clearings around lodges.

On the southern and western slopes the forest gradually merges into a belt of dense bamboo which often grows to 12 metres or more. This eventually gives way to more open woodland consisting of hagena and hypericum trees along with an undergrowth of flowering shrubs and herbs.

Further up still is a belt of giant heather which forms dense clumps up to four metres high interspersed with tall grasses. Open moorland forms the next zone and can often be very colourful because of the profusion of small flowering plants which thrive here. The only large plants to be found in this region – and then only in the drier, sandier parts such as the valley sides and the ridges – are those bizarre specimens of the plant kingdom, the giant lobelias and senecios. This moorland zone stretches right up to the snow line at between 4500 metres and 4700 metres though the vegetation gets more and more sparse the higher you go. Beyond the snow line, the only plants you will find are mosses and lichens.

The open woodland and moorland support various species of antelope, such as the duiker and eland, as well as zebra, but the most common mammal is the rock hyrax. Leopards also live in this region and have occasionally been observed as high as 4500 metres! Of the larger birds which you'll undoubtedly see up here are the verreaux eagles, which prey on hyrax, auger buzzards and the lammergeyer (or bearded vulture). Smaller birds include the scarlet-tufted malachite sunbird which feeds on nectar and

small flies and the friendly cliff chat which often appears in search of scraps.

As you might imagine, there are superb views over the surrounding country from many points, particularly the higher ones, though the summit is often clothed in mist by late morning which lasts until late afternoon.

It's not surprising that climbing to the top of this mountain is high on many travellers' priority list but many people rush the ascent and end up with very little appreciation of what the mountain has to offer other than a thumping headache and the thrill of having done it. I've even met people who have been up to the top and back again in just two days! If you take your time, on the other hand, you'll find that the mountain has a great deal more to offer than just an exhilarating climb.

The best times to go, as far as fair weather is concerned, is from mid-January to late February or from late August through September.

Books & Maps

Before you leave Nairobi we strongly recommend that you buy a copy of *Mt Kenya 1:50,000 Map & Guide* by Mark Savage & Andrew Wielochowski. It has a detailed topographical map on one side and full description of the various trails, mountain medicine, fauna and flora, accommodation, etc on the reverse. This is money well spent and contains everything which most trekkers will need to know. It's stocked by all the main bookshops.

Those who intend to do some climbing (as opposed to walking) should think seriously about getting hold of a copy of the Mountain Club of Kenya's *Guide to Mt Kenya & Kilimanjaro*, edited by Iain Allan. The last edition was published in 1981 but not too much has changed since then especially regarding the main trekking routes and climbing possibilities. This is a much more substantial guide but apparently out of print at the moment. If you want one then try the bookshops in Nairobi or the Mountain Club of Kenya, PO Box 45741, Nairobi. It may also be available from West Col Productions,

Goring-on-Thames, Reading, Berks RG8 9AA, UK, and from Stanford's Map Centre, 12/14 Long Acre, Covent Garden, London WC2E 9LP, UK.

The Survey of Kenya also print the map, *Mount Kenya* (1:125,000), which is sufficient for an overall view. It's available from the Public Map Office in Nairobi or from bookshops.

Preparations for Climbing Mt Kenya

Clothing & Equipment The summits of Mt Kenya are covered in glaciers and snow and the temperature at night often drops to below -10°C so you are going to need a good sleeping bag. An air mattress is also advisable if you are going to sleep on the ground as it provides the necessary insulation under your body and is far more comfortable than sleeping without one. A good set of warm clothes is equally important and that should include some sort of headgear and gloves. As it can rain at any time of year – and heavily – you will also need waterproof clothing. A decent pair of boots is an advantage but not strictly necessary. A pair of joggers is quite adequate most of the time though it's a good idea to have a pair of thongs or canvas tennis shoes available for evening wear if your main shoes get wet.

Remember that it's a good idea to sleep in clothes which you haven't worn during the day because the salt which your day clothes absorb from your skin keep them moist at night and so reduce their heat retention capabilities.

Those who don't intend to stay in the huts along the way will need a tent and associated equipment.

Unless you intend to eat solely canned and dried food along the way (not recommended) then you'll also need a tent, a stove (kerosene or gas stoves are to be preferred), basic cooking equipment and a water container with a capacity of at least one litre per person as well as water purifying tablets for use on the lower levels of the mountain. Except in an emergency, using wood gathered from the vicinity of camp sites to light open fires is prohibited within the confines of the national park and for good reasons. If you intend to engage porters then you'll also have to supply each of them with a rucksack to carry your gear and theirs.

Hiring Equipment All the sort of gear you need for the climb can be hired in Nairobi at Atul's (tel 25935, PO Box 43202), Biashara St, Nairobi or at the Naro Moru River Lodge (tel (0176) 22018, PO Box 18), Naro Moru. The gear at both places is good and well maintained. Advance booking of gear (from Atul's) is a good idea if you want to be absolutely sure but not normally necessary. Gear cannot be booked in advance at the Naro Moru River Lodge. Here it's first come, first served. Both places carry plenty of stock.

Examples of the sort of daily hire charges and deposits (in KSh) which you'll have to pay at Atul's are:

Item	Hire Cost	Deposit
sleeping bag	30-50	500-800
air mattress	18	800
air mattress pump	10	200
tent	60-180	1000-2000
gas stove	20	400
water containers	5	50
cooking pots	4-6	40-60
woollen socks	15	150
woollen gloves	15	150
climbing boots	40	400
raincoats	40	400

The hire charges at the Naro Moru River Lodge are consistently higher than those at Atul's.

Cooking In an attempt to cut down on baggage, quite a few people forgo taking a stove and cooking equipment and exist entirely on canned and dried foods. You can certainly do it so long as you keep up your fluid intake but it's not the best way to go about it. That cup of hot soup in the evening and pot of tea or coffee in the morning can make all the difference between enjoying the climb and hating it or, at least, feeling irritable.

There are, however, a few things to bear

in mind about cooking at high altitudes. The major consideration is that the boiling point of water is considerably reduced. At 4500 metres, for example, it boils at 85°C and at 5500 metres at 82°C. The latter is too low to sufficiently cook rice or spaghetti and you won't be able to brew a good cup of tea from it either (instant coffee is the answer). Cooking times are also considerably increased as a result (with consequent increased use of fuel).

The best range of suitable foods for the mountain is, of course, to be found in the supermarkets of Nairobi though it's quite a long way to cart food from there to the trail heads. On the western and northern sides of the mountain there's a good range of food at the stores in Nyeri and Nanyuki but precious little at Naro Moru. On the southern and eastern sides the best places to shop are Embu and Meru. Dehydrated foods are not all that easy to find and given the low boiling point of water at high altitudes you really need the precooked variety. Fresh fruit and vegetables are available in all reasonably sized towns and villages.

Take plenty of citrus fruits with you and/or citrus drinks as well as chocolate, sweets or dried fruit to keep your blood sugar levels high on the climb.

One last thing – and this is important to avoid altitude sickness as far as possible: drink at least three litres of fluid per day.

Getting to the Trail Heads

There are seven different routes to the summit but only the three main routes are covered here – Naro Moru, Sirimon and Chogoria. The other trails are much harder to follow and there's a real chance you can get lost without decent maps and the ability to read them, and if you have no experience with a compass.

If you intend to do the climb independently then public transport (buses or matatus) along the Mt Kenya ring road is the first step towards getting to the trail heads. For the Naro Moru Trail it's Naro Moru village where there's a prominent signpost on the right-hand side just outside the village

on the way to Nanyuki. For the Sirimon Trail, first go to Nanyuki and then take another matatu about 13 km up the main road to Isiolo where the trail is signposted off to the right. For Chogoria you have the choice of getting off the bus or matatu about three km before Chogoria village on the Embu-Meru road where there's a signpost for Meru Mt Kenya Bandas, or going into Chogoria village, walking through it, continuing on to where the tarmac ends and then a further two km where it joins the gravel road which you would have taken further south.

From where the buses or matatus drop you it's quite a walk to any of the park entry gates but there are possibilities of private (though relatively expensive) transport from the main roads to the park entry gates.

If you have your own transport, you can get up to all three of the national park entry gates in 2WD but to get to the road heads beyond that on the Naro Moru and Sirimon trails you will need 4WD. Don't attempt these last sections in anything other than that. And don't even expect a small Suzuki 4WD to make it up to the Meteorological Station on the Naro Moru Trail in wet weather. The road up there from the park entry gate is diabolical in wet weather.

On the Mountain

Park Entry Fees, Guides, Porters & Cooks Entry fees to the national park are KSh 220 per person per night (KSh 50 for Kenyan residents) plus KSh 50 for a vehicle (KSh 20 for Kenyan residents). If you take a guide and/or porters then you'll have to pay their entry fees too which are KSh 10 per person per night. Camping fees are an additional KSh 60 per person per night (KSh 20 for Kenyan residents).

The charges for guides, porters and cooks vary according to the route taken. On the Naro Moru route they are KSh 65, KSh 55 and KSh 65 per day respectively. On the Chogoria route they are KSh 100, KSh 90 and KSh 100 per day respectively. On the Sirimon route they are KSh 90, KSh 75 and KSh 90 per day respectively.

Porters will carry up to 18 kg for a three

Mt Kenya

day trip or 16 kg for a longer trip excluding the weight of their own food and equipment. If you want them to carry more then you'll have to negotiate a price for the extra weight. A normal day's work is regarded as one stage of the journey – from the Meteorological Station to Mackinders Camp on the Naro Moru Trail or from the Chogoria road head to Minto's Hut on the Chogoria Trail, for example. If you want to go further than this then you'll have to pay them two days' wages even if they don't do anything the following day.

Guides, porters and cooks can be engaged at the Naro Moru River Lodge or the Meru Mt Kenya Bandas and possibly at the park entry gates (though this isn't as reliable). They can also be found by contacting the Naro Moru Porters & Guides Association, PO Box Naro Moru, Naro Moru, or the Chogoria Porters (tel 88), PO Box 33, Chogoria. If you're staying at the Mt Kenya Hostel in Naro Moru, Joseph will fix you up if you ask him.

Places to Stay There are quite a lot of huts on the mountain but not all of them are available to the general public. Several are owned by and reserved exclusively for use by members of the Mountain Club of Kenya (MCK). Others are owned by lodges outside of the park and reserved for the use of people who go on their organised treks. Most of the other huts which are available to the general public have to be booked and paid for in advance. This is certainly true for the *Meteorological Station* and *Mackinders Camp* (otherwise known as the 'Teleki Valley Lodge') on the Naro Moru Trail. Both can be booked either through the MCK or the Naro Moru River Lodge (which can also book you other huts owned by the MCK).

MCK huts cost KSh 35 per person per night. Those at the Meteorological Station cost KSh 165 per person per night (KSh 110 for Kenyan residents), those at Mackinders Camp, KSh 275 per person per night (KSh 200 for Kenyan residents), and those at *Meru Mt Kenya Bandas*, KSh 200 per person per night.

Due to unauthorised use of the MCK huts open to the public in the past, the club has decided to fix locks to them so don't turn up without a booking voucher to show to the warden otherwise there may not be room for you. Negotiations are also in progress between the MCK and the Naro Moru River Lodge which will probably see all of the publicly accessible MCK huts taken over by the lodge. If that happens, *all* the huts will be staffed and there'll be a considerable price hike so don't turn up without booking vouchers.

Shipton's Camp (on the Sirimon trail) is owned by Bantu's Mt Kenya Leisure Lodge and the Meru Mt Kenya Bandas (on the Chogoria Trail) by the local county council. Bookings for Shipton's should be made through the Bantu Lodge in Nanyuki but it's not usually necessary to prebook Meru Mt Kenya Bandas.

The Trails

The normal weather pattern is for clear mornings with the mist closing in from 10 am though this sometimes clears again in the early evening. This means that if you want to make the most of the trek you should set off early every morning and, for the final assault on Point Lenana (the highest point for walkers), you need to make a 5 am start if you want to see the sunrise from the top.

Naro Moru Trail This is the most popular of the trails and the quickest but it's the least scenic. You should allow a minimum of four days for the climb or three if you have transport to and from Naro Moru and the Meteorological Station.

Your starting point here is the village of Naro Moru on the Nairobi-Nanyuki road where the turn-off for the mountain is well signposted just beyond the village. To get there, take one of the daily OTC buses from Nairobi to Naro Moru. The depot is at the junction of Cross Rd and Racecourse Rd. You can also get to Naro Moru from Nyeri by matatu though these are usually very crowded.

The first part of the trail takes you along a

relatively good gravel road through farm-lands for some 12 km (all the junctions are signposted) to the start of the forest where there's a wooden bridge across a small river. A further five km brings you to the park entry gate at 2400 metres. Having paid your fees, you continue on another eight km to the *Meteorological Station* at 3000 metres where you stay for the night.

If your time is limited you can cut out this part of the trek by taking the Naro Moru River Lodge's Land Rover all the way to the Meteorological Station. This costs KSh 960 plus KSh 15 for the driver's park entry fee and KSh 50 for the vehicle shared by up to eight people. You don't have to be on one of the lodge's organised treks to use this vehicle. Hitching is also possible but the chances of a lift *up* the mountain are limited – it's easier to get a ride on the way down.

On the second day you set out up the Teleki Valley along a well marked path past the radio relay station and up to the edge of the forest at around 3200 metres. From here you scale the so-called 'Vertical Bog' and up onto a ridge from where you can see Mackinders Camp. The trail divides into two here and you have the choice of taking the higher path which gives the best views but is often wet or the lower path which crosses the Naro Moru stream and continues gently up to Mackinder's Camp (4160 metres). This part of the trek should take you around 4½ hours. Here you can stay the night (bunk houses or camping) or continue on to the *Austrian Hut* (4790 metres). The Austrian Hut is a better choice if you want to be on Point Lenana at dawn the next day since it's only a one hour trek from there. On the third day you continue on up the valley past the rangers' station to where the track divides into two. The main track to the right takes you to the Austrian Hut and Point Lenana (4985 metres and the main summit for walkers) via a swampy area followed by a moraine and a long scree. The final part of the trek up to Point Lenana takes you across a snow-covered glacier though the going is fairly easy. Mackinders Camp to Point Lenana should take about four hours.

Those who are camping and not staying in the bunk houses at either Mackinders Camp or the Austrian Hut have a third choice of where to spend the second night. This is the so-called *American Camp* which you get to by branching off left along a minor track just before the swampy area and above the rangers' station. It's an excellent camp site on a grassy meadow.

From Point Lenana you have the choice of returning to the Meteorological Station back down the same route or continuing round the summit and down either the Chogoria Trail or the Sirimon Trail. Assuming you get to Point Lenana early in the day, you can reach the Meteorological Station the same day.

Sirimon Trail This is the least used of the three main trails but the driest. You should allow a minimum of five days to undertake this trek.

Take the same OTC bus as to Naro Moru but continue on to Nanyuki. If you want to start out up the mountain the same day as you leave Nairobi on this route, you need to take the earliest possible bus leaving Nairobi otherwise you'll probably have to stay in Nanyuki for the night and leave the following day.

To get from Nanyuki to the start of the Sirimon track take one of the frequent matatus going to Timau on the main Nairobi-Nanyuki road and tell the driver you want to be dropped off at the start of the track (signposted). If you go over a fairly large river (the Sirimon River) then you've gone too far. The start of the trail is about 13 km out of Nanyuki.

On the first day you walk from the main road to the park entrance gate (about 10 km) and on from there to the road head at 3150 metres (a further nine km). It's a fairly easy stroll and you don't gain much in altitude. At the road head there's a good camp site as well as a bunk house. There are no Land Rovers for hire along this part of the route as there are on the Naro Moru Trail. If you have your own vehicle then you'll need 4WD for the last five km as the road is in bad shape.

On the second day you walk from the road

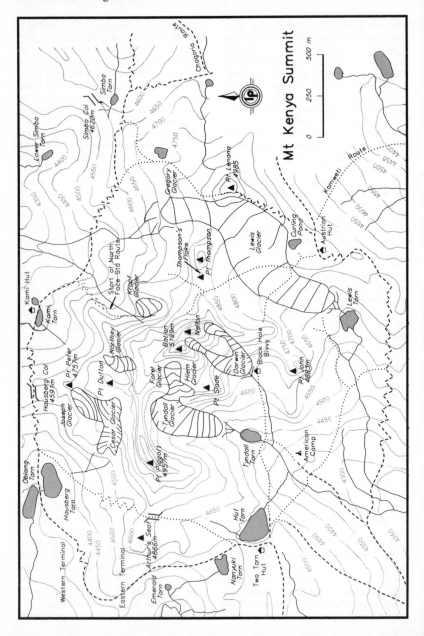

Mt Kenya Summit

head to Liki North Hut (3993 metres). It's an easy morning's walk along a gradually deteriorating trail. If it's still early in the day and you prefer to continue then don't take the trail off to the left at the Liki North stream (which takes you to Liki North Hut) but cross the stream and the ridge beyond and descend into Mackinder Valley. There is a clearly defined track from here which follows the eastern side of the valley, eventually crosses the main Liki stream and leads you to Shipton's Caves – a formation of obvious rock overhangs where you can camp for the night though it's a poor site. From the road head to Shipton's Caves takes about seven hours.

On the third day (assuming you start from Liki North Hut) take the same route as outlined above to Shipton's Caves and on to Kami Hut (4433 metres). Not far from Shipton's Caves the trail divides into two and you have a choice of routes. The right-hand fork takes you steeply up to Kami Hut and is the best place to head for if you intend to walk around the peaks. Taking this route you can stay in *Kami Hut* for the night or pitch a tent at any of the good camp sites on the ridge just above the hut.

If you take the left-hand fork it leads you further up the Mackinder Valley, past the Shipton's Camp and bunk house, and then up a long hard scree slope to Simba Col. From here you can reach Square Tarn and the junction of the Chogoria Trail and, after that, Point Lenana. The walk from Shipton's Camp to Square Tarn takes about two hours. If you take this route then you'll need a tent unless you intend to carry on to the Austrian Hut for the night – not recommended as this would be a very long day and you'd be exhausted by the end of it.

Assuming you stayed the night at Kami Hut, on the fourth day you go from there to the Austrian Hut via Two Tarn Hut. The first section takes you steeply up a scree slope to Hausberg Col and then down another to Hausberg and Oblong tarns. From here there's a choice of bearing to the right across screes to the Western Terminal or more steeply to the left up to Arthur's Seat from

which Two Tarn Hut can be seen. From the col along the Western Terminal route, head down and left towards the lower of the two tarns and then up a little further to Two Tarn Hut. Kami to Two Tarn Hut should take about two hours. There are superb views along this leg of the trail.

From Two Tarn Hut, descend to American Camp and then on down to the Naro Moru Trail leading to the Austrian Hut.

On the fifth day your options are the same as on the Naro Moru route.

Chogoria Trail This trail, from the eastern side of the mountain, is undoubtedly the most beautiful of the access routes to the summit and certainly the easiest as far as gradients go. From Minto's Hut there are breathtaking views of the head of the Gorges Valley and the glaciers beyond.

To get started on this trail, take an OTC bus from Nairobi direct to Chogoria village or one first to Embu and then a matatu to Chogoria. Unless you get to Chogoria village early on in the day you will probably have to spend the night in Chogoria before setting off up the mountain, as the first day's hike is a long slog (about 24 km) up the forest track with nowhere to stay en route.

The first day is spent walking up to the park entry gate at 2990 metres through superb rainforest and on into the bamboo zone. You have the choice here of staying at the *Meru Mt Kenya Bandas*, about ½ km from the park entry gate, or continuing on a further three km to the *Urumandi Hut* where you can stay free of charge (at present). At the road head itself (3200 metres), six km from the park entry gate, there's also an excellent camp site.

There are possibilities of hitching all the way to the park entry gate from Chogoria as there's at least one official vehicle which does the run daily between the village and the Meru Mt Kenya Bandas, leaving the Bandas between 6.30 and 7 am and returning between 9 and 10 am. There may also be people staying at the Bandas who can help out with lifts.

Alternatively, if you want guaranteed

transport, stay at the *Chogoria Cool Inn* (tel 35, PO Box 461, Chogoria) and speak to the proprietor, Francis Njoroge. He has a Peugeot and will take you up to the trail head for KSh 960 shared by up to four people.

The second day is spent walking from either the Meru Mt Kenya Bandas, the Urumandi Hut or the road head camp site to Minto's Hut with spectacular views all the way. The trail is well defined all along and first crosses the stream up to the ridge which it then follows all the way to Minto's Hut. You need to bring water with you as there are no sources en route. The road head to Minto's Hut should take you about 4½ to five hours. Stay at *Minto's Hut* for the night (recently rehabilitated by a team from Operation Raleigh – a British volunteer organisation) or head further up the valley where there are a number of sheltered camp sites.

On the third day you continue up to the head of the valley, across scree slopes to the right and then left up to Square Tarn. The last section of this leg of the trail is very steep. From the tarn the trail continues straight on to a col below Point Lenana after which it descends briefly and then goes up across a scree slope to the right and onto the Austrian Hut. The trail is well marked with cairns and should take you about 3½ hours. From the Austrian Hut you can scale Point Lenana the same day or stay there for the night and make the ascent the following morning. Point Lenana is about 1½ hours from the Austrian Hut.

The descent from Point Lenana to Minto's Hut should take about two hours after which it's a further three to five hours back down to the Meru Mt Kenya Bandas.

Organised Treks

If your time is limited or you'd prefer someone else to make all the arrangements for climbing the mountain, there are several possibilities.

The Naro Moru River Lodge (tel (0176) 22018, PO Box 18, Naro Moru) can do this for you at a cost of KSh 4200 per person which includes a guide/cook, porters, all meals, park entry fees, camping fees, and transport to and from the trail heads. You spend four nights on the mountain (one of them in a hut and the other three camping) and you go up the Sirimon Trail and come back down along the Naro Moru Trail. These treks take a minimum of seven people.

The Bantu's Mt Kenya Leisure Lodge (tel Burguret 1 or Nanyuki (0176) 22787, PO Box 333, Nanyuki), between Naro Moru and Nanyuki, also offer a range of organised treks, usually up the Sirimon Trail and down the Naro Moru Trail, taking from three to six days and they have their own huts on the Sirimon Trail where you stay for the night. Costs vary according to the number of days you wish to spend on the mountain and the number of people in the party, though it's cheapest if you can get eight or more people to go on the trek. A three day direct trip to Point Lenana via the Sirimon Trail costs KSh 4560 to KSh 2640 per person (one to eight people respectively), a four day trip along the same route KSh 5640 to KSh 32400 per person (one to eight people respectively) and a six day trip KSh 7200 to KSh 4380 per person (one to eight people respectively). All prices include park entry fees, guide and porters fees, food, transport to and from the trail heads, accommodation, and a special half board deal at the Lodge.

Other outfits which can organise walking safaris on Mt Kenya are Tropical Ice Ltd (tel 23649, PO Box 57341, Nairobi), which offer group and individual treks mainly on the Sirimon Trail, and East African Mountain Guides (tel 60728, PO Box 44827, Nairobi), which offers luxury safaris along the Chogoria Trail.

You need to be well prepared when climbing Mt Kenya. We received the following letter from a traveller who had a less than ideal trip:

I'm sure thousands of people agree that your books are extremely useful but the travel survival kit is very aptly named.

I went missing for five days on my own on the descent from Point Lenana. I lost my rucksack, sleeping bag and food. I managed to keep an army surplus bag with my camera, purse belt, hypothermia foil and guide book.

By the end of the fourth day the foil was ripped to shreds and gaining inspiration from the street dwellers in London I ripped out pages from the travel survival kit to cover myself with. I also ate some of the pages on Uganda!

Thanks for helping me survive!

Gillian Tree, UK

Western Kenya

Western Kenya is an area with many attractions, but is often overlooked by travellers, and you won't find a single safari minibus out this way either. For this reason alone it's worth spending a bit of time exploring out here, just to get the feel of Kenya without the tourists.

The countryside is, for the most part, beautiful rolling hills, often covered with the pale green bushes of the rambling tea plantations. Further west you have Lake Victoria and the regional capital of Kisumu on its shore. From here there are plenty of possibilities – just a short distance to the north lies the Kakamega Forest with its lush vegetation and abundant wildlife. Further north still, close to the sleepy regional town of Kitale, are the national parks of Mt Elgon (well worth climbing) and Saiwa Swamp, where the only way of getting around is on foot and the attraction is the rare sitatunga deer.

If you have your sights set on more distant horizons, head west for Busia and Uganda, or south to Isebania and across the border into Tanzania.

This area is the home of Kenya's Luo people. Numbering around two million they make up the third largest ethnic group in the country.

Getting Around

This is the most densely populated part of the country so the road system is good and there are hundreds of matatus of varying shapes and sizes plying the routes. Accidents are unnervingly common, but these seem to happen more amongst the very small matatus which are usually dangerously overloaded. The small-truck size matatus are a lot safer as they generally travel slower and can carry loads with greater ease.

One annoying factor of matatu travel in this region is the way the destination changes suddenly depending on how many passengers there are. So if your matatu is supposedly going from, say, Kakamega to Kitale and it gets to Webuye and everyone gets out, it's a fairly safe bet that you will have to as well. When this happens, and you have paid to the final destination, the driver will find you a seat in another vehicle and fix things with the driver. You will get there in the end, but it may take longer than you think. It took me three matatus to get from Kisumu to Kisii, despite being told when I boarded the first two that they were going all the way.

Lake Victoria

With an area approaching 70,000 square km, Lake Victoria is obviously the major geographical feature in this part of the continent. Unlike the lakes further west, Victoria is not part of the rift valley system, and so is wide and shallow (only 100 metres deep) compared with, say, Lake Tanganyika which is nearly 1½ km deep.

Lake Victoria touches on three countries – Uganda, Tanzania and Kenya – and it's just a pity that it's not possible to travel between any of the countries via the lake. The only possibilities for excursions are the ferries operating out of Kisumu.

Bilharzia is prevalent in Lake Victoria so don't swim in the water or walk in the grass along its shores – this is the hideout of the snails which are the host for the parasitic flukes which invade your body. Admittedly you face only a very small risk of contracting bilharzia if you spend only a short time here.

KISUMU

Although it hardly feels like it, Kisumu is Kenya's third largest town. It has a very easy-going, almost decaying, atmosphere, possibly partly due to the fact that with the cessation of international ferry services on

Western Kenya

0   50   100 km

Mt Elgon
Wagagai 4321m ▲ Endebess
Sigor
Cherongoni Hills
Tot
Kapsawar
Kitale
Kimilili
UGANDA
Maloba   Webuye
Eldoret
Busia
Kakamega
Asembo   Kisumu
Rusinga Island
Mfangano Island
Kendu Bay   Kericho
Lake Victoria
Homa Bay
Kisii
TANZANIA
Migori
Isebania

the lake, and the decline in through traffic to Uganda, it's a bit of a dead end these days. It was also a busy port from early this century right up until the East African Community split up in 1977, and it seems that from this point on the town has just been marking time.

Don't be put off by that though, as it's the ideal place to head for from the east of the country as the travel connections are excellent. There's also enough to do in the town itself to make it an interesting place to stop for a day or two.

If you've arrived from the higher country further east the first thing that you will notice is the heat and humidity. Kisumu is always a good few degrees hotter than say Nairobi and the steamy conditions only add to the general torporific air.

Orientation

Kisumu is sited on the gently sloping shore of Lake Victoria. Although it's a fairly sprawling town, everything you are likely to need is within walking distance. The main drag is Oginga Odinga Rd and along it are virtually all the shops, the banks and the post office.

The railway station and ferry jetty are

close together about five minutes walk from Oginga Odinga Rd, while the noisy bus and matatu station is on Jomo Kenyatta Highway behind the market, about 10 minutes walk from the centre.

Most of the cheap hotels are in the area between Oginga Odinga Rd and Otiena Oyoo St. The best access to the lake itself is at Dunga, a small village about three km south of town along Nzola Rd.

Information

The GPO is in the centre of town on Oginga Odinga Rd and is open Monday to Friday from 8 am to 5 pm and Saturday from 9 am to noon. If you need to make international calls there is a card phone outside and you dial direct. Phonecards are sold at the post office.

The British Council Library is also on Oginga Odinga Rd. It has newspapers and magazines and quite a good library. It is open from 9.30 am to 1 pm and 2 to 5 pm Monday to Friday, and 8.30 am to 12.45 pm on Saturday.

For car rentals see Shiva Travels (tel 43420) or Kisumu Travels (tel 44122), both on Oginga Odinga Rd. Both agencies have a limited number of cars available. Prices are not as good as you can get in Nairobi.

Kisumu Museum

It comes as something of a surprise to find this excellent museum here – it's probably the best in the country and is well worth a visit. It's on Nairobi Rd within easy walking distance of the centre and is open daily from 9.30 am to 6 pm; entry is KSh 20.

The displays are well presented and wide ranging in their variety. There's a very good collection of everyday items from the various different peoples of the area, including agricultural implements, bird and insect traps (including a white-ant trap!), food utensils, clothes, furniture, weapons, musical instruments, a fairly motley collection of stuffed birds and animals and an amazing centrepiece of a lion riding on a wildebeest – both stuffed also.

Outside there is a traditional Luo home-

stead consisting of the mud and thatch house of the husband and separate ones for each wife. There's usually a man hanging around who will show you around for a few shillings and point out the salient features. Also outside are the inevitable crocodile and tortoise enclosures which are small and a bit depressing.

Market

Kisumu's market is one of the more animated in the country, and certainly one of the largest. Whether you're in the market for a kg of potatoes or are just curious, it's worth a stroll around. You can cut through to the bus station through the hole in the back wall of the market compound.

Hippo Point

Hippo Point is at Dunga, about three km south of town, and the café on the point is a good place to head for. There were no hippos in evidence when I visited but it's a pleasant spot all the same. Known as Dunga Refreshments, it is well signposted once you get out of town along Nzola Rd. This place also has the only camp site in Kisumu.

Places to Stay – bottom end

Accommodation in Kisumu generally seems to be more expensive than similar places elsewhere in Kenya though there's no apparent reason for this. The cheapest option if you don't mind dorm accommodation is the *YWCA* on the corner of Omolo Agar Rd and Nairobi Rd. Beds cost KSh 40, or there are just a few rooms at KSh 120 per person.

As usual, the real budget hotels are brothels and are shabby and extremely basic. Typical of these places is the *PVU Lodge* on Accra St, which charges KSh 60/85/100 for a single/double/triple room with common facilities. A step up the scale is the *New Rozy Lodge* on Ogada St. Rooms here go for KSh 90/165 with common bath; the doubles are definitely overpriced.

On Apindi St there's a couple of places worth a try. *Mirukas Lodge* has small singles but reasonable doubles for KSh 80/110 – not bad value for Kisumu. Right next door is

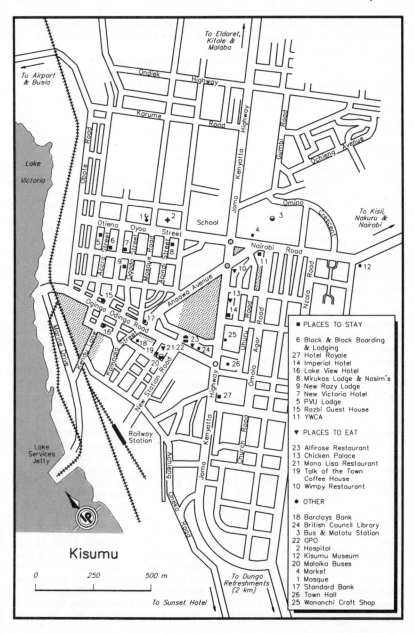

Kisumu

0   250   500 m

To Eldoret, Kitale & Malaba

To Airport & Busia

To Kisii, Nakuru & Nairobi

To Dunga Refreshments (2 km)

To Sunset Hotel

Lake Victoria

Lake Services Jetty

Railway Station

■ PLACES TO STAY

6 Black & Black Boarding & Lodging
27 Hotel Royale
14 Imperial Hotel
16 Lake View Hotel
8 Mirukas Lodge & Nasim's
9 New Rozy Lodge
7 New Victoria Hotel
5 PVU Lodge
15 Razbi Guest House
11 YWCA

▼ PLACES TO EAT

23 Alfirose Restaurant
13 Chicken Palace
21 Mona Lisa Restaurant
19 Talk of the Town Coffee House
10 Wimpy Restaurant

● OTHER

18 Barclays Bank
24 British Council Library
3 Bus & Matatu Station
22 GPO
2 Hospital
12 Kisumu Museum
20 Malaika Buses
4 Market
1 Mosque
17 Standard Bank
26 Town Hall
25 Wananchi Craft Shop

Nasim's which is even better value at KSh 110 for a double (no singles) and there's hot water in the common baths.

The pick of the bottom-end places, however, is the *Razbi Guest House* (tel 41312), upstairs on the corner of Oginga Odinga Rd and Kendu Lane. It's very secure (there's a locked grille at the top of the stairs), the rooms are spotless and a towel and soap are provided. The rates are KSh 100/155 for a single/double room with common bath (cold water only).

Right in the centre near Oginga Odinga Rd is the *Talk of the Town Coffee House* which also has rooms. These cost KSh 110/145 with common bath and are not terrific value considering what else is available. Another restaurant with rooms is the *Mona Lisa* on Oginga Odinga Rd but at KSh 90/125 it's worth paying the extra and staying at the Razbi.

Campers should head for *Dunga Refreshments* at Hippo Point, right on the water three km south of town. It takes nearly an hour to walk it, or you can take a taxi for KSh 70. Camping here costs KSh 60 per person, the only disadvantage being that there's no shade. You also need to bring all your own food with you unless you intend to eat in the restaurant as the only shops are in Kisumu. The restaurant offers Indian, Western and African food and is quite reasonably priced.

Places to Stay – middle

The *New Victoria Hotel* (tel 2909) on the corner of Kendu Lane and Gor Mahia Rd is good value, especially if you get one of the front rooms with balcony and views of Lake Victoria. The rates are KSh 165/305 for rooms with bath and breakfast. The hotel also has a good restaurant.

On the next corner down the hill is the *Black & Black Boarding & Lodging* where B&B is KSh 185/275. Bathrooms are shared by three rooms and there is hot water.

The *Lake View Hotel* is much closer to the lake but it barely seems to function as a hotel these days, although the bar is definitely still a bar. The rooms cost KSh 175/350 including bath and breakfast and, like the New Victoria, some rooms have views of the lake.

Places to Stay – top end

At the top of the range Kisumu has a few options. The *Hotel Royale* (tel 44240) on Jomo Kenyatta Highway exudes a certain creaking olde-worlde charm, but at KSh 300/480 for B&B with common facilities is not great value. With private bathroom the price jumps to KSh 505/720. Nonresidents can use the pool for KSh 20 per day.

The *Imperial Hotel* (tel 41485), also on Jomo Kenyatta Highway, is a much newer place and the prices reflect this – KSh 900/1140 for B&B. The hotel has a pool but it is tiny and is hemmed in by the building.

On the southern edge of town, the *Sunset Hotel* (tel 41100) does indeed have views of the sunset, and of the lake, from each room. There's also a swimming pool and a good, if expensive, restaurant. The room rates reflect the position and facilities; KSh 840/1020 for rooms with breakfast. It's part of the African Tours & Hotels Ltd chain and so can be booked in Nairobi in the City Hall Way office by the Hilton.

Places to Eat

For breakfast the best place is the airy restaurant in the *New Victoria Hotel*. For KSh 35 you get juice, papaya, eggs, toast, butter and tea or coffee. It's open for breakfast from 7 to 9 am and also serves standard dishes such as steak, chicken, chips, etc at other times. The *Mona Lisa Restaurant* on the main street also does good breakfasts and meals.

The *Talk of the Town Coffee House* just off Oginga Odinga Rd has good cheap meals and a couple of tables outside. For stand-up or takeaway greasy spoon there's the *Chicken Palace* or the *Wimpy*, both on Jomo Kenyatta Highway.

For something a bit better try the *Alfirose Restaurant* on Oginga Odinga Rd up near the British Council Library. The extensive menu includes good curries and fish dishes in the range of KSh 40 to KSh 90. This place is also licensed and is popular among local expats (mainly Peace Corps and VSO volunteers).

Bodega's is recommended for a cheap fish meal – huge portions of whole fresh fish for KSh 60 to KSh 85.

On Thursday evenings the *Hotel Royale* has a barbecue buffet for KSh 120 which is well worth the money.

If you take a walk out to Hippo Point, the *Dunga Refreshments* café has quite good Indian, Western and African meals and snacks and you can sit outside right on the water's edge.

Things to Buy
Kisumu is about the best place to buy Kisii soapstone carvings and there are pavement stalls set up on the northern side of Oginga Odinga Rd near the British Council Library.

The Wananchi Craft Shop near the town hall is a cooperative selling crafts made by the local women, and they have some interesting items.

Getting There & Away
Air Kenya Airways have 11 flights weekly to Nairobi. The trip takes one hour and costs KSh 650 one way.

Road There are plenty of buses and matatus to all over the place from the large bus station just north of the market. Destinations frequently served include Busia (KSh 50), Kakamega, Homa Bay, Kitale, Nakuru, Kericho and Nairobi. It's possible to book Nairobi buses in advance with Coast Bus at the bus station or Malaika buses in the town centre. Malaika have twice daily buses to Nairobi and Mombasa, and the charge is Kericho KSh 35, Nakuru KSh 60, Naivasha KSh 95, Nairobi KSh 110 and Mombasa KSh 240.

The quickest way to get to Kakamega and Kitale is in one of the fairly new minibuses which leave from right by Jomo Kenyatta Highway and not in the main part of the bus station. Peugeots to Nakuru and Nairobi also leave from here.

Train There are trains to Nairobi daily at 6.30 pm, arriving at 7.35 am the next day. Depending on demand there is often a second daily train. Fares to Nairobi are KSh 380 in 1st class, KSh 179 in 2nd class and KSh 90 in 3rd class. It's advisable to book in advance. The booking office at the station is open daily from 8 am to noon and 2 to 4 pm.

Lake Ferry With the demise of the international services, the Lake Victoria ferries now only go to places close to Kisumu such as Kendu Bay, Homa Bay, Asembo Bay and Mfangano Island. There are three classes on the ferries, none of them ever very crowded, so 2nd or 3rd class is quite OK.

The MV *Alestes* and MV *Reli* have the following services from Kisumu every day except Thursday:

	Arrival	Departure
Kisumu	–	9 am
Kendu Bay	11 am	11.10 am
Homa Bay	2 pm	2.30 pm
Asembo Bay	5 pm	8 am (next day)
Homa Bay	10.40 am	11 am
Kendu Bay	2 pm	2.45 pm
Kisumu	4 pm	–

The fares from Kisumu to Kendu Bay are KSh 50/40/25 in 1st/2nd/3rd class, to Homa Bay KSh 82/65/36, and to Asembo Bay KSh 133/108/52.

The MV *Kamondo* operates between Homa Bay and Mfangano and Rusinga islands twice a week, and between Homa Bay and Kisumu once a week.

AROUND THE LAKE
Kendu Bay
This small lakeside village has little to offer apart from a somewhat strange volcanic lake a couple of km from town. There's basic accommodation in the town, and the ferry jetty is about one km away.

Homa Bay
This is a very nondescript town on a small bay in Lake Victoria. If you've just got off the ferry from Kisumu you'll have to spend the night here, which is no great pleasure. For accommodation there's the *Asego Stores Guest House* which costs KSh 190 for a double with breakfast, or the expensive

Homa Bay Hotel (KSh 390/575). There's transport from here on to Kisii, Migori and Isebania (Tanzanian border) and back to Kisumu.

Rusinga Island

Mbita is the town on Rusinga Island and it is connected by a causeway to the mainland. The only remarkable thing about the island is the mausoleum of Tom Mboya on the northern side of the island – he was born here in 1930 and was shot dead by police in 1969 during political unrest.

There are matatus to Homa Bay, as well as the twice weekly ferry services to Mfangano and Homa Bay.

Mfangano Island

There's little to see here and very little in the way of facilities. The small fishing community is about as far off the beaten track as you can get in Kenya.

There is one cheap hotel and the island is connected to the mainland by twice-weekly ferries to Homa Bay.

Western Highlands

The Western Highlands are the agricultural heartland of Kenya and they separate Kisumu and Lake Victoria from the rest of the country. In the south around Kisii and Kericho lie the vast tea plantations, while further north around Kitale and Eldoret it's all fertile farming land.

The towns of the highlands are really just small agricultural service towns, much the same as you'd find in similar areas in Australia or the USA – and they're about as interesting. For visitors the attractions of the area lie outside these towns – the tea plantations around Kericho, Kakamega Forest near Kakamega, Mt Elgon and Saiwa Swamp national parks both near Kitale, and the Cherangani Hills which lie east of Kitale and Eldoret. They are dealt with in that order in this section.

KISII

As you might expect this is where Kisii soapstone comes from but it's not on sale here at all, the simple reason being that Kisii sees very few tourists and those that do come this way tend to just keep moving. You can, however, visit the quarries if you like. When you get there, ask for Abyce and he'll show you around. Not much happens in Kisii, and even the locals will tell you that it's 'a remote place'. On the other hand, people are friendly and interesting and as so few tourists come here you'll be regarded with curiosity.

Kisii is the main centre of the region known as the Gusii Highlands, home of the Gusii people. The Gusii, numbering around one million, are a Bantu speaking people in the middle of a non-Bantu area – the Maasai to the south, Luo to the west and north and Kipsigis to the east all speak unrelated languages.

The town centre is compact and, as usual, the market is the liveliest place in the town during the day.

Whilst you're here, it's worth making the four hour round trip to the top of nearby Manga Ridge from which the views – especially over Lake Victoria – are magnificent. You can also see Kisumu in the distance and the coffee plantations of Kericho behind you.

Places to Stay – bottom end

There are two excellent places to stay at in Kisii. The cheaper one is the new *Sabrina Lodge*, just around the corner from the matatu park. It's a very friendly place and has rooms with common facilities for KSh 90/145. The hotel also has a bar and restaurant. Somewhat more expensive is the *Safe Lodge* (tel 202950), opposite the BATA shop, which has friendly staff and costs KSh 130/180 for single/double self-contained rooms. There's hot water, soap and towel are provided and breakfast is included in the price. The single rooms have double beds so a couple could get away with this. It also has an excellent restaurant (dinner KSh 62) which is reminiscent of the sort of place you might find in a small French village. The hotel is also the main social focus of the town

Top: Approaching Lake Turkana (GP)
Bottom: Baragoi, Northern Kenya (GC)

Top Left: Baboon investigating Tuskers (beer), Tsavo National Park (GC)
Top Right: Mt Kilimanjaro from Amboseli National Park (GC)
Bottom: Amboseli National Park (GC)

Kisii

0   125   250 m

15 Akamba Buses
17 Barclays Bank
3 BP Station
5 EARS
16 Gusii Delux Buses
1 Highway Lodge
  & Kiango Lodge
4 Hospital
7 Market
8 Matatus to Kisumu
11 Matatus to Migori,
   Kericho & Tabaka
18 Kisii Mwalimu Hotel
13 Police Station
14 Post Office
6 Sabrina Lodge
12 Safe Lodge
9 Sarawa Towers Hotel
10 Standard Bank
2 Supermarket

– well, the video machine in the restaurant is, anyway.

There's also the *Highway Lodge*, one of the cheapest in town, which has clean, basic rooms for KSh 70/86 with common bath. The only problem here is that it's right on the main road, so the front rooms cop the noise. Right next door is the *Kiango Lodge* which is clean and costs KSh 95/145 for rooms with bath.

Places to Stay – middle

The modern high-rise building on the northern side of the market is the *Sarawa Towers Hotel*. Rooms here cost KSh 210/330 for a single/double with bath and breakfast.

Otherwise, there's the *Kisii Hotel* for KSh 240 or the *Kisii Mwalimu Hotel*, both slightly out of town. The Kisii Hotel is definitely the best of the two.

Places to Eat

For breakfast try the restaurant in the *Safe Lodge*. For KSh 33 you get juice, fruit, cereals, eggs, sausage, toast and tea or coffee – good value. They also serve good meals, and the fact that there is a video and they serve beer make this a gregarious and lively place, especially in the evenings.

For local tucker there are plenty of the usual sort of restaurant around the matatu station.

Getting There & Away

To make life confusing matatus leave from two separate locations. Matatus for Kisumu (KSh 50, three hours) leave from in front of the market, while those for everywhere else (Migori, Kericho, Tabaka) leave from the station up past the Standard Bank.

For direct buses to Nairobi Akamba has a night bus for KSh 150, and a day bus which also stops at Kericho (KSh 40), Nakuru (KSh 90) and Naivasha (KSh 120) en route. Tickets should be booked one day in advance. Gusii Deluxe Buses across the road has four nightly buses to Nairobi. The trip takes around 8½ hours. EARS also has a night bus to Nairobi at 9 pm for KSh 150.

TABAKA

This is the village where the soapstone is quarried and carved, and on arrival in the village it's easy enough to locate someone who can show you one of the workshops. It's almost just a cottage industry and there are few people who actually work the stone for a living – to most people it's just a handy way to supplement a meagre living made from agriculture.

To get there take one of the fairly infrequent matatus from Kisii.

KERICHO

Tea – it's everywhere! This is the real heart of Kenya's tea plantation area and the rolling hills are a uniform pale green. Kericho's climate is perfect for growing tea, the main aspect being the showers which fall every afternoon year-round. Yes, Kericho is a wet place but the showers are only brief and not unpleasant, and apart from benefiting the tea bushes, they make the town a green and pleasant land.

The town takes its name from the Maasai chief, Ole Kericho, who was killed by the Gusii in the 18th century in a battle over land – the Maasai had been in the area for years and didn't appreciate the Gusii moving into the area, although the Gusii themselves were being pushed by the advancing Luo. The area today is the home of the Kipsigis people, part of the greater Kalenjin group – a name (meaning 'I tell you') devised in the 1950s and given to the grouping of Nandi speaking tribes, including the Pokot, Kipsigis, Marakwet and Nandi.

The town itself has nothing to recommend it but it's not a bad place to stop for the night.

Information

The post office and the two main banks are all on Moi Highway. The banks are open Monday to Friday from 8 am to 1 pm and on Saturday from 8.30 to 11 am.

Tea Plantations

The closest plantation to town is behind the Tea Hotel, itself once owned by the Brooke Bond company. Walk through the hotel grounds behind what was the service station and out through the back gate. This path leads through the tea bushes to the hotel workers' huts. If you're lucky there may be picking in progress.

For a tour of a plantation and processing plant it may be possible to organise one through the Tea Hotel.

Places to Stay – bottom end

Kericho has the usual assortment of scruffy budget hotels at the bottom end of the market. The *Sugutek Hotel* on Tengecha Rd is about as basic as you can get but is cheap enough at KSh 60/95 for a single/double room with common bath. The hotel also has a restaurant.

The *Tas Lodge* is basically a mid-range place but it does have a few good single rooms for KSh 110 with common bath and hot water (in the morning only). Breakfast is also included. It's also possible to camp in the green gardens of this place for KSh 50 per person.

There are a few more basic boarding & lodging places on the road below the matatu station. None of them are up to much.

Places to Stay – middle

The *Tas Lodge* (tel 21112) on the Nakuru road is about the best. KSh 180/275 gets you a big bright room with bath and hot water, and breakfast is included. This hotel has a pleasant garden setting, including an open-air bar.

In the centre of town there's the characterless *Mwalimu Hotel* which charges KSh 215/300 for rooms with bath and breakfast. There's a restaurant and noisy bar in this place. Even more anonymous is the *Mid West Hotel* (tel 20611) on John Kericho Rd, where rooms go for KSh 450/580 with breakfast.

Places to Stay – top end

The *Tea Hotel* (tel 20280) has plenty of charm – it was built by the Brooke Bond

16 Barclays Bank
2 Bus & Matatus
18 Caltex Station
1 Cheap Hotels
19 Hindu Temple
20 Hospital
7 Kobil
12 Law Courts
3 Market
9 Mid West Hotel
11 Mother Hotel
10 Mwalimu Hotel
4 Police
13 Post Office
8 Shell
15 Standard Bank
14 Sugutek Hotel
6 Tas Lodge
5 Tea Hotel
17 Town Hall

To Nakuru

Kericho

0   100   200 m

To Kisii
& Kisumu

company in the 1950s but is now owned by African Tours & Hotels chain. At KSh 840/1020 for B&B, it doesn't do a lot of business, but it's worth a wander around and maybe have a drink (tea, perhaps?) in the lounge or on the terrace.

Places to Eat

For basic African stodge and stews the *Mother Hotel* on Uhuru Rd does as good a job as any, as does the restaurant in the *Sugutek Hotel* on Tengecha Rd – chips, chicken, ugali, etc.

The restaurant in the *Mwalimu Hotel* is a little more sophisticated, while the KSh 95 set lunch or dinner in the *Mid West Hotel* is good value.

For the full treatment you could try a meal at the *Tea Hotel* but don't expect to get out of it lightly.

Getting There & Away

The matatu station is fairly well organised, with matatus on the upper level and minibuses and buses on the lower level.

As is the case throughout the west, there is plenty of transport in any direction. To the town of Kisumu there are occasional Nissan

Gusii in traditional dress

A *kiinga* is a basket used for storing grain. It's made of long grass interwoven with string.

The Gusii

The Gusii number around one million and inhabit an area in the western highlands east of Lake Victoria. The area is dominated by Nilotic speaking groups with just this pocket of the Bantu speaking Gusii. Being a relatively small group, the Gusii were always on the move following influxes of other groups into their lands. After migrating to the Mt Elgon area sometime before the 15th century, the Gusii were gradually pushed south by the advancing Luo, and over the next couple of centuries came into conflict with the Maasai and the Kipsigis. They finally settled in the hills east of Lake Victoria as the high ridges were easier to defend. Having fought hard for their autonomy, the Gusii were unwilling to give it up to the British and suffered heavy losses in conflicts early this century. Following these conflicts the men were conscripted in large numbers into the British Army.

The Gusii family typically consists of a man, his wives and their married sons, all living together in a single compound. Large families served two purposes: with high infant mortality rates the survival of the family was assured, and the large numbers facilitated defence of the family enclosure. Initiation ceremonies are performed for both boys and girls, and rituals accompany all important events. Death is considered not to be natural but the work of 'witchcraft'. The Gusii were primarily cattle keepers but also practiced some crop cultivation and millet beer was often an important ingredient at big occasions.

As is the case with many of Kenya's ethnic groups, medicine men *(abanyamorigo)* had a highly privileged and respected position. Their duty was to maintain the physical and mental wellbeing of the group – doctor and social worker combined. One of the more bizarre practices was (and still is) the removal of sections of the skull or spine to aid maladies such as backache or concussion. ■

The Akamba

The traditional homeland of the Akamba people *(Ukumbani)* is the region east of Nairobi towards Tsavo National Park. They migrated here from the south several centuries ago in search of food, mainly the fruit of the baobab tree which was accorded great nutritional value.

The Akamba were great traders and ranged all the way from the coast to Lake Victoria and up to Lake Turkana. Ivory was one of the main barter items but locally made products such as beer, honey, iron weapons and ornaments were also traded. They used to obtain food stocks from the neighbouring Maasai and Kikuyu, as their own low altitude land was relatively poor and couldn't sustain the increasing population which followed their arrival in the area.

In colonial times, the Akamba were highly

regarded by the British for their intelligence and fighting ability, and were drafted in large numbers into the British Army. Thousands lost their lives in WW I. When it came to land, however, the British were not quite as respectful and tried to limit the number of cattle the Akamba could own (by confiscating them) and also settle more Europeans in Ukumbani. The Akamba response was the formation of the Ukamba Members Association, whose members marched en masse to Nairobi and squatted peacefully at Kariokor market in protest. After three weeks, the administration gave way and the cattle were eventually returned to the people.

All Akamba adolescents go through initiation rites to adulthood at around the age of 12, and have the same age-set groups common to many of Kenya's tribes. The various age-set rituals involve the men, and the women to a lesser extent, gaining seniority as they get older. Young parents were known as 'junior elders' (*mwanake* for men, *mwiitu* for women) and were responsible for the maintenance and upkeep of the village. Once his children were old enough to become junior elders themselves, the mwanake went through a ceremony to become a 'medium elder' (*nthele*), and later in life a 'full elder' (*atumia ma kivalo*) with the responsibility for death ceremonies and administering the law. The last stage of a person's life is that of 'senior elder' (*atumia ma kisuka*) who is responsible for the holy places.

Akamba subgroups include the Kitui, Masaku and Mumoni. ∎

Traditional weapons of the Akamba

The Luo

The Luo people live in the west of the country on the shores of Lake Victoria. Along with the Maasai, they migrated south from the Nile region of Sudan around the 15th century. Although they clashed heavily with the existing Bantu speaking people of the area, intermarriage and cultural mixing readily took place.

The Luo are unusual amongst Kenya's ethnic groups in that circumcision is not performed on either sex. This practice was instead replaced by something that one can imagine being almost as painful – the extraction of four or six teeth from the bottom jaw. Although it is not done that much these days, you still see many middle-aged and older people of the region who are minus a few bottom pegs.

Although originally cattle herders, the Luo have adopted fishing and subsistence agriculture. The family group consists of the man, his wife (or wives) and their sons and daughters-in-law. The house compound is enclosed by a fence, and includes separate huts for the man and for each wife and son. (There is a good reconstruction of a Luo village in the grounds of the Kisumu Museum.)

The family group is member of a larger grouping of families (*dhoot*), several of which in turn make up a group of geographically related people (*ogandi*),

Luo chief

each led by a chief *(ruoth)*. Collectively the ogandi constitute the Luo tribe. As is the case with many tribes, great importance is placed on the role of the medicine man and the spirits. ■

The Kalenjin

Kalenjin, which means 'I say to you' in Nandi, is a name formulated in the 1950s to describe the group of peoples previously called the Nandi by the British. The Nandi tag was erroneous as, although the people were all Nandi speakers (one of many dialects), they were not all Nandis; the other groups included the Kipsigis, Marakwet, Pokot and Tugen (arap Moi's people).

The Kalenjin people occupy the western edge of the central Rift Valley area which includes Kericho, Eldoret, Kitale, Baringo and the Mt Elgon area. They first migrated to the area west of Lake Turkana from southern Sudan around 2000 years ago and gradually moved south as the climate changed and the forests dwindled.

Although originally pastoralists, most Kalenjin groups took up agriculture. Some of them, however, such as the Okiek, stuck to the forests and to a hunter-gatherer existence. Beekeeping was a common practice and the honey was used not only in trade but also for brewing beer. As with most tribes, Kalenjin have age-sets into which a man is initiated after circumcision and remains for the rest of his life. Polygamy was widely practiced. Administration of the law is carried out at the *kok* – an informal gathering of the clan's elders and other interested parties in the dispute. Unusually, the doctors were mostly women and they used herbal remedies in their work. Other specialist doctors practiced trepanning (taking out pieces of the skull to cure certain ailments), which is also practiced by the Bantu speaking Gusii of the Kisii district. ■

Kalenjin in traditional dress

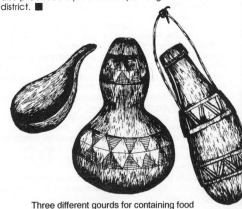

Three different gourds for containing food

minibuses as well as regular matatus. The companies running buses to Nairobi have small offices at the matatu station.

If you are hitching, the turn-off to Kisumu is about two km south of town along the Kisii road, so you need to get there first, either on foot or by matatu.

KAKAMEGA FOREST RESERVE

The Kakamega Forest Reserve is a superb slab of virgin tropical rainforest in the heart of an intensive agricultural area. It is home to a huge variety of birds and animals and is well worth the minimal effort required to get to it.

The Forest Department maintains a beautiful four room rest house here, as well as a large nursery for propagating trees and shrubs for planting both in this district and for ceremonial occasions around the country. The workers are very amenable and it's no problem to get shown around.

The forest near the rest house is very dense and there are paths leading all over the place. For that reason, and certainly for a greater appreciation of the forest flora and fauna, it's worth engaging one of the staff to guide you around. The most well known man, Leonard (known to some as Light-Fingered Lenny for reasons I won't go into), is amenable and his knowledge of the trees and birds is extensive. Binoculars are virtually essential, as is wet weather gear as it usually pisses down every afternoon for a couple of hours or so. For that reason also it's best to try and arrive in the morning as you usually have to walk a few km to reach the rest house. The driest period here is from December to April, but even then it rains daily.

Places to Stay & Eat

The *Forest Rest House* is a superb place to put your feet up for a few days. It's an elevated wooden building with a verandah which looks directly on to the seemingly impenetrable forest. There are only four double rooms, and surprisingly they all have a bathroom and toilet. Blankets are supplied but you need to have your own sleeping bag or sheet. It costs KSh 6 to camp here, or KSh

35 per person in the rooms. If the rest house is full when you arrive it is usually possible to sleep on the verandah for KSh 18. If you want to be sure of a room, book in advance through the Forest Officer, PO Box 88, Kakamega.

The only problem here is food. Basically you need to bring your own and preferably something to cook it on, although it is possible to cook on a fire. There is a small kiosk which sells beer, tea and sodas and also cooks basic meals at lunch time, and on request in the evenings – beans or corn and rice is about the limit, but you won't starve. The kiosk closes at 6.30 pm so you need to make sure they know you are coming. There is a small group of dukas about two km back towards Shinyalu, and you can get basic meals and supplies here.

Getting There & Away

The Forest Rest House lies about 12 km east of the A1 Kisumu-Kitale road, about 30 km north of Kisumu. Access is possible either from Kakamega village on the main road when coming from the north, or from Khayaga also on the main road when coming from the south. From both places dirt roads lead east to the small market village of Shinyalu, from where it's a further five km to the rest house, signposted to the left. There are matatu from Kakamega to Shinyalu (KSh 12), and even the occasional one from Khayaga to Shinyalu. If you want to walk – and it is beautiful walking country – it's about seven km from Khayaga to Shinyalu, about 10 km from Kakamega to Shinyalu. These roads become extremely treacherous after rain and you may prefer to walk when you see how the vehicles slip all over the road. There's very little traffic along either of the roads but you may get a lift with the occasional tractor or Forest Department vehicle. Whatever means you employ to get there, allow half a day from Kitale or Kisumu. From the turn-off to the rest house the dirt road continues on to Kapsabet so you could also come from that direction but it is a long walk if you can't get a lift.

KAKAMEGA

The town of Kakamega is on the A1 route, 50 km north of Kisumu and 115 km south of Kitale. About the only reason to stay here is if you are heading for the Kakamega Forest and arrive too late in the day to walk or get a vehicle in. It's also the last place to stock up with supplies if heading for a forest sojourn.

The town has the usual facilities – a couple of banks, post office, market and the ubiquitous boardings & lodgings.

Places to Stay

The *New Garden View Lodge* is conveniently close to the matatu station. It is a typical basic Kenyan hotel, and therefore serves as a brothel as well, but is not too bad at KSh 60/85 for a single/double. There is a couple of other places if this one doesn't appeal.

At the absolute other end of the scale is the *Golf Hotel* where rooms go for KSh 660/935 for B&B. The draw card of this place is the attached golf course, and your room rate includes temporary membership.

Getting There & Away

The matatu station is at the northern edge of town. There are buses, matatus or Peugeots to Kisumu, Webuye, Kitale, Nairobi and Busia. Hitching is not too difficult.

ELDORET

There is little to see or do in Eldoret but it may make a convenient stop for the night in your peregrinations around the western highlands, particularly if you are heading to or from the Cherangani Hills which lie to the north of Eldoret.

The town has benefited hugely from the new university here and so it seems likely that it will become one of the few expanding towns in the west.

Information

The post office is on the main street, Uganda Rd, and is open Monday to Friday from 8 am to 5 pm and Saturday from 9 am to noon. There are branches of both Barclays and the Standard Chartered banks, also both on the main street.

For car rental, check out the Eldoret Travel Agency (tel 33351) on Kenyatta St.

Places to Stay – bottom end

Right at the bottom of the range are the two *Sikh Temples* west of the town centre, where I was assured travellers could stay. If you do make use of this hospitality be sure to leave a donation.

For a regular hotel, try the *New Paradise Bar & Lodging* on the corner of Uganda Rd and Oginga Odinga St, or the *Top Lodge*, also on Oginga Odinga St. As usual, the prime function of these cheap places is as brothels but they are quite happy for you to stay a whole night.

Places to Stay – middle

The *Mahindi Hotel* is conveniently close to the bus and matatu station and is good value at KSh 155/215 for rooms with bath and hot water. They also have cheaper rooms at KSh 120 for singles with common bath. The hotel has a restaurant, and the noise from the Silent Night Bar (!) downstairs can sometimes be distracting. A similar place and also close to the bus station is the *New Miyako Hotel* (tel 22594) which charges KSh 120 for a single with common bath, and KSh 145/215 for singles/doubles with bath.

The *New Lincoln Hotel* (tel 22093) is much quieter and has parking spaces if you're driving. Self-contained rooms with breakfast included are a good bargain at KSh 205/310. The hotel also has its own restaurant and bar.

Places to Stay – top end

Eldoret's top-end offerings are the *Eldoret Wagon Hotel*, which charges KSh 360/540 for rooms with bath and breakfast, and the more modern *Sirikwa Hotel* (tel 31655) which has rooms for KSh 720/900 including breakfast. This place has the only swimming pool in Eldoret.

Places to Eat

A popular lunch time spot is *Otto Cafe* on

Eldoret

0   150   300 m

To Kitale & Uganda

To Sikh Temples (200 m)

To Nairobi

To Kisumu

18	Akamba Bus
11	Barclays
14	Bus & Matatu Park
17	Eldoret Travel Agency & Sizzlers Cafe
1	Eldoret Wagon Hotel
7	Library
13	Mahindi Hotel
5	National Bank of Kenya
8	New Church
16	New Lincoln Hotel
15	New Miyako Hotel
9	New Paradise Bar & Lodging
12	Otto Cafe
4	Police
3	Post Office
2	Sirikwa Hotel
19	Spark Milk Bar
10	Standard Chartered Bank
20	Top Lodge
6	Town Hall

Uganda Rd. It offers good cheap Western-style meals such as steak, chicken, sausages,

eggs, chips and other snacks. Another good place for snacks is the *Spark Milk Bar* on Oginga Odinga St.

For a slightly more upmarket meal or snack try the flash new *Sizzlers Cafe* on Kenyatta St, near the Eldoret Travel Agency. Here they have a whole range of burgers, curries, steak and sandwiches. It's popular but certainly not the cheapest in town.

For over the top meals both the *Sirikwa* and *Eldoret Wagon* hotels have fancy restaurants.

Getting There & Away
Air Air Kenya Aviation have four weekly flights between Nairobi's Wilson Airport and Eldoret. They depart from Nairobi on Tuesday and Thursday at 7 am and 3.45 pm, and from Eldoret at 8.15 am and 5 pm; the trip takes around one hour and costs KSh 1500 one way.

Road The bus and matatu station is right in

the centre of town, just off Uganda Rd. There are bus, minibus, Peugeot and matatu departures throughout the day for Kisumu, Nakuru, Naivasha, Nairobi, Kericho and Kitale. Peugeots to Nairobi cost KSh 180 and take just 3½ hours.

Train There are services three times a week for Nairobi on Wednesday, Saturday and Sunday at 9 pm, arriving the next day at 9.30 am. To the Ugandan border at Malaba they depart on Wednesday, Saturday and Sunday at around 4 am.

CHERANGANI HILLS
The beautiful Cherangani Hills are part of the Rift Valley system and extend for about 60 km from the north-east of Eldoret. They form the western wall of the spectacular Elgeyo Escarpment. You could easily spend weeks exploring here, and never come across another mzungu.

The area is best explored on foot as the roads are rough and some of those which scale the Elgeyo Escarpment are incredibly steep. In wet conditions the roads in this area become treacherous. For serious exploration you would need to get copies of the relevant Survey of Kenya maps to the area. Otherwise just follow the dirt roads.

The hills are dotted with small towns and although none of them have any recognised accommodation, it should be possible to arrange something with the local people. If you have a tent it's just a matter of finding a good spot and asking permission.

From Eldoret it should be possible to hitch, or even find a matatu, as far as Kapsowar, 70 km to the north-east in the Kerio Valley and right in the heart of the hills. Coming from the north there is a road which starts from Sigor at the Marich Pass and finds its way to Kapsowar via Tot and the impossibly steep escarpment road, but don't expect much in the way of transport along it.

The hills are the home of the Marakwet (or Markweta) people, part of the greater Kalenjin grouping. They migrated here from the north and found the area provided good safety and the streams were ideal for agricul-ture, as the rainfall was low. To this end they have made good use of, and extended, the water distribution channels which were already in existence when the Marakwet first migrated to the area. The channels distribute the water to all the small shambas in the hills.

KITALE
Kitale is another in the string of agricultural service towns which dot the western highlands. It does have a vaguely interesting museum but its main function for travellers is as a base for explorations further afield – Mt Elgon, Saiwa Swamp National Park – and a take-off point for the trip up to Lake Turkana. As such it's a pleasant enough town and can make an enjoyable stopover for a couple of days.

Information
The post office is on Post Office Rd (surprise, surprise) and is open the usual hours. It's possible to make international calls but they have to go through the operator in Nairobi, and this takes time.

Kitale has the usual banks and a busy market.

Kitale Museum
The museum has a variety of indoor exhibits, including good ethnographic displays of the Turkana people. The outdoor exhibits include traditional homesteads of a number of different tribal groups, the inevitable tortoise enclosure and an interesting biogas display. Probably most interesting is the small nature trail which leads through some virgin forest at the back of the museum. There are numbered points along the way and a small guidebook available from the craft shop (KSh 5) explains the points of interest.

The museum is open Monday to Friday from 7.30 am to 6 pm, Saturday from 8 am to 6 pm and Sunday from 9 am to 6 pm; entry is KSh 20.

Places to Stay – bottom end
Best of the usual bunch of cheapies/brothels is the *Star Lodge*. Good sized rooms upstairs

To Eldoret & Kisumu

Nature Trail

8

Kitale

300 m

150

0

Kenyatta Street

Post Office Road

7

9

5

Askari Road

4

3

Street

Bank Street

10

11

22

21

23

Moi Avenue

12

20

Kenyatta Street

13

15

18

19

16

17

14

Engineering Shops

To Kapenguria & Lodwar

Railway Station

To Mt Elgon & Endebess

Bus & Matatu Park

To budget hotels

1

2

22 Akamba Bus
6 Alakara Hotel
12 Barclays
20 Bongo Hotel
1 Covered market
7 Delicious Restaurant
10 Executive Lodge
18 Hotel Mamboleo
16 Kahuruko Boarding & Lodging
19 Kenya Commercial Bank
8 Kitale Museum
23 Law Courts
4 New Kitale Hotel
15 New Mombasa Hotel
2 Open food market
3 Police
5 Post Office
14 Rock Hotel
11 Standard Chartered Bank
17 Star Lodge
9 Three Shade Bar
21 Town Hall
13 Wandi Cafe

are KSh 60/85 with common bath, although they are a bit noisy from the road below.

The *Kahuroko Boarding & Lodging* has double rooms for KSh 120 with common bath. These are in the back yard of the hotel (which has excellent mid-range single rooms upstairs) and are a bit gloomy and also noisy.

There's a stack of other cheap places, and a couple of the better ones are the *New Mombasa Hotel* and the *Hotel Mamboleo*, both on Moi Ave. The Mamboleo's rooms are also on the gloomy side but are not bad value at KSh 85/130 with bath. Up beyond the covered market there is a number of very basic places which charge around KSh 60/85 for basic rooms.

If you want to camp the only place in the area is the *Sirikwa Safaris*, about 20 km north of Kitale on the Kapenguria road. It's run by Mrs Barnley and her daughter and in fact is just their house – they have a couple of rooms (expensive) or you can camp in the garden. It's a very pleasant setting and is a good place to relax for a day or two. Camping costs KSh 60 per person and you need to bring your own supplies, although gargantuan meals are available for KSh 145 for dinner or KSh 110 for breakfast. There's no sign for this place but the matatu drivers usually know where to drop you – ask for Safari Lodge; the driveway is at the top of a rise on the eastern side of the road, and is flanked by three yellow concrete posts.

Places to Stay – middle
For singles, or couples who don't mind sharing a bed, the *Kahuroko Boarding & Lodging* is a good place. Modern rooms with a double bed, bath and hot water cost KSh 145. The *Executive Lodge* on Kenyatta St is similar – large singles with a big bed and bathroom for KSh 180; there are also cheaper rooms with common bath for KSh 95/180.

The *New Kitale Hotel* is the town's old colonial place but these days it's poor value – the whole place has an air of neglect and it seems they are generating a bit of income by letting out some rooms to businesses on a permanent basis. The tariff is KSh 180/300 with bath and breakfast.

The brand new *Alakara Hotel* on Kenyatta St is the best in this category, although it remains to be seen whether they can maintain the standard. Well appointed rooms with bathrooms and hot water cost KSh 215/300.

Places to Stay – top end
The new *Bongo Hotel* (tel 20593) on Moi Ave has good self-contained rooms for KSh 300/360 with breakfast. It's not bad value although the rooms are definitely on the small side.

The best place is Mrs Barnley's *Sirikwa Safaris* where a room with breakfast is KSh 575/865, or KSh 720/1150 with half board. See the bottom-end section for location details.

Places to Eat
The *Wandi Cafe* on Kenyatta St is a popular place at lunch time. They serve basic but tasty meals such as beef stew with rice, and chicken and chips. Another good place is the *Delicious Restaurant* on the same street.

The *Bongo Hotel* on the corner of Moi Ave and Bank St is a slightly more upmarket restaurant and a good place for an evening meal. They also serve alcohol. Right next door is the lively Bongo Bar and there's also a takeaway food section. Other lively bars include the *Three Shade Bar* on Kenyatta St and the *Rock Hotel*.

Getting There & Away
The bus and matatu park is fairly chaotic – it's just a matter of wandering around and finding a vehicle going your way. As is usually the case, competition for passengers is keen and you'll soon be spotted and pointed in the right direction.

For Lodwar and Kalekol in the Turkana district there is a daily JM bus at around 9 am, although it cruises up and down at lunatic speeds for at least two hours prior to that drumming up business. Get on early if you want a choice of seats, otherwise wait near the mosque near the budget hotels past the market (just ask) as they stop and load all the roof baggage there when they are ready to leave. The trip takes around seven hours to Lodwar and costs KSh 125. At around 3 pm (or soon after it arrives in Lodwar) the bus continues on to Kalekol close to the lake shore. This leg of the trip takes around one hour and costs KSh 25. On the Kitale-Lodwar route there is usually at least one large matatu doing the trip daily. They also leave Kitale at around 9 am, but take only around five hours. Every second day there is a minibus doing the trip and this takes only four hours. Although the JM bus is slowest, it is also the most interesting as local Turkana tribespeople in traditional gear get on and off, seemingly in the middle of nowhere.

On the Nairobi route there is a variety of transport – bus, matatu, Peugeot – so it's a matter of finding which suits you. The bus companies have their offices mainly around the bus station area. The exception is Akamba which has its office on Moi Ave. They have daily buses to Nairobi at 9 am and 9 pm; the fare is KSh 155.

For Kakamega there are matatus (KSh 55) and minibuses, the latter en route to Kisumu. For Mt Elgon take one of the frequent matatus to Endebess.

SAIWA SWAMP NATIONAL PARK
This small park north of Kitale is a real delight. The swamp area is the habitat of the sitatunga antelope (*Tragelaphus spekii*), known in Swahili as the Nzohe, and this park has been set aside to protect this habitat.

What makes this park unique is that the only way around inside the park is on foot. There are marked walking trails which skirt the swamp, duckboards right across the swamp in places, and some extremely rickety observation towers. The sitatunga is fairly elusive and really the only way to spot one is to sit atop one of these towers armed with a pair of binoculars and a hefty dose of patience. As is the case in most of the parks, the best time for animal spotting is in the early morning or late afternoon.

This shy antelope is not unlike a bushbuck in appearance, although larger, and has elongated hooves which are supposed to make it

easier for it to get around in swampy conditions – it's hard to see how, but no doubt nature has it all worked out. The colouring is basically grey-brown, with more red noticeable in the females, and both sexes have white spots or stripes on the upper body. The males have long twisted horns which grow up to a metre in length.

The park is also home to the impressive black-and-white colobus monkey (*Colobus polykomos*). It inhabits the higher levels of the trees and, not having the gregarious nature of many primates, is easy to miss as it sits quietly in the heights. When they do move, however, the flowing 'cape' of white hair is very distinctive. Birdlife within the park is also prolific.

With all this on offer it's surprising how few people visit Saiwa Swamp.

Places to Stay
It is possible to camp at the ranger's station inside the park but there is nothing in the way of facilities, otherwise the nearest accommodation is at Kitale or the *Sirikwa Safaris* house of the Barnley family, some few km along the main road to the north (see the Kitale section).

Getting There & Away
Saiwa Swamp National Park lies five km east of the main A1 road, 18 km north of Kitale. Any of the matatus running between Kitale and Kapenguria will let you off at the signposted turn-off, from where you'll probably have to walk to the park as there is little traffic along the dirt road.

MT ELGON NATIONAL PARK
Mt Elgon sits astride the Kenya-Uganda border and, while it offers similar trekking possibilities to Mt Kenya, its location makes it a far less popular goal. The lower altitude also means that the weather on the upper slopes is not quite as severe.

The mountain is an extinct volcano and the national park extends from the lower slopes right up to the border. The highest peak of Elgon, Wagagai (at 4321 metres the 4th highest in Africa) is actually on the far side of the crater in Uganda; the highest peak on the Kenyan side is Koitoboss. There are warm springs in the crater itself, the floor of which is around 3500 metres above sea level.

As access to the national park, which covers 170 square km, is only officially allowed with a vehicle, those of independent means can take advantage of two other trekking routes to the north and south of the national park.

The mountain's biggest attraction is the elephants, renowned the world over for their predilection for salt, the major source of which is in the caves on the mountain slopes. The elephants are such keen excavators that one school of thought has it that it is the elephants that are totally responsible for the caves. Sadly the numbers of these saline-loving creatures has declined over the years, mainly due to incursions by poachers from the Ugandan side. There are three caves which are open to visitors – Kitum, Chepnyali and Mackingeny. Kitum is the one which you are most likely to see elephants in, Mackingeny the most spectacular. Obviously a good torch (flashlight) is essential.

Less obvious attractions are the ranges of vegetation found on the mountain, starting with forest at the base, then as you ascend it changes to bamboo jungle and finally alpine moorland with the bizarre giant groundsel and giant lobelia plants. The lower forests are the habitat of the impressive black and white colobus monkey along with many other species of birds and animals. Those most commonly sighted include buffalo, bushbuck, giant forest hog and Sykes monkey.

Access to the park is from Endebess, west of Kitale. This is as far as matatu transport goes and is where the bitumen stops. In the dry season it is possible to hire a matatu to take you to the park entrance at Chorlim Gate, but from there you'll have to wait for a lift – and you could be waiting a long time as this is not a popular park. In the wet season the only way in is to have your own 4WD. Elgon can be a wet place at any time of the year, but the driest months seem to be

December, January and February. As well as waterproof gear you are going to need warm clothes as it gets bloody cold up here at night.

If you want to walk in the park, the most popular route is from Kimilili, a small village 36 km south of Kitale on the main A1 road to Webuye and Kisumu. There's basic accommodation here, and matatus going on the seven km to Kapsakwany, from where you start walking. The Kimilili Forest Station is about five km past Kapsakwany and from there it's a further 20 km to the Chepkitale Forest Station, and another seven km past this station to the mountain hut. Obviously it's a long day's walk from Kapsakwany to the hut (32 km for those of you who can't add up) but the rangers at either of the forest stations shouldn't mind if you camp there.

From the hut it takes around four hours to reach the lake known as Lower Elgon Tarn, and from here it's a further one hour walk along a marked trail (cairns and white blazes) to Lower Elgon peak. The pass at the foot of Koitoboss peak and the Suam hot springs are around the crater rim to the right (north-east) and once here you are in the national park. If you reach this point and descend via the park entrance (Chorlim Gate), which is in fact illegal as you're not supposed to walk in the park, expect some difficult questions and be prepared to pay the KSh 220 park entry fee. The options are to return the same way, or via the third route, known as the Masara route, which goes to the small village of Masara on the northern slopes of the mountain, a trek of about 25 km.

Places to Stay

Apart from a very on again/off again lodge, there's no accommodation on the mountain so you need to be fully self-contained. The *Mt Elgon Lodge* officially charges KSh 540/980 for full board – if it's open (don't count on it).

Getting There & Away

As described above, access to the national park is by vehicle only and there's very little traffic so hitching is not an option.

Northern Kenya

This vast area, covering thousands of square km to the borders with Sudan, Ethiopia and Somalia, is an explorer's paradise hardly touched by the 20th century. The tribes which live here – the Samburu, Turkana, Rendille, Boran, Gabra, Merille and El-Molo – are some of the most fascinating people in the world. The whole area is a living ethnology museum. Like the Maasai, most of them have little contact with the modern world, preferring their own centuries-old traditional lifestyles and customs which bind members of a tribe together and ensure that each individual has a part to play. Many have strong warrior traditions and, in the past, it was the balance of power between the tribes which defined their respective areas.

As late as 1980 there was a clash between the Samburu and the Turkana over grazing land near South Horr which required army intervention. Since most of the tribes are nomadic pastoralists these sort of conflicts have a long history. Nevertheless, the settlement of disputes between the tribes is based on compensation rather than retribution so wholesale violence is a rare occurrence.

Change is slowly coming to these people as a result of missionary activity (there are an incredible number of different Christian missions, schools and aid agencies, many of them in very remote areas), employment as rangers and antipoaching patrols in national parks and game reserves, the construction of dams and roads, and the tourist trade. You may well be surprised, for example, to see a young man dressed smartly in Western-style clothes doing some business in a small town and then later on the same day meet him again out in the bush dressed in traditional regalia. It might even turn out that he's a college student in Nairobi for much of the year. Pride in their heritage is one thing these people are very unlikely to lose.

Yet, such examples of sophistication apart, not only are the people another world away from Nairobi and the more developed areas of the country but the landscapes are tremendous. Perhaps no other country in Africa offers such diversity. Much of it is scrub desert dissected by *luggas* (dry river beds which burst into brief but violent life whenever there is a cloud burst) and peppered with acacia thorn trees which are often festooned with weaver bird nests. But there are also extinct and dormant volcanos, barren, shattered lava beds, canyons through which cool, clear streams flow, oases of lush vegetation hemmed in by craggy mountains and huge islands of forested mountains surrounded by sand deserts. And, of course, the legendary 'Jade Sea' (Lake Turkana) – Kenya's largest lake and, as a result of the Leakeys' archaeological digs, regarded by many as the birthplace of mankind.

A long narrow body of water, Lake Turkana stretches south from the Ethiopian border for some 250 km, yet is never more than 50 km wide. While it looks fairly placid most of the time, it is notorious for its vicious squalls which whip up seemingly out of nowhere, and these are largely responsible for the fatalities among the local Turkana and El-Molo people who live along the lake shores.

It was first reached by Europeans in the late 19th century in the form of two Austrian explorers, von Hehnel and Teleki, who named it Lake Rudolf and it wasn't until the early 1970s that the name was changed to Turkana. The Leakeys' fossil discoveries of hominid skulls here are thought to be around 2½ million years old. At that time it is believed that the lake was far more extensive than it is today and supported a richer plant and animal life. Around 10,000 years ago the water level was high enough for the lake to be one of the sources of the Nile, which accounts for the presence of the huge Nile perch still found in the lake.

The contrasts are incredible in this part of Kenya and the climate mirrors this. By

Northern Kenya

0   50   100 km

midday on the plains the temperature can reach 50°C without a breath of wind to relieve the sweat pouring from your brow. Mirages shimmer in the distance on all sides. Nothing moves. Yet in the evening, the calm can suddenly be shattered as the most violent thunderstorm you have ever experienced tears through the place taking all before it. And, just as suddenly, it can all be over leaving you with the clearest, star studded skies you have ever seen. It's adventure country *par excellence*.

A remote region like this with such diverse geographical and climatic features naturally supports a varied fauna. Two species you will see a lot of here (but not elsewhere) are Grevy's zebra, with their much denser pattern of stripes and saucerlike ears, and the reticulated giraffe. Herds of domestic camel are commonplace in the area and often miraculously emerge from a mirage along with their owner when you are bogged down to the axles in soft sand or mud in the middle of the desert. A rope is all you need, although it's a seller's market of course. Lake Turkana also supports the largest population of Nile crocodile in Kenya which feed mainly on the fish living in the lake but which will quite happily dine on incautious humans swimming there. The giant eland finds a sanctuary in the forested hills around Marsabit.

There are several national parks and game sanctuaries in the area, three of them along the Ewaso Nyiro River just north of Isiolo. Further north are the national reserves of Maralal, Losai and Marsabit and right up near the Ethiopian border on the eastern shores of Lake Turkana is the Sibiloi National Park. Others are in the planning stages particularly one in the Mathew's Range north of Wamba which is currently a rhino and elephant sanctuary.

The national parks and game reserves of Marsabit, Maralal, Samburu, Buffalo Springs, Shaba and Meru, on the eastern side, and Saiwa Swamp, on the western side, are all accessible by a combination of public transport and hitching.

Getting There & Around

Hitching Apart from three routes, Kitale-Lodwar, Nyahururu-Maralal-Baragoi and Isiolo-Marsabit-Moyale, there is no public transport in this area of Kenya. You can certainly hitch as far as Maralal or Marsabit (from Nyahururu or Isiolo) on the eastern side and Lodwar (from Kitale) on the western side but that's about the limit of reliable hitching possibilities. There is *very* little traffic on any other routes though I have seen obvious hitchhikers atop trucks heading south out of Loyangalani and met others attempting to hitch north from there to North Horr and Marsabit.

The mission stations/schools invariably have their own Land Rovers (and some have their own light aircraft) but they usually only go in to regional centres of population once a week or once a fortnight. Even so, although most will try to help out if you're stuck, you cannot be guaranteed a lift. The vehicle might be full of people who need urgent medical assistance or (on the return journey) full of supplies. It can be done, of course, but you must have no deadlines to meet and you must be the sort of person who is quite happy to wait around for days for a ride. In some ways, this could be a very interesting way of getting around and you'd certainly meet a lot of local people but if it is lifts you want you can only do this along the main routes.

You could, of course, buy a camel and do a John Hillaby but this isn't something to approach lightly. It is, however, a distinct possibility especially if you are part of a small group. You'd have the adventure of your life!

Driving For most travellers who want freedom of movement and to see a lot of places it comes down to hiring a vehicle or going on an organised safari. Remember if you are taking your own vehicle to bring a high-rise jack, sand ladders, a shovel, a long, strong rope or chain (that you can hitch up to camels or other vehicles) plus enough fuel and water. The only regular petrol pumps you will find are at Isiolo, Maralal and Marsabit. Elsewhere there's usually nothing except religious mission stations which will reluctantly sell you limited amounts of fuel at up to three times the price in Nairobi. You can't blame them – they have to truck it in in barrels in the back of their Land Rovers or pay for someone else to do it in a truck. A 4WD vehicle is obligatory and you'd be extremely foolhardy to attempt such a journey in anything else except for Samburu National Park and Buffalo Springs National Reserve.

Organised Safaris Most of these last eight to nine days and they all seem to follow much the same route. Starting from Nairobi, they head up the Rift Valley to Lake Baringo, over to Maralal and then up the main route to Loyangalani on Lake Turkana via Baragoi and South Horr. On the return journey, again via Maralal, they take in Samburu National Park and Buffalo Springs National Reserve. Only one or two of them take in Marsabit National Reserve since the only way of getting there from Loyangalani is directly across the Koroli Desert (hazardous after rain) or via the long loop north through North Horr and Maikona. Even this involves crossing the Chalbi Desert which, like the Koroli, is hazardous after rain. There are also the restrictions on the Marsabit-Isiolo road to contend with – all transport must go in convoy at a certain time of day, usually 10 to 11 am.

The cost of the safaris varies between KSh 3300 and KSh 3960 and includes transport, all meals, park fees and necessary camping equipment. There are all-camping safaris which use open-sided 4WD trucks and are not, therefore, for those in search of luxury. Everyone has their favourite company but a lot depends on the people you find yourself with, what you see en route and the drivers and guides. The following companies all offer Turkana tours, usually once a week but sometimes once a fortnight:

Best Camping
    PO Box 40223, Nanak House, 2nd floor, corner Kimathi and Banda streets, Nairobi (tel 28091, 27203)

Birds Paradise Tours & Travel Ltd
    PO Box 22121, Nairobi (tel 25898)
Safari Camp Services
    PO Box 44801, corner Koinange and Moktar Daddah streets, Nairobi (tel 28936, 330130)
Special Camping Safaris
    PO Box 51512, Gilfillan House, 3rd floor, Kenyatta Ave, Nairobi (tel 338325)
Zirkuli Expeditions
    PO Box 34548, Banda St, Nairobi (tel 23949, 20848)

Some companies also offer flying safaris to Lake Turkana using twin-engined aircraft but they cost more than the truck tours. Two companies which offer this are Birds Paradise Tours & Travel Ltd (address above) and Turkana Air Safaris (tel 26623, 26808), PO Box 41078, Nairobi. These usually go to the western side of the lake and use Lake Turkana Lodge on Ferguson's Gulf as a base. A five day tour costs KSh 6960. You can also combine the Turkana safari with one to Masai Mara but the five day safari then goes up to KSh 9240.

West of Turkana

From Kitale the road north winds through the fertile highlands, passing the turn-off for the tiny Saiwa Swamp National Park (well worth a visit) before reaching Kapenguria, the town most famous for being the place where Jomo Kenyatta and five associates were held and tried in 1953 for their part in the Mau Mau uprising.

The road then snakes its way through the narrow northern gorges of the Cherangani Hills, emerging on to the desert plains through the Marich Pass. The change in scenery is dramatic and there are some fantastic views of the plains. The only town in this part of the hills is Ortum, just off the road. There is basic accommodation in the town if you want to stop and explore the area but the best place to stay in this area is the Marich Pass Field Studies Centre (see below).

Shortly after leaving the Marich Pass is a

turn-off to the left to the Turkwel Gorge. There is a huge hydroelectric project nearing completion here and when finished it should supply electricity to a large area of the densely populated highlands – the northern areas will still have to rely on generators.

After km of endless plains and dry creek beds Lokichar is little more than a collection of dismal dukas by the side of the road. The heat here is oppressive and the settlement seems to be gripped by a permanent torpor. The one redeeming feature of the place is that it is possible to buy the basketware and other Turkana trinkets cheaper than you'll find them further north.

MARICH PASS
The best place to stay in this area is the *Marich Pass Field Studies Centre* (tel (0321) 31541), PO Box 2454, Eldoret. This is essentially a residential facility for groups pursuing field courses in geography, botany, zoology, ecology, conservation, geology and rural development, but it's also open to independent travellers who want to spend a day, a week or a month in a little-known corner of Kenya.

The Centre covers an area of 12 hectares and is surrounded by dense bush and woodland. Birdlife is prolific, monkeys and baboons are 'in residence', while wart hog, buffalo, antelope and elephants are regular visitors. Facilities include a secure camp site (KSh 50 per person per night) with drinking water, toilets, showers and firewood, and several bandas with beds, mattresses and blankets provided (KSh 85 per person per night). English speaking Pokot and Turkana guides are available on request. A dormitory block and basic restaurant are due to be completed shortly.

Most necessities and fresh food are available in local shops and markets but you need to bring with you canned and packet foods if required. Those with their own vehicles should bring sufficient supplies of petrol as there are no service stations between Kapenguria and Lodwar. If you intend walking in the vicinity then you need to be adequately prepared for a variety of weather conditions.

Excursions from the Marich Pass
A few km to the north-west, Mt Sekerr (3326 metres) can be climbed comfortably in a three day round trip via the agricultural plots of the Pokot tribe, forest and open moors. The views from the top are magnificent when the weather is clear.

To the south are the Cherangani Hills, which offer some of the best hill walking possibilities anywhere in Kenya ranging from half-day excursions to week-long safaris by vehicle and on foot. Possibilities include a half-day walk along the old road perched high on the eastern side of the Marich Pass to a local Pokot trading centre; a hard day's slog up the dome of Koh which soars some 1524 metres above the adjacent plains; a safari of several days' duration along the verdant Weiwei Valley to Tamkal and then up to Lelan Forest and the main peaks of the Cherangani.

The Elgeyo Escarpment, which rises in places to more than 1830 metres above the Kerio Valley and offers spectacular views and waterfalls, is only 1½ hours away from the Centre along a road that passes through several local market centres and intensively farmed garden plots.

The South Turkana National Reserve in dry and rugged hills north-east of the Centre is the domain of Turkana herdsmen and rarely visited by outsiders. The 50 km drive there traverses grazing lands of the pastoral Pokot.

Lastly, the Turkwel Gorge hydroelectric project is only 30 km away along a fine tarmac road. Much of the gorge with its towering rock walls has not been affected by the construction while the dam (the highest of its type in Africa) and connecting road up a sheer mountain face is itself spectacular. The 35 km long lake will eventually be available for fishing, sailing and other water sports.

Getting There & Away
To reach the Field Studies Centre, leave the

main Kitale-Lodwar road at the Centre's signpost two km north of the Sigor-Tot junction at Marich Pass and continue south for one km down a clearly marked track. There are three approaches to Marich Pass:

1. The easiest is through Kitale and Kapenguria and then a further 67 km down a tarmac road (described as possibly Kenya's most spectacular tarmac road'). There are daily bus services from Nairobi to Kapenguria and matatus (KSh 35) from there to Marich Pass.

2. Through Iten either from Eldoret or via Kabarnet using the new and very scenic road across the upper Kerio Valley from Kabarnet. The all-weather Cherangani Highway can be picked up from Iten to cross the main pass of the Cherangani Hills and join up with the Kitale-Lodwar road near Kapenguria.

3. The roughest of the three approaches is the road from Lake Baringo through the Kito Pass and across the Kerio Valley to Tot but it gives you the chance of a diversion to the hot waterfalls at Kapedo. From Tot, the track skirts the northern face of the Cherangani Hills and involves fording numerous streams which may be impassable after heavy rain.

LODWAR

The hot and dusty administrative town of Lodwar is the only town of any significance in the north-west. With a bitumen road connecting it with the highlands, and air connections with Nairobi, it is no longer the isolated outpost of the Northern Frontier District that it was during colonial days but is certainly lagging a few steps behind the rest of the country.

Lodwar is also the base for any excursions to the lake from the western side and you will probably find it convenient to stay here for a night at least. There's little to do in the town itself but it has an outback atmosphere which is not altogether unpleasant and just watching the garrulous locals is entertainment in itself. The Turkana have suddenly found that tourists are a good touch when it comes to selling trinkets and they approach with alarming audacity and don't conceal their disgust when you don't want to buy. They are also remarkably persistent. The small market is a good place to watch women weaving the baskets.

Information

The town has a post office and a branch of the Kenya Commercial Bank.

Places to Stay – bottom end

Lodwar is one place where it's worth spending a bit more on accommodation – mainly to get a room with a fan. The rooms in the cheaper places are all hellishly hot and as the mosquitoes are fierce you need to cover up or burn coils if you don't have a net. It seems the recently surfaced road from the south has put Lodwar on the map, and there are new hotels springing up all the time.

Best of the cheapies is the *Mombasa Hotel*, almost next door to the JM Bus office which is where you'll be dropped if arriving that way from Kitale. The friendly Muslim owners charge KSh 60 for single rooms and KSh 95 for doubles. The singles are cooler (it's all relative though) as they have high ceilings. If you have a mosquito net you can sleep in the courtyard.

The *Marira Boarding & Lodging* is a new place and could be worth a try. Another bottom-end cheapie is the *Ngonda Hotel*. Both charge around KSh 60/95 for singles/ doubles without fan.

Places to Stay – middle

The *Turkwel Hotel* (tel 21201) is the town's social focus and also has the best accommodation. Single rooms with fan and common bath go for KSh 100, while singles/doubles with fan and bath cost KSh 180/240. There are also a few spacious cottages which are very pleasant and cost KSh 360 for two including breakfast.

Directly opposite the Turkwel is the *New Lodwar Lodge* which has concrete and bamboo cottages situated where they catch the breeze, although they are somewhat overpriced at KSh 180/360.

It is rumoured that a luxury hotel of the

African Tours & Hotels chain is to be built on the southern side of the Turkwel River on the approach into town.

Places to Eat

The restaurant at the *Mombasa Hotel* does reasonable local food and has excellent fresh mandazis early in the morning. The *Marira Boarding & Lodging* has little variety but their chips are excellent and freshly cooked to order. For something a bit more sophisticated the *Turkwel Hotel* restaurant does standard Western fare such as steak, chips, etc. Breakfast here consists of a couple of eggs and a sausage and nonresidents are not served until all the hotel guests have finished. The bar here is also a popular place.

Getting There & Away

There are daily JM buses to Kitale at 7 am. The trip takes around seven hours and costs KSh 125. There are also matatus covering this route but they tend to operate on a supply and demand basis. If you can find one they are much quicker than the bus.

The JM bus arriving from Kitale daily at around 3 pm continues on to Kalekol near the lake at around 4 pm. The fare is KSh 20 and the trip takes one hour. If you want to hitch to Kalekol the place where the locals wait is under the tree about 200 metres north of the Kobil station. To give an indication of how long you can expect to wait, there is a chai stall here which also sells mandazis.

KALEKOL

Most travellers head on from Lodwar to Kalekol, a fairly dismal little town a few km from the lake shore. The main building in the one street town is the fish processing factory built with Scandinavian money and expertise and, although fairly new is currently not operating. There is also an Italian sponsored plant closer to the lake shore.

Places to Stay & Eat

A good place to stay is the rudimentary but friendly *George Oyavi's Hotel*. It is right next to the bus office and George meets all incoming buses. The rooms are only rough grass

constructions and so thankfully get some breeze. There's a rough and ready shower rigged up and George and his staff somehow muddle through and cook meals although you need to order in advance. Warm beer and sodas are also available. If you want anything more sophisticated to eat than rice, chapatis or fish you'll need to bring it from Lodwar.

There's a second hotel called *Skyway Bar & Lodge* on the right-hand side as you enter Kalekol from the south. Rooms here cost KSh 35/120 a single/double with shared bathroom facilities. Next door is the *Safari Hotel* which has a reasonable restaurant.

Getting There & Away

There is a daily JM Bus to Lodwar and Kitale at 5 am. There is no danger of missing it as the driver revs the engine and honks the horn in plenty of time. The fare to Lodwar is KSh 24, and to Kitale KSh 145.

To get out to the lake it's a hot 1½ hour walk. Someone at George's will guide you, or just walk to the Italian fishing project and cut across the lake bed from there to the lodge.

FERGUSON'S GULF

This is the most accessible part of the lake shore but really it's not particularly attractive, although the sense of achievement in just getting there usually compensates. The water has receded greatly, mainly due to drought in Ethiopia, so you have to walk a long way over the lake bed to actually get to the water. The birdlife along the shore is prolific with flamingos and wild birds. There are also hippos and crocodiles so seek local advice before having a refreshing dip.

There is a small fishing village of grass huts on the far side of the Turkana Lodge and that's about the limit of things.

To get out on the lake you can hire the launches from the lodge to take you to Central Island National Park. By all accounts the trip is worthwhile but it's not cheap. A covered cruiser which takes eight people costs KSh 2340, while the open four-seater long boat costs KSh 1740. Talk to the fishers and they might take you out for a good deal less but make sure their craft is sound – the danger posed by the lake's squalls is not to be taken lightly.

Places to Stay

If you don't mind really roughing it the local villagers will put you up for a few bob, otherwise you'll have to come here just for a day trip from Kalekol or stay at the lodge.

The *Lake Turkana Lodge* is supposedly on an island but the level of the lake has fallen so far in recent years that it's now possible to drive to the lodge, in the dry season at least. It takes around 1½ very hot hours to walk out there from Kalekol – follow the track to the Italian fishing project then head across the lake bed from there. There are children with canoes who will paddle you across the 20 metres or so of channel. By car you just follow the main road through Kalekol and it takes a circuitous route to the far side of the lodge.

Although reportedly busy on weekends, the lodge was deserted when I visited on a weekday and the underworked staff were happy to pass the time playing darts in the bar. The cottages are all self-contained and cost KSh 1020/1585 for full board. If you're just out at the lodge for the day a somewhat meagre plate of fish and chips will set you back KSh 70. Although the water once used to lap at the edge of the bar terrace, it is now more than 100 metres away across a blinding expanse of sand.

ELIYE SPRINGS

This is a far more attractive place than Ferguson's Gulf but, unless you have a 4WD, is inaccessible. The small village here has an army post, a couple of dozen grass huts and a lodge which is of marginal status to say the least. The springs however do provide moisture enough for a curious variety of palm tree to grow here which gives the place a very misplaced tropical island feel. This particular palm tree has an unusually shaped fruit which the locals eat.

If you do make it here you will be greeted by a number of Turkana girls and young women selling trinkets at absurdly cheap prices. With an average of one vehicle a week, it's a real buyer's market. Items for sale include fossilised hippo teeth and fish backbones threaded into necklaces!

Places to Stay & Eat

The *lodge* here is in a state of semidisrepair and, although closed, it still had a full complement of workers milling about. They assured me that the lodge would be reopening but check this in Nairobi in advance before relying on being able to stay. It is possible to camp here at any time. Meals are sporadically available although baked beans from a tin and chapatis was the limit of it and while I sat there and ate, part of the thatch roof gave way and fell to the ground at my feet – which certainly didn't do anything for my confidence about the place ever reopening.

Getting There & Away

The turn-off for Eliye Springs is signposted about halfway along the road from Lodwar to Kalekol. There are a few patches of heavy sand so a 4WD is advisable although you'd probably get through in a conventional vehicle. As there are so few vehicles, hitching is not an option and it's 35 long hot km if you plan to walk it.

LOKICHOKIO

This frontier town is the last on the Pan African Highway before the Sudan border. The road has been sealed all the way here and is in excellent condition but you can't get beyond Lokichokio without a police permit. Even if this was forthcoming the area is not safe as long as the civil war in southern Sudan continues.

Places to Stay

There's a *hotel* of sorts here with a couple of mud huts out the back, and there's a bar in town.

East of Turkana

There are two main routes here. The first is the A2 highway from Nairobi to Marsabit, via Isiolo and Laisamis, and north from there to Moyale on the Ethiopian border. The other is from Nakuru to Maralal, via Nyahururu and north from there to Loyangalani on Lake Turkana, via Baragoi and South Horr. From Loyangalani you can make a loop all the way round the top of the Chalbi Desert to Marsabit via North Horr and Maikona.

Getting There & Away
Bus & Matatu Mwingi runs buses to Marsabit and Moyale from Isiolo on Tuesday, Thursday and Saturday which take about six hours to Marsabit and the same, on the following day, to Moyale. The fare for each stage of the journey is KSh 180. These buses only go when full and, consequently, departures are frequently delayed by up to a day. There's no alternative except to simply hang around and wait or either negotiate a ride on a truck (relatively easy and usually somewhat less than the bus fare) or walk out to the police checkpoint north of town where the tarmac ends and hitch a ride with tourists (not so easy). A convoy system is in operation in order to deter shiftas from stopping and robbing trucks, buses and cars.

Mwingi also operate buses to Maralal every second day (depending on demand) which cost KSh 180.

North of Maralal, the only public transport is a matatu which plies between Maralal and Baragoi once daily if demand warrants it.

Driving None of the roads in this region are surfaced and the main A2 route is corrugated piste which will shake the guts out of both you and your vehicle depending on what speed you go at. The road connecting Isiolo with Maralal (which branches off the A2 north of Archer's Post) is similarly corrugated but otherwise in good shape. The road from Maralal to Loyangalani, however, is surprisingly smooth though there are bad patches here and there including a diabolical several km section down to Lake Turkana from the plateau.

The main cross route between the two is via Wamba and Parsaloi (though you don't actually go through Wamba itself). This road leaves the main A2 about 20 km north of Archer's Post and joins the Maralal-Loyangalani road about 15 km south of Baragoi. Though a very minor route, this road is very smooth most of the way though there are occasional rough patches. Its main drawback is the steep-sided luggas, none of which are bridged. In the dry season you won't have any problems with a 4WD (impossible with a 2WD) but you can forget about it in the wet season. The worst of these luggas is just outside of Wamba and there's a way around it by taking the Maralal road from Wamba and turning first right along a dirt road once you've crossed an obvious bridge. You'll probably only use it if you want to visit the Mathew's Range.

Forget about the Maralal-Parsaloi road marked on the Survey of Kenya's maps. It's all washed out and you won't even make it in 4WD.

NATIONAL PARKS & GAME RESERVES
Just north of Isiolo are three national reserves, Samburu, Buffalo Springs and Shaba, all of them along the banks of the Ewaso Nyiro River and covering an area of some 300 square km. They are mainly scrub desert and open savannah plain, broken here and there by small rugged hills. The river, however, which is permanent, supports a wide variety of game and you can see elephant, buffalo, cheetah, leopard and lion as well as dik-dik, wart hog, Grevy's zebra and the reticulated giraffe. Crocodiles can also be seen on certain sandy stretches of the river bank. You are guaranteed close-up sightings of elephant, reticulated giraffe and various species of smaller gazelle in both Samburu and Buffalo Springs but other game is remarkably thin on the ground and particularly on the route into Samburu from Archer's Post. The rhino were wiped out years ago by poachers.

Samburu & Buffalo Springs
Game Reserve

If you are driving round these parks in your own vehicle it's useful to have a copy of the Survey of Kenya map, *Samburu & Buffalo Springs Game Reserves* (SK 85) which costs KSh 80.

The roads inside Buffalo Springs and Samburu are well maintained and it's easy to get around even in 2WD though you might need a 4WD on some of the minor tracks.

Entry to all three parks or game reserves costs KSh 220 per person plus KSh 50 for a vehicle per day. Even though they're contiguous, if you drive from Buffalo Springs to Samburu (or vice versa) in one day then you'll have to pay two lots of park entry fees though, if it's very late in the afternoon when you cross the boundary, the guards will generally postdate your ticket for the following day.

These parks are much less touristed than Amboseli or Masai Mara so, once you're out of the immediate vicinity of the lodges and camp sites, you'll frequently have the place to yourself.

Places to Stay

In Buffalo Springs National Reserve there are four *public camp sites* close to the Gare Mara entrance gate (the nearest to Isiolo and accessible from the main Isiolo-Marsabit road) but none of them are particularly safe as far as robberies go so stick with a group and make sure your tent is guarded when you're out on game drives or pack it up and take it with you. There's also a *special camp site* further west. Camping costs KSh 35 per person per night.

For those with adequate finances, there's the *Buffalo Springs Tented Lodge* (tel 2234, PO Box 71, Isiolo) up at the north-eastern end of the reserve just south of the Ewaso Nyiro River. The lodge consists of 30 tents shielded from the sun by makuti roofs and each with its own bathroom facilities. There are also eight cottages which sleep two to four people. The lodge has a swimming pool and a bar and restaurant overlooking a natural spring where you can sit and observe the wildlife. In the high season, tents or cottages cost KSh 1800/2280 for singles/doubles with full board. In the low season, the costs are KSh 840/1680 with full board. Advance bookings can be made through African Tours & Hotels Ltd (tel 336858, PO Box 30471, Nairobi). The best access to the lodge is either from the Gare Mara Gate or the Buffalo Springs Gate just south of Archer's Post.

In Samburu National Reserve, the most convenient places to stay are the *public camp sites* close to the Samburu Game Lodge and close to the wooden bridge which connects the western extremity of Buffalo Springs to Samburu across the Ewaso Nyiro River. The sites themselves are fairly pleasant and adjacent to the river but the facilities are minimal and the 'toilets' are nothing short of pigsties. The only advantage to staying at them if you don't want to cook for yourself is that they're very close to the lodge with its restaurant and bar. There are also two *special camp sites* further west. Camping costs KSh 35 per person per night.

For those with money, there's a choice of three top-range lodges/tented camps. The most popular is perhaps the *Samburu Game Lodge* which is part of the Block Hotels chain (tel 335807, PO Box 47557, Nairobi). It's built right alongside the river and consists of a main stone and makuti roof restaurant, bar and reception area, and a series of self-contained cottages strung out along the river bank. The tariff depends on the season. In the high season it's KSh 1870 to KSh 2400 a single and KSh 2100 to KSh 3070 a double with breakfast, whereas in the low season it's KSh 960 a single and KSh 1410 a double. Rates in the shoulder season are intermediate. Lunch and dinner are KSh 275 each and nonresidents are welcome to eat here.

The supposed 'highlights' of any evening here are the appearance of a leopard across the other side of the river and the crocodiles which crawl up onto a sandy bank adjacent to the bar. The leopard, which is lured by a hunk of meat strung up from a tree by two very blasé employees just before dusk, is extremely contrived but Kodak make a fortune supplying film to fools who think they can get anything but a picture of midnight in the bush with an Instamatic from about 100 metres. The crocodile 'show' is equally contrived but at least it takes place right in front of you even if pieces of dead meat in the sand don't encourage dynamism. The lodge is the only place in the two parks where petrol can be bought. Game drives through the park can be organised at the lodge.

Further east and also alongside the river is *Larsens* which is a luxury tented camp also owned by the Block Hotels chain. The rates depend on the season. In the high season (16 December to 31 March and 1 July to 31 August) full board costs KSh 5590/7505 for singles/ doubles whereas in the low season (1 April to 30 June) the corresponding rates are KSh 4090/5360. For the rest of the year the costs are intermediate. All these rates include two game drives.

The other lodge is the *Samburu River Lodge* (tel Nairobi 338656) further upstream on the southern side of the river and, though actually outside the park boundary, is still quite close to it.

You can take any of the access gates into the parks to get to these lodges but remember that if you drive through Buffalo Springs Reserve and into Samburu on the same day then you'll be up for two lots of park entry fees. You can avoid this by entering through the Archer's Post gate.

WAMBA

Wamba is a small, essentially one-street town off the Isiolo-Maralal road north of Samburu National Reserve and a sort of provincial headquarters for the surrounding area. There's precious little here for the traveller and its only 'claim to fame' is that it was from here that John Hillaby organised his camel trek to Lake Turkana which resulted in his book, *Journey to the Jade Sea*.

It has quite a few well stocked dukas, a butchery, a hospital, schools and a large police station but no bank and no electricity despite its proximity to Isiolo.

Places to Stay & Eat

There's only one lodge in the village and that is the *Saudia Lodge* run by Jamal which is at the back of the main street off to the right-hand side coming into town (signposted). Jamal – and indeed his whole family – is very friendly and helpful. You get a very pleasant, clean room here with new beds, mosquito nets and soap, towel and toilet paper provided for just KSh 60 a single and KSh 95 a double. Bathroom facilities are communal. A wholesome breakfast can be provided for you if you order it in advance.

There's a very lively bar on the main street, on the right-hand side as you enter the main part of town, where you can drink your fill though there's no refrigeration. You can't miss it – just listen for the cassette player blaring away!

MARALAL

Maralal is high up in the hills above the Lerochi Plateau (essentially a continuation of the Central Highlands), north of Nyahururu and Nanyuki and north-west of Isiolo, and connected to all these towns by gravel roads. Surrounding it is the Maralal National Sanctuary which is home to zebra, impala, eland, buffalo, hyaena and wart hog, all of which you can see from the road leading into Maralal from the south or at the Maralal Safari Lodge which has the only permanent water hole in the area.

It's an attractive area of grassy undulating plains and coniferous forests which was once coveted by White settlers in the colonial era. However, their designs for taking it over were scotched by the colonial authorities due to anticipated violent opposition from the Samburu for whom it holds a special significance.

The town itself, while a regional headquarters, retains a decidedly frontier atmosphere with a sense of excitement blowing in the wind which frequently sweeps the plains and whips up the dust in the somewhat ramshackle, but very lively, township with its wide streets and Wild West-type verandahs. It's also the preferred

12 Buffalo Lodge
9 Bus Stand
15 Corner Bar Boarding
   & Lodging
1 Council Offices
16 Jamhuri Boarding
   & Lodging
14 Kenya Commercial Bank
13 Kimaniki Boarding
   & Lodging
17 Maralal Safari Hotel
3 Market
7 Mid Point Hotel
8 New Dynamic Starlight
   Bar & Restaurant
5 New Garden Hotel
2 Police
4 Post Office
10 Samburu Restaurant
11 Petrol Stations
6 Wananchi Hotel

Maralal

route and overnight centre for the safari companies which take people up to Lake Turkana. People here are very friendly and it's a great place to buy Samburu handicrafts.

There's a post office (with telephone), petrol stations, mechanics, the only bank north of Isiolo other than in Marsabit, shops with a good range of stock, hotels, bars, one of the best camp sites in Kenya, a surprising number of butchers' shops and regular bus transport to Isiolo. There are also matatus to Baragoi which leave from the Shell station. If you're not travelling with a safari company you may well consider spending a few days here. It's a bizarre but captivating place.

Information
The Kenya Commercial Bank is open Monday to Friday from 8.30 am to 1 pm and on Saturday from 8.30 to 11 am. This is the last bank going north apart from those in Marsabit so stock up on cash.

The post office is open normal hours and the staff are very helpful should you want to make national or international calls.

There are two petrol stations (Shell and Total) in the centre of town where you can be assured of getting what you need at regular prices. North of here you will only find petrol at Baragoi and Loyangalani – if they have it and always at a high price.

Safaris
Regular camel (five days, KSh 6600) and walking safaris (KSh 720 per day including food and accommodation with English speaking Samburu guides) depart from the Maralal Hostel & Campsite and they can also arrange safaris to Lake Turkana by truck (eight days, KSh 6600 including all food and equipment).

Places to Stay – bottom end
The best place to stay here and one which is very popular with travellers is the *Maralal*

Hostel & Campsite, three km south of town on the Isiolo-Nyahururu road (signposted). Here you have a choice of camping, staying in a dormitory or renting a self-contained banda. It's been thoughtfully constructed with local materials and is set amongst Samburu manyattas. Facilities include a lounge/library, reference room, self-service restaurant serving local dishes, a shop selling vegetables and canned goods, etc and a bar with cold beers.

The camp site has its own showers and toilets plus there's a manyatta where you can stay the night if you wish. Camping costs KSh 70 per person per night. The dormitories, of which there are two with a total capacity of 30 beds, cost KSh 85 per person. You don't have to be a Youth Hostel member to stay here even though it's affiliated to the IYHF, but if you are there's an 8% discount on the price of a bed. The self-contained bandas cost KSh 360 a single and KSh 565 a double which includes breakfast.

The hostel and camp site are owned and run by Yare Safaris (tel 559313, PO Box 63006, Nairobi) and it's probably a good idea to make advance bookings for the bandas whilst you're in Nairobi though this isn't normally necessary for the dormitories or the camp site.

There are dances by local tribespeople on Thursdays.

If you wish to head straight there from Nairobi, there's transport from the Heron Court Hotel on Milimani Rd every Saturday at 9 am, returning every Friday from Maralal around 8 am, which is free if you're booked on one of Yare Safaris tours. Otherwise, the charge is KSh 190 one way.

In Maralal itself the most popular place to stay is the *Buffalo Lodge* which is a fairly modern structure offering rooms for KSh 145 a single and KSh 290 a double. It's a lively place and there's a video room at the back. Sammy, the barman here, is a real live wire and very friendly. Cheaper but excellent value is the *Kimaniki Boarding & Lodging* which is a two storey wooden building offering good rooms for KSh 60 per person. Clean sheets are provided as well as hot showers (if

requested) and vehicles can be parked safely in the hotel compound. There's also the *Mid Point Hotel* which has beds for KSh 60 per person.

Other possibilities include the *Corner Bar Boarding & Lodging*, *Jamhuri Boarding & Lodging*, *Maralal Safari Hotel*, *New Garden Hotel* and *Wananchi Hotel* – all rather basic.

Places to Stay – top end
The only top-range hotel in Maralal is the *Maralal Safari Lodge* (tel 25641, 25941; PO Box 42475, Nairobi) which consists of a main building housing a restaurant, bar and souvenir shop and a series of cottages. It costs KSh 1680 a single, KSh 2630 a double and KSh 3700 a triple for full board. The watering hole, which attracts a varied selection of game, is right in front of the bar's verandah so you can watch the animals whilst sipping a cold beer. You don't have to be a resident to drink or eat here but you will need transport to get there as it's quite a way from the centre of Maralal (about three km), off the road to Baragoi (signposted).

Places to Eat
The liveliest bar in town – and one where you can get good, tasty, cheap food – is the improbably named *New Dynamic Starlight Bar & Restaurant* which, nevertheless, lives up to its name. The inside rooms are painted with the most bizarre and florid representations of African bush life and there's even a traditionally dressed Samburu hooker here most evenings who does a roaring trade. Unfortunately, there's no refrigeration so the beers are warm but the company makes up for it and some of the characters who come in here have walked straight out of a Breugel canvas. It's a great spot to meet local live wires, get completely out of it and have numerous animated conversations.

An alternative place to eat is the *Samburu Restaurant* near the petrol stations.

There's also the occasional disco in town – ask around when you get there.

Getting There & Away
If you're not coming in on Yare Safaris'

transfer bus, Mwingi operate buses every second day to Isiolo which cost KSh 180. They leave from the dirt patch in front of the New Garden Hotel.

There are also matatus to Nyahururu daily which leave early in the morning, and usually one to Baragoi, though this only runs when there's sufficient demand. Matatus leave from in front of the Shell station.

MATHEW'S RANGE

North of Wamba, off the link road between the Isiolo- Marsabit road and the Maralal-Loyangalani road via Parsaloi, is the Mathew's Range. Much of this area is thickly forested and supports rhino, elephant, lion, buffalo and many other species. The highest peak here rises to 2285 metres. The whole area is very undeveloped and populated by Samburu tribespeople but the government is in the process of making it into a game sanctuary especially for the rhino. Some of the tribespeople are already employed to protect the rhino from poachers and there's a game warden's centre.

A few km from this centre (which you have to report to on the way in though there are no charges as yet) is a *camp site* with no facilities other than river water and firewood. At one time it was a well set-up research centre, as the derelict huts indicate. It's a superb site and a genuine African bush experience. You are miles from the nearest village and elephants are quite likely to trundle through your camp in the middle of the night – lions too. During the day, traditionally dressed Samburu warriors will probably visit you to see if you need a guide (which you will if you want to see game or climb to the top of the range as we did). Agree on a reasonable price beforehand (about KSh 60 per person per day) plus a similar amount for the one who stays behind to guard your vehicle. Don't forget that the rules of hospitality will oblige them to provide them with a beer, soft drink or cup of tea, a few cigarettes and perhaps a snack when you get back to camp. They're extremely friendly people. One or two will be able to speak English (the

nearest school is in Wamba) but most can converse in Swahili as well as Samburu.

Getting There & Away

Getting to this camp site is not at all easy even with 4WD. There are many different tracks going all over the place and you are going to have to stop many times to ask the way. Perhaps the best approach is from the Wamba-Parsaloi road. Just before Wamba you will get to a T-junction. Instead of going into Wamba, continue north and take the first obvious main track off to the right, several km after the junction. If there are tyre tracks in the sand – follow them. There are two religious mission stations down this track and both have vehicles. You will be able to ask the way at either. One of them is right next to a large river course which generally has some water flowing through it and which you have to ford. If you get lost, ask a local tribesman to come along and guide you but remember that you will have to drive him back to his manyatta after you have found the place. No-one in their right mind walks around in the bush after dark except in large groups – it's too dangerous. It might sound like a *tour de force* getting to this place but it's well worth it!

PARSALOI

Further north, Parsaloi (sometimes spelt Barsaloi) is a small scattered settlement with a few very basic shops but no petrol station. It has a large Catholic Mission which may or may not offer to accommodate you or allow you to camp. There are no lodges. The EEC is funding the building here of quite a large school which was scheduled to finish in 1990.

There are two very rugged and steep-sided luggas at this point on the road, one on either side of the village, and you'll definitely need 4WD to negotiate them.

BARAGOI

Next on is Baragoi, a more substantial settlement full of tribespeople, a couple of very basic lodges, and a few shops. There's also a derelict petrol station but petrol can usually be bought here from a barrel – the local people will show you where to go for it. If you're White, you'll probably be the only one in town and therefore an object of considerable curiosity. Quite a few people speak English around here. The town seems to get rain when everywhere else is dry so the surroundings are quite green.

Be careful not to take photographs in the town as it's supposedly forbidden and the local police are keen to enforce the rule and are not at all pleasant about it.

Places to Stay & Eat

If you ask at any of the restaurants in town they'll usually come up with accommodation but it will be very basic – just a bed in a bare room with no toilet facilities. Some will also allow you to camp in their back yards.

For those with camping equipment, the best place to stay is the *camp site* at the water pumping station about four km to the north of town. To get there, take the road north towards South Horr. After a while you'll go through a small gully and then, a little further on, across a usually dry river bed. Take the next track on the right-hand side and follow this for about one km. It will bring you to a concrete house and a fairly open patch of ground. This is the camp site and there's always someone around. Facilities include toilets and showers and your tent will be guarded by Samburu warriors. It costs KSh 35 per person per night. Trips can be arranged to nearby manyattas for a small fee and you'll be allowed to take photographs.

For food in the town itself, the best is the *Wid-Wid Inn* run by Mrs Fatuma. It's on the top side of the main street and you'll know you've got the right place because all the staff wear garishly pink pinafores! She'll cook you up an absolutely delicious meat stew and chapatis for dinner as well as pancakes, omelettes and tea for breakfast. Either meal costs just KSh 30 per person.

There are also two bars in the town but only one of them – the *Sam Celia Joy Bar*, at the end of the main street going north – usually has beers. The other, on the back street, usually only has conyagi (local firewater) and other spirits.

SOUTH HORR

The next village is South Horr which is set in a beautiful lush canyon between the craggy peaks of Mt Nyiro (2752 metres) and Mt Porale (1990 metres) and Mt Supuko (2066 metres). It's a lively little place with a huge Catholic Mission but there's no petrol available.

Places to Stay & Eat

There are two small and very basic hotels on the main street – the *Mt Nyiro Hotel* and the *Good Tourist Hotel* – where you can find accommodation of sorts as well as a reasonably tasty meal of meat stew, mandazi and tea for around KSh 30 per person. The hotels will generally need up to two hours notice if you want to eat but tea is generally immediately available.

For those with camping equipment, there's a really pleasant *camp site* at the top end of town next to a mountain stream and above the Catholic Mission. The access road for this is on the outskirts of town coming in from the south. Look for signs on the left-hand side before you get to the concrete ford across the stream which read, 'South Horr Forest Station' and 'Veterinery Office South Horr' and turn off there. The site is used by safari companies going to Loyangalani and there doesn't appear to be any fee at present though this could soon change.

There's another *camp site* (signposted 'Camping' but easy to miss) about 12 km out of town going north on the right-hand side. It's a pleasant site (though the discarded beer bottles and tyres aren't too pretty) and facilities include showers and toilets. There's also plenty of firewood. The charge is KSh 35 per person per night. This site used to be called Kurungu Camp Site and was where most of the safari companies used to put their people up for the night. They no longer stop here and the bandas which used to offer fairly good accommodation have been demolished. Guards can be arranged to watch your tent if you're not cooking your own food and want to eat in town.

South Horr also sports a very lively bar – the *Serima Bar* – on the main road heading north out of town. It's only open in the evenings and seems to have a plentiful supply of beer though there's no refrigeration.

LAKE TURKANA (THE JADE SEA)

Going further north, the lushness of the Horr Valley gradually peters out until, finally, you reach the totally barren, shattered lava beds at the southern end of Lake Turkana. Top the ridge here and there it is in front of you – the Jade Sea. It's a breathtaking sight – vast and yet apparently totally barren. You'll see nothing living here except a few brave, stunted thorn trees. When you reach the lake shore, you'll know why – it's a soda lake and, at this end, highly saline. The northern end of the lake isn't anywhere near as saline because it's fed by the Omo River from Ethiopia (is that where the name of the washing powder came from!?). At this point, most people abandon whatever vehicle they're in and plunge into the lake. If you do this watch out for crocodiles. They're quite partial to a meal of red meat as a change from Nile perch.

LOYANGALANI

A little further up the lake shore and you are in Loyangalani – Turkana 'city'. There is an airstrip, post office, fishing station, luxury lodge, two camp sites, a Catholic Mission (which may reluctantly sell petrol at up to three times the price in Nairobi) and all of it surrounded by the yurtlike, stick and doum-palm dwellings of the Turkana tribespeople. Taking photographs of people or their houses here will attract 'fees'.

If you're an independent traveller, the Oasis Lodge can organise trips to the village where the El-Molo live. Otherwise, ask the drivers of safari trucks at the camp sites if they have room for you – organised safaris to this part of Kenya usually include a trip to the El-Molo village. They're one of the smallest tribes in Africa and quite different

from the Turkana though it seems their days are numbered as a distinct tribe. Tourism has also wrought inevitable changes in their life-style and you may feel that the whole thing has been thoroughly commercialised. You'll also pay handsomely for taking photographs. As one traveller who felt the tribe had totally prostituted their traditional way of life to make money from tourists put it, 'If they live on fish it must be smoked salmon and caviar'.

Trips to Mt Kulal and Mt Porr can also be arranged at the Oasis Club but they're expensive. The Mt Kulal trip is a part drive, part walking trip up to the forest there and Mt Porr is a well known fossicking spot. A better thing to do would be to get in touch with Francis Langachar who is a very friendly young Turkana man and ask him to organise something similar for you. He speaks fluent English and his father went on John Hillaby's 'Journey to the Jade Sea' saga.

Places to Stay & Eat

Of the two camp sites, it's hard to favour one over the other though only one has a restaurant and bar. Both are staffed by very friendly people and theft doesn't appear to be a problem at either of them. The first you come to is *El-Molo Camp* (tel 724384, PO Box 34710, Nairobi) which has excellent facilities including good showers and toilets, a swimming pool (KSh 50 fee for use), a large dining hall and bar (with cold beers!) and electricity up to 9.30 pm at night (kerosene lanterns after that). Camping costs KSh 60 per person per night. They also have 20 self-contained bandas for rent which cost KSh 2370 a double with full board.

Meals can be ordered at short notice in the dining room here whether you are staying on the site or not but they take a long time to arrive: 1½ hours is normal. The food, on the other hand, is very good. A dinner of mushroom omelette, boiled potatoes and dressed salad, for instance, cost KSh 95 whereas a breakfast of two fruit salads and a pot of tea or coffee cost KSh 60. Cold beers naturally cost more than in Nairobi but are still very reasonably priced.

Skull 1470

In the early 1970s archaeologist Richard Leakey (now head of Kenya's Ministry of Wildlife) made a significant fossil find on the shores of Lake Turkana. It was the discovery of a fossilised skull, which came to be known somewhat prosaically as 1470 (its Kenya Museums' index number).

The almost complete, but fragmented, skull was thought to be from an early hominid. It was hoped that it would back up earlier fossil discoveries made by the Leakeys at the Olduvai Gorge in Tanzania during the '60s which suggested that the direct human ancestral line went back further than the 1½ million years that was the common theory at the time.

The pieces of the skull were painstakingly fitted together – a demanding task in itself which kept two people fully occupied for over six weeks. The completed jigsaw confirmed what they had suspected: here was an evolutionary sophisticated hominid, named *Homo habilis*, which was a direct ancestor of *Homo sapiens* and 2½ million years old.

Since then, *Homo* fossil finds have been made which push the date of the direct human ancestral line back even further, but at the time 1470 was a very important 'person'! ■

The Turkana

The Turkana are another of Kenya's more colourful (and warlike) people. Originally from the Karamajong district of north-eastern Uganda, the Turkana number around 250,000 and live in the virtual desert country of Kenya's north-west. Due to their isolation, the Turkana are probably the least affected by the 20th century of all Kenya's people.

Like the Samburu and the Maasai (with whom they are linguistically linked), the Turkana are cattle herders first, and more recently they have taken up fishing the waters of Lake Turkana and even growing the occasional crops, weather permitting. But unlike the other two tribes, the Turkana have discontinued the practice of circumcision.

The traditional dress of the Turkana people is amazing, as is the number of people who still wear it – catching a bus up in the north-west is a real eye-opener for a first-time visitor. The men cover part of their hair with mud which is then painted blue and decorated with ostrich and other feathers. The main garment they wear, despite the blast-furnace heat of the region, is a woollen blanket (usually a garish modern checked one) which is worn around one shoulder.

Traditional accessories include a small wooden stool carved out of a single piece of wood (used either as a pillow or a stool), a wooden stick with a distinctive shape, and a wrist knife. Both the men and the women wear with great flourish the lip plug through the lower lip which looks a bit gruesome to tourists. The women wear a variety of beaded and metal adornment, much of it indicating to the trained eye events in the woman's life. A half skirt of animal skins and a piece of black cloth are the only garments worn, although these days pieces of colourful cloth are not uncommon for use as baby slings.

Tattooing is also surprisingly common and usually has special meaning. Men are tattooed on the shoulders and upper arm each time they kill an enemy – the right shoulder for killing a man, the left for a woman; it's surprising the number of men you still see with these markings. Witch doctors and prophets are held in high regard and tattooing on someone's lower stomach is usually a sign of witch doctors' attempts to cast out an undesirable spirit rather than any sort of decoration. ■

Turkana women (HF)

The Samburu

Closely related to the Maasai, and in fact speaking the same language, the Samburu occupy an arid area directly north of Mt Kenya. It seems that when the Maasai migrated to the area from Sudan, some headed east (and became the Samburu) while the bulk of them continued south to the area they occupy today.

As is often the case, age-sets are an integral part of the society and the men pass through various stages before becoming a powerful elder at the top of the ladder. Circumcision is practiced in both sexes; with the girls it is only done on the day of marriage, which is usually when she is around 16 years old. Men are often in their thirties by the time they pass out of warriorhood and become elders qualified to marry. ■

Samburu women - South Horr (GC)

The other camp site adjacent to El-Molo is *Sunset Strip Camp,* which also costs KSh 60 per person per night. Facilities include showers and toilets and covered dining areas but you cannot buy food and drink here and there's no electricity.

Neither camp site has firewood so you'll have to bring your own from further south.

Whichever place you camp at, beware of sudden storms which can descend from Mt Kulal. If there is a storm, stay with your tent otherwise it may not be there when you get back and neither will anything else.

Other than the camp sites there is the luxury *Oasis Lodge* (tel 339025, 750034/6, PO Box 14829, Nairobi) which has 25 self-contained double bungalows with electricity (own generator) at KSh 1860 a single and KSh 2640 a double with full board. It's a beautiful place with two spring-fed swimming pools, ice-cold beers and meals available. The only trouble is, if you are not staying there but want to use the facilities, it's going to cost you KSh 200 entrance fee which gives you the use of the bar and swimming pools. It's a lot of money to pay for a brush with luxury but you won't wring any concessions out of the owner (Wolfgang) who can be quite belligerent about this. Basically, he doesn't want what he considers to be 'riffraff' marring the tone of the place and mingling their sweaty bodies with his otherwise very chic guests.

Other than the El-Molo Camp, there are a couple of basic *tea houses* on the main street of Loyangalani and, if you ask around, you'll meet villagers who will cook up a meal of Nile perch for you in their houses.

Getting There & Away

It's unlikely you'd use the service but Air Kenya (not to be confused with Kenya Airways) operates flights to Loyangalani from Nairobi's Wilson airport three times a week in either direction on Wednesday, Friday and Sunday. The fare is KSh 3600 one way and KSh 6600 return. If there are more than five of you, it's cheaper to charter your own 'plane'.

NORTH HORR

North of Loyangalani the road loops over the lava beds to North Horr. There is a short cut across the desert through the village of Gus.

There are no lodges here and no petrol available but the Catholic Mission is very friendly and will probably offer you somewhere to stay for the night if you are stuck. It's staffed by German and Dutch people.

MAIKONA

Next down the line is Maikona where there is a large village with basic shops (but no lodges) and a very friendly Catholic Mission and school, staffed by Italian people, where you will undoubtedly be offered a place to stay for the night. Please leave a donation before you go if you stay here. The mission usually has electricity and the Father goes into Marsabit once a fortnight in his Land Rover.

MARSABIT

South of Maikona is Marsabit and you are back in relative civilisation. Here there are three petrol stations, a bank, post office, dry cleaners, shops, bars and lodges, buses and an airport. The main attraction here though is the Marsabit National Park & Reserve centred around Mt Marsabit (1702 metres).

The hills here are thickly forested and in stark contrast to the desert on all sides. Mist often envelopes them in the early morning and mosses hang from tree branches. The views from the communications tower on the summit above town are magnificent in all directions. In fact, they're probably as spectacular as any of the views from Mt Kenya or Kilimanjaro. The whole area is peppered with extinct volcanoes and volcanic craters (called *gofs*), some of which have a lake on the crater floor.

One of the most memorable sights in Marsabit is the colourful mix of tribespeople who you'll see thronging the streets and roads into town. Most noticeable are the Rendille, with their elaborate braided hairstyles and dressed in skins, fantastic multicoloured beaded necklaces and bracelets. These people graze camels and, like the

To Maikona & North Horr
To Moyale
To Isiolo & Nairobi
To Karantin Summit & Communications Tower
To Lake Paradise & Marsabit Lodge
Park Gates
Park Gates
To Park Headquarters

1 Airstrip
5 Badassa Hotel
12 Camp Site
10 Catholic Mission
11 D C's Office
2 Esso
13 Hospital
7 Hotel Al-Jazeera
9 Kenya Commercial Bank
3 Kenya Lodge
4 Marsabit Highway Hotel
8 Post Office
14 Prison
6 Shell & Bus Stand

Marsabit

0   0.5   1 km

Approximate scale

Samburu and Maasai, show little interest in adopting a more sedentary lifestyle, preferring to roam the deserts and only visiting the towns when necessary for trade. They are the major non-Muslim people in what is otherwise a largely Muslim area.

The other major tribes are the Boran and the Gabbra, both of them pastoralists, though with these people it's cattle which they graze rather than camels. They're allied to the Galla peoples of Ethiopia from which areas they originated several hundred years ago. Many have abandoned their former transient customs and settled down to more sedentary

activities. In the process, many have adopted Islam and the modes of dress of the Somalis with whom they trade and who have also migrated into the area. There are also quite a few Ethiopians in town as a result of that country's tragic and turbulent recent past.

Marsabit National Park & Reserve
The Marsabit National Park & Reserve is home to a wide variety of the larger mammals including lion, leopard, cheetah, elephant, rhino, buffalo, wart hog, Grevy's zebra, the reticulated giraffe, hyaena, Grant's gazelle, oryx, dik-dik and greater kudu

among others. Because the area is thickly forested, however, you won't see too much game unless you spend quite some time here and, preferably, camp at Lake Paradise. The lake, which occupies much of the crater floor of Gof Sokorte Guda, is appropriately named. It's an enchanting place and right out in the bush. Entry to the park, which is open from 6 am to 7.15 pm, costs KSh 220 per person plus KSh 50 for a vehicle.

The Survey of Kenya's map, *Marsabit National Park & Reserve* (SK 84), KSh 35, is a good buy if you are touring this park.

Places to Stay
In the Park Few camp sites in Kenya would rival the one at *Lake Paradise*. There are no facilities (except lake water and firewood) so bring everything with you. A ranger has to be present when you camp here so it costs more than an ordinary site (KSh 360 per group and only one group at a time) but you can arrange all this at the park entrance gate. There's also another good *camp site* next to the entrance gate (water and plenty of firewood) but the so-called showers are a joke. You would die of thirst waiting for enough water to wet the back of your ears here. Camping at this site costs KSh 35 per person.

There's also the *Marsabit Lodge*, a luxury safari lodge overlooking a lake in another gof, Sokorte Dika. This costs KSh 980 a single, KSh 1625 a double and KSh 2135 a triple with full board except from 1 April to 15 July when there's a considerable discount. Bookings can be made at Msafiri Inns (tel 29751, 330820; PO Box 42013), 11th floor, Utalii House, Uhuru Highway, Nairobi.

In the Town If you have no camping equipment there's a good choice of lodges available in the town of Marsabit. One of the best is the *Kenya Lodge*. It's very clean and pleasant and costs KSh 60 a single and KSh 85 a double with soap and toilet roll provided. The showers are communal and the hotel has its own bar and restaurant at the front. The restaurant offers excellent Ethiopian food.

Almost as good is the *Marsabit Highway Hotel* which costs KSh 60 a single, KSh 100 a double and KSh 145 a triple with shower and toilet. It's a large place and very clean. Breakfast costs KSh 30. The hotel has its own bar/restaurant open from 11 am to 2 pm and 5 pm to midnight. There is a disco on Friday and Saturday nights.

The cheapest place, though not such good value, is the *Hotel Al-Jazeera* which costs KSh 35 per person with communal showers. There's a bar and restaurant at the front. For something vaguely mid-range, try the *Badassa Hotel*.

Getting There & Away
Air Most of the small private airline companies which operate out of Wilson Airport fly from Nairobi to Marsabit and Moyale depending on demand.

Bus Buses run from Marsabit south to Isiolo and north to Moyale on the Ethiopian border. They depart around 10 am on Wednesday, Friday and Sunday but can be delayed by up to a day if there are not sufficient passengers. The fare to either Isiolo or Moyale is KSh 180 and the trip takes about six hours. All vehicles including buses travelling between Marsabit and Isiolo or Marsabit and Moyale must travel in convoy. The reason for this is to minimise the danger of attack from shiftas.

Unless you are Kenyan or Ethiopian you will need special permission to cross the border into Ethiopia at Moyale. This is relatively easy to obtain so long as you only intend to stay briefly.

MOYALE
Straddling the Kenyan-Ethiopian border, Moyale lies some 250 km north of Marsabit across the Dida Galgalu desert. It's a small town of sandy streets, bars, a post office, police station, several shops selling basic commodities and with a small market area. Unlike Marsabit, however, where most of the roofs these days are of corrugated iron, there are still a large number of traditionally built houses here with sturdy pole frames supporting mud and stick roofs which can be up to half a metre thick thus ensuring that the

To Maikona & North Horr

To Moyale

Gof Redo

Airstrip

Marsabit National Park

0   2.5   5 km

Marsabit Town

Gof Mude

Gate & Camp Site

Gate

Karatin 1707 m

Sokorte Dika

Park Headquarters

Marsabit Lodge

To North Horr & South Horr

Mt Marsabit

Gof Sokorte Guda (Lake Paradise)

Gof Bongole

To Laisamis Isiolo

interiors stay cool even when the outside temperature is 30°C and more.

There's not a great deal to do here though the town attracts the occasional intrepid traveller either just for the hell of it or for the sake of an exotic passport stamp.

There is no bank in Moyale and only derelict petrol stations so come prepared.

The Ethiopian side of the town is somewhat larger and the facilities are much better – tarred roads, electricity, a number of bars and small restaurants, a hotel, lively market area and plenty of Marxist-Leninist slogans as well as caricatures of the big three theoreticians.

Crossing into Ethiopia

Although this border is open to Kenyans and Ethiopians, it's officially closed to other nationalities but as it's so far from anywhere else the rules can generally be twisted slightly. At the Kenyan border post this normally requires a little *chai* (small bribe) and a promise to return before the day is out. At the Ethiopian border post you'll be asked for a visa (which you won't have unless you got one in Nairobi on the pretext of flying into Addis Ababa). Tell the border guards you only want to visit for the day and would like to talk to customs and immigration. They *may* let you in and even permit you to stay overnight but it's very unlikely you'll be allowed to go any further. If you're let in, cameras have to be left with customs officials and you can expect a thorough search of whatever else you are carrying.

Places to Stay & Eat

There are only three places to stay on the Kenyan side of Moyale and they're all pretty basic. Probably the best of the bunch is the *Barissah Hotel* which also has the town's bar. Out at the back surrounding an earth compound there are several basic cubicles without locks where you can rent a bed for KSh 35 per person. There are no showers (though you can order a bucket of water) and the place is far from clean but the staff are friendly. The Barissah is also the preferred

place to eat, the usual fare being meat stew and chapatis.

If it's full, head for the *Bismillahi Boarding & Lodging* across from the Barissah and up behind the derelict Esso station. It's a family run place and you'll find yourself sharing the same roof. A bed here costs KSh 30 and facilities are absolutely minimal.

On the Ethiopian side of Moyale, the best place to stay is the *Bekele Molla Hotel* which is government owned and about two km from the border. It has a very lively bar – especially in the evenings – and the rooms are clean and self-contained.

For somewhere to eat closer to the border, try the *Negussie Hotel*, up on the hill to the left after you've crossed the border. They offer the standard Ethiopian fare of wat (a fierce hot sauce) and injera (bread made of millet flour), and there's also a bar here.

Kenyan shillings are acceptable when paying for meals and drinks.

Getting There & Away

Buses between Marsabit and Moyale are detailed in the Marsabit section.

The North-East

Like the north of Kenya, the north-east up to the border with Somalia covers a vast area of desert and semidesert with very few centres of population and limited public transport possibilities. The main towns are Garissa and Wajir. Most of the area is relatively flat yet it's through here that one of Kenya's major rivers flows – the Tana. The river enters the ocean about halfway between Malindi and Lamu and is the territory of the Orma, Pokomo and Bajun tribes. Straddling this river just north of Garsen is the Tana River Primate Reserve which is included on a few safari companies' itineraries but otherwise difficult to get to. The reserve was set up to protect the red colobus and crested mangabey monkeys both of which are endangered species. The other main river, the Ewaso Nyiro which flows through Samburu and

Buffalo Springs national reserves, eventually peters out into the Lorian Swamp, never reaching the ocean.

Few travellers come this way except those taking the back route to Lamu via Garissa and Garsen and those going overland to Somalia via Liboi. It's still possible to enter Somalia via Liboi en route to Kismayu but hardly recommended at present because of internal tensions within Somalia which have led to a lot of fighting and dislocation of the population. There's also been quite an increase in the activities of shiftas as a result both of the fighting and the efforts of the Kenyan government to rid the eastern national parks of poachers who have decimated the elephant and rhino populations. The Somalis have been blamed for much of this and justifiably but the poachers and shiftas have proved hard to control.

There's big money in the sordid ivory and rhino horn business which is fuelled by the refusal of several Arab nations – notably the two Yemens, the United Arab Emirates, Oman and Kuwait – to ban imports and the insatiable appetite of the Chinese market for these animal products. As a result, those who procure the ivory and rhino horn are well armed with automatic weapons and, often, high speed vehicles. They're people to be dealt with very seriously and cautiously and are not averse to taking on units of the Kenyan army or police let alone game wardens and trackers. And, when denied ivory, tourists are an acceptable substitute.

You should think twice before driving a vehicle around Meru National Park (or even taking an organised safari) until the situation is resolved because tourists have been robbed at gunpoint and some of them actually shot dead. If you do go there and you're held up, don't mess about! Get your money and cameras out and hand them over. Any prevarication will invite a bullet in the head. The same possibly applies on the overland route to Somalia through Liboi though we've had no reports of this – maybe because very few people are currently doing this trip. It's unlikely much will change until Seyyed Barre (the Somali president) is replaced and

there's some sort of resolution of the Ethiopian conflicts.

Other than a visit to Meru National Park, which is worth it if security can be guaranteed, and the Tana River area, the north-east isn't a particularly interesting area even for desert fans though Wajir, with its predominantly Somali population, 'Beau Geste' fort and market, would definitely have the edge over Garissa, itself quite a nondescript town hardly worth stopping over in.

MERU NATIONAL PARK

On the lowland plains east of the town of Meru, the Meru National Park is a complete contrast to its more northerly sisters – Samburu, Buffalo Springs and Shaba – where open bush is the norm. Here, abundant rainfall and numerous permanent streams flowing down from the Mt Kenya massif support a luxuriant jungle of forest, swamp and tall grasses which, in turn, provide fodder and shelter to a wide variety of herbivores and their predators. As in other parks, such as Marsabit, where the vegetation is dense, the wildlife is not so easily sighted so you need to spend a few days here if you're to fully appreciate what the park has to offer. If you do that then you are virtually guaranteed sightings of large herds of elephant, buffalo and reticulated giraffe and, in the more open bush, Grevy's zebra, ostrich and gerenuk. The large predators – leopard and lion, in particular – are only rarely sighted even though there are considerable numbers of them, though lions occasionally visit the Leopard Rock Lodge area. Monkeys, crocodiles and a plethora of bird species are common in the dense vegetation alongside the watercourses.

Meru National Park was also the home of Kenya's only herd of white rhinos which were imported from the Umfolozi game park in South Africa. Jealously guarded 24 hours a day by rangers to protect them from poachers, these huge animals were quite unlike their more cantankerous cousins, the black rhino, in being remarkably docile and willing to allow their keepers to herd them around the camp sites and park headquarters

To Garba Tula

To Meru, Nanyuki & Nairobi

Kinna Plains

Bisanadi Plains

Bisanadi Gate

Murera Gate

Murera Plains

Leopard Rock Lodge

Meru Mulika Lodge

Meru National Park

0   5   10 km

Rojewero Plains

Park Headquarters

Rhino Plains

Bwatherongi Plains

Kiolu Plains

Punguru Plains

Ura Gate

Kampi ya Game

Kampi ya Kiko

To Meru, Embu & Nairobi

Kampi ya Elsa

Kampi ya Teziwa

area during the day and pen them up at night. Sadly, that's all gone now. Heavily armed poachers shot the lot of them and, for good measure, killed their keepers too.

The park is also famous for being Joy and George Adamson's former base where they raised orphaned lion and leopard cubs until they were old enough to be returned to the wild. Both paid for their efforts with their lives – Joy several years ago when she was murdered in Meru park by poachers and George in 1989 when he too met the same fate along with two of his assistants in the nearby Kora National Reserve.

Security in the park has been beefed up since George Adamson was murdered but there is still a real risk of encountering poachers and bandits here so you need to bear this in mind especially if you're driving your own vehicle. It's true to say, however, that the chances of running into bandits is just as great in Masai Mara or Tsavo as it is in Meru. The one major plus about Meru National Park is that you're unlikely to come across another safari vehicle anywhere in the park except outside the lodges.

The tracks through the park are well maintained and signposted though it's a good idea to have with you a copy of Survey of Kenya's map, *Meru National Park*.

Places to Stay

There are several *public camp sites* close to the park headquarters and airstrip where there's plenty of firewood as well as shower and toilet blocks. If you don't have a tent then there are also several simple *bandas* for rent in the same area.

More expensive are the self-contained bandas at *Leopard Rock Lodge* which have electricity, hot water, mosquito nets and fully equipped kitchens. There's a shop at the site which sells basic commodities including canned goods and beer.

At the top of the range is the *Meru Mulika Lodge* (tel 29751, PO Box 42013, Nairobi) which has all the usual facilities of a luxury lodge including a swimming pool (KSh 30 for nonresidents) and where full board costs KSh 1285 a single, KSh 1780 a double and KSh 2300 a triple.

Getting There & Away

Getting to Meru National Park by public transport is a problem. There are no buses or matatus which will take you either to the lodges or the camp sites and park headquarters. Likewise, attempting to hitchhike is basically a waste of time since so few vehicles come into the park and those that do are mainly tour groups so they won't pick you up. It's almost essential to have your own vehicle or be part of a tour group. Quite a few safari companies include Meru National Park on their itineraries but they are all liable to cancel visits at short notice if there has been any trouble with shiftas in the park. Dead or robbed tourists are no good for business.

TANA RIVER PRIMATE SANCTUARY

Well south of Garissa and not too far north of Garsen is the Tana River Primate Sanctuary which, as its name suggests, is a reserve for a number of endangered species of monkey. It's possible to get close to the sanctuary by public transport but there's still a lot of walking involved and the facilities have long fallen into disrepair so you need to take everything with you. Very few safari companies include the reserve on their itineraries. The only one which presently does is Bushbuck Adventures (tel 728737, PO Box 67449, Nairobi) which operates a once-a-year, 12 day Tana River safari taking in the Kora National Reserve, the Primate Reserve, the Tana River delta and Lamu by foot, vehicle, boat and air. Accommodation is in lodges and special camp sites and costs US$2640.

GARISSA

The only reason you would come to Garissa is if you were going overland to Somalia or taking the back route to Lamu direct from Nairobi via Garsen. There's nothing much to see or do here and the heat and humidity are unrelenting but there's a bank (normal hours), petrol stations, bars and a fair choice of places to stay plus the streets are tarmacked.

Places to Stay & Eat

Perhaps the best place to stay for the night is the *Safari Hotel* which offers clean rooms with running water for KSh 60 a single and KSh 95 a double. It has reasonable food in the attached restaurant. The *Garissa Guest House* is somewhat more expensive at KSh 120 per person for B&B with bathroom but the rooms are nothing special and it's quite a walk from the centre of town. If both are full then there's the more basic *Nile Lodging* or the *Kenya Hotel & Lodging*.

Getting There & Away

Air It's possible to fly direct to Garissa from Nairobi's Wilson Airport with one of the small private airlines if there's sufficient demand.

Bus Garissa Express operates a bus from the Kenya Bus Depot in Eastleigh, Nairobi, to Garissa on Monday, Wednesday, Friday and Sunday at 8 am. The depot is a 10 minute matatu ride from Ronald Ngala St (Route No 9). The fare is KSh 95 and the journey takes about eight hours.

Garissa

0   250   500 m

5 Barclays Bank
8 Garissa Guest House
1 Kenya Hotel & Lodging
2 Mosque
4 Nile Lodging
7 Petrol Station
6 Post Office
3 Safari Hotel

Tana River

To Garissa & Nairobi

To Liboi & Wajir

There's also a daily Garissa Express bus from the Lamu mainland (Mokowe) to Garissa which leaves at 7 am, costs KSh 180 and takes eight to 10 hours when the weather is dry.

Going further afield, Garissa Express operate buses to Wajir on Tuesday, Thursday and Saturday which arrive the same day and cost KSh 145. These buses continue on the next day to Mandera at the junction of the Kenyan, Ethiopian and Somalian borders. The fare from Garissa to Mandera is KSh 290.

LIBOI
Liboi, right on the Kenya-Somalia border, is a staging post in the *qat* (drug) trade to Somalia. It has only one place to stay, the *Cairo Hotel*.

GARSEN
If you're heading towards Lamu from Garissa then you may have to stay here overnight as it's necessary to change buses – there are none direct from Garissa to Mokowe on the mainland opposite Lamu. There's nothing at all special about Garsen but there are several basic hotels to choose from. The best is the *3-in-1 Lodging & Restaurant* which is fairly clean and has its own restaurant.

For details of buses passing through Garsen, see either the Malindi or Lamu sections.

Amboseli, Masai Mara & Tsavo

AMBOSELI NATIONAL PARK

Amboseli is the next most popular park after Masai Mara, mainly because of the spectacular backdrop of Africa's highest peak, Mt Kilimanjaro, which broods on the southern boundary of the park.

At 392 square km Amboseli is not a large park, and it certainly doesn't have the profusion of game which you find in Masai Mara. The western section of the park is the dry bed of Lake Amboseli, and although it is occasionally flooded in the wet season, for the majority of the time it is a dry, dusty, shimmering expanse.

Probably the best reason for visiting Amboseli is that it is here that you stand the best chance of spotting a black rhino. Amboseli also has huge herds of elephant, and to see a herd of them making their way sedately across the grassy plains, with Kilimanjaro in the background, is a real African cliché but one which leaves a lasting impression.

Other animals which you are likely to see here include buffalo, lion, gazelle, cheetah, wildebeest, hyaena, jackal, wart hog, Masai giraffe, zebra and baboon.

Amboseli more than any other park has suffered hugely from the number of minibuses which drive through each day. It has a much drier climate than Masai Mara and so for much of the year is a real dust bowl. If you are driving through the park, stick to the defined tracks, and hopefully others will follow suit.

Places to Stay – bottom end

Once again the only budget option is a *camp site*. This one is right on the southern boundary of the park. The only facilities are a couple of long-drop toilets and a kiosk which sells warm beer and sodas, and where you pay the camping fees. The water supply here is extremely unreliable so bring some with you. Elephants are a real problem in this camp site at night and practically everyone

who has stayed here has an elephant story to relate – there are some hilarious (and not so hilarious) ones doing the rounds. At night make sure all food is locked away inside your vehicle. *Don't* keep food in your tent as elephants have a habit of investigating.

Places to Stay – top end

The group of lodges in the centre of the park are strategically situated for views of Kilimanjaro; they (the lodges) couldn't be called pretty. The *Kilimanjaro Safari Lodge* and the *Amboseli Lodge* are both run by the Kilimanjaro Safari Club in Nairobi (tel Nairobi 337510). Prices are around KSh 2640/3600 for a single/double with full board. Also in this group are the *Ol Tukai Lodge* (tel Nairobi 334863) self-catering cottages, but even these aren't cheap.

The *Amboseli Serena Lodge* (tel Nairobi 339800) is of a much more sensitive design and construction; it blends in well with the landscape and the nearby Enkongo Narok Swamp ensures constant bird and animal activity. Room charges are KSh 2880/3480 for a single/double with full board.

Getting There & Away

Air Air Kenya Aviation have daily flights between Wilson Airport and Amboseli. These depart Nairobi at 7.30 am and Amboseli at 8.30 am; the trip takes about 45 minutes and costs KSh 1250 one way.

Road The usual approach to Amboseli is through Namanga, 165 km south of Nairobi on the A104 and the main border post between Kenya and Tanzania. The road is in excellent condition from Nairobi to here. This is the last fuel stop before the park and outside the town's petrol station is a couple of shops selling Maasai crafts. First prices asked are totally ridiculous so bargain fiercely. There's accommodation in Namanga (at the *Namanga Hotel* and others)

if you're stuck, and the petrol station is a good place to ask around for lifts.

The 75 km dirt road from Namanga to the Namanga Gate is fiercely corrugated and is guaranteed to shake your fillings loose. If you'd been wondering up until now why the suspension in your minibus was shot to pieces, here is the answer. The whole trip from Nairobi takes around four hours.

It's also possible to enter Amboseli from the east via Tsavo.

MASAI MARA GAME RESERVE

This is it – the big one. Virtually every person who visits Kenya goes to Masai Mara, and with good reason as this is the Kenyan section of the wildly evocative Serengeti Plains and the wildlife abounds. This is also traditionally the lands of the Maasai, but these people have been displaced in favour of the animals.

The Mara (as it's often abbreviated to) is a 320 square km slab of basically open rolling grassland dotted with the distinctive flat-topped acacia trees tucked away in the south-west corner of the country. It is watered by the tree-lined Mara River and its tributary the Talek River. The western border of the park is the spectacular Oloololo Escarpment and it's at this edge of the park that the concentrations of game are the highest. It must also be said that it's the most difficult area of the park to get around in as the swampy ground becomes impassable after heavy rain. Conversely, the concentrations of tourist and minibuses are highest at the eastern end of the park around the Oloolaimutia Gate and Talek Gate as it's these area which are the most accessible by road from Nairobi.

Wherever you go in the Mara, however, the one certain thing is that you'll see an astonishing amount of game, often in the one place at the one time. Of the big cats, lions are found in large prides everywhere and it's not at all uncommon to see them hunting. Cheetahs and leopard are harder to spot but are still fairly common. Elephant, buffalo, zebra and hippo also exist in large numbers within the reserve. Of the antelopes, the black-striped Thomson's gazelle (Tommys) and the larger Grant's gazelle are found in huge numbers, while the impala, topi and Coke's hartebeest and of course the wildebeest are also profuse. Rhinos do exist in the park but are rarely seen. Other common animals include the Masai giraffe, baboon (especially around the lodges), wart hog, spotted hyaena and grey (or side-striped) jackals.

The highlight of the Mara is no doubt the annual wildebeest migration when literally millions of these ungainly beasts stray north from the Serengeti in July-August in search of the lush grass, before turning south again around October. It is truly a staggering experience to be in the reserve at that time – and one which is likely to have a profound effect on your own feeling of insignificance.

Masai Mara doesn't have national park status. The fundamental difference between the two is that in a game reserve people (in this case the Maasai) can graze their animals and can also shoot animals if they are attacked. In a national park however, the entire area is set aside exclusively for the wildlife and the natural environment.

Just outside the Oloolaimutia Gate there's a Maasai village which has opened itself up as a tourist attraction. For KSh 120 per person you can walk around and take as many pictures as you like. As you might imagine, it's a real zoo when you have a couple of dozen tourists poking their video cameras and long lenses intrusively everywhere. If you can manage to visit when there are no other tourists it's not too bad and you can at least talk to the villagers.

Ballooning

If you can afford the KSh 4000 price tag, balloon safaris are definitely the way to go. For more details see the section on Ballooning under Activities in the Facts for the Visitor chapter.

Places to Stay – bottom end

There is no budget accommodation within the reserve so it's camp or pay high prices at the lodges and tented camps. It's possible to camp just outside the park at any of the gates for a small fee. There are no facilities but you can usually get water from the rangers. The Maasai run the *Oloolaimutia Campsite* between the gate of the same name and the Mara Sopa Lodge at the western extreme of the park. This place is very popular with the budget safari outfits and is usually pretty lively. For KSh 95 per person the Maasai provide firewood and an askari at night. The water supply here is very limited and if you need any you'll have to buy it from the Maasai. The staff canteen of the nearby Mara Sopa Lodge is usually a lively place and you can get meals and warm beer.

There are *official camp sites* along the Talek River by the Talek Gate on the northern border of the park, and just outside the reserve on the banks of the Mara River near the Oloololo Gate. If you want to use any of these sites it's advisable to book them in advance in Nairobi (at Nairobi National Park main gate) but people who roll up unannounced generally seem to have no problems. The only problem with using these sites is that they are none too secure – baboons and thieves can both take their toll on your gear.

What isn't widely known is that it's possible to camp at *Cottar's Mara Camp* (see below) for KSh 120 per person. They certainly don't encourage it but can't turn you away.

Places to Stay – top end

The lodges and tented camps are all pitched at the top end of the market and should all be booked in advance. For a night's accommodation you are looking at around KSh 2400/3600 for a single/double with full board. The lodges are separate bandas, while the tented camps are often almost identical, the difference being that the rooms have canvas walls – it's certainly stretching things to call them tents.

The *Mara Sopa Lodge* (tel Nairobi 336088) by Oloolaimutia Gate is one of the newer ones and has a commanding view. *Keekorok Lodge* (tel Nairobi 335807) is an older lodge on a grassy plain. The *Mara*

Sarova Camp (tel Nairobi 333233) is not far from the Sekenani Gate and has the works, including a swimming pool. The charge here is KSh 2580/3120 for full board. In the centre of the reserve is the *Mara Serena Lodge* (tel Nairobi 339800) with a superb outlook over the Mara River. *Governor's Camp* (tel Nairobi 331871) is the focus of activity in the western part of the reserve. The *Fig Tree Camp* (tel Nairobi 20592) is on the northern boundary of the reserve by Talek Gate.

Other accommodation outside the park north of Oloololo Gate includes the *Kichwa Tembo Camp* (tel Nairobi 335887), the *Mara River Camp* (tel Nairobi 331191) and the *Mara Buffalo Camp*. *Cottar's Mara Camp* (tel Nairobi 882408) is another tented lodge about 15 km from Sekenani Gate. The 'cottages' are dotted around a beautiful green clearing with shady trees, sweeping lawns and flowers. There's an open bar and dining room and a roaring log fire at night. Although it's not actually in the reserve there is a lot of game around the camp itself. They have a baited hide nearby and there's a good chance of seeing leopards. Dawn walks (KSh 140) and night time spotlight game drives (KSh 420) are also organised from the camp.

Even if you can't afford to stay in one of these places, they are usually great places to drop in for a cleansing ale and perhaps a snack although, not surprisingly, prices are high. On a more practical level, the Mara Sarova Camp, Keekorok Lodge and Mara Serena Lodge all sell petrol (KSh 10 per litre) and will usually part with it to nonguests.

Getting There & Away

Air Air Kenya Aviation Ltd has twice daily flights between Nairobi's Wilson Airport and Masai Mara, departing Nairobi at 10 am and 3 pm, and from the Mara at 11 am and 4 pm. The one-way fare is KSh 1585, but to these you have to add the cost of chartering a vehicle in the park.

Road The Mara is not a place you come to without transport. There is no public transport to or within the park, and even if there was there's certainly no way you could do a

Masai Mara
National Park

game drive on a matatu! If you are patient and persistent you should be able to hitch a ride with other tourists, but get yourself to Narok first.This is the main access point to the reserve and is a small provincial town a few hours drive west of Nairobi. As most vehicles stop to refuel here (it's the last place to do so before the park itself) the town is chocker with souvenir shops and hawkers. There are a couple of banks and a few basic budget hotels if you get stuck for the night. There are frequent buses and matatus buzzing between Nairobi and Narok.

From Narok onwards the bitumen runs out and public transport dries up. It's almost 100 km from here to any of the park gates.

It's also possible to approach the reserve from Kisii and the west along reasonably well maintained dirt roads. You can get closer to the park by public transport but there are far fewer tourist vehicles to hitch with. Matatus run as far as Kilkoris directly south of Kisii, or Suna on the main A1 route close to the Tanzanian border.

TSAVO NATIONAL PARK

At just over 20,000 square km Tsavo is the largest national park in Kenya, and for administrative purposes it has been split into Tsavo West National Park, with an area of 8500 square km, and Tsavo East National Park, which covers 11,000 square km.

The northern area of Tsavo West, west of the Nairobi-Mombasa A109 road, is the most developed and has some excellent scenery. Tsavo East is much less visited and consists of vast rolling plains with scrubby vegetation. The entire area north of the Galana River, and this constitutes the bulk of the park, is off limits to the general public. This is due to the ongoing campaign against poachers, who still find the relative remoteness of Tsavo a good prospect. Happily it seems the authorities are winning the battle, but in the meantime the rhino population has been absolutely decimated – from around 8000 in 1970 to less than 100 today.

When driving around the park, all track junctions have a numbered cairn which makes navigation fairly simple.

Tsavo West National Park

The focus here is the watering holes by the Kilaguni and Ngulia Lodges. Both attract huge varieties of animals and birds, particularly during the dry season when water may be scarce elsewhere.

The Mzima Springs are not far from Kilaguni Lodge and the pools here are favourite haunts of both hippo and crocodile. The much vaunted underwater viewing chamber was designed to give you a view of the hippos' submarine activities but they have retreated to the far end of the pool. The springs are the source of the bulk of Mombasa's fresh water and there is a direct pipeline from here to the coast.

Also in the area of the lodges is the spectacular Shaitani lava flow and caves. Both are worth investigating although for the caves you need to exercise caution and carry a torch (flashlight). The Chaimu Crater just south of Kilaguni Lodge can also be climbed. It's worth remembering while walking on any of these nature trails that the park animals are far from tame, and while there's little danger, you do need to keep your eyes on what's happening around you. These nature trails are also the only places where you are permitted to get out of the vehicle.

There is an information centre at the Kilaguni Lodge and if it's open it may be worth checking to see where the most recent animal sightings have been.

Places to Stay – bottom end Tsavo West has a number of *camp sites*, namely at each of the three gates (Tsavo, Mtito Andei and Chyulu) and the *Ziwani Campsite* on the western boundary of the park.

The self-service accommodation at the *Ngulia Safari Camp* and the *Kitani Safari Camp* (tel Nairobi 340331 for both) is, by park standards, quite cheap at KSh 120 per person in the fully equipped bandas.

Places to Stay – top end The *Ngulia Lodge* (tel Nairobi 336858) charges KSh 2400/ 3000 for singles/doubles for full board. The water hole here is a constant attraction, both for the animals and therefore the visitors.

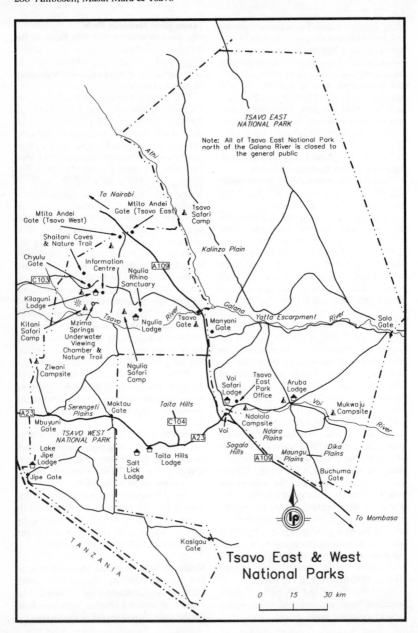

Tsavo East & West
National Parks

The *Kilaguni Lodge* (tel Nairobi 336858) is slightly more expensive at KSh 2520/3240, also for full board. Here is a recent visitor's account of a day spent at Kilaguni Lodge:

The lodge is beautifully situated looking out over the rolling hills. The large water hole, floodlit at night, is right in front of the lodge and you can sit in the bar or restaurant, or on the verandah in front of your room, and watch the wildlife. You can even lie in bed with your binoculars to hand – every room faces a water hole. All this luxury, including a swimming pool and lush garden, doesn't come cheap, but where else do you need a pair of binoculars and a field guide at hand while you eat?

We arrive in time for lunch and watch the comings and goings at the water hole. To the left there are impala and a couple of waterbuck; back from the water there's a small group of ostrich, and off to the right there's a herd of oryx. Marabou storks lounge around in the foreground while right in front of the restaurant are groups of smaller birds and mongoose. There's so much activity it's hard to concentrate on lunch – and this is just after the wet season when the game are less concentrated at the water holes!

The scene is only spoilt by the idiots who persist, in spite of numerous posted warnings, in throwing bread out to the animals. This has already taught some of the storks (notoriously efficient scavengers) to line up in front of the restaurant wall. It would be all too easy to turn this wonderful scene into a cheap zoo with animals begging for handouts. This is the same Africa of Ethiopia and Mozambique and there's something obscene about dumb tourists hurling whole bread rolls just for amusement and a better shot with the Instamatic.

After lunch we watch from the verandah of our room – some zebra and two more ostrich appear but all the storks have left and gradually the animals wander off as the afternoon wears on. By 4.30 pm there's only the solitary waterbuck left; even the ostrich finally troop off in a stately line.

Down at the north end of the lodge grounds there's a tree full of weaver bird nests with twittering hordes of the bright yellow birds furiously at work. Some of their nests, mainly older ones, have fallen out of the tree, and on close examination they are amazingly intricate and neatly woven; coconut-size with a funnel-like entrance underneath. Right in front of our room a small squad of mongooses appear, cavort around for a few minutes, then wander away. By 5 pm it's baboon time again and the tribe wanders down to the water hole again for their evening visit. A few of them come up to our room to hassle us but soon give it away. Rock hyrax scamper around, one even coming right into our room, and the mongooses come and go. Gradually the impala reappear.

Dinner time, unhappily, is the one blot on the perfect experience. Once again there are the idiotic food hurlers at work and a hyaena trots up and waits expectantly for handouts, joined by a slender mongoose-like genet. With much shouting, loud conversation and cameras flashing madly there's a distinct theatre-restaurant feel to the whole meal and we're glad to get back to the quiet of our rooms.

The baboons leave soon after dark and by bedtime it's basically the impalas and zebras. I get up several times in the night to check what's up but, apart from bats swooping around, the scene seems static until dawn. The impala keep watch all night long.

At dawn the zebra wander off, the oryx reappear, the whole baboon tribe wanders back and immediately start carousing merrily. A couple of pairs of impala bucks square off for a morning duel and the whole cycle starts again.

Although we didn't see elephants or lions we still enjoyed every minute of it. Now if only they could put those 'don't feed the animals signs' on every table...

Tony Wheeler

In a fairly isolated spot on the western boundary of the park and almost on the Tanzanian border, the *Lake Jipe Lodge* (tel Nairobi 27623) is one of the cheaper places, with a tariff of KSh 1920/3000 for a single/double with full board.

Getting There & Away The main access is through the Mtito Andei Gate on the Mombasa-Nairobi road at the northern end of the park. The park HQ is here and there's a camp site. From the gate it's 31 km to the Kilaguni Lodge. A further 48 km along the main road away from Nairobi is the Tsavo Gate, where there's another camp site. This gate is 75 km from the Kilaguni area, so if you're hitching the Mtito Andei Gate is much closer and far busier.

From Voi there is access past the Hilton-owned Taita Hills and Salt Lick lodges (tel Nairobi 334000 for both) via the Maktau Gate. This road cuts clear across the park, exiting at the Mbuyuni Gate, to Taveta from where it's possible to cross into Tanzania and the town of Moshi at the foot of Kilimanjaro.

Tsavo East National Park
The southern third of this park is open to the public and the rolling scrub-covered hills are

home to huge herds of elephants, usually covered in red dust.

The Kanderi Swamp, not far into the park from the main Voi Gate and park HQ, is home to a profusion of wildlife and there's a camp site here. Further into the park, 30 km from the gate, is the main attraction in this part of the park, the Aruba Dam built across the Voi River. Here too you'll encounter a wide variety of game – without the usual hordes of tourists; very few people visit Tsavo East.

Places to Stay – bottom end There are *camp sites* at the Voi Gate, Kanderi Swamp (Ndololo Campsite), Aruba Lodge and the *Makwaju Campsite* on the Voi River 50 km in from the main gate.

Places to Stay – top end The *Voi Safari Lodge* (tel Nairobi 336858) is five km inside the park from the Voi Gate. As you might imagine, things are a good deal more peaceful here than at the lodges in Tsavo West. Charges for a rooms are KSh 1980/2640 in the high season for full board.

The *Aruba Lodge* (tel Nairobi 340331) is in a good shady location by the dam. The small shop here sells basic provisions.

Getting There & Away The main access point and the park HQ is Voi Gate on the Nairobi-Mombasa road. Further north near the Tsavo Gate entrance of Tsavo West is the Manyani Gate. The murram road from here cuts straight across to the Galana River and follows the river clear across the park, exiting at Sala Gate on the eastern side, a distance of 100 km. From Sala Gate it's a further 110 to Malindi.

Index

ABBREVIATIONS

SG Safari Guide
Ug Uganda

MAPS

TEXT

294

This Book

To the following travellers who wrote in after using either *Africa on a shoestring* or *East Africa – a travel survival kit*, I'd like to express my sincere thanks for the time and effort which you put in. The information contained in your letters has been an extremely valuable source of original material and for cross-reference. Please keep it up! It all gets read personally and used.

Sal Aisene (USA), Judith Allsopp (UK), Rodney Bartlett (A), Miriam Basten (C), Tina Birkemose (Dk), Martin Bohnstedt (Aust), Dr Adam Booth (UK), Norbet Brockman (K), Stephanie Brookes (USA), Nick Broughton (UK), Marco Burstein (B), Piet van Bussel & Aliky de Kort (Nl), Suzanne Chapman (NZ), Rob Cheves (G), Hugh Cobbett (UK), John B Cronin (K), David Daly (A), Sam Dalley (UK), Christer Danielsson & Liz Kristiansson (Sw), Pierre Deseyn (B), Stan & Jenny Doolan (A), Duncan Dunlop (UK), Andrew Eade (UK), Janfrans van der Eerden (Nl), Saidi M Famao (U), Susanne France (A), Tom Gehrels (Nl), Charlie Gillet (UK), Caroline & Michel Guichon (F), Hilary Guite (UK), Iain Hardy (Z), Kate Harrison (A), Mark A Hilton (UK), Achim Hoffmann (D), Ted Horbulyk (C), Johanna Hortensius (Nl), Kate Jennings (UK), Tony Jonges (Nl), G Michael Junge (USA), C & T Kaiser (Swit), Craig Knight (A), Carol Lawson (A), C Leong (UK), Tonso M Luisa (It), Vicky Luke (C), Stephen Mahon (A), Amy Mall (USA), William Markey (K), Coralie Mason & Gavin Buckley (A), Enrico Michelon (It), Susanne Moller (Dk), Patricia Molloy (Ir), Hilary Moore (UK), Tony Muller (UK), Pilar Alonso Murga (Sp), George Musser Jr (USA), Juliet Nachman (USA), Mike Naylors (A), Cheryl Neckritz (USA), Kala Nobbs (UK), Mark O'Brien (A), J Brian O'Day (USA), Uffe Just Pedersen (Dk), Michael & Liliane Perefais (A), Alison Petit (UK), Kevin Quin & Anne Quigley (USA), Richard & Jeri Ringold (USA), George & Lorna Sether (K), Benny Shanon (Is), Dr G Shaw (UK), Brian Shelley (Zi), Ulla & Olle Siljeholm (Sw), Amy Silverston (UK), John Skirrow (UK), Shane Sleeman (NZ), Nick Smedley (UK), Diccon Smeeton (UK), Una Song (USA), Ashley Spivaek (UK), David Stanley (C), Judi Stellingwerf (UK), Rosalind Sutton (UK), S J Tan (Sin), Karen Tebay (NZ), N R Varley (UK), Susan Vaughan (USA), David Wall (NZ), Dr Bruno Watschinger (Aust), Liz Watters (A), Brooke Wentz (USA), Florian Wick, Graeme Yeoman (UK), Lieve Youques (B).

A - Australia, Aust - Austria, B - Belgium, C - Canada, D - Germany, Dk - Denmark, F - France, G - Greece, Ir - Ireland, Is - Israel, It - Italy, K - Kenya, Nl - Netherlands, NZ - New Zealand, Sin - Singapore, Sp - Spain, Sw - Sweden, Swit - Switzerland, U - Uganda, UK - United Kingdom, USA - United States of America, Z - Zaïre, Zi - Zimbabwe

For the technically minded and those interested in the possibilities of living without another Chernobyl, this book was written on a solar-powered computer using a Kaypro 4 microprocessor, eight Solarex X100 GT solar panels, a Santech 2000 watt inverter and 12 BP PVSTOR 1000 AH lead-acid batteries. The only thing which broke down during the writing of the book was the computer. Lucky I had a spare even though the keyboard wouldn't type 'z' – an easy thing to fix later with the approriate software but fortunate that I didn't have to type 'Zanzibar' too often!

Safari
Guide

Safari Guide

ANTELOPES

The large, striped bongo antelope is rarely seen. About your only chance of sighting one is in Aberdare National Park. They live close to water in dense forest, only leaving the forest cover to graze at night in open clearings.

The bongo stands around 120 cm high at the shoulder and measures around 250 cm from head to tail. Mature males are a beautiful dark mahogany-brown colour, while the females are a much lighter reddish-brown. Both sexes have distinctive vertical white stripes on the body, never less than nine, never more than 14. Horns are sported by both males and females, and these are slightly spiralling with yellow tips, with those on the male being slightly shorter and sturdier than on the female.

The bongo grazes mainly on leaves and will often stand on its hind legs to increase its reach. It also digs for roots with its horns. They are usually found in small family herds although bulls often lead a solitary existence, meeting up with other animals only to mate.

Bongo

Scientific name: *Tragelaphus eurycerus*

Swahili name: *Bongo*

Although the small bushbuck antelope exists in fairly large numbers in most of Kenya's game parks, it is a shy solitary animal which is rarely sighted.

Standing at about 80 cm at the shoulder, the bushbuck is chestnut to dark brown in colour with a variable number of white vertical stripes on the body between the neck and rump, as well as (usually) two horizontal white stripes lower down which give the animal a 'harnessed' appearance. There are also a number of white spots on the upper thigh and a white splash on the neck. Horns are usually only grown by males but females have been known to grow them on rare occasions. They are straight with gentle spirals and average about 30 cm.

Bushbuck are rarely found in groups of more than two and prefer to stick to areas with heavy brush cover. When startled they take off and crash loudly through the undergrowth. They are nocturnal animals and browsers yet rarely move far from their chosen spot. Though shy and elusive they can be aggressive and dangerous when cornered. Their main predators are leopard and python.

Bushbuck

Scientific name: *Tragelaphus scriptus*

Swahili name: *Pongo*

Dik-dik

Full name: *Kirk's dik-dik*
Scientific name: *Rhynchotragus kirki*
Swahili name: *Dik-dik*

Kirk's dik-dik is the more common of the two dik-diks found in Kenya (the other is Gunther's dik-dik, found only in Marsabit National Reserve) and is commonly seen in Nairobi, Tsavo, Amboseli and Masai Mara reserves. Its name comes from the 'zic-zic' call it makes when alarmed.

The dik-dik is a tiny antelope, standing only around 35 cm at the shoulder. It is a reddish-brown colour on the back, with lighter flanks and white belly. Size is usually the easiest way to identify a dik-dik, but other telltale marks are the almost total lack of a tail and the tuft of dark hair on the forehead. Horns (found on the males only) are so short (around six cm) that they are often lost in the hair tuft.

Dik-diks are usually seen singly or in pairs and are often found in exceedingly dry places – it seems they don't have a great dependence on water. They are territorial creatures, each pair occupying an area of around five hectares. They are mainly nocturnal but can be seen grazing in acacia scrub in the early morning and late afternoon; like so many animals they rest in the heat of the day.

The females bear a single offspring twice a year. After six months the young dik-dik reaches sexual maturity and is then driven out of the home territory.

Duiker

Full name: *Grey (or common) duiker*
Scientific name: *Sylvicapra grimmia*
Swahili name: *Nsya*

This is the most common of the duikers, of which there are at least 10 species. Even so, they are not often sighted as they are largely nocturnal, usually only live in pairs and prefer areas with good scrub cover. They are known to exist in Marsabit, Tsavo, Nairobi, Amboseli, Meru and Masai Mara reserves.

The duiker stands only 60 cm at the shoulder, is a greyish light-brown colour with white belly and a dark brown vertical stripe on the face. The horns (males only) are very short (around 20 cm), pointed, and grow straight.

Duikers are widely distributed and can be found in a variety of habitats ranging from open bush to semidesert and up to the snow line of the highest mountains except for bamboo forest and rain forest. This ability to survive in many different habitats explains their survival in cultivated areas where other species of herbivore have been exterminated.

They are almost exclusively browsers and only rarely eat grasses though they appear to supplement their diet with insects and guinea fowl chicks. They are capable of doing without water for long periods of time but will drink it when available.

The eland looks similar to some varieties of cattle seen on the Indian subcontinent, and is found in Nairobi, Marsabit, Tsavo and Masai Mara reserves.

The biggest of the antelopes, the eland stands about 170 cm at the shoulder and a mature bull can weigh up to 1000 kg. Horns are found on both sexes and these are spiralled at the base, swept straight back and grow to about 65 cm. Males have a much hairier head than the females, and their horns are stouter and slightly shorter. They are a light greyish-brown in colour, and bear as many as 15 vertical white stripes on the body, although these are often almost indistinguishable on some animals.

The eland prefers savannah scrub to wide open spaces, but also avoids thick forest. They graze on grass and tree foliage in the early morning and late afternoon, and are also active on moonlit nights. They need to drink once a day, but can go for a month or more without water if diet includes fodder with high water content.

Eland are usually found in groups of around six to 12, but there may be as many as 50 in a herd. A small herd normally consists of several females and one male, but in larger herds there may be several males, and there is a strict hierarchy. Females reach sexual maturity at around two years and can bear up to 12 calves in a lifetime. The young are born in October-November.

Eland

Scientific name: *Taurotragus oryx*
Swahili name: *Pofu*

The gerenuk is probably the easiest of all antelopes to identify because of its inordinately long neck, which accounts for its Swahili name, meaning gazelle-giraffe. Its distribution is limited to Meru, Samburu, Tsavo and Amboseli national parks.

Growing to around 100 cm at the shoulder, the gerenuk is a dark fawn colour on the back which becomes much lighter on the sides and belly. The horns (found on the male only) curve gently backward and grow up to 40 cm long.

The gerenuk's habitat ranges from dry thorn bush country to semidesert and its food consists mainly of the tender leaves and shoots of acacia bushes. It is quite capable – in the same way as goats – of standing on its hind legs and using one of its forelegs to pull down the higher branches of bushes to get at the leaves and shoots. Also like goats, they are quite capable of doing without water.

Gerenuk

Scientific name: *Litocranius walleri*
Swahili name: *Swala twiga*

Grant's Gazelle

Scientific name: *Gazella granti*
Swahili name: *Swala granti*

This is one of the most common antelopes and exists in large numbers in Nairobi, Amboseli, Masai Mara, Tsavo and Marsabit reserves.

Grant's gazelle are most easily identified by their colouring and long horns: sandy brown on the back, clearly demarcated from a lighter colour on the flanks and white belly, and white around the tail and hind legs. They are not a large gazelle, standing around 90 cm at the shoulder. Horns are found on both sexes and are heavily ridged with around 25 rings; in the male they grow to around 60 cm (although they often appear longer because of the relatively small body) and curve gracefully and evenly up and back, usually with some outward curving as well; in the female the horns are much shorter but follow the same pattern.

You usually come across herds of Grant's gazelle in open grassy country where there is some forest cover, although they are also occasionally found in heavily wooded savannah country. Herd size is usually between 20 and 30, with one dominant male, does and young. Food consists mainly of leaves and grass. As water is obtained through dietary intake these gazelles do not need to drink.

Greater Kudu

Scientific name: *Tragelaphus
                  strepsiceros*
Swahili name: *Tandala mkubwa*

The greater kudu is one of the largest of the antelopes but it's a rare sight and only found in any numbers in Marsabit National Reserve. Elsewhere kudu prefer hilly country with fairly dense bush cover. The kudu stands around 1.5 metres at the shoulder and weighs up to 250 kg, yet it's a very elegant creature, light grey in colour, with broad ears and a long neck. The sides of the body are marked by six to 10 vertical white stripes and there is a white chevron between the eyes. Horns are carried only by the males and are both divergent and spiralling.

Kudu live in small herds of up to four or five females with their young but these often split up during the rainy season. The males are usually solitary though occasionally they band together into small herds.

They are mainly browsers and only seldom eat grasses but are capable of eating many types of leaves which would be poisonous to other animals.

Although somewhat clumsy animals when on the move, they are capable of clearing well over two metres when jumping.

The hartebeest is a medium sized antelope and is found in Nairobi, Tsavo, Amboseli and Masai Mara parks. It is easy to recognise as it has a long, narrow face and distinctively angular short horns (on both sexes) which are heavily ridged. Colouring is generally light brown on the back, becoming paler towards the rear and under the belly. The back slopes away from the humped shoulders. They prefer grassy plains for grazing but are also found in lightly treed savannah or hills.

The hartebeest feeds exclusively on grass, and usually drinks twice daily, although it can go for months without water if necessary.

They are social beasts and often intermingle with animals such as zebra and wildebeest. Their behaviour is not unlike the wildebeest's, particularly the head tossing and shaking.

Sexual maturity is reached at around 2½ years and calving goes on throughout the year, although there are peak periods in February and August. Predators are mainly the large cats, hyaenas and hunting dogs.

Hartebeest

Scientific name: *Alcelphus buselaphus*

Swahili name: *Kongoni*

The graceful impala is one of the most common antelopes and is found in virtually all national parks and reserves in large numbers.

A medium sized antelope, it stands about 80 cm at the shoulder. The coat is a glossy rufous colour though paler on the flanks with the underparts, rump, throat and chin being white. A narrow black line runs along the middle of the rump to about halfway down the tail and there's also a vertical black stripe on the back of the thighs but, unlike in Grant's gazelle, this does not border the white buttocks. It's also distinguishable from Grant's gazelle by having a tuft of long black hairs above the heels of the hind legs. Only the males have horns which are long (averaging 75 cm), lyre-shaped and curve upwards as they spread.

Impala are gregarious animals with each male having a 'harem' of up to 100 females, though more usually around 15 to 20. Males without such a 'harem' form bachelor groups. There is fierce fighting between males during the rutting season but otherwise they are fairly placid animals.

One of the most noticeable characteristics of impala is their speed and prodigious ability at jumping. They are quite capable of clearing 10 metres in a single jump lengthwise or three metres in height and this they frequently do even when there are no obstacles in their path.

Impala are both browsers and grazers and are active during the day and by night. They are quite highly dependent on water but are capable of existing on just dew for fairly long periods of time.

Their main predators are leopard, cheetah and wild dog.

Impala

Scientific name: *Aepyceros melampus*

Swahili name: *Swala pala*

Klipspringer

Scientific name: *Oreotragus oreotragus*
Swahili name: *Mbuzi mawe*

The distinctive klipspringers inhabit rocky outcrops in Tsavo, Amboseli, Masai Mara, Marsabit and Meru reserves.

Standing about 50 cm at the shoulder, they are easily recognised by their curious 'tip-toe' stance (the hooves are designed for balance and grip on rocky surfaces) and the greenish tinge of their speckled coarse hair. Horns (found on the male only) are short (10 cm) and widely spaced.

Klipspringers are most often seen on rocky outcrops, or in the grassland in the immediate vicinity, and when alarmed they retreat into the rocks for safety. They are amazingly agile and sure-footed creatures and can often be observed bounding up impossibly rough rock faces. These antelope can also go entirely without water if there is none around, getting all they need from the greenery they eat. They are most active just before and after midday, and single males often keep watch from a good vantage point. The klipspringer are usually found in pairs, or a male with two females, and they inhabit a clearly defined territory.

Klipspringers reach sexual maturity at around one year, and females bear one calf twice a year. Calves may stay with the adult couple for up to a year, although young males usually seek their own territory earlier than that.

Predators are mainly the leopard and the crowned eagle, but also include jackals and baboons.

Lesser Kudu

Scientific name: *Tragelaphus imberbis*
Swahili name: *Tandala ndogo*

The lesser kudu is a smaller model of the greater kudu, the major differences being the lack of a beard, more numerous and more pronounced vertical white stripes on the body, and two white patches on the underside of the neck. As with the greater kudu, only the males have horns. The coat colour varies from brownish grey to blue grey. It stands around a metre high at the shoulder.

These kudu usually live in pairs accompanied by their fawns though females occasionally form small herds. It's a very shy animal and spends much of the day hiding in dense bush, only moving out of cover to feed in the early morning and at dusk. This makes it difficult to spot.

Kudu are browsers and feed on a mixture of leaves, young shoots and twigs and, though they drink regularly if water is available, they are capable of doing without it for relatively long periods of time – more so than the greater kudu.

The most likely places you will find them are Tsavo and Marsabit where they prefer the drier, more bushy areas.

Not unlike a duiker in appearance, the small oribi is relatively uncommon, and your best chance of spotting one is in the Masai Mara reserve.

The oribi's most distinguishing mark, although you'll need binoculars to spot it, is a circular batch of naked black skin below the ear – it is actually a scent gland. Another useful indicator is the tuft of black hair on the tip of the short tail. Otherwise the oribi is a uniform golden brown with white on the belly and insides of the legs. Short straight horns about 10 cm in length are found in the males only.

Oribi usually graze in grassy plains with good shelter. If water is available they will drink willingly but can also go without entirely. When alarmed they bolt and then make bouncing jumps with a curious action – all four legs are kept completely stiff. It is thought this helps them to orient themselves in places with poor visibility. After 100 metres or so they stop and assess the danger.

The oribi are usually found in pairs and are territorial. Sexual maturity is reached at around one year, and the females bear one calf twice a year.

Being quite small, the oribi has many predators, including the larger cats.

Oribi
Scientific name: *Ourebia ourebi*
Swahili name: *Taya*

The oryx (or beisa) is a large reddish-grey antelope which is most commonly seen in the Marsabit National Reserve and along the Tana River. The related fringe-eared oryx *(oryx callotis)* is more widespread and can be seen in Amboseli and Tsavo national parks.

Oryx are large antelopes standing around 120 cm at the shoulder. The coat is a sandy fawn with a black stripe along the spine down to the tip of the tail. The underparts are white and separated from the lower flanks by another black stripe. There are also two black rings just above the knee of the forelegs. Both types of oryx have ovate, pointed ears with the main distinguishing feature being, as the name suggests, a tuft of black hairs on the ears of the fringe-eared one. Oryx are easy to distinguish from other antelopes due to their straight, very long and heavily ridged horns which are carried almost parallel. Both the males and females have horns. These horns come into their own when the animal is forced to defend itself. Held down between the forelegs, they are formidable weapons and used to impale an enemy.

Oryx are principally grazers but will also browse on thorny shrubs. They are capable of doing without water for long periods of time but will drink daily if it is available.

Herds vary from five to 40 individuals and sometimes more though the bulls are usually solitary. Oryx are often found in association with zebra and Grant's gazelle.

Oryx
Scientific name: *Oryx beisa*
Swahili name: *Choroa*

Reedbuck

Full name:	*Bohor reedbuck*
Scientific name:	*Redunca redunca*
Swahili name:	*Tohe*

The best places to spot the dusty brown reedbuck is in Nairobi and Amboseli national parks, and they are occasionally seen in Tsavo National Park.

The reedbuck is a medium sized antelope, standing around 80 cm high at the shoulder. The most distinctive features are the forward curving horns (found on the males only) and the bushy tail. The underbelly, inside of the thighs, throat and underside of the tail are white.

The reedbuck frequent open grassy plains or hills and are never found more than around eight km from a water supply. They are very territorial and are found in small groups of up to 10 animals. The groups usually consist of an older male and accompanying females and young. Their diet consists almost exclusively of grass but does include some foliage.

At mating time males fight spiritedly. After reaching sexual maturity at around 1½ years, females bear one calf at a time.

The bohor reedbuck's main predators include the big cats, hyaena and hunting dog.

Roan Antelope

Scientific name:	*Hippotragus equinus*
Swahili name:	*Korongo*

The roan antelope is one of Kenya's less common species and the best place for seeing one these days is in the Shimba Hills National Reserve, where they have been translocated from other parts of the country, although there are still a few small herds in Masai Mara.

The third largest of the antelopes after eland and kudu at up to 150 cm at the shoulder, roan bear a striking resemblance to a horse – hence their name. The coat varies from reddish fawn to dark rufous with white underparts and there's a conspicuous mane of stiff, black-tipped hairs which stretches from the nape to the shoulders. Under the neck, there's another mane of sorts consisting of long dark hairs. The ears are long, narrow and pointed with a brown tassel at the tip. The face is a very distinctive black and white pattern. Both sexes have curving backswept horns which can measure up to 70 cm.

Roan are aggressive by nature and fight from a very early age – a characteristic which frequently deters predators. For most of the year they live in small herds of up to 20 and sometimes more, led by a master bull, but in the mating season, the bulls become solitary and take a female out of the herd. The pair stay together until the calf is born after which the females form a herd by themselves. They eventually return to their former herd. Herds congregate during the dry season.

Being principally grazers, roan rarely move far when food is plentiful but they are susceptible to drought and during such periods they may be constantly on the move.

Also found only in the Shimba Hills National Reserve, the sable antelope is slightly smaller than its cousin the roan, but is more solidly built. The colouring is dark brown to black, with white face markings and belly. Both sexes carry long back-swept horns which average around 80 cm, those of the male being longer and more curved.

The sable antelope is active mainly in the early morning and late afternoon, and is found in herds of up to 25 and sometimes more in the dry season. They are territorial and each group occupies a large area, although within this area individual males have demarcated territories of up to 30 hectares. Sables feed mainly off grass but leaves and foliage from trees account for around 10% of their diet.

Females start bearing calves at around three years of age, and the main calving times are January and September.

Like the roan, the sable is a fierce fighter and has been known to kill lions when attacked. Other predators include the leopard, hyaena and hunting dog.

Sable Antelope
Scientific name: *Hippotragus niger*
Swahili name: *Pala hala*

The sitatunga is a swamp antelope with unusual elongated hooves which give it the ability to walk on marshy ground without sinking. It is restricted solely to the Saiwa Swamp National Park near Kitale, and it's well worth a visit to this small, walkers-only park.

Very similar to the bushbuck in appearance, except that the coat of the male is much darker and the hair of both sexes much longer and shaggier, the sitatunga stands something over one metre at the shoulder. The males have twisted horns up to 90 cm long. It is a fairly shy antelope and sightings are not all that common. A good swimmer, the sitatunga will often sub-merge itself almost completely when alarmed.

It feeds largely on papyrus and other reeds and is usually nocturnal though in places where it remains undisturbed it can be diurnal. Animals normally live singly or in pairs but sometimes come together in small herds numbering up to 15.

Sitatunga
Scientific name: *Tragelaphus spekei*
Swahili name: *Nzohe*

Thomson's Gazelle

Scientific name: *Gazella thomsonii*
Swahili name: *Swala tomi*

The small and frisky Thomson's gazelle is instantly recognisable by the black slash across the side which separates the brown back from the white underbelly. They are very common in the plains country – Amboseli, Masai Mara and Nairobi reserves, but very rare in different habitats such as Tsavo National Park.

Standing around 60 cm at the shoulders, the 'Tommy' is one of the smaller antelopes. Horns on the male grow to about 30 cm and almost straight with just a gentle curve towards the tips; in the female the horns are straighter and much shorter. Another easy to identify characteristic is the short black tail which seems to be constantly twitching. Along with the oribi, Tommys also do the stiff legged bouncing jump when alarmed.

Group size varies: one old (largely territorial) male may be accompanied by anything from five to 50 females, or there may be herds of up to 500 young males without territory. When food is plentiful the herds tend to be smaller and more territorial. In times of drought herds of several thousand may gather and roam for food. They are often found in close proximity to other animals, including Grant's gazelles and wildebeest.

Sexual maturity is reached at around one year but males only mate after establishing their own territory, which occurs sometime after two years of age. Calving occurs throughout the year though tends to peak at the end of the rainy season.

Being a small animal, Tommys have many predators, including the big cats, hunting dog, hyaena and serval.

The topi is not unlike the hartebeest in appearance, but is a dark almost purplish colour and has black patches on the rear thighs, front legs and face. Its horns, which are found on both sexes, also differ in shape from the hartebeest in curving gently up, out and back. Although fairly widely distributed in East Africa, in Kenya it is only found in Masai Mara where it exists in large numbers.

A highly gregarious antelope which lives in herds numbering from 15 up to several hundred individuals, topi congregate at certain times of year in gatherings of up to 10,000 in preparation for a migration to fresh pastures. They are often found mingling with wildebeest, hartebeest and zebra.

In the mating season, bulls select a well defined patch of ground which is defended against rivals and this is where mating takes place. At this time females are free to wander from one patch to another. After mating, the herds split into single sex parties.

Topi are exclusively grazers and prefer flood plains which support lush pasture though they are capable of thriving on dry grasses which other antelopes will not eat. When water is available they drink frequently but they are also capable of surviving long periods without water so long as there is sufficient grass available.

Their main predator is the lion.

Topi
Scientific name: *Damaliscus topi*
Swahili name: *Nyamera*

Waterbuck

Full name: *Defassa (or common) waterbuck*
Scientific name: *Kobus ellipsiprymus*
Swahili name: *Kuru*

The defassa waterbuck is a fairly solid animal and is easily recognisable by its thick, shaggy, dark brown coat, and white inner thighs. They are fairly common and are easily seen in Nairobi and Nakuru national parks, and in Masai Mara. A second variety, the ringed waterbuck (also *kobus ellipsiprymnus*), so called because of the white ring around its rump, is also seen in Marsabit, Tsavo and Amboseli parks. Both varieties have white facial and throat markings.

Only the males have horns, and these curve gradually outwards then grow straight up to a length of about 75 cm. As you might expect from the name, waterbuck are good swimmers and readily enter the water to escape from predators. Their habitat is always close to water and males have marked territories by the water's edge. Females and younger males tend to wander at random through male territories. Herds are small and usually consist of cows, calves and one mature bull – the other bulls live in small groups apart from the herd.

The bulk of the waterbuck's diet is grass but it does eat some of the foliage of trees and bushes.

Sexual maturity is reached at just over one year, although a male will not become the dominant bull in the herd until around five years of age.

Waterbuck are usually only preyed on when other food is scarce. The reason being that when mature the flesh is tough and has a distinct odour. Predators such as lion, leopard and hunting dog go for the young calves and females.

Wildebeest are to the African savannah what the bison once were to the American prairies. Numbering in their millions in certain areas, particularly Masai Mara and over the border in Serengeti, they are unmistakable for their prehistoric appearance. Wildebeest are well known for their eccentric behaviour which includes loud snorting, tossing and shaking of the head, bucking, running around in circles and rolling in the dust (thought to be a reaction to the activity of the botfly larva which manage to find their way right up into their nostrils). They are heavily built with a massive head and wild mane, somewhat clumsy, and have been described as having the forequarters of an ox, the hind parts of an antelope and the tail of a horse.

Their sheer numbers, nevertheless, are testimony to their superb adaptation to the environment.

Almost entirely grazers, they are constantly on the move in search of good pasture and water, and their annual migration between the Serengeti and Masai Mara (and vice versa) has to be one of the world's most spectacular sights. Thousands lose their lives in this annual event, either drowned fording rivers or taken by crocodiles and other predators or just through sheer exhaustion. The migration north from Serengeti takes place in July and the return trip from Masai Mara in October.

They're very gregarious animals and are usually seen in large herds numbering up to tens of thousands in association with zebra, Thomson's gazelle and other herbivores.

During the mating season, groups of up to 150 females and their young are gathered together by one to three bulls which defend a defined territory against rivals even when on the move. There's apparently no hierarchy amongst the bulls and, at the end of the mating season, the breeding herds are reabsorbed into the main herds.

Although they graze in a scattered fashion without any apparent social organisation during the rainy season, they coalesce around water holes and remaining pasture in the dry season. Wildebeest prefer to drink daily and will walk up to 50 km to secure water but are capable of surviving for up to five days without it. They're also a noisy animal when grazing, constantly producing a series of snorts and low pitched grunts.

Their main predators are lion, cheetah and wild dog though hyaenas are also very partial to young calves.

Wildebeest (Gnu)

Full name:	*Bridled wildebeest*
Scientific name:	*Connochaetes taurinus*
Swahili name:	*Nyumbu*

Scientific name: *Syncerus caffer*
Swahili name: *Mbogo*

BUFFALO

The buffalo is another animal which appears in great numbers in all the major parks, with the exception of Nairobi National Park.

The massive animal is said to be the most dangerous (to humans) of all African animals and should be treated with caution, although for the most part they will stay out of your way. Females protecting young calves, and solitary rogue bulls, are the most aggressive, and having 800 kg of angry animal thundering towards you is no joke.

Both sexes have the distinctive curving horns which broaden and almost meet over the forehead, although those in the female are usually smaller. The buffalo's colour varies from dark reddish brown to black.

Buffalo are often found in herds of 100 or more and never stray too far from water, especially in the dry season. When food and water are plentiful the herds often disperse. They are territorial in that they have a home range of about 50 km outside of which they don't stray.

CARNIVORES

The carnivores are the animals which are most affected by the number of tourists to the game parks – you try to catch your dinner with half a dozen minibuses bringing up the rear. Although the temptation and excitement are great, keep your distance if animals are obviously hunting.

The civet is a medium sized omnivore around 40 cm high at the shoulder and 90 cm long (excluding the tail), with some canine features and short, partially retractile claws. Its coat of long coarse hair is basically grey but with a definite and variable pattern of black spots over most of the body, along with two black bands stretching from the ears to the lower neck and two black bands around the upper part of the hind legs. The tail is bushy at the base becoming thinner towards the tip, held out straight when the animal is on the move, and black except for three to four greyish bands near the base. The head is mostly greyish white and the ears are quite small, rounded and tipped with white hairs.

Civets are solitary, nocturnal animals which hide in thickets, tall grass or abandoned burrows during the day and so are rarely sighted. The most likely places to spot one are in Marsabit or Tsavo West reserves, although they are also known to inhabit Nairobi, Amboseli and the Masai Mara.

It has a very varied diet consisting of rodents, birds and their eggs, reptiles, amphibians, snails, insects (especially ants and termites) as well as berries, the young shoots of bushes and fruits.

Litters consist of up to four cubs and these have a similar colouring to the adults only slightly darker.

The other conspicuous feature of the civet is the presence of musk glands in the anal region which produce a foul smelling oily substance used to mark territory. This musk is used in the manufacture of perfumes though in Western countries it is collected from animals held in captivity.

Civet

Scientific name: *Viverra civetta*
Swahili name: *Fungo*

Cheetah

Scientific name: *Acinonyx jubatus*
Swahili name: *Duma*

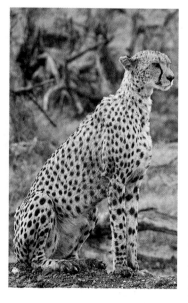

The cheetah is one of the most impressive animals you can hope to come across – sleek, streamlined and menacing. They are found in small numbers in all the major game reserves – Nairobi, Amboseli, Masai Mara, Tsavo, Samburu, Buffalo Springs, Marsabit and Meru.

Similar in appearance to the leopard, the cheetah is longer and lighter in the body, has a slightly bowed back and a much smaller and rounder face. It stands around 80 cm at the shoulder, measures around 210 cm in length (including the tail) and weighs anything from 40 kg to 60 kg.

When undisturbed the cheetah hunt in early morning or late evening, although these days with the number of tourist vehicles around, they are often found hunting at midday when the rubbernecks are back in the lodges stuffing their faces and the poor animal has a chance of stalking some dinner undisturbed. This forced change in habit is particularly stressful for the cheetah as it relies on bursts of tremendous speed for catching its prey, and this speed (up to 110 km/h) is only sustainable for a very short time. Obviously as the midday heat is much greater than morning or afternoon, hunting for the cheetah becomes much more difficult. During a hunt the cheetah stalks its prey as close as possible and then sprints for 100 metres or so; if by that time it hasn't caught its victim, it will give up and try elsewhere. The prey (usually small antelope) is brought to the ground often with a flick of the paw to trip it up. Other food includes hares, jackals and young wart hogs.

Cheetah cubs reach maturity at around one year but stay with the mother much longer than that as they have to learn hunting and survival skills. Cubs are usually born in litters numbering from two to four, and the main breeding period is from March to December.

The cheetah rarely fights but predators (mainly of cubs) include lion, leopard and hyaena.

Unlike the civet, the genet distinctly resembles the domestic cat though the body is considerably more elongated and the tail longer and bushier. The coat is long and coarse with a prominent crest along the spine. The basic colour varies from grey to fawn and is patterned from the neck to the tail with roundish dark brown to blackish spots. The tail is banded with nine to 10 similarly coloured rings and has a whitish tip.

The genet lives in savannah and open country and is a very agile tree climber but not frequently sighted since it is entirely nocturnal. During the day it sleeps in abandoned burrows, rock crevices, hollow trees or up on high branches and seems to return to the same spot each day. The animals live singly or in pairs.

Its prey is generally hunted on the ground though it will climb trees to seek out nesting birds and their eggs. Like the domestic cat, it stalks prey by crouching flat on the ground. Its diet consists of a variety of small animals (mostly rodents), birds, reptiles (including snakes), insects and fruits. It is well known for being a wasteful killer, often eating only a small part of the animals which it catches.

Litters typically consist of two to three kittens.

Like the domestic cat, the genet spits and growls when angered or in danger.

Genet

Scientific name: *Genetta genetta*
Swahili name: *Kanu*

The hunting dog is the size of a large domestic dog and is of a medium build. It is found in Kenya anywhere where there is a high concentration of game animals, and so is seen in all the reserves.

The dog's unusual coloration makes it quite an ugly creature – the black and yellowish splotches are different in each animal, ranging from almost all black to almost all yellow. The only constant is the white tail tip. Prominent physical features are the large rounded ears.

Hunting dogs tend to move in packs ranging from four or five up to as many as 40. They are efficient hunters and work well together. Once the prey has been singled out and the chase is on, a couple of dogs will chase hard while the rest pace themselves; once the first two tire another two step in and so on until the quarry is exhausted. Favoured animals for lunch include gazelle, impala and other similar sized antelope. They rarely scavenge, preferring to kill their own.

Hunting dog cubs are usually born in grass lined burrows in litters averaging seven, although litters of up to 15 are not unheard of. By six months they are competent hunters and have abandoned the burrow.

The hunting dog has no predators, although unguarded cubs sometimes fall prey to hyaenas and eagles.

Hunting Dog

Scientific name: *Lycaon pictus*
Swahili name: *Mbwa mwitu*

Hyaena

Scientific name: *Crocuta crocuta*
Swahili name: *Fisi*

The spotted hyaena is a fairly common animal throughout most of Kenya and especially where game is plentiful. Bearing a distinct resemblance to dogs, it is a large, powerfully built animal with a very sloping back, broad head and large eyes but with rather weak hindquarters. The sloping back is what gives the animal its characteristic loping gait when running. Its coat is short, dull grey to buff and entirely patterned with rounded blackish spots except on the throat. Its powerful jaws and teeth enable it to crush and swallow the bones of most animals except the elephant.

Hyaenas are mainly nocturnal animals but are frequently seen during the day, especially in the vicinity of lion or cheetah kills impatiently waiting for their turn at the carcass along with vultures. Otherwise, the days are spent in long grass, abandoned aardvark holes or in large burrows which they dig out up to a metre below the surface of the soil. It's a very noisy animal and when camping out in the bush at night you'll frequently hear its characteristic and spine chilling howl which rises quickly to a high-pitched scream. This is only one of the sounds which the spotted hyaena emits. Another is the well known 'laugh', though this is generally only produced when the animal finds food or is mating.

The hyaena has highly developed senses of smell, sight and sound, all important in locating food (carrion or prey) and for mutual recognition among pack members and mating pairs.

Hyaenas are well known as scavengers and can often be seen following hunting lions and wild dogs, usually at a respectable distance, though they will occasionally force these animals to abandon their kill. On the other hand, although carrion does form an important part of their diet, hyaenas are also true predators and are more than capable of bringing down many of the larger herbivores. To do this they often form packs to run down wildebeest, zebra and gazelle, and are able to reach speeds of up to 60 km/h. They also stalk pregnant antelope and, when the female gives birth, snatch and kill the newly born foal and occasionally the mother too. Domestic stock are also preyed on.

In the mating season, hyaenas assemble in large numbers especially on moonlit nights. All hell breaks loose on these occasions and the noise is incredible. The gestation period is about 110 days and litters number up to four though usually less. The young are born in the mother's burrow. The pups are weaned at around six weeks old and become independent shortly afterwards.

The hyaena's main enemy is man, though lions and wild dogs will occasionally kill or mutilate them if they get too close to a kill. Although they are reputed to be cowardly, you're advised to keep your distance from them as they do occasionally attack humans sleeping in the open.

The black-backed jackal is a common sight in the major reserves. The black back which gives it its name is usually more silvery than black, is wide at the neck and tapers to the tail. Although the jackal is in fact a dog, the appearance is more that of a fox with its very bushy tail and long ears.

The jackal is for the most part a scavenger and so is commonly seen in the vicinity of a kill. If food is not forthcoming from that direction the jackal will hunt for itself – insects, small mammals and birds, even the occasional small antelope. They are also found on the outskirts of human settlements and will attack sheep, poultry and young calves or foals.

Jackals are territorial and a pair will guard an area of around 250 hectares. Cubs are born in litters of five to seven and, although they don't reach maturity until almost a year old, they usually leave the parents when just two months old.

Enemies of the black-backed jackal include the leopard, cheetah and eagles.

Jackal

Full name:	*Black-backed jackal*
Scientific name:	*Canis mesomelas*
Swahili name:	*Bweha*

The leopard is perhaps the most graceful and agile of the large cats. A powerfully built animal which uses cunning to catch its prey, it is present in all the major game reserves but is difficult to find as it is nocturnal and spends the day resting on branches of trees, often up to five metres above the ground. It is as agile as a domestic cat in climbing such trees and this is also where it carries its prey so that it's out of the way of other scavengers which might contest the kill.

The leopard's coat is usually short and dense with numerous black spots on a yellowish background, though some are black all over. The underparts are white and less densely spotted. In addition, the coats of leopards found in open country are generally lighter than those in wooded country.

Leopards are solitary animals except during the mating season when the male and female live together. The gestation period is three months and a litter usually consists of up to three cubs.

They prey on a variety of birds, reptiles and mammals including large rodents, rock hyrax, wart hogs, smaller antelopes and monkeys (especially baboon), though they occasionally take domestic animals such as goats, sheep, poultry and dogs. This wide range of prey explains why they are still able to survive even in areas of dense human settlement long after other large predators have disappeared. But their presence is generally unwelcome since they do occasionally turn human-eater. It also explains why they are found in very varied habitats ranging from semi-desert to dense forest and as high as the snow line on Mts Kenya and Kilimanjaro.

Leopard

Scientific name:	*Panthera pardus*
Swahili name:	*Chui*

Lion

Scientific name: *Panthera leo*
Swahili name: *Simba*

Lions are one of the main attractions of the game reserves and are found in all the main ones. They spend most of the day lying under bushes or in other attractive places and when you see a pride stretched out in the sun like this, they seem incredibly docile. It is possible to drive up very close to them in a vehicle – they either don't sense humans or realise that humans in vehicles are not a threat. Whatever the case, don't be tempted to get out of a vehicle at any time in the vicinity of a lion. Loud noises and sudden movement also disturb them. They're at their most active for around four hours in the late afternoon, then spend the rest of the time laying around.

Lions generally hunt in groups, with the males driving the prey towards the concealed females who do most of the actual killing. Although they cooperate well together, lions are not the most efficient hunters – as many as four out of five attacks will be unsuccessful. Their reputation as human-eaters is largely undeserved as in most circumstances they will flee on seeing a human. However, once they have the taste for human flesh, and realise how easy it is to make a meal of one, lions can become habitual killers of people. This mostly occurs among the old lions which no longer have the agility to bring down more fleet-footed animals.

Lions are territorial beasts and a pride of one to three males and accompanying females (up to 15) and young will defend an area of anything from 20 to 400 square km, depending on the type of country and the amount of game food available.

Lion cubs are born in litters averaging two or three. They become sexually mature by 1½ years and males are driven from the family group shortly after this. Lions reach full maturity at around six years of age. Unguarded cubs are preyed on by hyaenas, leopards, pythons and hunting dogs.